CAPODIMONTE
AND I VERGINI

DECUMANO MAGGIORE

SPACCANAPOLI

TOLEDO AND
CASTEL NUOVO

| 0 metres | 500 |
| 0 yards | 500 |

**Capodimonte and
I Vergini**

Spaccanapoli

Decumano Maggiore

NAPLES
&
THE AMALFI COAST

EYEWITNESS TRAVEL

NAPLES
& THE AMALFI COAST

DK

Penguin
Random
House

Produced by Fabio Ratti Editoria Libraria
e Multimediale Milano, Italy

Project Editor Giovanni Francesio
Editors Barbara Cacciani, Giorgia Conversi, Elena Marzorati,
Michele Di Muro
Designers Paolo Gonzato, Carlotta Maderna, Stefania Testa
Maps Paul Stafford

Dorling Kindersley Ltd
Project Editor Fiona Wild
Editors Francesca Machiavelli, Naomi Peck, Rosalyn Thiro

Contributors Patrizia Antignani, Mariella Barone, Ciro Cacciola, Angela Catello, Daniela
Lepore, Emilia Marchi, Kirsi Viglione, Beatrice Vitelli
Illustrators Giorgia Boli, Paola Spampinato, Nadia Viganò

English Translation Richard Pierce

Printed and bound in China

Published for the first time in Italy in 1997, under the title
Guida Mondadori: Napoli e Dintorni.
© Fabio Ratti Editoria, Milan 1997
© Dorling Kindersley Ltd, London 1997

First American Edition 2000
17 18 19 20 10 9 8 7 6 5 4 3 2 1
Published in the United States by DK Publishing,
345 Hudson Street, New York, New York 10014

**Reprinted with revisions 2000, 2001, 2003, 2005, 2006, 2007,
2009, 2011, 2013, 2015, 2017**

Copyright © 1998, 2017 Dorling Kindersley Ltd, London
A Penguin Random House Company

ISSN 1542-1554
ISBN 978-1-4654-6000-4

Floors are referred to throughout in accordance with European usage; ie the "first floor"
is the floor above ground level.

MIX
Paper from
responsible sources
FSC™ C018179
www.fsc.org

**The information in this
DK Eyewitness Travel Guide is checked regularly.**
Every effort has been made to ensure that this book is as up-to-date as possible
at the time of going to press. Some details, however, such as telephone numbers,
opening hours, prices, gallery hanging arrangements and travel information, are
liable to change. The publishers cannot accept responsibility for any consequences
arising from the use of this book, nor for any material on third party websites, and
cannot guarantee that any website address in this book will be a suitable source of
travel information. We value the views and suggestions of our readers very highly.
Please write to: Publisher, DK Eyewitness Travel Guides, Dorling Kindersley,
80 Strand, London, WC2R 0RL, UK, or email: travelguides@dk.com.

Front cover main image: Afternoon in the port of Cetara, on the Amalfi Coast

◀ The town of Positano on the Amalfi Coast

Contents

How to Use This Guide **6**

The Farnese Hercules

Introducing
Naples

Fresco by Francesco Solimena in the
sacristy of San Domenico Maggiore

The Li Galli Archipelago, just off of the Sorrento coast

A pavement café in the historic Piazza Bellini

Pizza Napoletana

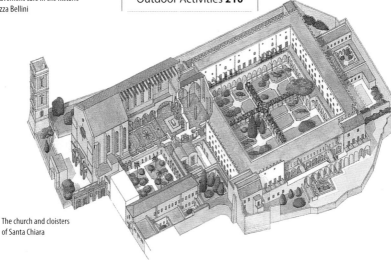

The church and cloisters of Santa Chiara

HOW TO USE THIS GUIDE

This guide helps you to get the most out of your visit to Naples. It provides both expert recommendations and advice as well as useful practical information. The first chapter, *Introducing Naples*, sets the city in its rich and varied geographical and historical context. *Naples at a Glance* gives you a brief overview of the main sights in the city, as well as cultural background. *Naples Through the Year* describes events and festivals season by season. *Naples Area by Area* describes the main sightseeing areas in detail, with maps, illustrations and photographs. *Pompeii and the Amalfi Coast* covers this region's splendid archaeological sites and also features an itinerary for a coastal boat trip. Information on hotels, shops, restaurants and bars is covered in *Travellers' Needs*, while the *Survival Guide* contains practical advice – for example, how to use the local transport networks.

Finding Your Way Around the Sightseeing Section

The city has been divided into six colour-coded areas, each with its own chapter. A description of the history and features of each area is followed by a Street-by-Street map focusing on the main attractions. The sights are numbered for easy reference. The most important sights in each area are described in detail in two or more pages.

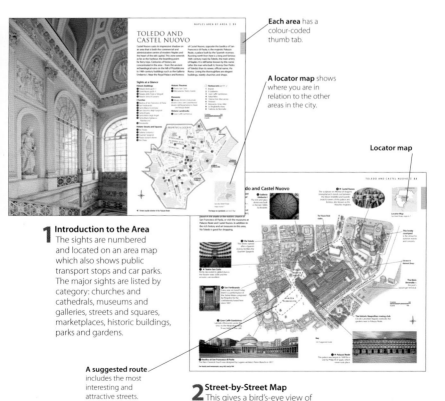

Each area has a colour-coded thumb tab.

A locator map shows where you are in relation to the other areas in the city.

Locator map

1 Introduction to the Area
The sights are numbered and located on an area map which also shows public transport stops and car parks. The major sights are listed by category: churches and cathedrals, museums and galleries, streets and squares, marketplaces, historic buildings, parks and gardens.

A suggested route includes the most interesting and attractive streets.

2 Street-by-Street Map
This gives a bird's-eye view of the heart of the sightseeing area. The numbers refer to the fuller descriptions provided on the following pages.

Naples Area Map

The coloured areas on this map *(see inside front cover)* correspond to the seven main sightseeing areas. Each area is covered in full either in the *Naples Area by Area (see pp48–133)* section or in the *Pompeii and the Amalfi Coast (see pp134–177)* chapter. The map showing the centre of Naples *(pp18–19)* also locates all of the major sights and monuments in the city.

Numbers refer to each sight's position on the area map and its place in the chapter.

Practical information provides all the information you need to visit the sights, including map references to the *Street Finder (see pp224–39).*

The Visitors' Checklist provides all the practical information needed to plan your visit.

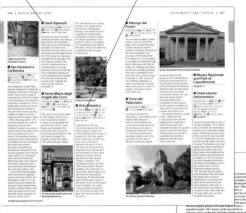

3 Detailed Information on Each Sight
All the most important sights in Naples are described individually. They are listed in order, following the numbering on the area map, which appears at the beginning of each chapter. The key to the symbols used is shown on the back flap for easy reference.

Stars indicate the features you should not miss.

The timeline lists the most important events in the history of the building.

4 Naples' Top Sights
Historic buildings are dissected to reveal their interiors. Museums and galleries have colour-coded floorplans to help you locate the major works exhibited.

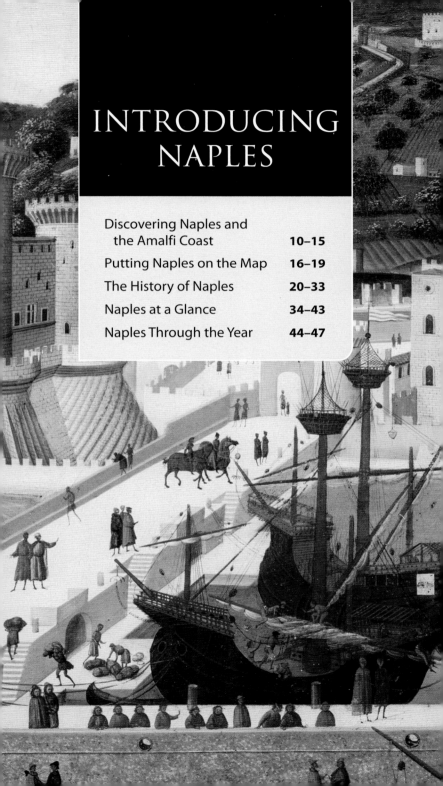

INTRODUCING NAPLES

DISCOVERING NAPLES AND THE AMALFI COAST

The following tours have been designed to take in as many of Naples' and the Amalfi Coast's highlights as possible, while keeping back-tracking to a minimum. First comes a three-day introductory tour of Italy's most life-affirming city, Naples, with a day trip to the sights surrounding Caserta. Next comes a five-day tour of the volcanic area to the west of Naples, the Phlegraean Fields,

and the nearby islands of Procida and Ischia. Finally, a spectacular eight-day trip heads southeast of Naples to explore the best of the Amalfi Coast, along with the archaeological wonders of Pompeii and Paestum, the Sorrento Peninsula and the incomparable island of Capri. Pick, combine and follow your favourite tours, or simply dip in and out and be inspired.

3 Days in and Around Naples

- Experience **Naples** on foot, uncovering its layers of history and superstitions.

- Devour the world's best **pizza** in its home city.

- Climb the seaside citadel **Castel dell'Ovo** for stunning views over the Bay of Naples.

- Saunter along the waterfront promenade and dip into the harbour-side restaurant scene at **Borgo Marinaro**.

- Discover vibrant and powerful artworks including **Santa Chiara's** joyous majolica-tiled courtyard and brooding **Caravaggio** masterpieces.

- Visit the stunning collection at the **Museo Archeologico Nazionale** and stroll through its beautiful grounds.

5 Days Exploring the Phlegraean Fields and Islands

- Trace the footsteps of emperors and gladiators at the Amfiteatro Flavio in **Pozzuoli**.

- Venture to the ancient towns of **Baia** and **Bacoli** and bathe in its thermal springs.

- Discover ancient **Cumae** where a mysterious tunnel is associated with Virgil's mythical soothsayer, Sibyl.

- Sail to the island of **Procida** whose fishing villages, crater bays and sandy beaches are loved by film-makers.

- See the best on the island of **Ischia** from the top of Monte Epomeo, then bathe in its volcanic springs.

- Marvel at Greek relics at Museo di Pithecusae in **Lacco Ameno** on Ischia.

◄ *Ferdinand of Aragon's Fleet in Naples Harbour* by Francesco Pagano

Royal Palace of Caserta
In 1752, the prominent architect Luigi Vanvitelli began building the 1,200-room Reggia Caserta and the extensive gardens, which overflow with fountains and cascades.

The island of Capri
This glamorous resort-island offers luxurious accommodation and stunning island scenery, such as the I Faraglinoni rock formations.

8 Days on the Amalfi Coast and Capri

- Spend an unforgettable day at the ruins of **Pompeii** and **Stabiae**, getting up close to Roman bars, graffiti and artwork.

- See the best of the **Sorrento Peninsula** including the picturesque gardens of Villa Comunale.

- Swim below **Capri's** limestone cliffs in secluded coves once frequented by Roman emperor Tiberius.

- Lounge around the seaside resorts of chic **Positano** and more down-to-earth **Praiano**.

- Wind along the famous coastal **Amalfi Drive**, for dizzying views of the sea.

- Walk amid the columns of Greek temples at **Paestum**.

Pompeii

Stabiae

Cava de' Tirreni

Salerno

Ravello

Vietri sul Mare

Vico Equense

Cetara

Positano

Vettica Maggiore

Amalfi

Praiano

Li Galli

Golfo di Salerno

Paestum

Agropoli

Key

— 3 Days in and Around Naples

— 5 Days Exploring the Phlegraean Fields and Islands

— 8 Days on the Amalfi Coast and Capri

3 Days in and Around Naples

- **Arriving** Arrive at Naples Capodichino (NAP) airport, 6 km (4 miles) northeast of the city centre and linked by a shuttle bus.
- **Transport** Take public transport and walk in Naples. Trains run to Caserta for the Royal Palace, but for other sights near Caserta a car is best as buses are unreliable.

Day 1

Morning Begin with a visit to a Neapolitan coffee legend, the historic **Gran Caffè Gambrinus** (p56) – ask for a seat *al banco*, at the bar. Then explore the monumental sights around Piazza Plebiscito. Note the rulers of Naples on the façade of **Palazzo Reale** (pp54–5) and explore the vast palace containing a wonderful opera museum, **Memus** (p57), dedicated to the adjoining **Teatro San Carlo** (p57). Walk under the glass dome of **Galleria Umberto I** (p57) then discover the tales of battle-worn **Castel Nuovo** (pp58–9) and its Sala dei Baroni.

Afternoon Stroll along the partly pedestrianized **Lungomare** promenade (pp118–19) to **Castel dell'Ovo** (p120) for rooftop battlement views of the bay. Have lunch at a seafood restaurant by the boats below at **Borgo Marinaro** (p119). Relax by the palms and fountains of **Villa Comunale**

(p121) and examine the bay's sea creatures at the **Stazione Zoologica** (p121). If time and energy allow, walk to **Mergellina** (p123) and continue along Via Posillipo for its seaside architecture. Alternatively, take the Mergellina funicular to Via Manzoni for wonderful sunset views and gelato stalls. The evening is also the perfect time to shop in swanky **Chiaia** (p62).

Day 2

Morning Start early to explore the ancient heart of Naples, walking from Piazza del Gesù Nuovo along buzzing **Spaccanapoli** (pp66–7), taking in the majolica-filled cloisters of **Santa Chiara** (pp70–71), the exquisite statuary of **Cappella Sansevero** (p72; closed Tue), numerous historic monuments and spires, and the cool and calm respite offered by many of the area's churches. For a mix of Neapolitan artistry, religion and superstition head to the nativity scene workshops of Via San Gregorio Armeno. Be certain to visit the impressive **Duomo** (pp86–7) and **Pio Monte di Misericordia** (p85) to see a Caravaggio masterpiece.

Afternoon The best Neapolitan DOC pizza can be found on Decumano Maggiore; try Sorbillo at No. 32 or Di Matteo at No. 94, both legendary *pizzerie* (pp190–91). On your way, dare to touch the metallic skull and crossbones outside **Santa Maria delle Anime del Purgatorio ad Arco**

The peaceful gardens in the cloisters of Santa Chiara

(p83). For more rest and refreshment options walk to leafy **Piazza Bellini** (p82) near the old Greek city walls. Dedicate a few hours to the mind-boggling collection of antiquities at the **Museo Archeologico Nazionale** (pp90–93). A contemporary contrast can be found at **Museo MADRE** with its more challenging art (p88).

Day 3

Morning A full morning can be spent at the **Museo Nazionale di Capodimonte** (pp102–5), with its world-class art collection and leafy grounds. Highlights include Caravaggio's *Flagellation of Christ* and Titian's *Danaë*.

Afternoon Head to Vomero to conquer **Castel Sant'Elmo** (p110–11). Be sure to visit **Certosa di San Martino** (pp112–13) for its sumptuous artworks and views. If there's time, stroll around the exotic gardens and ceramic museum at **Villa la Floridiana** (p110), before some evening shopping and a meal along elegant **Via Scarlatti** (p110).

To extend your trip…
Take a train north to **Caserta** (pp168–71) to explore the Royal Palace with its fountain-filled gardens and lavish interior. Don't miss the Giardino Inglese (English Garden) dotted with Roman statuary and curious follies. **Caserta Vecchia** (p168) is worth a visit for its medieval atmosphere and the impressive Duomo di San Michele Arcangelo.

The ancient Castel dell'Ovo, jutting into the Bay of Naples

5 Days Exploring the Phlegraean Fields and Islands

- **Arriving** Arrive at Naples Capodichino (NAP) airport, 6 km (4 miles) northeast of the city centre and linked by a shuttle bus.
- **Transport** Travel by bus and local train; ferry and hydrofoil to and from the islands.

Day 1

Morning Start your trip in **Pozzuoli** *(p140)* where you can examine the remnants of the Roman trading centre Puteoli and the volcanic caldera **Solfatara** *(p141)*. Walk around the Anfiteatro Flavio and the Temple of Serapis, an ancient food market. Bubbling mud, steaming fumaroles and hollow-sounding footsteps make a walk around the snoozing volcano hot and disorientating – it's a spellbinding experience.

Afternoon Marvel at the Roman patricians' lavish villas that run down to the sea at **Baia** and **Bacoli** *(p141)*, and bathe in the hot thermal springs. A boat trip from Baia reveals sunken ancient structures. Among the monuments to see at Bacoli is the atmospheric underground cistern **Piscina Mirablis** *(p142)*, which supplied drinking water to the Roman fleet stationed nearby. At sunset follow the footsteps of Pliny the Younger to panoramic headland **Capo Miseno** *(p142)*, where the Roman writer witnessed the AD 79 eruption of Vesuvius.

The Sybil's Cave, a mysterious tufa tunnel at Cumae

Colourful buildings at Marina Grande on the island of Procida

Day 2

Morning Explore the Greek and Roman temples at the archaeological site of **Cumae** *(pp142–3)*. Try and work out the mysterious origins of Sibyl's Cave, a trapezoid tunnel, which was mentioned by Virgil.

Afternoon Head back to Pozzuoli's port to take a boat to the island of **Procida** *(pp176–7)*. After checking into your hotel wander its narrow lanes, market gardens and hidden coves with sandy beaches.

Day 3

Morning Take a leisurely tour of the island of Procida. Early risers should head to Marina Corricella to watch the fishermen at work and the sun rise over Ischia's Mont Epomeo nearby. Head up to Terra Murata to see the **Abbey of San Michele** *(p176)* and the fantastical exhibits and icons used in the Good Friday procession.

Afternoon Tour the island on foot or hire a bike from Marina Grande. Climb the verdant hill behind Chiaolella port for views over the **Vivara Nature Reserve** *(p173)* and out to sea. Marina Corricella is a wonderful place for a seafood dinner by the harbour.

Day 4

Morning Take the boat to **Ischia** *(pp174–5)* and spend the morning exploring Ischia Porto and Castello Aragonese.

Those seeking healing waters should take time out at spa resort Cassamicciola Terme.

Afternoon Cool off in **Museo di Pithecusae** *(p175)*, the municipal museum at Lacco Ameno, to see some Greek relics and Roman foundations. Discover the tropical microclimate, water features and foliage at the undulating **Giardini La Mortella** *(p174)*.

Day 5

Morning Scale Ischia's highest peak **Monte Epomeo** *(p177)* and enjoy walking on the sculpted, weathered rock of this extinct volcano with its splendid views.

Afternoon Have a leisurely lunch at a shoreline restaurant in Sant' Angelo, then sun yourself on nearby Maronti beach. Or hail a taxi boat and spend the rest of the day at a secluded cove.

The stronghold of Castello Aragonese, just offshore of the island of Ischia

8 Days on the Amalfi Coast and Capri

- **Arriving** Arrive at Naples Capodichino (NAP) airport 6 km (4 miles) northeast of the city centre. Take the bus run by Curreri *(see p219)* straight to Pompeii, Castellammare or Sorrento.

- **Transport** Drive or take buses and trains, including the funicular railway line. To extend your trip to Paestum, hop on the summer boat service from Amalfi to Agropoli.

The ruins of Pompeii's forum, with Vesuvius rising behind

Day 1

Morning Start your tour at the fascinating, poignant site of **Pompeii** *(pp150–55)*, whose citizens were engulfed and suffocated in the AD 79 eruption of Vesuvius. Allow at least three hours to explore the extensive ruins, booking a guide or tagging onto a group tour to gain access to many of the best-preserved interiors, kept under lock and key by the site caretakers *(custodi)*. Bring a picnic with refreshments and find somewhere quiet and shady to rest – the arcaded Great Gymnasium is a good spot *(p153)*.

Afternoon Hop on the funicular train to explore **Ancient Stabiae** *(p156)* just outside of Castellammare di Stabia. It was decimated in the same eruption as Pompeii, and its remains

can be seen at two Roman villas: 13-room Villa di Arianna and lavish Villa San Marco with a swimming pool.

Day 2

Morning Next stop on the funicular railway and coastal road is **Vico Equense** *(p157)* famed for its 14th-century Gothic church Santissima Annunziata. It is also the birthplace of *pizza a metro* (pizza by the metre), making it a very good spot for lunch. While in town, you might also want to visit the small archaeological museum, Museo Antiquarium Equano, or the Museo Mineralogico Campano, filled with geological finds from Vesuvius and dinosaur fossils.

Afternoon Travelling past scented terraces of lemon and olive trees, the railway line and road reach the popular tourist resort of **Sorrento** *(pp158–9)*. It's packed with touristy shops and attractions, such as the gardens of Villa Comunale, and a couple of small museums hold interesting collections: the Museo Bottega della Tarsia Lignea showcases Sorrento's marquetry craftsmen, and the Museo Correale displays the collection of a noble family, including early photographic equipment, artworks and period costume.

Wander over to Sedile Dominova, where locals play cards beneath the frescoed walls, and take a walk to one of

the nearby rocky beaches such as Bagno della Regina Giovanna where you'll find Roman ruins.

Day 3

Morning Take the hydrofoil or ferry from Sorrento to the island of **Capri** *(pp172–3)*, allowing at least two days to enjoy the relaxed glamour of island life. The approach to Capri's limestone cliffs is unforgettable and Marina Grande is a bustling and vivid introduction. Take the funicular up to Capri Town to explore whitewashed lanes draped in flowers.

Afternoon Walk Capri's quiet lanes and paths, heading for the lighthouse at Punta Tragara, which overlooks the rock formations of I Faraglioni. Here you will find a rocky beach and a great choice of restaurants. Alternatively, head for Emperor Tiberius's notorious cliff-top retreat, **Villa Jovis**.

The stacked white-washed buildings of the town of Capri

Lemons and chilli peppers on display outside a produce shop, Sorrento

Day 4

Morning Bathe at rocky Marina Piccola or far-flung lighthouse outpost Faro; the former has a tiny pebbly beach backed by seafood restaurants, while the latter has a rocky shore and deeper waters popular with divers and snorkellers.

Afternoon Board a bus to **Anacapri** *(p172)*, holding tight while it negotiates the road's bends. Explore Anacapri's shops and lanes, and take the chair lift up to lofty Monte Solaro.

Day 5

Morning Spend another laid-back morning on Capri, sipping a cool *caffè shakerato* in the Piazzetta. Keep the pace relaxed with a stroll to the 14th-century **Certosa di San Giacomo** *(p172)*. The monastery's gardens and cloisters offer further serenity before the dash to catch the boat.

Afternoon Return on the boat to Sorrento and explore the coastline of **Massa Lubrense** *(p157)*. Adventurous types can scramble over the wild cliffs at **Punta della Campanella** to the ancient temple of Minerva *(p160)*. **Marina del Cantone** *(p156)* is a gorgeous sheltered bay perfect for bathing and sampling local seafood.

Day 6

Morning Weave your way down and around the pastel-hued houses and shops to the beach of **Positano** *(p162)*, with its coarse pebbly sand dotted with colourful parasols, deckchairs and boats. Be sure not to miss the Santa Maria dell'Assunta church with its vibrant majolica-tiled cupola and Byzantine Black Madonna. Boat trips set off from here to Arienzo, a secluded cove where film director Franco Zeffirelli had a villa, and **Li Galli** *(p161)*, a rocky archipelago where ballet dancer Rudolf Nureyev saw out his final years.

Afternoon Those with a car can sweep along the Amalfi Drive, the SS163, stopping to admire

Ruins of the Temple of Ceres, built around 500 BC, Paestum

the views and pausing in scenic **Vettica Maggiore** *(p163)*. Be wary of buses also occupying this busy road. Stop at **Praiano** *(p163)*, descending on foot to the Marina di Praia for a glimpse of the fishing fleet. Stay for a dip and dine on the sea's bounty.

Day 7

Morning Spend a morning in handsome **Amalfi** *(p163)*, visiting the Duomo di Sant'Andrea near the port and Museo della Carta at the top of the town. Those with time should hike the verdant **Valle dei Mulini** *(p163)* in the hills above town.

Afternoon At 350 m (1,150 ft) above sea level, lofty **Ravello** *(p164)* will take your breath away. Visit the exquisite Duomo and the terraced garden villas Rufolo and Cimbrone. Linger

until late for a tranquil evening meal with stunning views, high above the hubbub below.

Day 8

Morning Those with a car can explore the remaining harbours and villages along the coast including **Vietri sul Mare** *(p165)*, famed for its colourful majolica tiles, and **Cetara** *(p165)* home of the *colatura di alici*, a piquant anchovy sauce.

Afternoon After lunch at Cetara head inland to the lush wooded valley surrounding the town of **Cava de' Tirreni** *(p165)*. Stroll around the handsome porticoed streets and visit the 11th-century Benedictine abbey Santissima Trinità. From Cetara it's a speedy hour's drive along the A3 back to Naples, or if you crave more coastal road drama, retrace your route along the SS163.

To extend your trip...

Take a boat from Amalfi to Agropoli in summer or drive past the city of Salerno to the ancient ruins of Greek-founded **Paestum** *(pp166–7)*. You can spend hours among the wild flower meadows and columned temples; an excellent museum offers cool respite in the summer. En route pick up some of the area's renowned buffalo mozzarella from one of the local producers.

Picturesque Positano, overlooking the Gulf of Salerno

Putting Naples on the Map

Naples is the third largest city in Italy after Milan and Rome, and the largest city in Southern Italy. The population of the city proper *(see pp18–19)* is around one million, rising to more than three million when the suburbs are taken into account. The city faces the great sweep of the splendid Bay of Naples, extends into the fertile Campania plain, and occupies high ground and hollows formed by ancient volcanic craters.

Cassino
Campobass
A1
S87
Appennii
S372
S7
Caserta
Benevento
Campan
NAPLES
Avel
Pozzuoli
Isola
d'Ischia
Pompeii
Sorrento
Salerno
Battipac
Isola di
Capri
Paestu

Key

— Motorway
— Major road
— Railway line
— Regional border

Cagliari

Tyrrhenian
Sea

Genoa,
Civitavecchia

Cagliari,
Tunis

Ustica

Isole Eolie
or Lipari

Palermo
Cefalù
A20
Trapani
A29
Alcamo
S121
A19
Monti Nebro
Marsala
A29
S115
S121
Sicily
Sciacca
S118
Enna
A19
Catar
S640
Caltanissetta
Mediterranean
Sea
Agrigento
S417

Gela
Val di Noto

S115

Modica
Isola di
Pantelleria

Isole Pelagie

Foggia

Barletta

Cerignola

Molfetta

Bari

Dubrovnik

Greece

A14

A16

Le Murge

S96

S655

Melfi

S100

S16

Fasano

S658

Altamura

Puglia

Potenza

S99

A14

Appennino

S407

Matera

S172

Brindisi

Greece, Albania

Basilicata

Taranto

S7

Penisola Salentina

Lecce

Lucano

S598

S106

Galatina

S16

Maratea

A3

Sibari

Ionian Sea

S18

Rossano

Cosenza

Calabria

Crotone

Lamezia Terme

Catanzaro

Vibo Valentia

A3

S106

Reggio di Calabria

azzo

ssina

ormina

↑ *Naples*

sta

↘ *Malta*

acusa

0 kilometres 100

0 miles 100

Europe

NORWAY

SWEDEN

ESTONIA

North Sea

LATVIA

DENMARK

LITHUANIA

REP. OF IRELAND

UNITED KINGDOM

NETH.

POLAND

BELARUS

BELGIUM

GERMANY

UKRAINE

CZECH REPUBLIC

SLOVAKIA

Atlantic Ocean

FRANCE

SWITZ.

AUSTRIA

HUNGARY

SLOV.

ROMANIA

CROATIA

BOSNIA HERZ.

SERBIA

ITALY

MONTEN.

KOS.

BULGARIA

MAC.

SPAIN

Naples

ALBANIA

GREECE

PORTUGAL

MOROCCO

ALGERIA

TUNISIA

Central Naples

The old town is divided into six distinct areas. From the 16th century on, the administrative and commercial centre of Naples developed around Toledo and Castel Nuovo. The old city centre is described in the chapters on Spaccanapoli and Decumano Maggiore. The Vergini district, immediately north of the Foria gorge, leads to the park of Capodimonte with its Royal Palace. The Certosa di San Martino and Castel Sant'Elmo dominate the Vomero hill. In the Chiaia area, a few steps from the most elegant shops in Naples, places such as Castel dell'Ovo and Mergellina are surrounded by greenery and the sea. To the west are the lovely inlets and villas of Posillipo.

The Certosa di San Martino, on the Vomero

The Cappella Caracciolo di Vico in San Giovanni a Carbonara

Key

Major sight

Castel Nuovo, known locally as Maschio Angioino

Reggia di
Capodimonte

PIAZZA
S. EFRAMO
VECCHIO

CAPODIMONTE
AND
I VERGINI

ORTO
BOTANICO

PIAZZA
CARLO III

PIAZZA
ANSEVERO

VIA TENORE

VIA FORIA

CORSO GARIBALDI

ZZA
ANITÀ

L.GO
MIRACOLI

VIA DEI CRISTALLINI

VIA PIAZZI

PIAZZA
MIRACOLI

S. Giovanni a
Carbonara

P.ZA TEATRO
S. FERDINANDO

P.ZA
VOLTURNO

ONTE

P.ZA
PAGANO

P.TTA S. CARLO
ALL'ARENA

P.TTA
DEI LEPRI

P.ZA
STELLA

P.TTA
SETTEM-
BRINI

P.ZA
S. ANNA
A.CAPUNA

PIAZZA
CAVOUR

M Cavour

M Museo

PIAZZA
DE NICOLA

PIAZZA
PRINCIPE
UMBERTO

gico
ale

P.TTA
D. DAME

S. ANDREA

LARGO
DONNAREGINA

CUMANO
AGGIORE

L.GO
REGINA
COELI

VIA

Duomo

PIAZZA
S. GAETANO

PIAZZA SISTO
RIARIO
SFORZA

P.ZA
MIRAGLIA

S. Lorenzo
Maggiore

P.ZA
BELLINI

S. Gregorio
Armeno

P.ZA
CALENDA

S. Domenico
Maggiore

PIAZZA
S.ʰMARIA
LA SCALA

Gesù Nuovo

P.ZA
S. DOMENICO
MAGGIORE

P.TTA
SCACCHI

P.TTA
S. ELIGIO

Santa Chiara

PIAZZA
NICOLA
AMORE

P.TTA
DE
OMO

PIAZZA
MERCATO

SPACCANAPOLI

DUOMO

CORSO UMBERTO I

PIAZZA
MASANIELLO

P.ZA
PORTA-
NOVA

P.TTA
PRINCIPESSA
MARGHERITA

NUOVA MARINA

P.TTA
PORTO

PIAZZA
BOVIO

MOLO
C. PISACANE

Università M

LEDO AND
TEL NUOVO

VIA C.

M Municipio

AZZA
NICIPIO

Castel
Nuovo

MOLO
BEVERELLO

MOLO
ANGIOINO

INI
ICI

The tiled cloister of Santa Chiara

0 metres		500
0 yards		500

The fountain of Christ and the Samaritan in the cloister
of the convent of San Gregorio Armeno

Castel dell'Ovo, seen from the bay

For keys to symbols *see back flap*

THE HISTORY OF NAPLES

In Greek mythology, Naples was built where the Siren Parthenope was washed ashore after she had been rejected by Odysseus. Greek colonists founded a settlement overlooking the Bay of Naples as early as the 4th century BC, calling it Parthenope. As the settlement continued to expand, they established *Neapolis* (new city) next to the *Palaeopolis*, or old city. Neapolis was a leading commercial centre, and the Greek language and customs survived even during the Roman period, when this was a favourite area of the elite.

After the fall of the Roman Empire and a wave of invasions, the city, though it retained some independence, came under Byzantine influence and went through a period of rebirth. In the 12th century, the invading Normans succeeded in conquering the whole of Southern Italy, a kingdom initially ruled from Palermo, under Roger II. In 1266, Charles of Anjou was crowned King of the Two Sicilies, an event that began the Angevin (French) and Aragonese (Spanish) dynasties. Naples itself became a capital, and the court began to attract famous artists. The 1400s were a golden era for Naples, but there followed two centuries of direct rule by Spain. The Spanish viceroys were oppressive rulers and the era is remembered for unjust taxation, the Inquisition, the plague, overpopulation and the rebellion of Masaniello. Creativity flowered, however, despite the widespread poverty.

In 1734 King Charles began the period of Bourbon hegemony. With the exception of the short-lived republican government in 1799 and the subsequent decade of French dominion, the Bourbons ruled Naples until 1860.

Since the unification of Italy, in the mid-19th century, the city's problems have become national issues – for example, the markedly different level of development between Northern and Southern Italy.

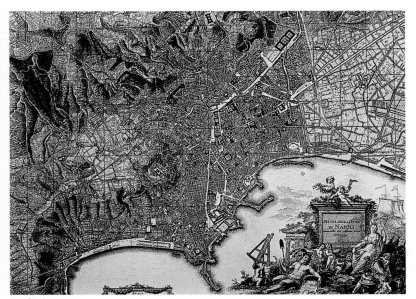

Map of Naples in 1790

◀ *Paquius Proculus and His Wife*, 1st-century AD wall painting from Pompeii

Greco-Roman Naples

By the 8th century BC, Greeks had founded a settlement at Cumae, one of the earliest Greek colonies in Italy. From there they established a new town on Pizzofalcone hill, known as Parthenope, and trade prospered. Population growth led to the founding of *Neapolis*, or "new city", nearby, and victory over the Etruscans in 474 BC brought further expansion. *Neapolis* came into contact with the growing power of Rome during the latter's protracted wars with the Samnites, and in the 4th century BC the citizens agreed to become an "allied city" of Rome. In AD 79 an erupting Vesuvius buried a number of ancient Roman cities, including Pompeii.

Extent of the city
☐ 8 BC ☐ Today

Bedrooms and living rooms

Temple of the Dioscuri
This 16th-century print shows the Roman temple that once stood on the site of San Paolo Maggiore *(see p83)*. The temple façade collapsed in the 1688 earthquake.

Via Anticaglia
The "street of ruins" acquired its name from the brick arches connecting the Ancient Roman bath house and the theatre *(see p88)*.

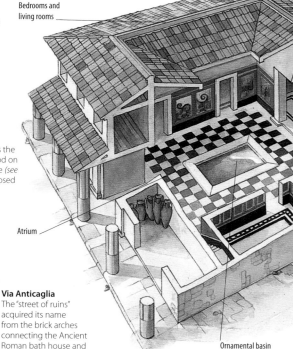

Atrium

Ornamental basin *(impluvium)*

1000–900 BC According to Greek myth, city of Parthenope founded

328 BC War with Rome; Naples is defeated but a treaty sanctions the city's freedom

90–89 BC People of Campania become Roman citizens

900 BC   **600 BC**   **300 BC**   **100 BC**

600 BC Greeks from Cumae found *Neapolis* or "new city"

Red-figure vase (5th century BC)

100 BC Tunnel built in Posillipo hill connecting city with Phlegraean Fields area and its trade and military ports

The Houses of Pompeii

The Roman houses in Pompeii (see pp154–5) are among the best-preserved examples of Roman civilization in Campania. This illustration shows a typical patrician house in Pompeii, displaying characteristic features of Roman and Greek domestic architecture. The houses were generally rectangular. To ensure privacy, they faced inwards, as can be seen by the few windows on the outer walls, and the rooms were built around an atrium or courtyard, which was the focal point of domestic life. Wealthier houses were richly decorated.

Where to See Greco-Roman Naples

Beneath the cloister of San Lorenzo *(see p84)* layers of the ancient city are still visible.

Although not much is left of Greco-Roman *Neapolis*, some traces are visible in Piazza Bellini *(see p82)*, around Santa Chiara *(see pp70–71)* and under the Duomo *(see pp86–7)*. Outside the city, Pompeii and Herculaneum are vivid records of ancient Roman life. The Museo Archeologico Nazionale *(see pp90–93)* in Naples houses rich finds. Amphitheatres survive at Pozzuoli *(see p140)* and Santa Maria Capua Vetere *(see p169)*, and Greek ruins at Cumae *(see p142)* and Paestum *(see pp166–7)*.

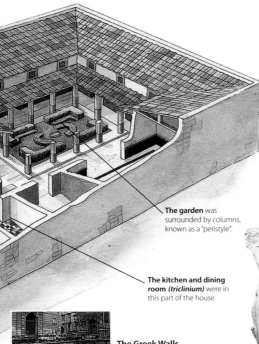

The garden was surrounded by columns, known as a "peristyle".

The kitchen and dining room *(triclinium)* were in this part of the house.

The Greek Walls
Made of large tufa blocks, the city walls date from the 5th century BC. Remnants can be seen in present-day Piazza Bellini *(see p82)*.

The Diadumeno Torso from Castel Capuano

Statue of Aphrodite, Museo Archeologico

305 San Gennaro decapitated in Pozzuoli; his remains are placed in the city catacombs *(see p98)*

500 Construction of first parish church, now San Giorgio Maggiore *(see p74)*

AD	AD 300	400	500

79 Vesuvius erupts; Pompeii and Herculaneum destroyed

The Siren Parthenope on a Roman coin

476 Romulus Augustulus, last Roman emperor of the West, imprisoned in the Castrum Lucullanum *(see p120)*

536 Byzantine General Belisarius wins Naples, entering city via the aqueduct

From Byzantine Rule to the Aragonese Dynasty

In the 6th century AD, Naples became part of the Byzantine (Eastern Roman) empire. Despite incursions into Southern Italy by Goths, Lombards and Saracens, it remained a semi-independent duchy, nominally under Byzantine rule, until it became part of the Norman kingdom of Sicily in the 12th century. By the 13th century the French House of Anjou had taken over and Naples became the capital of the Angevin kingdom. Ambitious schemes were begun: land reclamation and the building of new castles, churches and monasteries. In 1421 the last Angevin queen, Joan II, named Alfonso V of Aragon as her successor.

Growth of the city
▢ AD 500   ▢ Today

Tombs in Santa Chiara
The Angevin rulers were buried in Santa Chiara, which contains superbly crafted tombs such as this one by an unknown artist (first half of the 14th century).

Tomb of Ladislas of Durazzo
This tomb is in San Giovanni a Carbonara *(see p100)*, chosen by Ladislas to house the tombs of the Angevin kings.

Louis of Anjou took vows after refusing the crown of Naples and was canonized in 1317.

The Pietrasanta Bell Tower
This is among the few remaining examples of medieval architecture in Naples *(see p82)*.

553 Naples again under Byzantine rule

7th-century Byzantine fibula

915 After many attempts to conquer Naples, the Saracens are defeated at Garigliano

600	700	800	900

600 Naples resists Lombard siege and remains an independent duchy

763 The duchy becomes hereditary and independent

Statue of Frederick II, Holy Roman Emperor

Frescoes of the Giotto School
Giotto lived in Naples from 1328–33. His influence can be seen in the frescoes in Santa Maria di Donnaregina Vecchia (see p88).

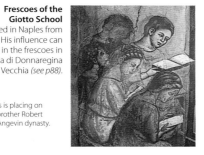

The crown Louis is placing on the head of his brother Robert legitimized the Angevin dynasty.

St Louis of Toulouse
This Gothic portrait was probably painted in 1317, after Louis of Anjou was canonized. Louis is shown as a Franciscan saint crowning his younger brother Robert King of Naples. Simone Martini's masterpiece is now in the Museo Nazionale di Capodimonte (see pp102–5).

Robert of Anjou

Where to See Angevin and Aragonese Naples

Evidence of this period is everywhere in Naples, although successive reconstructions have often obscured the original architectural styles. Rather than civic buildings such as Castel Capuano (see p85), it was the churches that changed the face of the city: Santa Chiara (see pp70–71), San Lorenzo Maggiore (see p84), San Domenico Maggiore (see p72), and Santa Maria di Donnaregina Vecchia (see p88) with its wonderful cycle of frescoes painted by the school of Giotto.

Castel Nuovo, originally Angevin, also has Aragonese elements (see pp58–9).

King Roger II
The Norman king of Naples is depicted in one of the eight statues placed in the niches of the Palazzo Reale façade in 1888 (see pp54–5).

1140 Neapolitans consign city to Roger II, Norman king of Sicily

1165 Castel Capuano built in a position to control communications with interior

1194 The city ruled by Henry VI Hohenstaufen, Roger II's son-in-law

1224 Frederick II founds the University

1266 Charles I of Anjou enters Naples and makes it the capital of the new Angevin kingdom

1279 Construction of Castel Nuovo begins

1341 Petrarch stays at Castel Nuovo

1443 Alfonso of Aragon enters Naples

Bust of Alfonso V

1421 Joan II, last Angevin sovereign, names Alfonso V of Aragon her heir

1496 Threatened by France and Spain, the king cedes Naples to the French

1486 The Barons' Conspiracy fails

1100 | **1200** | **1300** | **1400**

The Spanish Viceroyalty

In 1503 Naples ceased to be an independent kingdom, and became a colony of Spain, ruled by a viceroy. The city began to expand unchecked in the suburbs and beyond the walls. Palazzo Reale was built near Castel Nuovo, and courts assembled at Castel Capuano. With the construction of Via Toledo and the restructuring of Via Chiaia in the mid-1500s, the focus of city development shifted: aristocratic palaces were built along the Riviera and Toledo, and the need to accommodate the troops led to the building of the Quartieri Spagnoli district. New churches and monasteries were built. By now Naples was the largest city in Italy, with consequent problems of overcrowding and poverty. A famous figure in this period is Masaniello, the revolutionary who was first considered a hero, and then killed by the people who had supported him. Spanish rule came to an end in 1707 when, with the Treaty of Utrecht, the Kingdom of Naples was ceded to Austria.

Growth of the city
1500   Today

Santa Maria del Carmine
(see p77), which gave the square its name.

Don Pedro de Toledo
Don Pedro was viceroy from 1532 to 1553. He promoted new town planning, but also wanted to bring the Inquisition to Naples, triggering a revolt by the landed nobility.

Masaniello, born Tommaso Aniello in 1622, was an illiterate fisherman.

1503 Gonzalo Fernández de Cordóba, sent by the King of Spain, enters the city

1532–52 The first modern town plan of Naples is put into effect

1600 Construction of Palazzo Reale, by Domenico Fontana

The Eruption of Vesuvius by Philipp Hackert

1631 Eruption of Vesuvius

1500

1600

1536 Via Toledo opened

1547 Viceroy Don Pedro fails to bring the Inquisition to Naples

1606–7 Caravaggio in Naples

1637–60 Construction of Guglia di San Gennaro to thank the patron saint for saving the city from the eruption of Vesuvius

Palazzo Reale

Statue of San Gennaro
The Neapolitans gave their venerated patron saint credit for having stopped the eruption of Vesuvius in 1631.

This memorial stone was to record all the concessions obtained from the viceroy by Masaniello.

Where to See Viceroyal Naples

The original 17th-century façade of the Palazzo Reale (see pp54–5) has changed little over the centuries. The Cappella del Tesoro di San Gennaro, or Duomo, (see pp86–7) is one of the richest Baroque monuments in Naples. A short distance from the Duomo is a small area with a wealth of 17th-century treasures: the Guglia di San Gennaro (see p85) and Pio Monte della Misericordia (see p85), which houses the canvas that marked a turning point in 17th-century Neapolitan painting – The Seven Acts of Mercy by Caravaggio, who stayed in Naples in 1607.

Masaniello's uprising

This painting by Micco Spadaro depicts Piazza Mercato (see p77) during the 1647 riot. A tax levied on fruit sparked the riot, which rapidly grew into a fully fledged uprising against the aristocracy. However, the attempt was soon crushed, as the city's moderates managed to persuade people to rebel against their revolutionary leader. Masaniello was killed the same year on 16 July.

The Certosa di San Martino (see pp112–15) was extended and decorated in the late 1500s.

At San Gregorio Armeno (see p84), the cloister is decorated with this striking fountain.

Giambattista Vico
The famous philosopher and historian, author of *La Scienza Nuova (The New Science)*, was born in Naples in 1668, the son of a bookseller.

The plague in a painting by Micco Spadaro (detail)

1647 Masaniello's uprising

1707 Beginning of Austrian viceroyalty

1723 Pietro Giannone flees to Vienna after publishing his *Civic History of the Kingdom of Naples*, which is banned by the Church

1700

1656 Devastating plague epidemic; Naples loses one-third of population

1701 Failure of Prince of Macchia's conspiracy to overthrow Spanish rule

1697 Giambattista Vico becomes professor of rhetoric at Naples university

1688 Earthquake damages most of old city

Bourbon Naples

In 1734 the much-abused Kingdom of Naples changed hands once more, with the arrival of King Charles of Bourbon, who set out to make Naples into a metropolis. He suspended church building in favour of large-scale public works and new industries. He also built a Royal Palace in Caserta modelled on Versailles, which was to be the focal point of an entire city. At the same time, art, antiquities, music and even the *lazzaroni* (street people) attracted travellers making the Grand Tour. The royal schemes lacked a coherent plan, however, and fundamental problems failed to be addressed. Bourbon rule ended in 1860, when Garibaldi arrived in Naples, having won over Sicily and Calabria. In the same year Naples became part of the new Kingdom of Italy.

Growth of the city

⬜ 1700   ⬜ Today

The Palace of Capodimonte

Charles's Porcelain
The king founded a porcelain factory in 1743 *(see p105).* After Charles returned to Spain his son, Ferdinand, opened his own factory.

The Beheading of Ettore Carafa
This relief in the Museo di San Martino depicts the execution of one of the martyrs of the Parthenopean Republic on 17 August 1799.

Antonio Genovesi (1713–69)
A leading figure in the Neapolitan Enlightenment movement, he became the first professor of political economics in Italy in 1754.

Statuette found in Herculaneum

1738 Beginning of excavations at Herculaneum

1777 The university moves to the Jesuit College, now a banished society. Ferdinando Fuga turns Palazzo degli Studi into a museum

1700

1750

1740 Church building suspended

1734 King Charles establishes the Bourbon dynasty in Naples

1759 Charles returns to Spain; his son Ferdinand becomes king

Ancient finds at Herculaneum transferred to Palazzo degli Studi

Cappella di San Gennaro
19th-century Neapolitan painting often featured landscapes and picturesque settings, as seen in this work by Gigante (1806–76), showing the chapel of San Gennaro, as well as the rural scenes of Palizzi (1818–88) and the realism of Morelli (1826–1901).

Where to See Bourbon Naples

The most important architectural achievements of the Bourbons are the Teatro San Carlo *(see p57)*, the Palace of Capodimonte *(see pp102–5)* and the Albergo dei Poveri *(see p101)*. Urban projects such as the Foro Carolino and the Villa Reale at Chiaia also date from the Bourbon period. The passion for antiquity inspired collecting and the setting up of the Museo Archeologico *(see pp90–3)*. But Bourbon influence is mainly to be seen outside the city, where kings built hunting lodges as well as royal palaces, such as Caserta *(see pp168–9)*.

The Duke of Noja's map

This was the first modern relief map, the work of Duke Giovanni Carafa di Noja in 1775. The map shows the full extent of the city of Naples and the monumental buildings in the newly developed districts. In this detail the impressive Royal Palace of Capodimonte dominates the city skyline.

Naples appears as a chaotic muddle of buildings here.

The Bourbon court out hunting in a painting by Jakob Philipp Hackert (1783).

The Naples-Portici Railway

The first Italian railway was inaugurated in 1839, when the Bayard locomotive took 9 minutes 30 seconds to travel about 7.5 km (4.5 miles). This painting of the Vesuvio by Fergola is in the Museo di San Martino.

1806 Napoleon gives the role of king of Naples to his brother Joseph Bonaparte

1815 Murat executed at Pizzo Castle, in Calabria. Ferdinand returns to throne as King of the Two Sicilies

1839 First railway in Italy, Naples–Portici, inaugurated

1860 Garibaldi enters city on 7 September; after plebiscite, Naples becomes part of newly united Kingdom of Italy

1800

1850

1808 Bonaparte goes to Spain and is replaced by Joachim Murat. The French promote great public works and administrative reforms

1820 Constitution granted but it is repealed the following year

1848 Popular revolt restores constitution but it is annulled by Parliament in 1849

1799 Birth of Neapolitan Republic, overthrown six months later by the counter-revolution. Its leaders are executed in Piazza Mercato

Giuseppe Garibaldi

Naples after Unification

In a crowded, densely populated city, the 1884 cholera epidemic brought ancient problems to a head. An attempt to face them was made with the Urban Renewal Plan. Slum clearance was carried out around the port and new districts were created in the centre and towards the hills. However, the Plan failed to solve many basic problems, work took much longer than expected, and triggered a wave of corruption. The Fascist regime contented itself with a new series of public works and the creation of more built-up areas. A leading local figure of the time was the philosopher Benedetto Croce, one of the few Italian intellectuals who openly opposed Fascism.

Growth of the city

▨ 1850 ☐ Today

The ILVA Steelworks in Bagnoli

This plant, later known as Italsider, was built near the beach and the ancient hot springs in 1907 (see p140). Renovated for the last time in 1987 and now closed, it has become a symbol of modern development carried out with total disregard for the natural context and scenic beauty of the area.

Santa Chiara
After being damaged in the 1943 bombardments, Santa Chiara was restored to its presumed original appearance.

Matilde Serao (1856–1927)
"Naples must be gutted" declared the prominent author on the eve of the Renewal Plan. A few years later, disappointed by the results, she described Corso Umberto I as a "screen" concealing old and new misery.

1880 Inauguration of Vesuvius funicular, which inspires the famous song *Funiculì Funiculà*

The Mount Vesuvius funicular

1891 First city funicular connecting Vomero with centre becomes operative

1860	1875	1890

1868 Via Duomo begun with first city demolition and finished in late 1800s as part of Urban Renewal Plan

1885 Special law for Urban Renewal Plan: demolition of slum areas begins

1899 First stretch of Cumana railway built

1884 Cholera epidemic

The Rettifilo
This eclectic and stately avenue, officially called Corso Umberto I and built after the Urban Renewal projects ended, is a good example of late 19th-century bourgeois Naples.

Where to See Post-Unification Naples

The Gran Caffè Gambrinus *(see p56)* was the haunt of Italian avant-garde artists, such as the Futurists, as well as such illustrious visitors as Oscar Wilde. During the Urban Renewal period that changed the face of civic Naples, the Art Nouveau style prevailed in the new residential districts and the small villas in Chiaia *(see pp116–23)* and Vomero *(see pp106–15)*. Monumental Fascist architecture is represented by the Palazzo delle Poste e Telegrafi *(see p61)* and the Stazione Marittima (the port). Via Toledo *(see p57)* boasts an important Novecento-style building constructed in 1939 to house the main offices of the Banco di Napoli.

The Gran Caffè Gambrinus was popular in the early 1900s.

The Mostra delle Terre d'Oltremare
This huge exhibition and recreational complex was one of the Fascist regime's most notable architectural achievements. Work on the site began in 1937 after the demolition of the Fuorigrotta quarter.

01 Saredo judicial inquiry reveals government–camorra rapport

Benito Mussolini

1925–7 Naples incorporates surrounding towns, formerly independent

Entrance to Mostra d'Oltremare

1940 Mostra delle Terre d'Oltremare – a huge exhibition, recreational and sports complex built by the Fascist regime – opens

1905

1920

1935

1922 On October 24, Fascists meet in Naples on eve of "March on Rome"

1928–41 Rione Carità district replaces old San Giuseppe quarter

1943 *"Quattro giornate"* uprising: Germans driven out of Naples

1944 Last eruption of Vesuvius

Present-day Naples

At the end of World War II the city had to cope with the appalling damage inflicted by all the bombardments. The 1950s and 1960s were marked by the large-scale, indiscriminate building activity promoted by politicians seeking short-term gain. The closure of some large factories in the 1980s aggravated the acute unemployment problem. However, Naples has always distinguished itself by its irrepressible vitality and creativity, especially in the fields of music and theatre. Today the city is rediscovering its past, and there is a commitment to city regeneration, as well as a resurgence of cultural programmes and the creation of contemporary art galleries.

Growth of the city
▨ 1945   ☐ Today

Vesuvius
This work by Andy Warhol was produced in 1985 for an exhibition held at the Museo di Capodimonte, where a copy is now on display. It is the American artist's tribute to the most recurrent artistic motif relating to Naples – an erupting Vesuvius.

San Paolo Stadium
Built in the 1960s, this football stadium has a seating capacity of 60,000. Famous former players for Naples include Dino Zoff and Diego Maradona.

1952 Shipowner Achille Lauro, leader of the monarchist party, becomes mayor. Period of building speculation begins

Achille Lauro

1972 Town-planning regulations (still partly in force) protect historic old town

1975 Inauguration of bypass road for fast traffic at edge of old town

1950	1960	1970	1980

1949 Curzio Malaparte's novel *La Pelle*, set in Naples, causes a scandal with its raw descriptions

1945 Eduardo De Filippo writes *Napoli milionaria*. Town council approves reconstruction project

1963 Francesco Rosi directs film *Hands over the City (see p41)*

1962 Centre-left coalition governs city

1980 The earthquake Campania and Basilica also causes damage in Naples. Reconstructio includes a plan to revi the outskirts

Posillipo Today

Among the many examples of building malpractice in Naples, Posillipo is one of the most tragic. The hill, known the world over for its ancient history and lovely scenery, has been defaced by unchecked and unscrupulous development.

A pedestrian avenue runs between the buildings: cars use underground roads.

Skyscrapers are a novelty in Neapolitan architecture.

Centro Direzionale

This district of futuristic administrative office buildings in the heart of the city, near the central railway station, is an example of "rational" modernization. The original plan dates from the 1960s, but in 1982 the famous Japanese architect Kenzo Tange began a new design. The layout of the area is such that traffic, which runs along underground streets, is separated from pedestrians.

The planting of trees softens the stark modern aesthetic and improves the environment for workers.

Montagna di Sale

Mimmo Paladino's *Montagna di Sale* (*Salt Mountain*) was installed in Piazza del Plebiscito for New Year's Day 1996. The square, restored for the G7 summit and now a pedestrian zone, has become a symbol of the new Naples.

1995–6 Mimmo Paladino's temporary sculpture *Montagna di Sale* is placed in Piazza del Plebiscito

2001 Antonio Bassolino, famous for restoring historic centre of Naples, stands down as mayor. Rosa Russo Iervolino takes over

2006 Giorgio Napolitano, Naples native, elected 11th president of Italy; Iervolino re-elected mayor

Antonio Bassolino

| 990 | 2000 | 2010 | 2020 |

1994 G7 summit opens in July in Naples. First stage of hill metro becomes operative

2002 Station Art project sees the work of emerging artists on show in city metro stations

2012 20 km (12 mile) cycle path added to the beach front, giving Naples one of the best cycle-path networks in Italy

2001 Thousands of anti-globalisation demonstrators take to the streets while the G8 leaders are in town

NAPLES AT A GLANCE

Naples is filled with evidence of many centuries of occupation blended into the fabric of the present-day city. This complex heritage, from ancient Greeks and Romans to the dukes, kings and queens of the Middle Ages and beyond, has contributed to a rich store of galleries and museums, ancient amphitheatres and ruins, as well as churches, monasteries, royal palaces and monuments. While the *Area by Area* section *(pp48–133)* describes the various places of interest in detail, the following ten pages will provide some background and cultural context. Each corner of Naples has something different to offer, but below is a selection of attractions that no visitor to the city should miss.

Naples' Top Tourist Attractions

Castel Nuovo
See pp58–9

Santa Chiara
See pp70–71

Museo di Capodimonte
See pp102–5

Certosa di San Martino
See pp112–15

Mergellina
See p123

Castel dell'Ovo
See p120

Museo Archeologico Nazionale
See pp90–93

Posillipo
See pp128–33

 The glass-vaulted ceiling of Galleria Umberto I, built in 1890

Naples and the Bay

Formed by an immense crater, the Bay of Naples is both sheltered and exposed; sheltered by the curve of hills to the east which create a natural semi-circular amphitheatre, but open to the sea. The zone is volcanic, shaped by cones and craters of all ages, some submerged, some still bubbling with thermal springs and jets of steam. Now that Vesuvius is quiet (the last smoke trail was seen in 1944), the most active crater in the region is the Solfatara at Pozzuoli *(see p141)*. The living, breathing quality of the land led Homer to choose the coastline as the setting for parts of the *Odyssey*. Chaotic development along the coast has not deterred visitors from seeking out and appreciating the beauty of the bay.

The Ischia waterfront is built up with many restaurants and historic buildings

Gaiola is the largest of the three islands facing the Gaiola quarter. The coastline is rocky and precipitous with natural caves.

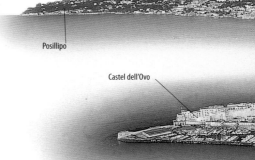

Posillipo

Castel dell'Ovo

The Bay of Naples

Mount Vesuvius stands guard over a bay that owes its beauty and characteristic curves to the violent and often deadly explosions of a series of volcanoes. The conical shape of Monte Epomeo on Ischia still shows its volcanic origin; one submerged crater now does service as the port of Ischia and hot springs abound. Capri, once joined to the mainland, is geologically an extension of the Sorrento peninsula; time has carved beautiful caves along the island's precipitous coastline. Just beyond Punta Campanella are islands known to Homer as the home of the Sirens.

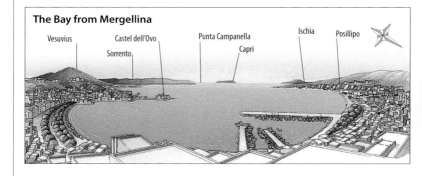

The Bay from Mergellina

Vesuvius   Castel dell'Ovo   Punta Campanella   Ischia   Posillipo

Sorrento   Capri

The fertility of the soil in Naples was proverbial in ancient times. To this day you can still find unexpected pockets of terraced cultivation in built-up areas.

The port of Naples, once a disembarkation point for transatlantic ships, is now the centre of intense ship, ferry and hydrofoil traffic for tourists along the coast and to the islands of Capri, Ischia and Procida. The Angioino wharf is also important commercially.

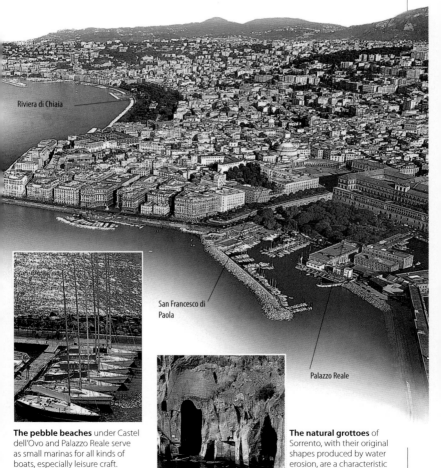

Riviera di Chiaia

San Francesco di Paola

Palazzo Reale

The pebble beaches under Castel dell'Ovo and Palazzo Reale serve as small marinas for all kinds of boats, especially leisure craft.

The natural grottoes of Sorrento, with their original shapes produced by water erosion, are a characteristic feature of the southern stretch of the bay.

The Architecture of Naples

One feature of the architecture of Naples is the way in which traces of various epochs and styles can be seen in one short section of street, from Roman foundations and remains to the turn-of-the-century galleria made of iron and glass. Little remains within Naples of its Greek heritage, yet in the heart of the city you can still discern the regular grid layout adopted in 5th-century BC *Neapolis*: the three main streets going east–west – present-day Via Anticaglia *(see p88)*, Via dei Tribunali *(see pp80–81)* and Via San Biagio dei Librai – and the north–south roads that intersect them at right angles. Along the waterfront (Lungomare) and the Riviera di Chiaia, more modern buildings can be found, elegant palazzi alternating with villas and splendid luxury hotels.

The ancient grid layout of *Neapolis* (red lines) over a plan of the modern city

Via Foria

Caserma Garibaldi, 1843

Via Duomo

1956–7

Riviera di Chiaia

The wide, elegant Riviera di Chiaia, flanked by fine buildings, mostly dating from the 18th and 19th centuries   1940–41

Lungomare

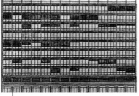
1955–6

Faculty of Business Administration, 1934

Hotel Royal, 1956

A Multi-Layered City

San Lorenzo Maggiore *(see p84)* is one example of a layered building. Remains of the ancient city are visible under the monastery. The church itself is also the result of a series of reconstructions; the Angevin basilica, built over the ruins of a 6th-century church, was completely rebuilt in the 1700s, and then restored to its original medieval state in the last century. The 18th-century façade still has the original 14th-century wooden doorway.

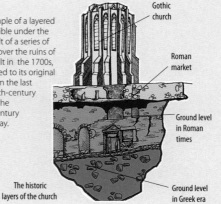

Gothic church

Roman market

Ground level in Roman times

Ground level in Greek era

The historic layers of the church

Greco-Roman remains

The Galleria Principe di Napoli, built in 1883, the oldest galleria in Naples

San Giuseppe a Chiaia, dating from 1666–73

The Neo-Classical Villa Pignatelli, 1826, designed by Pietro Valente, now a museum *(see p122)*

Hotel Continental, 1955

Hotel Vesuvio (reconstruction), 1948

Santa Lucia, 1902

Writers in Naples

The beauty of the Bay of Naples and the fascination of Vesuvius have inspired writers and artists for over 2,000 years. The Greeks wove stories around the landscape, seeing in it a variety of mythological creatures; volcanic activity was regarded as the work of the gods. The poet Virgil so loved Naples that he spent his last years there while writing the *Georgics* and the *Aeneid*. The city's rich Classical inheritance again attracted travellers with the advent of the Grand Tour, over 17 centuries later, when no young man could be considered well educated without a visit to Italy.

Portrait of Giacomo Leopardi

From Classical Writers to the Renaissance

Before the eruption in AD 79 Vesuvius had been quiet for 1,200 years, but inhabitants were nonetheless aware of the living nature of the land. Pliny the Elder, author of *Naturalis Historia*, died at Pompeii; his curiosity tempted him to go closer to the volcano and he was suffocated by the fumes. His nephew, Pliny the Younger, provides in his letters an eyewitness account of the eruption.

The Renaissance brought a revival of interest in Greek and Latin culture. In the 14th century writers and artists including Boccaccio, Giotto and the great lyric poet and scholar Petrarch were attracted to the court of Robert of Anjou. Torquato

Petrarch

Tasso, a native of Sorrento, worked on his epic poetry at the monastery of Monteoliveto at the end of the 1500s.

Travellers and the Grand Tour

The Grand Tour first became a custom in the 16th century and by the 18th century it was English fashion. Young aristocrats were expected to study Europe's Classical past to complete their education and the Tour took them to Rome and Naples. Excavations at Herculaneum in 1711 and at Pompeii in 1733 added to the enormous appeal of this part of Italy. Sir William Hamilton, an archaeologist, collector and envoy to Naples from 1764, entertained Grand Tour travellers at the embassy. The Tour inspired journals, letters and guide books and Goethe, overwhelmed by his visit to the city in 1775 with the painter Tischbein, wrote of Naples in *Italian Journey*.

Romantic Naples

Stendhal departed Naples in 1817 smitten with Toledo and Teatro San Carlo, the glories of the "most beautiful city in the universe". In 1812 Alphonse de Lamartine recalled his experiences of Naples in *Graziella*, which featured a

Tischbein, *Goethe in the Country* (Museo di San Martino)

girl from Procida, and the *Gulf of Baia*. In 1828 the American author James Fenimore Cooper was so taken by the city he managed to find good qualities even in its negative aspects. In his description of the Castel Nuovo area he declares: "This was the area of the *lazzaroni*; and it is no easy task to find lovelier or happier vagabonds than the ones here". Charles Dickens' 1844 observations were published in the *Daily News* and in his book, *Pictures from Italy*.

To the 20th–21st Centuries

Neapolitan Matilde Serao wrote vividly of the hectic city and hopes and passions inspired by the lottery in *Il Paese di Cuccagna* (1891). Curzio Malaparte, whose red villa is a landmark on Capri *(see p172)*, wrote in *La Pelle* (1948): "Naples is the most mysterious city in Europe. It is the only city of the ancient world that has not perished… It is not a city: it is a world – the ancient pre-Christian world – which has survived intact on the surface of the modern world". More recently, a reclusive Neapolitan author working under the pseudonym Elena Ferrante achieved international success with her four-part *Neapolitan Novels* series. Published between 2012 and 2015, the books richly evoke life in Naples through the changing fortunes of the story's characters during the 20th century.

Naples and the Arts

Naples was famous in the 19th century for its spectacular operas and the magnetism of its popular songs, and in more recent times, Neapolitan performers such as Eduardo De Filippo, Totò and Sophia Loren, have all gained worldwide acclaim. The arts scene is still alive today, with creative experiments ranging from variations on the *sceneggiata* to avant-garde theatre, and from traditional song to modern cinema.

Eduardo De Filippo and Totò

Opera and Theatre

Opera may be the preserve of the elite elsewhere, but in Naples passion for opera knows no social boundaries and even permeates street life. Historic Teatro San Carlo *(see p57)* is one of Italy's most prestigious opera houses. The season is well subscribed and performances often sell out. Rossini's opera *Otello* was first performed at the San Carlo, as were two other of his world premieres: *Mosè in Egitto* (1818) and *La Donna del Lago* (1819), based on Sir Walter Scott's *The Lady of the Lake*. Donizetti's *Lucia di Lammermoor* made its debut at the San Carlo in 1835.

Theatre has a broad popularity in Naples. Cinemas forced to close because of dwindling attendance have even been reborn as theatres. Neapolitans are proud of their dialect, used to great effect by beloved comic actors like Eduardo Scarpetta (1853–1925), Totò (1898–1967) and Eduardo De Filippo (1900–84). Comedies by actor-playwrights De Filippo and Raffaele Viviani (1888–1950) affectionately expose the ironies and petty concerns of daily life. They are performed as much today as when they were written.

Experimental theatre has been active in Naples since the establishment of the "Falso Movimento" in 1977.

Its founders are now involved in the Teatri Uniti, staging avant garde plays at the Teatro Nuovo and Galleria Toledo.

The Sceneggiata

Gioacchino Rossini

The *sceneggiata* (popular Neapolitan melo-drama) dates from the turn of the 20th century. Simple plots and characters embroiled in tragedy and farce delighted audiences that cheered heroes and booed villains. Music played a vital part in the show and there was always a rousing title song, the *pezzo forte*. This lively genre temporarily fell into disfavour, but was revived in the 1970s and is still performed today.

Neapolitan Songs

Enrico Caruso remains Naples' most famous tenor, though opera singers from far and wide are lured by the beauty, power and melancholy of Neapolitan songs. The songs' romantic melodies have had a profound influence on the development

Massimo Troisi on the set of *Ricomincio da Tre* (1981)

of Italian music and are familiar worldwide. Best known of all is *O Sole Mio*, composed in 1898 (and modified for Elvis Presley's *It's Now or Never*). Present-day masters of the tradition include Sergio Bruni, who achieved fame with *Carmela*, and Roberto Murolo. Less well-known traditional forms include the *macchietta* (a comic song routine) and *tammorriate* (dances accompanied by songs).

Cinema

Although Lombardo Film was founded in the Vomero district in the early 1900s, the first major film produced in Naples was *Assunta Spina* (1915). More familiar however are the films made in the 1950s. Neapolitan stage actors that made the crossover into film included Eduardo De Filippo and Totò. Pozzuoli native Sophia Loren starred in *The Gold of Naples* (1954) and *Marriage Italian Style* (1964). Roberto Rossellini's portrait of the city in *Viaggio in Italia* (1954) is unsentimental, while in 1963 Francesco Rosi attacked corrupt politicians and developers in *Mani sulla Città*. Despite its flaws, Naples is not easy to leave, as Massimo Troisi showed in *Ricomincio da Tre* and Mario Martone in *L'Amore Molesto*. More recently, Caserta's Royal Palace *(see pp170–71)* was the setting for Star Wars: Episode I (1999) and II (2002), and *Mission Impossible III* (2006).

Symbols of the City

Naples is a city that defies rational explanation, yet visitors have always found a wealth of sights and sounds that sum up aspects of its character. Some are positive: the beauty of the bay, the romantic melodies of Neapolitan songs, the craftsmanship of the cribs in the churches. Others are quite the opposite. Northern Europeans (and Northern Italians) are often shocked by the contrast between the city's general air of *dolce far niente* and its widespread poverty and superstition. All these things have become clichés, making it even harder to distinguish the true nature of Naples.

The pazzariello and his band

Street life: stalls with colourful wares in a city market

First Impressions

Naples has always been famous for the vivacity of its alleyways, streets and squares. The zest for life in the Toledo district amazed foreign visitors such as Goethe and Stendhal *(see p40)*. The *lazzaroni* (ruffians) lounging around on street corners made such a strong impression on foreign visitors to Naples in the 18th and 19th centuries, that they became more or less synonymous with the city. Ferdinand I, King of the Two Sicilies from 1759 to 1825, was even nicknamed the *Re Lazzarone*.

Today, many people are struck by the ubiquitous street pedlars. There have been many attempts to regulate their activities, but most have come to nothing.

Old water-seller's marble stand

The Water-Seller

The Neapolitan water-seller *(l'acquaiolo)* was once a very common sight on the streets of the city, offering refreshing drinks to passers-by on torrid summer afternoons. The water often came from the sulphurous springs of Chiatamone, which used to rise near the church of Santa Lucia *(see p120)*. It was kept cool in clay jugs, known as *lummare*. If you paid extra, you could have lemon or orange juice added to make a *spremuta*. In some parts of the old city you can still spot a *banco dell'acqua* or water stand with its solid marble counter and decorative citrus fruit. Most, however, have been modernized by the addition of stainless steel and sell cans of Coca-Cola as well as traditional drinks.

The Pazzariello

A curious and unique figure, sadly now defunct, the *pazzariello* could be seen dressed in an old-fashioned military uniform, wielding a long ceremonial baton with a gold pommel at one end and leading a small marching band. The amusing and immensely popular character, he was originally a town crier, but his duties were later extended to include leading parades on local feast days and advertising goods for sale in a new shop. The *pazzariello* was immortalized by Totò in Vittorio De Sica's film *The Gold of Naples* *(see p41)*.

The Scugnizzo

The stereotype of the cheeky, but basically good, street urchin, plays a major part in the folklore of the city. Living by his wits, ready to run errands for anybody who would give him money or food, he made an indelible impression on the American troops based in Naples during World War II. The true *scugnizzo* no longer really exists. Yet one can perhaps sense his streetwise spirit in the many young men who now whizz about the city on mopeds.

A *scugnizzo*

Pulcinella

The character of Pulcinella, stupid, yet at the same time cunning, dogged by chronic bad luck and always hungry, is the stock comic figure of a Neapolitan. One can never be quite sure, as the philosopher Benedetto Croce remarked, whether he represents a faithful portrait, a caricature or an ideal to which Neapolitans aspire. Either as a puppet (he was the model for the English Mr Punch) or in the theatre, Pulcinella has always made people laugh. With his crazy schemes, wild grimaces and the comic effects of his permanently empty stomach, he personifies the city's age-old scourge of famine.

The character of Pulcinella, as we know him today, first appeared in about 1600, but he may well have had a Classical ancestor in the equally hungry Macchus, a character from the ancient farces of Atella, a town northeast of Naples.

The greatest interpreters of the role within living memory were naturally the two actors who most fully represented the spirit of Naples – Eduardo De Filippo and Totò *(see p41)*. Their performances were especially poignant in the period of famine during and after World War II.

The Christmas Crib

Nobody knows when the custom of representing the nativity of Christ in a sculpted tableau began. One of the earliest examples is the 13th-century sculpture by Arnolfo di Cambio at the Basilica of Santa Maria Maggiore in Rome, but the tradition may well be much older. In Naples it became such an important feature of the Christmas celebrations that

Detail of historic crib scene at the Museo di San Martino *(see p115)*

Pulcinella

people came to think of the crib *(il presepe)* as a Neapolitan institution. The traditional local craftsmen, who, in many cases, have produced magnificent works of art *(see p115)*, do not limit themselves to the central figures of the nativity grouped around the baby Jesus in the manger. The scene expands to become a miniature representation of the whole of Naples, with all its characteristic sights and personalities. Look closely at the figures in a modern crib scene and you may spot Pulcinella, Totò or even reality show contestants and unpopular politicians.

The Lottery

The drawing of the lottery, in which a blindfolded child extracts the winning numbers, has remained unchanged, but the lottery is not quite the force it once was. Founded by Ferdinand I in 1774, *il lotto* can be said, without exaggeration, to have ruled the lives of many 19th-century Neapolitans. It is still very popular and *La Smorfia*, a book that claims to interpret dreams and events to help you choose the winning numbers, has been reprinted many times *(see p75)*.

Ingredients for the topping of a pizza Margherita

Pizza and Pasta

The gastronomic symbols of Naples, pizza and pasta, were not always the city's staple foods. Before the population explosion of the 1600s, the poor lived mainly on cabbage and other vegetables. These were then replaced as the staple food by wheat flour, which was less perishable, and the Neapolitans acquired the nickname "macaroni eaters".

Pizza, in its present form, dates from the end of the 18th century. It may not have been a Neapolitan invention, but it was Naples that gave the world the Napoletana and the Margherita, its two most enduring varieties.

Period print showing the traditional lottery drawing ceremony

NAPLES THROUGH THE YEAR

There is no single ideal season for visiting Naples; the temperate climate means a pleasant stay at any time of year. However, every season has its particular attractions. In May, more churches and monuments are open to the public; while July and August are perfect for the beach. The miracle of the city's patron saint San Gennaro is celebrated in May and September. In December, craftsmen create traditional Christmas crib scenes. Events in Naples are sometimes changed or cancelled at short notice due to a lack of funds or organizational problems so check at local tourist offices.

Spring

The mild spring climate is perfect for enjoying drinks at an outdoor café, walking around the town centre, or visiting the surrounding countryside, which is relatively uncrowded during this season compared with summertime. At Easter it may be warm enough to swim in the sea, although traditionally 1 May marks the beginning of the bathing season. The months of March and April can be unsettled, however, and a brief spell of fine weather may be interrupted by a cold snap or even hailstorms. According to a local proverb, the weather experienced in Naples on 4 April will continue for the following 40 days.

San Giuseppe's day zeppole

March
Feast of San Giuseppe
(19 March). The Italian equivalent of Father's Day, with zeppole (doughnuts) in every bar, bakery and home. At one time the festival marked the change from winter clothes to the spring wardrobe.

Easter
In many outlying districts and in some quarters of Naples there are **Good Friday** processions. One of the most interesting takes place on the island of

Madonna dell'Arco, Easter Monday

Procida. The cortege of priests and parishioners leaves at dawn from the top of Terra Murata and ends up at Marina Grande.

Easter Monday, or "Pasquetta" is the day for outings, when the whole family goes for a meal in a trattoria out of town. For the more traditional, a ceremony is held at the sanctuary of Madonna dell'Arco, near Sant'Anastasia, 15 km (9 miles) east of the city. Barefooted men, known as fuijenti, ask for alms, and a statue of the Madonna is carried on flower-laden carts into the countryside. Here the occasion turns into a lively "pagan" feast.

The Inghirlandata ceremony

Trotting races at the Agnano racetrack

April
The Agnano racetrack hosts trotting races for the **Gran Premio della Lotteria di Agnano** in April.

May
One of the two annual celebrations of the miracle of **San Gennaro** (see p87) takes place on the Saturday before the first Sunday in May. The procession starts off at the cathedral with the statue of San Gennaro, the patron saint of Naples, being carried from the church. The procession is known locally as the Inghirlandata (garlanding) because it was traditionally accompanied by flowered decorations, and the faithful would throw rose petals over the saint's statue. During May visitors can make the most of the **Maggio dei Monumenti**, when buildings and churches which are normally closed are open to the public. Some offer special tours or concerts too. The scheme, also known as Napoli Porte Aperte, was started in 1992 by the Fondazione Napoli '99. Since 1995 it has been sponsored by the Naples city council to encourage the "rediscovery" of historic Naples. May is also the month of the **Vela Longa** regatta, open to any type of sailing boat.

Average Daily Hours of Sunshine

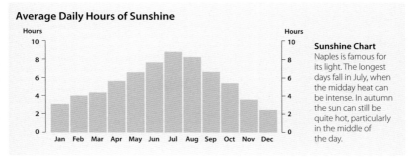

Hours

Sunshine Chart
Naples is famous for its light. The longest days fall in July, when the midday heat can be intense. In autumn the sun can still be quite hot, particularly in the middle of the day.

The Vela Longa regatta is held every May

Summer

This season can be quite muggy, especially in July, when the temperature sometimes exceeds 40°C (104°F). However, after mid-August the heat is sometimes interrupted by a brief, heavy and often violent thunderstorm that is known all along the coast as the *tropea*.

Summer nights in the city can be spent at the **Estate a Napoli** festival, which from late July to September features various performance art events and films. The week of the Assumption, or *Ferragosto* (15 Aug), is ideal for those who prefer a semi-deserted, if hot, city.

Outside Naples, interesting cultural events are held at the Pompeii amphitheatre *(see p153)*, and the Vesuvian Villa Campolieto *(see p144)* also host various events. For music-lovers, there are the **Estate Musicale Sorrentina** at Sorrento, and the well-known **Ravello Festival**, which takes place at Villa Rufolo in Ravello *(see p208)*.

June

The feast of **San Giovanni** (24 Jun), linked to the summer solstice, used to be celebrated with magicians, feasting, and night bathing. Out in the countryside people still gather walnuts to make the traditional liqueur *nocino* that will be ready by late autumn.

The popular book fair **Un'Altra Galassia** runs for three days in June each year in the Decumano Maggiore area, with free talks by authors from Italy and beyond. From late June to mid-July, the Mostra d'Oltremare *(see p31)* features the **Fiera della Casa**, when furniture, interior furnishings and local handicrafts are on sale.

July

Piazza Mercato *(see p77)* plays host to the feast of the **Madonna del Carmine** (16 Jul), an ancient tradition. The *Madonna Bruna* is kept inside the church of Santa Maria del Carmine: according to legend she miraculously saved the bell tower from a fire. Fireworks are used to re-enact the miracle wrought by the Madonna; the ceremony ends with the so-called "burning" of the bell tower.

Sant'Anna is celebrated in Ischia on 26 July with a night procession of illuminated boats and a firework display.

August

August is the traditional holiday month in Italy and you may find many city restaurants, as well as shops, local services and bars, closed until September. Throughout the region the traditional "fast" held on the Eve of the Assumption (the night of 14–15 August) is helped along by helpings of watermelon, eaten on the beach. At Positano, a ceremony in period costume celebrates the landing of the Saracens.

Fireworks at the Madonna del Carmine feast

Average Monthly Rainfall

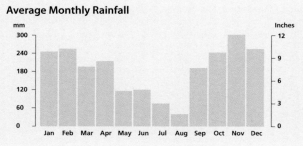

Rainfall Chart
The wettest months of the year are November and February. The rainfall does not last for long, but it comes in brief, violent downpours. The driest month is August, but this can also be interrupted by heavy thunderstorms near the end of the month.

Autumn

Autumn in Naples is quite mild; with September and October perfect for outings and long hikes in the countryside. The sea is warm enough for swimming well into September and even in early October. Nature lovers and amateur photographers will enjoy the splendid soft autumn light and clear days. Then there are popular local feast days, known as *sagre*, in nearby towns, such as the famous wine festivals *(sagra del vino)*, that coincide with the harvesting of the grapes.

Naples itself also comes back to life after the quiet and empty summer months. From September onwards football fans can spend Sunday afternoons in the San Paolo stadium, following the Neapolitans' favourite sport.

The procession of San Gennaro, the patron saint of Naples

September
The **Madonna di Piedigrotta** feast is held in the first half of the month. The ancient cave next to the sanctuary *(see p122)*, which has been closed for many years, was once the venue for popular rituals. Today, the festival has once again become fashionable. According to an old proverb, the date of the festival of Piedigrotta marks the beginning of the rainy season.

An increasingly popular festival is the **Settembrata Anacaprese**. During the first week of September, shows, games and gastronomic contests are held in Anacapri, Capri's second town.
The 19th marks the second celebration of the miracle of the blood of **San Gennaro** in Naples' Duomo. For centuries this ceremony, in which the congealed blood of the saint becomes liquid, has attracted scholars, tourists, local worshippers and city authorities.

Napoli Pizza Village, which takes place at Lungomare in the first week of the month, involves all the best pizza restaurants, with a competition for the best pizza.

October
The **Classical music season** begins at the Teatro San Carlo.

November
On **All Souls' Day** (1 Nov), also called the Day of the Dead, families take flowers to the graves of their loved ones. This was traditionally followed by a family meal at a trattoria outside town. This is the time of year when confectioners make the delicious *torrone dei morti* almond nougat.

The bright green turf of the San Paolo football stadium

Average Monthly Temperature

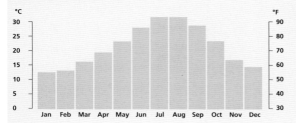

Temperature Chart
This chart gives the average minimum and maximum temperatures for each month. July and August are the hottest months, February the coldest. During the winter, relatively cold days may alternate with a spell of very mild and sunny days.

Winter

The month of December and the holiday season is rarely accompanied by any snow (except on the mountaintops). However, December and January are not usually cold, and the days can be bright and sunny. February sometimes brings rain and cold. Although the rainfall is not persistent, heavy showers may occur. The "land of the sun" is not in fact warm all year around, as many think, and the few cold days can be really cold.

December

The day of the **Immacolata** (Immaculate Conception, 8 Dec) opens the Christmas holiday season. People prepare the *presepe* (nativity scene) in their homes with moss and statuettes of figures such as Mary, the ox and donkey, the Wise Men and Jesus in the crib. The Cardinal and Mayor of the city lay wreaths on the Guglia dell'Immacolata *(see p69)*.

Christmas is celebrated with dinner and presents on Christmas Eve followed by midnight mass. The streets are illuminated and the stands on Via San Gregorio Armeno have crib figures on display *(see p43)*. A few days before New Year's Day the fireworks stalls start to appear and the traditional bagpipers add colour to the street scene.

A bagpipe player, a tradition at Christmas

January

New Year's Eve is celebrated with an impressive display of fireworks. For an enjoyable midnight outdoors, go and join in the merrymaking in the central Piazza del Plebiscito.

On **Epiphany** (6 Jan) the Befana witch arrives in Piazza del Plebiscito. This is a feast for children and stalls sell sweets and "gifts from the Befana", particularly in Via Foria. Naughty children are brought (sweet) "lumps of coal".

Traditionally the year begins with **Sant'Antuono** (Sant' Antonio Abate, 17 Jan) and in the old centre *cippi* or old things are thrown in bonfires.

February

Masked festivities for **Shrove Tuesday** and **Carnival** are accompanied by lasagna. Beginning in late February, the Mostra d'Oltremare, which hosts cultural events year-round, presents **Nauticsud**, one of the largest boating exhibitions in Europe.

Pulcinella, the protagonist of the Naples Carnival

Public Holidays

New Year's Day (1 Jan)

Epiphany (6 Jan)

Easter Sunday and Monday

Liberation Day (25 Apr)

Labour Day (1 May)

Republic Day (2 Jun)

Ferragosto (15 Aug)

All Saints' Day (1 Nov)

Immaculate Conception (8 Dec)

Christmas Day (25 Dec)

Santo Stefano (26 Dec)

A Christmas feast in a square illuminated with fairy lights

The cloister of Santa Chiara church and convent ▶

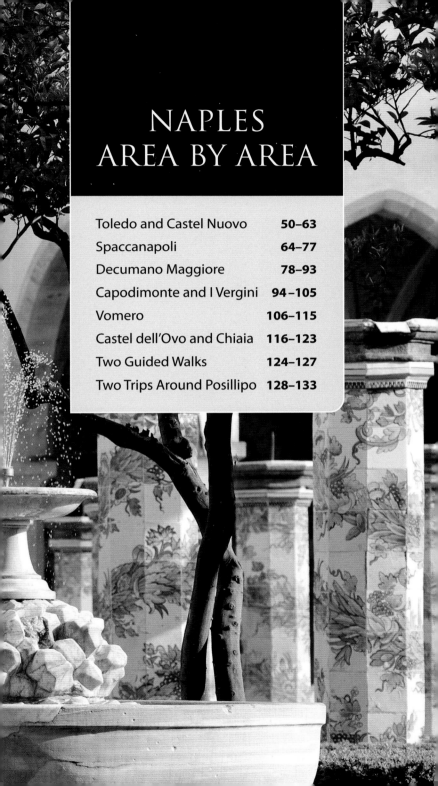

NAPLES
AREA BY AREA

TOLEDO AND CASTEL NUOVO

Castel Nuovo casts its impressive shadow on an area that is both the commercial and administrative centre of modern Naples and the heart of the old capital. This zone extends as far as the harbour, the boarding point for ferry trips. Centuries of history are concentrated in the area – from the ancient archaeological ruins on the hill of Pizzofalcone to 19th-century buildings such as the Galleria Umberto I. Near the Royal Palace and fortress

of Castel Nuovo, opposite the basilica of San Francesco di Paola, is the majestic Palazzo Reale, a palace built by the Spanish viceroys. Running north from here is a long and famous 16th-century road, Via Toledo, the main artery of Naples. It is still better known by this name (after the man who built it, Viceroy Don Pedro of Toledo) than its newer, official name, Via Roma. Lining the thoroughfare are elegant buildings, stately churches and shops.

Sights at a Glance

Historic Buildings
1 Palazzo Reale pp54–5
8 Castel Nuovo pp58–9
14 Palazzo delle Poste e Telegrafi
19 Palazzo Serra di Cassano

Churches
2 Basilica di San Francesco di Paola
4 San Ferdinando
10 Santa Maria Incoronata
11 San Giacomo degli Spagnoli
12 Santa Brigida
17 Santa Maria degli Angeli
18 Santa Maria Egiziaca a Pizzofalcone
20 Nunziatella

Historic Streets and Squares
5 Via Toledo
6 Galleria Umberto I
13 Quartieri Spagnoli
15 Piazza Giovanni Bovio
16 Via Chiaia

Historic Theatres
7 Teatro San Carlo
9 Mercadante, Teatro Stabile

Museums
21 Museo Artistico Industriale
Museo Civico (see Castel Nuovo)
Museo dell'Appartamento Reale (see Palazzo Reale)

Historic Landmarks
3 Gran Caffè Gambrinus

Restaurants pp191–2
1 Brandi
2 Il Gobbetto
3 Gran Caffè Gambrinus
4 Kukai Nibu
5 Osteria Don Maccarone
6 Pintauro
7 Ristorante Amici Miei
8 La Sfogliatella Mary
9 Trattoria da Nennella

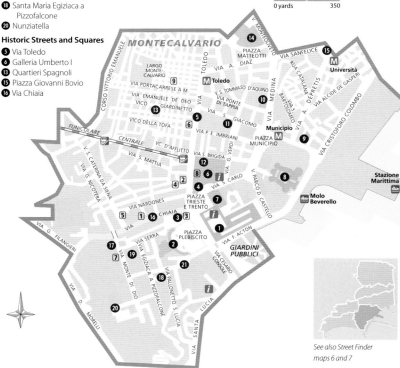

| 0 metres | | 350 |
| 0 yards | | 350 |

See also Street Finder maps 6 and 7

◄ Ornate marble interior of the Palazzo Reale

For keys to symbols see back flap

Street-by-Street: Toledo and Castel Nuovo

Naples is a city of contrasting moods: the quiet solemnity of Piazza del Plebiscito, a symbol of the city's rebirth, is very different from the animation – you might even call it confusion – of the surrounding streets. It is a pleasure to mingle with the crowd in Via Toledo, drop in at the Gran Caffè Gambrinus or Galleria Umberto I, pause in the shade of the historic church of San Francesco di Paola, or visit the museums at Palazzo Reale and Castel Nuovo. In addition to the rich history and art treasures in this area, Via Toledo is good for shopping.

❻ Galleria Umberto I
The iron and glass dome was built in the late 1800s by Boubée.

❺ Via Toledo
This street, named after a Spanish viceroy, borders the Quartieri Spagnoli.

PIAZZA TRIESTE E TRENTO

PIAZZA PLEBISCITO

❼ ★ Teatro San Carlo
Richly decorated in gilded stucco, the theatre seats 3,000 and the acoustics are excellent.

❹ San Ferdinando
Every year on Good Friday there is a performance of the *Stabat Mater* composed by Pergolesi for the confraternity based here since 1837.

❸ Gran Caffè Gambrinus
Gabriele d'Annunzio wrote the lyrics to the Neapolitan song *"A vucchella"* in this café.

❷ Basilica di San Francesco di Paola
This Neo-Classical church was designed by Lugano architect Pietro Bianchi in 1817.

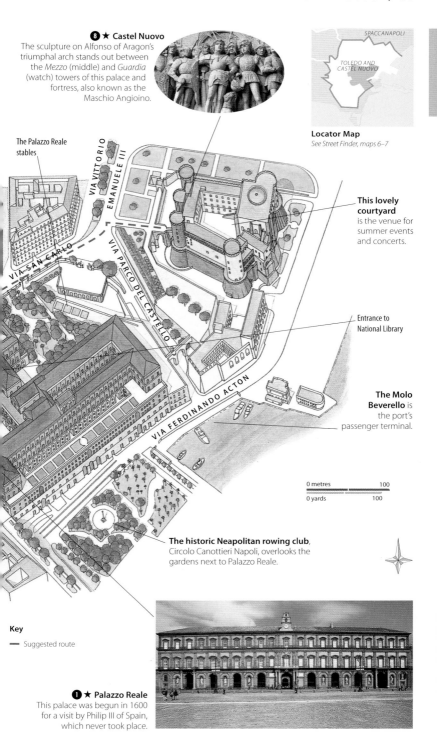

❽ ★ Castel Nuovo
The sculpture on Alfonso of Aragon's triumphal arch stands out between the *Mezzo* (middle) and *Guardia* (watch) towers of this palace and fortress, also known as the Maschio Angioino.

SPACCANAPOLI

TOLEDO AND CASTEL NUOVO

Locator Map
See Street Finder, maps 6–7

The Palazzo Reale stables

VIA VITTORIO EMANUELE III

VIA SAN CARLO

VIA PARCO DEL CASTELLO

VIA FERDINANDO ACTON

This lovely courtyard is the venue for summer events and concerts.

Entrance to National Library

The Molo Beverello is the port's passenger terminal.

0 metres	100
0 yards	100

The historic Neapolitan rowing club, Circolo Canottieri Napoli, overlooks the gardens next to Palazzo Reale.

Key

— Suggested route

❶ ★ Palazzo Reale
This palace was begun in 1600 for a visit by Philip III of Spain, which never took place.

❶ Palazzo Reale

The layout and size of the Palazzo Reale befit its role as one of the most important royal courts in the Mediterranean. Designed by Domenico Fontana at the request of the viceroy Fernández Ruiz de Castro, construction began in 1600. Building continued for centuries and the palace was only finished in 1843 by Gaetano Genovese. The Ala delle Feste wing, used in the 19th century for entertaining, now houses the Biblioteca Nazionale, the library named after King Vittorio Emanuele III, who donated the wing.

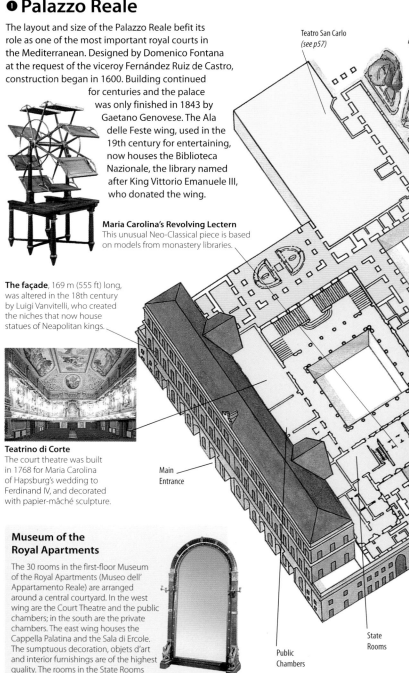

Teatro San Carlo *(see p57)*

Maria Carolina's Revolving Lectern
This unusual Neo-Classical piece is based on models from monastery libraries.

The façade, 169 m (555 ft) long, was altered in the 18th century by Luigi Vanvitelli, who created the niches that now house statues of Neapolitan kings.

Teatrino di Corte
The court theatre was built in 1768 for Maria Carolina of Hapsburg's wedding to Ferdinand IV, and decorated with papier-mâché sculpture.

Main Entrance

Museum of the Royal Apartments

The 30 rooms in the first-floor Museum of the Royal Apartments (Museo dell' Appartamento Reale) are arranged around a central courtyard. In the west wing are the Court Theatre and the public chambers; in the south are the private chambers. The east wing houses the Cappella Palatina and the Sala di Ercole. The sumptuous decoration, objets d'art and interior furnishings are of the highest quality. The rooms in the State Rooms house 16th- to 19th-century paintings.

A mirror in the Museo

Public Chambers

State Rooms

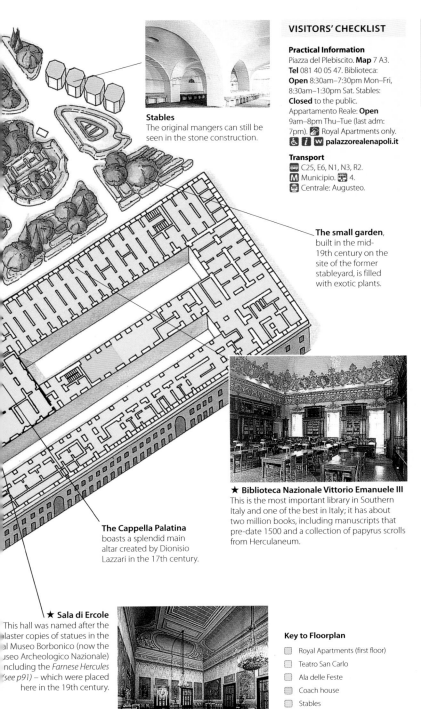

Stables
The original mangers can still be seen in the stone construction.

The small garden, built in the mid-19th century on the site of the former stableyard, is filled with exotic plants.

★ **Biblioteca Nazionale Vittorio Emanuele III**
This is the most important library in Southern Italy and one of the best in Italy; it has about two million books, including manuscripts that pre-date 1500 and a collection of papyrus scrolls from Herculaneum.

The Cappella Palatina boasts a splendid main altar created by Dionisio Lazzari in the 17th century.

★ **Sala di Ercole**
This hall was named after the plaster copies of statues in the al Museo Borbonico (now the useo Archeologico Nazionale) ncluding the *Farnese Hercules* *(see p91)* – which were placed here in the 19th century.

Key to Floorplan
- Royal Apartments (first floor)
- Teatro San Carlo
- Ala delle Feste
- Coach house
- Stables
- Non-exhibition space

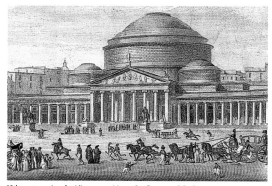

19th-century print of a riding competition at San Francesco di Paola

❷ Basilica di San Francesco di Paola

Piazza del Plebiscito. **Map** 7 A3. **Tel** 081 764 51 33. C25, E6, N1, N3, R2. Municipio. Centrale: Augusteo. **Open** 8:30am–noon, 4–7pm Mon–Sat; 8:30am–1pm, 4–7pm Sun.

Joachim Murat, Napoleon's brother-in-law, ruled the city of Naples from 1808 to 1815. Dissatisfied with the chaotic jumble of buildings opposite the Palazzo Reale, he decided to rebuild the whole area. The Largo di Palazzo, now called the Piazza del Plebiscito, was meant to play a major role in city life and was used for festivities, ceremonies and military parades. The first buildings to go up were the palace built for the Prince of Salerno, and the palazzo that is now the home of the Prefecture. Both were laid out symmetrically. Murat did not see the final results of his scheme, only managing to see Leopoldo Laperuta's design for the Doric colonnade and the initial construction work before the French were driven out of Naples.

In 1815 Ferdinand of Bourbon was reinstated to the throne and set about completing the project begun by Murat. He commissioned the architect Pietro Bianchi to design the central royal basilica, which was dedicated to San Francesco di Paola. Inspired by the Pantheon in Rome, the church has a circular plan with radiating chapels, a large cupola 53 m (174 ft) high and 34m (112 ft) wide, complete with rosettes. The sculpture and paintings inside the church are mostly Neo-Classical except for the high altar, which was re-built in 1835 with semi-precious stones and multi-coloured marble, and lapis lazuli taken from a 17th-century altar in the church of Santi Apostoli *(see p100)*. The cool, formal interior can have a rather chilling effect on visitors. According to architectural historian Renato De Fusco:

Statue of Charles III by Canova

"Despite the large size of the interior and the rich marble, stucco and garlanding decoration, the overall impression is not that of Neo-Classical rigour, but rather a lack of harmony between man and the setting, a funereal coldness compared to the exterior". The sobering effect is soon dispelled by emerging into the lovely open space of Piazza del Plebiscito, which is pedestrianized. The two equestrian statues of Charles III and Ferdinand I are the work of Antonio Canova and Antonio Calì.

❸ Gran Caffè Gambrinus

P.za Trieste e Trento. **Map** 7 A3. **Tel** 081 41 75 82. C25, E6, N1, N3, R2. Municipio. Centrale: Augusteo. **Open** 7am– 1am daily (to 2am Fri, to 3am Sat). grancaffegambrinus.com

The café dates from 1860; its walls decorated by the leading Neapolitan painters of the time. It soon became the haunt of politicians, artists and writers, including Guy de Maupassant and Oscar Wilde, as well as the local composers Roberto Murolo and Giovanni Bovio. When the literary café also became popular with opponents of the Fascist regime, the prefect closed it down, initiating a long period of decline and neglect. Fortunately, its lavish *belle époque* decor has been restored and this landmark is once again a favourite. Neapolitans drop in for coffee and cakes, or for ice cream.

Interior of the historic Gran Caffè Gambrinus

❹ San Ferdinando

Piazza Trieste e Trento 5. **Map** 7 A3.
Tel 081 41 81 18. 🚌 C25, E6, N1, N3, R2.
Ⓜ Municipio. 🚊 Centrale: Augusteo.
Open 8am–7pm daily (also 4:30–6pm
Sat). 🔾

This church was founded
in 1665 as San Francesco
Saverio. In 1769 Ferdinand I
dedicated it to his namesake
saint. The Baroque interior
contains frescoes by Paolo
De Matteis and sculptures by
Vaccaro as well as the tomb
of Lucia Migliaccio, the
Duchess of Floridia. Ferdinand
gave her his estate on the
Vomero hill, which became
Villa Floridiana (see p110). Until
1919 the square was called
Piazza San Ferdinando.

Pintauro's pastry shop in Via Toledo

❺ Via Toledo

Map 3 A5, 7 A1 (9 B4). 🚌 E1, R4, 201.
Ⓜ Toledo, Dante. 🚊 Centrale: Augusteo.

Commissioned by the Spanish
viceroy Don Pedro de Toledo in
1536, this 1.2 km- (0.75 mile-)
long street boasts many famous
buildings with rich histories.
Inside Palazzo Cirella (No. 228),
for example, artists planned
an insurrection against the
Bourbon king in 1848, while
Gioacchino Rossini (see p41)
lived at the Palazzo di
Domenico Barbaja (No. 205).

Shopping in Via Toledo
caters to all tastes and budgets.
Locals stop at Gay Odin for
home-made chocolates and
at Pintauro's for the excellent
sfogliatelle pastry.

The marble floor of the Galleria Umberto I

❻ Galleria Umberto I

Via San Carlo, Via Verdi, Via Santa
Brigida, Via Toledo. **Map** 7 A2.
🚌 C25, E6, N1, N3, R2. Ⓜ Municipio.
🚊 Centrale: Augusteo.

The galleria was built as part of
the Urban Renewal Plan, drawn
up after the cholera epidemic
which struck the city in 1884
(see pp30–31). The impressive
iron and glass roof and elegant
patterned marble pavement fill
the large open space with light.
The arcade soon became the
haunt of local composers and
musicians. From the galleria one
could gain entry to the Salone
Margherita, which, until 1912,
was a famous *café chantant*, and
considered the heart of cabaret
entertainment in Naples.

❼ Teatro San Carlo

Via San Carlo 98d. **Map** 7 A3. **Tel** 081
797 23 31. 🚌 C25, E6, N1, N3, R2.
Ⓜ Municipio. 🚊 Centrale: Augusteo.
🕙 10am–5:30pm Mon–Sat, by appt
Sun. 🎭 See Entertainment in Naples
p206, p209. 🆆 teatrosancarlo.it
Memus: Piazza Trieste e Trento. **Tel** 081
797 24 49. **Open** 9am–5pm Tue–Sat,
9am–2pm Sun. 🎭 🆆 memus.org

This is one of the oldest opera
houses in the world. Designed
by Giovanni Antonio Medrano
for the Bourbon King Charles, it
was built in a few months and
officially opened on 4 November
1737, 40 years before La Scala in
Milan. It soon became one of
the most important opera

houses in Europe, known for its
magnificent architecture and
excellent productions. For many
years, a performance at the
San Carlo was considered the
high point in the career of a
singer or composer.

A fire in 1816 severely damaged
the interior, which was immediately rebuilt by Antonio Niccolini,
who modified the façade by
adding the foyer and balcony.
The focal point of the magnificent
auditorium, with its six tiers of
184 boxes, is the royal box, sur-
mounted by the crown of the
Kingdom of the Two Sicilies.

Many great musical figures,
including Gioacchino Rossini and
Gaetano Donizetti, were at one
time artistic directors here. The
world premieres of Donizetti's
Lucia di Lammermoor and Rossini's
Mosè were performed here.

Opera fans not lucky enough
to get a ticket to a performance
should head for the Museo e
Archivio Storico del Teatro di
San Carlo or **Memus**, located in
the Palazzo Reale (see pp54–5).
The museum is dedicated to
the history of the opera house
and all things opera-related.

Tiers of boxes in the auditorium of the
opera house Teatro San Carlo

❽ Castel Nuovo

The castle, also known as Maschio Angioino, was called *nuovo* (new) to distinguish it from two earlier ones, dell'Ovo and Capuano *(see p120 and p85)*, which were too small to accommodate the entire Angevin court. Charles I of Anjou began construction in 1279, but the Cappella Palatina is the only part remaining of the original building. Alfonso V of Aragon (who later became Alfonso I, King of Naples and Sicily) began to rebuild it completely in 1443, the year that marked his triumphant entry into Naples. To celebrate this event, he later ordered the construction of the superb Arco di Trionfo, one of the most significant expressions of early Renaissance culture in Southern Italy. The castle, with its five cylindrical towers, is designed on a trapezoidal plan facing onto a central courtyard. From here you can gain access to the most famous chamber in the castle, the Sala dei Baroni (Barons' Hall), now used by the town council. Since 1990 a small but fine art collection, the Museo Civico, has occupied part of the west wing.

The Renaissance doorway of the Cappella Palatina

Cappella Palatina

This is the only surviving part of the 13th-century building. An elegant Renaissance doorway leads to the chapel, which is dedicated to St Barbara. The portal itself is crowned with an elaborate rose window typical of the Catalan style of its creators. The portal is also adorned with a Madonna executed by Francesco Laurana (c.1430–1502) in 1474.

The walls inside the chapel were once decorated with frescoes by Giotto and his workshop; today, only small fragments on the splays of the lofty Gothic windows remain.

Sala dei Baroni

Next to the chapel, the Barons' Hall, which is reached by means of an outer stairway, owes its name to the grim events that took place there in 1486. Then, the great barons who had plotted a conspiracy against Ferdinand I

The imposing Castel Nuovo, with its stunning Renaissance triumphal arch

1200	1300	1400	1500	1600	1700	1800

1279 Charles I of Anjou begins construction of Castel Nuovo

1443–68 Building of Arco di Trionfo

1547 Popular revolt against the Inquisition

1647 Signing of pact between the viceroy and Masaniello after popular uprising

1329 Giotto and his assistants paint the Cappella Palatina frescoes

1443 Alfonso V's total rebuilding plan

1486 The Barons' conspiracy

1509–37 Reconstruction of the defence system with new battlements and moats

The Barricades at San Ferdinando during the 1848 uprisings (detail of a painting in the Museo Civico)

Sala dei Baroni: the splendid Spanish Gothic vault

of Aragon, were arrested and subsequently executed.

This elegant, yet grand and austere hall, 26 m (85 ft) wide and 28 m (92 ft) high, was built by the Spanish craftsman Guglielmo Sagrera, who was summoned to Naples for the purpose in 1446. It is now the main meeting room of the town council. Its principal features are the magnificent Catalan-inspired ribbed vault with intersecting ribs in the shape of a huge star, the monumental fireplace, and the large rectangular "cross windows".

19th-century Neapolitan painting, Museo Civico

Museo Civico

A large part of the south wing of Castel Nuovo and part of the Cappella Palatina are occupied by the Museo Civico (civic museum). Before visiting the museum, do not miss the opportunity to take in the splendid panoramic views of the Bay of Naples and Mount Vesuvius from the upper floors of the castle.

The museum houses paintings, sculptures and objets d'art that come from the castle itself, from neighbouring churches and other Neapolitan monuments. These works date from the 14th to the 19th century, but by far the largest section consists of 19th-century Neapolitan paintings.

Some of these – such as Vincenzo Caprile's *Vecchia Napoli* (Old Naples), depicting the famous Zizze fountain in its original state – offer views of a city that no longer exists.

Arco di Trionfo

The combination of white marble against the grey volcanic stone of Castel Nuovo is immediately striking, as is the contrast between the ornamental reliefs and the severe geometric form of the towers. The structure, with its two superimposed arches, takes its inspiration from ancient Roman architecture.

The monumental gateway of the *Arco di Trionfo* (Triumphal Arch) was built in 1443 in honour of Alfonso V of Aragon. The bas relief depicting the *Trionfo di Alfonso* (Triumph of Alfonso) lies above the lower section, while the upper arch, which was once intended to house a statue of the sovereign, now holds allegorical figures representing the Four Virtues (looking from left to right, Temperance, Justice, Fortitude and Magnanimity). On the tympanum, supporting two large symbolic statues of rivers, stands a figure of the archangel Michael. A number of Italian artists contributed to the final building of the arch, the most significant among them being the Neapolitan artist

VISITORS' CHECKLIST

Practical Information
Piazza Municipio. **Map** 7 B2.
Tel 081 795 77 22.
Open 8:30am–7pm Mon–Sat. 🖼
🛗 see attendants for assistance.

Transport
🚌 C25, N1, N3, R2, 201, 202, 256.
Ⓜ Municipio. 🚋 Centrale: Augusteo.

Upper section of Arco di Trionfo

Francesco Laurana, who also worked on the Cappella Palatina and sculpted the statues of Justice and the bas-relief of Alfonso I on his chariot. Another artist of note was Laurana's pupil and assistant Domenico Gagini.

Castel Nuovo in a painting by Antonio Joli

9 Mercadante, Teatro Stabile

Piazza Municipio 74. **Map** 7 B2. **Tel** 081 551 03 36. C25, N1, N3, R2. M Municipio. Centrale: Augusteo. *See Entertainment in Naples: p206, p209.*

Built in 1778 to a design by Francesco Securo, this theatre was originally known as *"del Fondo"* because money for its construction came from a fund created by the sale of confiscated Jesuit property. The three-tier façade, with eight caryatids supporting the cornice, dates from 1892. The theatre opened in 1779 with *L'Infedeltà Fedele* by Cimarosa, a Neapolitan composer.

Late 19th-century façade of the Mercadante, Teatro Stabile

10 Santa Maria Incoronata

Via Medina 60. **Map** 7 B2. **Tel** 081 552 04 57. N1, N3, N8, R2, R4, 202. M Municipio, Toledo. Centrale: Augusteo. **Open** 9am–6pm Mon–Sat.

This deconsecrated church was originally built to celebrate the coronation of Joan I of Anjou in 1352. It was doubled in size in 1460 by building an identical building and connecting the two.

It is immediately obvious that Santa Maria Incoronata is at a lower level than Via Medina. The reason goes back to the 16th century, when Charles V built the new moats for Castel Nuovo. Earth had been dug out to make room for the ditches and when it was dumped nearby it partially buried this small mid-14th-century church.

The two fresco cycles in the first bay of the main nave, for years attributed to Giotto, are in fact the work of his pupil Roberto Oderisi.

Detail of the portico of Santa Maria Incoronata

11 San Giacomo degli Spagnoli

Piazza Municipio. **Map** 7 A2. **Tel** 081 552 20 89. N1, N3, N8, R2, R4, 201, 202. M Municipio, Toledo. Centrale: Augusteo. **Open** limited during restoration.

Part of the 19th-century Palazzo San Giacomo (now the town hall), the church of San Giacomo dominates Piazza Municipio and is sometimes called Nostra Signora del Sacro Cuore (Our Lady of the Sacred Heart). In 1540 Don Pedro Alvarez de Toledo, the viceroy responsible for the present appearance of the city centre, built the church and adjoining hospital for the Spanish community. This was the church of the local aristocracy and although rebuilt in 1741, it still belongs to the Real Hermandad de Nobles Hespanoles de Santiago, a confraternity founded more than four centuries ago.

San Giacomo contains tombs of Spanish nobles, including that of Don Pedro and his wife Maria. They were never buried in their sumptuous tomb, however: Don Pedro died in Florence and is buried there in the cathedral.

The marble tomb of Don Pedro Alvarez de Toledo in San Giacomo degli Spagnoli

12 Santa Brigida

Via Santa Brigida 72. **Map** 7 A2. **Tel** 081 552 37 93. C25, E6, N1, N3, R1, R2. M Municipio, Toledo. Centrale: Augusteo. **Open** 7am–12:30pm, 5–7:30pm daily.

The curious aspect of this 17th-century church is the dome, which could not be more than 9 m (30 ft) high because it would have obstructed artillery fire from Castel Nuovo. However, the fresco of a vivid sky created by Luca Giordano (1634–1705) on the cupola makes the most of boldly conceived perspective and creates a feeling of immense space.

The artist, nicknamed Luca Fapresto (Luca the Swift) because he worked so rapidly, painted the dome in exchange for his tomb, which can be found in the left transept.

13 Quartieri Spagnoli

Map 7 A2. E3, E6. M Toledo. Centrale: Augusteo.

The Spanish Quarter is one of the city's working-class districts; densely populated and rather run-down (tourists should take care when visiting the area). Built in the 16th century to the west of Via Toledo to house Spanish troops, its origins live on in the name, but today it is difficult to appreciate the original grid layout. Alleys are festooned with laundry, shielding the streets from the light.

Despite the state of neglect, there is still some fine architecture, such as the church of

The atmospheric 17th-century Quartieri Spagnoli district

Montecalvario (founded in 1560), which gives its name to one of the area's districts, and Santa Maria della Concezione, a Baroque masterpiece by Domenico Antonio Vaccaro.

The great Italian poet Leopardi once lived at No. 24 Via Santa Maria Ognibene, and the local playwright Eduardo De Filippo *(see p41)* used the area as a setting for his plays.

⑭ Palazzo delle Poste e Telegrafi

Piazza Matteotti 2. **Map** 7 B1 (9 B5). ▨ C25, E1, N3, N8, R4, 201. Ⓜ Toledo. **Open** 8am–6:30pm Mon–Fri, 8am–12:30pm Sat.

The post office building was designed in 1935 by Giuseppe Vaccaro as part of an Urban Renewal and Development Plan that resulted in the demolition of the San Giuseppe quarter. The bombastic style of the civic architecture of this period (also found in the police headquarters, the tax office and the provincial administration building) is typical of buildings constructed during the Fascist era. The Post Office combines emphatic features with other innovative elements of the European Modern Movement.

The curvilinear façade and broad staircase make this one of the most interesting examples of 20th-century Neapolitan architecture. In striking contrast to the Post Office is the nearby cloister of Monteoliveto *(see p68)*, sadly now dilapidated.

⑮ Piazza Giovanni Bovio

Map 7 B1 (9 C5). ▨ E1, N1, N3, N8, R2, 202. Ⓜ Università.

Neapolitans call this square Piazza della Borsa after the former Stock Exchange *(Borsa)* that dominates it. Built in 1895 when taste was eclectic, the old exchange is reminiscent of 16th-century buildings in the Veneto. It is now the home of the Chamber of Commerce. Incorporated into the left side of this building is the small church

of Sant'Aspreno al Porto, originally medieval but totally rebuilt in the 1600s.

The square marks the beginning of Corso Umberto I, also known as the *Rettifilo*. This grand avenue was built after slum clearance around the harbour, to connect the city centre and the central railway station, giving a new look to early 20th-century Naples *(see pp32–3)*. The 17th-century Fountain of Neptune has been moved, temporarily, to the corner of Piazza Municipie and Via Medina. Frequently altered, the fountain was moved several times before finding its final home in Piazza Bovio in 1898. It was the work of three artists: the statue of Neptune was sculpted by Michelangelo Naccherino, the balusters and lions were by Cosimo Fanzago, and the monsters at the base by Pietro Bernini.

The former stock exchange in Piazza Giovanni Bovio

⑯ Via Chiaia

Map 6 F2, 7 A3. 🚌 E6. Ⓜ Municipio.

In Neapolitan dialect, *chiaia* means "beach", and in fact this street was opened in the 16th century to connect Largo di Palazzo (now Piazza del Plebiscito) with the coast. Together with Via Toledo (*see p57*), Via dei Mille and Via Calabritto, this is one of Naples' smartest shopping streets. While browsing, it is worth stopping to see the Ponte di Chiaia, a 17th-century gateway restored in the 1800s. Nearby is Palazzo Cellamare, built in the 16th century and enlarged in the 18th century, when it became known for the magnificent banquets and receptions held there.
The impressive portal was designed by Ferdinando Fuga. Near the Ponte, a lift affords easy access to Piazza Santa Maria degli Angeli and the Pizzofalcone hill.

Via Chiaia and Ponte di Chiaia

The portal of the church of Santa Maria degli Angeli

⑰ Santa Maria degli Angeli

Piazza Santa Maria degli Angeli. **Map** 6 F2. **Tel** 081 764 49 74. 🚌 E6. **Open** 7:30–11am, 5–7pm Mon–Sat, 8:30am–1:30pm Sun. ✝

Construction of this church began in the 17th century on land donated to the devout Theatine religious order by Donna Costanza del Carretto Dira, the Princess of Melfi. The building was designed by the Theatine cleric Francesco Grimaldi, and it is clearly visible from any point overlooking the city. The three-nave interior is so well designed that Francesco

Milizia, the author of an 18th-century guide to Naples, said that it "is perhaps the most well-proportioned church in the city".
The frescoes on the vaults, which depict episodes from the life of the Virgin Mary, are the work of Giovan Battista Beinaschi (1638–88).

⑱ Santa Maria Egiziaca a Pizzofalcone

Via Egiziaca a Pizzofalcone 30. **Map** 7 A3. **Tel** 081 19 56 06 32. 🚌 E6. **Open** 9–11am, 5:30–7:30pm Tue–Sun. ✝

The portal on Via Egiziaca opens out onto the area in front of this Baroque church.

Its construction began in 1661 at the request of the nuns who lived nearby in the Sant'Agostino convent. The building's design was entrusted to Cosimo Fanzago (1593–1678), a Lombard architect and sculptor who was to become one of the most prestigious creators of the local Baroque style. The octagonal plan of the church was greatly admired by his contemporaries. The paintings in the main chapels are by Paolo De Matteis (1662–1728), while the sculptures are by Nicola Fumo (1647–1725). The high altar is in pure Rococo style.

⑲ Palazzo Serra di Cassano

Via Monte di Dio 14–15. **Map** 6 F2. **Tel** 081 795 11 11. 🚌 E6. **Open** 11am–4pm daily; by appointment only.

The main doorway to Prince Aloisio Serra di Cassano's palace is no longer the main entrance to one of the most beautiful examples of 18th-century Neapolitan civic architecture. To express his grief over the execution of his son Gennaro – one of the leaders of the 1799 revolution in Naples – the prince ordered the original entrance (at No. 67 Via Egiziaca) to be closed that same year. The originality of

Interior of the cupola of Santa Maria Egiziaca a Pizzofalcone

The impressive double staircase in Palazzo Serra di Cassano

this building, which was designed by one of the leading architects of the time, Ferdinando Sanfelice (1675–1748), lies in the majestic staircase with its double flight of steps *(see p97)*. Set in the entrance hall that opens on to the courtyard, it is decorated with white marble that contrasts beautifully with the building's imposing, grey volcanic stone.

The *piano nobile* (upper floor) of the palazzo is now the home of the Istituto Italiano per gli Studi Filosofici, a leading international cultural institution.

⓴ Nunziatella

Via Generale Parisi 16. **Map** 6 F2. **Tel** 081 764 15 20. 🚌 E6. **Open** 9–10am for occasional Mass, by appt at other times. 🕐 9:30am–1pm Mon, Wed & Fri; phone and ask for Secretaría to book. 🚹 🚻 **w** nunziatella.it

The façades of the church and former convent of the Nunziatella, which has been occupied since 1787 by the military college of the same name, converge at a right angle to form a beautiful little square. At the beginning of the 18th century, the Jesuits at the Nunziatella asked architect Ferdinando Sanfelice – who was working on the nearby Palazzo Serra di Cassano – to build the church and restore the convent, which dates from the 16th century. Entering the little

church, visitors are struck by the harmonious balance between the architectural space and the decorative elements. The most important frescoes were painted by Neapolitan artist Francesco de Mura (1696–1782); in the apse is the *Adoration of the Magi*, the *Assumption of the Virgin* is on the ceiling, and on the inside of the façade is *Rest during the Flight to Egypt*. The altar, by Giuseppe Sanmartino (1720–93), is one of the main examples of Neapolitan Baroque in existence.

㉑ Museo Artistico Industriale

Piazza Demetrio Salazar 6 (off Via Solitaria). **Map** 7 A3. **Tel** 081 764 74 71. 🚌 E6. **Open** 9am–3pm Mon–Fri by appt only. 🕐 ask at Art Institute; May: 9am–2pm daily. 🚻 🚻 **w** mai.museum.com

Founded in 1882 by Gaetano Filangieri, who also founded the Filangieri Civic Museum *(see p74)*, and Demetrio Salazar, this school started out as workshops to train young people in applied arts such as pottery, cabinet-making, goldsmithery and metalwork. Set on the third floor of the Istituto D'arte Palizzi, the museum now houses over 6,000 works of art. The most important are the ceramics, including two large tile panels designed by the 19th-century Neapolitan artists Domenico Morelli and Filippo Palizzi.

The Birthplace of Parthenope

Ancient ruins on Pizzofalcone

In the 7th century BC, Greek colonists from Rhodes founded the first urban settlement in Naples on the hill of Pizzofalcone: Parthenope, renamed Palaepolis (old city) three centuries later when *Neapolis* (new city) was founded to the east. The old city was later abandoned and by the Middle Ages the area had reverted to farmland. The site of ancient Naples was revived however in the 16th century, when it became a residential neighbourhood favoured by aristocrats and important officials, who were attracted by the beauty of the site and its proximity to the Royal Palace. In the 18th century Via Monte di Dio was one of the most important residential streets in Naples, and to this day it retains some of its original character.

Imposing façade of the Nunziatella Military School, overlooking the bay

SPACCANAPOLI

The straight street called Spaccanapoli corresponds to the lower *decumanus*, one of the three main thoroughfares in Greco-Roman Naples; the other two being present-day Via Anticaglia *(see p88)* and Via dei Tribunali *(see pp80–81)*. At the end of the 13th century, after the construction of Castel Nuovo *(see pp58–9)*, the administrative hub of the city began to shift towards the seafront. Commercial activity developed in the Piazza Mercato zone, while in the old

centre there was a concentration of churches and convents, notably Santa Chiara. When the city expanded around the newly built Via Toledo *(see p57)* during the era of the Spanish viceroyalty, the area which is now Piazza del Gesù Nuovo became the junction point between the old and modern cities. From here, the bustling pedestrian street runs east from Via Benedetto Croce and is crammed with lively eateries, shops and some of Naples' most fascinating sites.

Sights at a Glance

Historic Buildings
7 Palazzo Filomarino
13 Palazzo Carafa Santangelo
14 Monte di Pietà
17 Archivio di Stato

Churches
1 Santa Maria La Nova
2 Sant'Anna dei Lombardi
3 Gesù Nuovo
5 *Santa Chiara pp70–71*
6 Santa Marta
9 San Domenico Maggiore
10 Cappella Sansevero
11 Sant'Angelo a Nilo
15 San Giorgio Maggiore
18 Santi Severino e Sossio

19 Santi Marcellino e Festo
20 Gesù Vecchio
22 Pappacoda Cappella
23 Santissima Annunziata
24 Santa Maria del Carmine
25 Sant'Eligio Maggiore

Historic Streets and Squares
8 Piazza San Domenico Maggiore
21 Corso Umberto I

Spires and Statues
4 Guglia dell'Immacolata
12 Statue of the Nile

Museums
16 Museo Civico Filangieri

☐ Restaurants *p191*
1 L'Antica Pizzeria da Michele
2 Ecomesarà
3 Osteria il Garum
4 Palazzo Petrucci
5 Pizzeria Trianon da Ciro
6 La Taverna dell'Arte

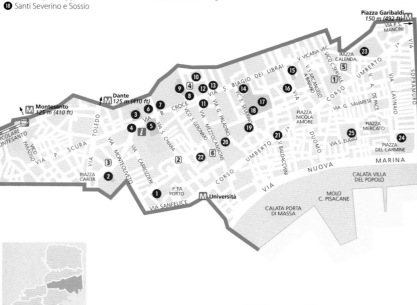

See also Street Finder
maps 3, 9 and 10

◄ A typical narrow street in Spaccanapoli

For keys to symbols *see back flap*

Street-by-Street: Spaccanapoli

The long street commonly known as Spaccanapoli is divided into seven sections bearing different names. Because of its rich array of churches, squares and historic buildings it has been called an "open-air museum", like nearby Via dei Tribunali. It is also one of the most lively and atmospheric places in Naples, with shops, crafts and cafés. Piazza San Domenico Maggiore, near the University, is always crowded with young people. Those with a sweet tooth can enjoy the excellent pastries at the Scaturchio pasticceria.

❽ Piazza San Domenico Maggiore
A siren with two tails is sculpted on the base of the spire.

❾ San Domenico Maggiore
This church was built in 1283 by Charles I of Anjou.

Cappella Sansevero

❸ ★ Gesù Nuovo
The rusticated façade of the church was once part of Palazzo Sanseverino.

VIA S. SEBASTIANO

VIA BENEDETTO CROCE

PIAZZA DEL GESÙ NUOVO

VIA S. CHIARA

CALATA TRINITÀ MAGG.

❼ Palazzo Filomarino
The philosopher Benedetto Croce died here in 1952.

⓫ Sant'Angelo a Nilo
The interior houses the tomb of Cardinal Brancaccio, sculpted by Donatello and Michelozzo.

❹ Guglia dell'Immacolata
Erected in the 1700s, this spire was named after the statue of the Virgin at its pinnacle.

❻ Santa Marta
This small church dates from the 15th century.

❺ ★ Santa Chiara
Robert of Anjou was responsible for building this church. The tiled cloister was designed by Domenico Antonio Vaccaro between 1739 and 1742.

⑩ ★ Cappella Sansevero
This moving *Veiled Christ* sculpture by Neapolitan artist
Giuseppe Sanmartino is in the di Sangro family chapel.

Locator Map
See Street Finder, maps 3, 9, 10

⑫ Statue of the Nile
This statue, erected in honour of the
Egyptian god Nile, gives its name to
the square in which it stands.

Palazzo
Marigliano

San Nicola a Nilo

Ospedale delle Bambole,
the dolls' hospital, is a
unique place where dolls
and puppets are repaired.

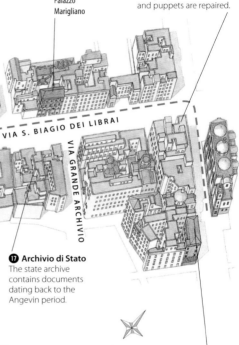

VIA S. BIAGIO DEI LIBRAI

VIA PALADINO

VIA GRANDE ARCHIVIO

**⑬ Palazzo Carafa
Santangelo**
Diomede Carafa designed this
palazzo in the 15th century.

⑰ Archivio di Stato
The state archive
contains documents
dating back to the
Angevin period.

Key
— Suggested route

| 0 metres | | 100 |
| 0 yards | | 100 |

⑭ Monte di Pietà
This majestic building and the
adjoining chapel were designed
by Giovan Battista Cavagna.

**⑯ Museo Civico
Filangieri**
Prince Filangieri's art
collection in elegant
Palazzo Como includes
detailed mosaic floor
tiles like these.

❶ Santa Maria La Nova

Piazza Santa Maria La Nova 44. **Map** 7 B1 (9 C5). **Tel** 081 552 15 97. 🚌 C25, E1, N1, N3, R2. Ⓜ Toledo. 🚇 Montesanto. **Open** 9:30am–3pm Mon–Fri, 9:30am–2pm Sat & Sun. 🚻 Ⓦ santamarialanova.info

In order to make room for Castel Nuovo *(see pp58–9)*, a Franciscan church devoted to the Virgin Mary had to be demolished. In exchange, Charles I of Anjou had a new church built at his own expense, Santa Maria La Nova. The richly decorated wooden ceiling was painted by the leading artists of the time (such as Imparato and Corenzio), creating a gallery of 16th- and 17th-century Neapolitan painting. In the fourth chapel on the right is Giovanni da Nola's (1488–1558) altarpiece of Sant'Eustachio. Other chapels contain works by Caracciolo, Teodoro d'Errico and Santacroce. In the former monastery, now the seat of the provincial government, there are two cloisters; the smaller one (No. 44) has Renaissance frescoes and marble tombs, while the other (No. 43) contains a garden.

❷ Sant'Anna dei Lombardi

Piazza Monteoliveto. **Map** 7 A1 (9 B5). **Tel** 081 551 33 33. 🚌 E1, N3, N8, R4, 139, 201. Ⓜ Toledo. 🚇 Montesanto. **Open** 10am–1pm, 4–6pm Mon–Sat, 10am–noon Sun. 🛉

Founded in 1411 as Santa Maria di Monteoliveto, this was the favourite church of the Aragonese kings, who summoned the leading artists of the time to decorate it. Its name changed when it was assigned to the Confraternity of Lombards (to whom it still belongs), whose church had collapsed in the 1805 earthquake. The roof was damaged during World War II and has not been restored, but the interior contains some examples of Renaissance sculpture.

Dancing angels, Sant'Anna dei Lombardi

The amazingly realistic sculptural tableau *Lamentation over the Dead Christ* was created by Guido Mazzoni (1450–1518) in 1492. It displays seven life-size terracotta figures leaning over the body of Christ in mourning. Their grief-stricken faces are said to be modelled on those of the Aragonese kings. In the Vasari Sacristy, the stunning ceiling frescoes were painted by the Tuscan artist Giorgio Vasari (1511–74) in 1545; while the Tolosa Chapel was decorated by the della Robbia workshop in Florence. The church also contains the tomb of the architect Domenico Fontana.

At No. 3 Via Monteoliveto is the 16th-century Palazzo Gravina, now occupied by the Faculty of Architecture.

The intricately carved busts of the reliquary, Gesù Nuovo

❸ Gesù Nuovo

Piazza del Gesù Nuovo 2. **Map** 3 B5 (9 B4). **Tel** 081 557 81 51. 🚌 E1. Ⓜ Dante. 🚇 Montesanto. **Open** 8:30am–12:30pm, 4:30–7pm daily. 🛉 Ⓦ gesunuovo.it

The façade, covered in diamond-point rustication, was once part of a 15th-century palazzo. It was retained by the Jesuits when they bought the building and in 1584 transformed it into the large church seen today. The 17th-century doorway incorporates the original Renaissance entrance to the palazzo. The Baroque interior is richly decorated with multi-coloured marbles and ornate works of art, including statues, vivid frescoes and a two-sided reliquary from 1617 decorated with 70 busts of martyred saints. In the chapel of St Ignatius of Loyola, founder of the Society of Jesus, are two of Cosimo Fanzago's finest

The smaller cloister in the former monastery of Santa Maria La Nova

The spectacular ceiling of Gesù Nuovo

works: the sculptures of *David* and *Jeremiah*. The cupola, frescoed by Lanfranco, collapsed in the 1688 earthquake; the only survivors were the corbels showing the four Evangelists in flight. Above the main entrance is Francesco Solimena's huge fresco, *Expulsion of Heliodorus from the Temple* (1725). The statue of the Virgin, on a lapis lazuli globe above the altar, dates from the mid-1800s. The second chapel on the right houses the remains of the physician San Giuseppe Moscati (1880–1927), who was canonized in 1987. On its walls are silver images of specific body parts, which were purchased by worshippers wishing to be healed.

❹ Guglia dell'Immacolata

Piazza del Gesù Nuovo. **Map** 3 B5 (9 B4). 🚌 E1. Ⓜ Dante. 🚇 Montesanto.

The Jesuits commissioned this gigantic marble spire as a symbol of devotion to the Virgin Mary, and as a tangible sign of their power. The monument, modelled on ancient Egyptian obelisks and designed by Giuseppe Genoino, was begun in 1747. The complex stone ornamentation, depicting the Jesuit saints and stories of Mary, was sculpted by Francesco Pagano and Matteo Bottigliero and is regarded as a key work of

18th-century Neapolitan sculpture. The statue of the Madonna is the centre of festivities on the Feast of Immaculate Conception.

❺ Santa Chiara

See pp70–71.

❻ Santa Marta

Via San Sebastiano 42. **Map** 3 B5 (9 B3). 🚌 E1. Ⓜ Dante, Cavour-Museo. 🚇 Montesanto. **Open** occasionally.

This small church was founded by Margherita di Durazzo in the 15th century and became the headquarters of one of the city's most important confraternities, whose members included kings, viceroys and high-ranking officials. The church stands opposite the bell tower of Santa Chiara *(see pp70–71)*. The doorway still retains its original depressed arch structure. On the high altar is a painting by Andrea and Nicola Vaccaro (1670), depicting Santa Marta, to whom the church is dedicated. The *Codice di Santa Marta (Codex of St Martha)*, with its valuable miniatures, came from this church and is now kept in the Archivio di Stato, or state archive *(see p74)*. You can get to the underground cemetery from the room next to the sacristy. Santa Marta is usually closed to the public, but it does open its doors from time to time.

❼ Palazzo Filomarino

Via Benedetto Croce 12. **Map** 3 B5 (9 C4). **Tel** 081 551 71 59. 🚌 E1. Ⓜ Dante. 🚇 Montesanto. Library: **Open** 9am–1pm, 4–7pm daily.

This is the first of many noble buildings you will see in the Spaccanapoli and Decumano Maggiore areas. These mansions and palaces are often in a bad state of preservation yet have retained an air of splendour and stateliness, and still bear traces of the lives of the generations of aristocrats who built and lived in them. The original Palazzo Filomarino dates back to the 14th century, but the building was substantially altered in the 16th century. It then underwent restoration in the following century after being damaged during Masaniello's uprising *(see pp26–7)*. The 18th-century doorway is the work of the architect Sanfelice. The philosopher Benedetto Croce, a leading figure in Italian culture and politics in the first half of the 20th century *(see p30)*, lived in this palazzo in the latter part of his life. The Italian Institute of Historical Studies, founded by Croce, takes up the whole of the first floor with its 40,000-volume library. Croce's apartment and personal library, however, are closed to the public.

The library of philosopher Benedetto Croce on the first floor of Palazzo Filomarino

❺ Santa Chiara

In 1310 Robert of Anjou laid the first stone of the convent and church that the Angevin rulers later chose as the site for their tombs. Santa Chiara was where the kingdom's assemblies were held, as well as ceremonies, such as the one celebrating the miracle of San Gennaro's blood *(see p44)*. In the mid-1700s, the church's Gothic lines were obscured by the addition of elaborate Baroque ornamentation. After the church was totally destroyed by fire in 1943, restoration work tried to recover as much as possible of the original; the present interior is simple and austere, typical of a Franciscan church. Near the apse are the fine sculpture groups of the royal Angevin tombs; a beautiful wooden 14th-century crucifix executed by an unknown artist is on the altar. The lovely cloisters are an oasis of calm and a convenient meeting place for Neapolitans.

Poor Clares' Choir
Built by Leonardo Di Vito, this choir is a great example of Neapolitan Gothic. It was frescoed by Giotto and his assistants, but only fragments of the original remain. The choir is closed to the public.

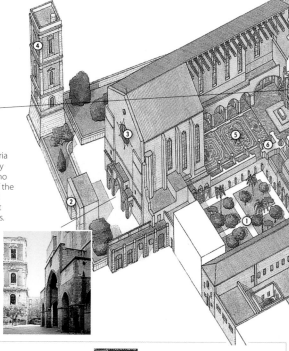

★ Royal Tombs
The tombs of Charles of Calabria (shown here) and his wife Mary of Valois (c.1285–1337) are by Tino da Camaino. In the centre of the rear wall is the tomb of Robert of Anjou, one of Italy's greatest medieval funerary monuments.

Projecting Porch
This massive structure in piperno stone stands out against the yellow tufa façade. On the marble portal is the coat-of-arms of Queen Sancia of Majorca, the wife of Robert of Anjou.

1340 Santa Chiara consecrated and declared a royal church

1742 Building of the tiled cloister

Detail of the cloister

1943 4 Aug: fire caused by bomb destroys church

1300   **1600**   **1900**

1343 Giovanni and Pacio Bertini sculpt the Tomb of Robert of Anjou

1769 Church rebuilt in Baroque style

1995 Museo dell'Opera opens to the public

1310 Robert of Anjou lays the first stone

Robert of Anjou

1953 4 Aug: restored church reopens for worship

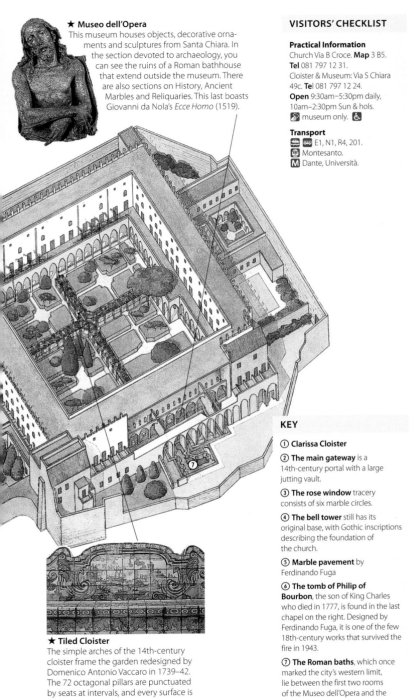

★ Museo dell'Opera
This museum houses objects, decorative ornaments and sculptures from Santa Chiara. In the section devoted to archaeology, you can see the ruins of a Roman bathhouse that extend outside the museum. There are also sections on History, Ancient Marbles and Reliquaries. This last boasts Giovanni da Nola's *Ecce Homo* (1519).

VISITORS' CHECKLIST

Practical Information
Church Via B Croce. **Map** 3 B5.
Tel 081 797 12 31.
Cloister & Museum: Via S Chiara
49c. **Tel** 081 797 12 24.
Open 9:30am–5:30pm daily,
10am–2:30pm Sun & hols.
🖼 museum only. ♿

Transport
🚌 🚐 E1, N1, R4, 201.
Ⓜ Montesanto.
Ⓜ Dante, Università.

KEY

① **Clarissa Cloister**

② **The main gateway** is a 14th-century portal with a large jutting vault.

③ **The rose window** tracery consists of six marble circles.

④ **The bell tower** still has its original base, with Gothic inscriptions describing the foundation of the church.

⑤ **Marble pavement** by Ferdinando Fuga

⑥ **The tomb of Philip of Bourbon**, the son of King Charles who died in 1777, is found in the last chapel on the right. Designed by Ferdinando Fuga, it is one of the few 18th-century works that survived the fire in 1943.

⑦ **The Roman baths**, which once marked the city's western limit, lie between the first two rooms of the Museo dell'Opera and the outer courtyard.

★ Tiled Cloister
The simple arches of the 14th-century cloister frame the garden redesigned by Domenico Antonio Vaccaro in 1739–42. The 72 octagonal pillars are punctuated by seats at intervals, and every surface is decorated with majolica tiles painted by Donato and Giuseppe Massa.

Guglia di San Domenico

❽ Piazza San Domenico Maggiore

Map 3 B5 (9 C3). ▣ E1. Ⓜ Dante, Università. 🚋 Montesanto.

This piazza was the result of a rare Renaissance town-planning project in Naples. In the 1500s the area, once crossed by the Greek city walls, was still being used for kitchen gardens. Rebuilding by the Aragonese rulers transformed the zone into a setting appropriate for the church of San Domenico, which had been chosen to house the royal tombs. They also wanted to improve the area around the statue of the Nile, the aristocratic residential district. The top of the piazza is dominated by the apse of San Domenico. Imposing buildings line the other sides of the square. Opposite the church (at No. 17) is the 17th-century Palazzo Sangro di Casacalenda; to the left (No. 3) is Palazzo Petrucci, with its 15th-century portal; to the right (Nos. 12 and 9) are Palazzo Corigliano, now home to the Oriental Studies department of the University of Naples, and Palazzo Sangro di Sansevero. In the centre stands the Guglia di San Domenico, built in gratitude for release from the plague of 1656. The spire was designed by Cosimo Fanzago and finished only in 1737 by Domenico Antonio Vaccaro.

❾ San Domenico Maggiore

Vico San Domenico Maggiore 18. **Map** 3 B5 (9 C3). **Tel** 081 45 91 88 or 081 442 00 39. ▣ E1. Ⓜ Dante, Cavour-Museo. 🚋 Montesanto. **Open** 9:30am–noon, 5–7pm daily. 🚻 ♿.

In 1283 Charles I of Anjou ordered the construction of a new church and monastery for the Dominican order. The Gothic three-nave building was built onto the pre-existing church of Sant'Arcangelo a Morfisa, which was the original seat of Naples' University of Theology, headed by Saint Thomas Aquinas. A relic of the saint's arm is said to be kept inside the monastery. In 1850–53 Federico Travaglini rebuilt the interior in Neo-Gothic style, removing much of the original spirit of the building. In the second chapel are some 14th-century frescoes ascribed to Pietro Cavallini, a pupil of Giotto. The sacristy houses 42 coffins arranged along the

Corradini's *Modesty* in the Cappella Sansevero

Fresco by Francesco Solimena in the sacristy of San Domenico Maggiore

balcony. Some contain the embalmed corpses of the Aragonese kings, including Alphonse and Ferdinand I. The ceiling fresco was painted by Francesco Solimena in 1707.

❿ Cappella Sansevero

Via Francesco de Sanctis 19 (off Via San Severo). **Map** 3 B5 (9 C3). **Tel** 081 551 84 70. ▣ E1. Ⓜ Dante, Cavour-Museo. 🚋 Montesanto. **Open** 9:30am–6:30pm Wed–Mon (last adm 6pm). 🎟 📷 ♿ limited. 🔲 **museo sansevero.it**

The lavish decoration in the family chapel was planned by Raimondo di Sangro (1710–71), Prince of Sansevero, in the second half of the 18th century. In each sculpture group a member of the powerful family is represented by an allegorical figure. Antonio Corradini's *Modesty*, located to the left of the altar, is set on the tomb of the prince's mother. On the tomb of his father, said to be a dissolute man who later repented his ways, is Francesco Queirolo's *Deception*, located to the right of the altar. The chapel's focal point is the extraordinary *Veiled Christ*, the masterpiece of Neapolitan sculptor Giuseppe Sanmartino (1720–93). Sculpted from a single block of marble, the recumbent figure of Christ is draped with a translucent veil. In the chapel crypt are two "anatomical machines", perhaps creations of the mysterious di Sangro himself. He headed the city's Masonic Lodge and was excommunicated from the Church; he was later re-admitted, probably due to the influence of his family. The stories about the famous prince – inventor, alchemist, lover of science and the occult – have engendered legends depicting him as a demon or a sorcerer.

⓫ Sant'Angelo a Nilo

Piazzetta Nilo. **Map** 3 B5 (9 C3).
Tel 081 211 08 60. 🚌 E1. Ⓜ Dante,
Cavour-Museo, Università.
🚇 Montesanto. **Open** 9am–1pm,
4:30–7pm Mon–Sat, 9am–1pm Sun &
hols. 🚻 ♿

Built in the early 15th century by
Cardinal Brancaccio next to his
family palace, this church was
remodelled four centuries later
by Arcangelo Guglielminelli. It
houses the earliest Renaissance
work in Naples: the cardinal's
funerary monument, sculpted
in Pisa by Donatello and
Michelozzo in 1426–7 and
sent to Naples by ship. On the
front of the sarcophagus, in
the bas-relief representing the
Assumption of the Virgin, Donatello
created one of the first examples
of his revolutionary "stiacciato"
technique – the relief receding
gradually from the foreground
to give the illusion of depth.
From the church you can visit
the courtyard of Palazzo Brancaccio
where the first public library in
Naples was founded in 1690.

⓬ Statue of the Nile

Largo Corpo di Napoli (off Via Nilo).
Map 3 B5. 🚌 E1, E2. Ⓜ Dante,
Cavour-Museo, Università.
🚇 Montesanto.

An 18th-century inscription
informs the reader that the
Alexandrian merchants who
worked in this area of the Greco-
Roman city had this statue
sculpted in honour of the
Egyptian god Nile. The statue
disappeared after the merchants
left Naples; and when found in
the 1400s, its head was missing.
At that time the recumbent
putti next to the god, symbols
of the many tributaries of the
river god, were interpreted as
babies at their mother's breast,
so the sculpture was called "the
Body of Naples", the
mother-city
suckling her

The frescoed ceiling in the Monte di Pietà chapel

children. The statue has kept
this name despite the addition
of a bearded head in the
17th century.

⓭ Palazzo Carafa Santangelo

Via San Biagio dei Librai 121. **Map** 3 C5
(10 D3). 🚌 E1, E2. Ⓜ Dante, Cavour-
Museo, Università. **Open** 7am–1pm,
4–7pm Mon–Sat (courtyard only).

This important example of
Neapolitan Renaissance architecture is known as Palazzo della
Capa di Cavallo because of the
terracotta copy of a horse's head
(now in the courtyard). This was
a gift from Lorenzo de' Medici to
his friend Diomede Carafa in
1471 to embellish his new
palace. The original sculpture, a
Roman bronze, has been in the
Museo Archeologico (*see pp90–
91)* since 1809.

The marble portal, similar to
that of Palazzo Petrucci in Piazza
San Domenico (*see p72*), and the
façade with its shallow rustica-

tion are examples of the
new Renaissance style. In late
15th- century Naples this look
merged with the late Gothic
style, as can be seen in the form
of the arches and pilasters and
the inlay in the wooden doors
with the Carafa family coats
of arms. Opposite the palace is
the animated Baroque façade
of the church of San Nicola a
Nilo, which is also the site of
a second-hand dealer's stall.

⓮ Monte di Pietà

Palazzo Carafa, Via San Biagio dei Librai
114. **Map** 3 C5 (10 D3). 🚌 E1, E2.
Ⓜ Dante, Cavour-Museo, Università
Open 9am–7pm Sat, 9am–2pm Sun.

This majestic building was built in
the late 1500s for the charitable
institute set up to grant loans
to people in debt to money-
lenders. The Cappella della
Pietà at the end of the courtyard
has a late Renaissance façade
with sculptures on either side
of the entrance by Pietro
Bernini, father of the great
Baroque sculptor Gian Lorenzo
Bernini; the sculptures on the
tympanum are by Michelangelo
Naccherino. The church interior
was frescoed by Belisario
Corenzio and the young
Battistello in the early 1600s.
It includes many works by
Naples' Baroque artists, among
them Giuseppe Bonito and
Ippolito Borghese.

Statue of the Egyptian god Nile, known as the "Body of Naples"

⓯ San Giorgio Maggiore

Via Duomo 237a. **Map** 3 C5 (10 E3).
Tel 081 28 79 32. 🚌 C57, E1, E2, N1,
N3, R2. **Open** 8am–noon, 5–7pm
daily, 8am–1pm Sun & public hols. 🛈

San Giorgio Maggiore,
originally an early Christian
basilica, is one of the city's
oldest churches. It was
completely rebuilt in the mid-
1600s to a design by Cosimo
Fanzago. The only surviving
part of the original church is
the semi-circular apse with
Corinthian columns at the
entrance of the 17th-century
church, originally built facing
a different direction. The right-
hand nave of the rebuilt church
was demolished in the late
19th century to make room
for the extended Via Duomo.
The frescoes in the third chapel
are by Francesco Solimena.
Before visiting the church,
pause for a moment at Palazzo
Marigliano (at No. 39 Via
Duomo). Though run-down, it
is one of the most important
examples of 16th-century
Neapolitan civic architecture.

⓰ Museo Civico Filangieri

Via Duomo 288. **Map** 3 C5 (10 E3).
Tel 081 20 31 75. 🚌 C57, E1, E2, N1,
N3, R2. **Open** 10am–4pm Tue–Sat,
10am–2pm Sun.

The building now occupied by
the Civic Museum was built in
the late 15th century as the
Como family residence in the
Florentine Renaissance style.

One of the cloisters in the Archivio di Stato

It became a monastery in the
late 1500s, was demolished
during work on Via Duomo
(1879) and then faithfully
rebuilt 20 m (66 ft) from its
original site.

In 1882 Prince Gaetano
Filangieri established his fine art
collection there and donated it
to the city in 1888. Much of the
collection was scattered during
World War II and was reassem-
bled through private donations.
Today it consists of objects from
various sources, including
weapons, furniture, paintings,
medallions, porcelain, coins and
costumes. The spiral staircase
leads from the ground floor
to the Sala Agata (named after
the founder's mother), which in
turn leads to the prince's library
via a suspended passageway.

⓱ Archivio di Stato

Piazzetta del Grande Archivio 5. **Map** 3
C5 (10 D3). **Tel** 081 563 81 11. 🚌 C57,
E1, E2, N1, N3, R2. **Open** 8am–7pm
Mon–Fri, 8am–1:30pm Sat.
🅦 archiviodistatonapoli.it

In 1835 Ferdinand II decided
to use the former Benedictine
monastery of Santi Severino e
Sossio to house the enormous
quantity of documents relating
to the administration of the
kingdom that had accumulated
since the Angevin period. The
old monastery, built in the 9th
century and enlarged in 1494,
was remodelled to allow for its
new function.

The huge complex has four
cloisters and a number of rooms
containing numerous works
of art. One cloister is known as
the *Chiostro del platano*, named
after an ancient plane tree
(felled in 1959 because it was
dying) which, according to
tradition, had been planted by
St Benedict himself. The mid-
16th century frescoes depicting
the life of the saint are the work
of Antonio Solario, known as
Lo Zingaro or "gypsy". The State
Archive contains over a million
files, registers, documents and
parchments, and is one of the
most important in Europe.

By the entrance to the former
monastery is the 17th-century
Fontana della Selleria.

The Sala Agata in the Museo Civico Filangieri, Palazzo Como

For hotels and restaurants in this area see p182 and pp190–91

Marco Pino, *Adoration of the Magi*

⓲ Santi Severino e Sossio

Via Bartolomeo Capasso 22. **Map** 3 C5
(10 D4). 🚌 E1, N1, N3, R2, 202.
Ⓜ Università. **Open** Church: 9:15am–
noon daily; Cloister: 9am–7pm daily. 🕆

Founded in the 9th century
together with the adjoining
monastery (which became the
Royal Archives in 1835), this
church was rebuilt from the late
1400s on, and finished in 1571.
The façade is the result of
restoration after the 1731
earthquake. In the interior of
both the church and monastery
are some excellent works of art
from the 16th, 17th and 18th
centuries. Among the paintings
are beautiful canvases by the
Sienese painter Marco Pino (first,
third and sixth chapels on the
right). The sculptures include
the tomb of Andrea Bonifacio
(who died at the age of six), a
masterpiece by the Spanish
sculptor Bartolomeo Ordoñez,
in the vestibule of the sacristy.

⓳ Santi Marcellino e Festo

Largo San Marcellino 10. **Map** 3 C5
(10 D4). 🚌 E1, N1, N3, R2, 202.
Ⓜ Università. Monastery: **Tel** 081 253
72 31. **Open** 9am–7pm Mon–Fri.
Museum: **Tel** 081 253 75 16. **Open**
9am–1:30pm Mon–Fri (also 2:30–
4:45pm Mon & Thu). 🅿 ♿

The two adjacent monasteries
of Santi Marcellino e Pietro and

A Number for Every Occasion

At noon every Saturday life stands still for a few minutes in the streets
and alleyways of Old Naples in anticipation of an important event –
the lottery draw. In the hall of the lottery office (Ufficio Lotto e
Lotterie) at No. 17 Via del Grande Archivio, a crowd will be waiting
impatiently for the result. Devised in Genoa in the 16th century, the
lottery was legalized the following century and grew rapidly in
popularity in the 1800s. Neapolitans were immediately hooked.
As Matilde Serao wrote in the late 19th century: "Even Neapolitans
who can't read know *La Smorfia* by heart and immediately apply
it to any dream or real-life event whatsoever".
La Smorfia is a guide to the significance of
numbers and is the lottery "bible". It can
be found in any Lotto office.

There are about 60,000 entries in
alphabetical order, and each entry has
a corresponding number. The book was
first published in the 19th century and is
regularly updated in order to offer readers
interpretations of even the most modern
events and dreams. For example, should
you dream of owning a computer, you
will find that the number to choose is 45.

The lottery in a
19th-century print

of Santi Festo e Desiderio date
from the 8th century. In the
mid-15th century they were
combined to create a single
large complex. The church, built
the following century, is adorned
with refined 18th- century
marble inlay. Luigi Vanvitelli,
architect of the Royal Palace of
Caserta *(see p170)* worked on its
renovation in 1770. The building
is now used as a congress
centre. The spacious cloister
with piperno stone arches has

a pretty garden in the centre;
from the south-facing side there
is a splendid panoramic view of
the Bay of Naples. By royal
decree, the complex became
the property of the University
of Naples in 1907, and it is still
used as a centre of study today.
The building next to the church
is open to the public. It is
occupied by the Museum of
Palaeontology, which has a fine
painted majolica floor and more
than 50,000 artifacts on display.

The airy cloister of the San Marcellino monastery

Courtyard of Gesù Vecchio, part of the University of Naples

⑳ Gesù Vecchio

Via Giovanni Paladino 39. **Map** 3 C5 (10 D4). 🚌 E1, N1, N3, R2, 202. Ⓜ Università. **Open** 9am–6:45pm Mon–Fri. Church: **Tel** 081 552 66 39. **Open** 7:30am–noon, 4:30–6:30pm daily. Anthropology Museum, Zoology Museum, Mineralogy Museum Library: **Tel** 081 253 75 87. Museums: **Open** 9am–1:30pm Mon–Fri (also 2:30–4:45pm Mon & Thu). 🎦 ♿

The home of the University of Naples since 1777, this late 16th-century building was the first Jesuit college in the city. In the late 19th century, thanks to the Urban Renewal Plan *(see pp30–31)*, the University expanded with the addition of a large factory building looking out over Corso Umberto I. One part remaining of the original college are the rooms occupied by the university library since 1808, and home to 1 million

volumes. In 1801 the large hall that was once the Jesuits' library was turned over to the Mineralogy Museum, the most important in Italy and one of the most famous in the world. Other sections house the Anthropology Museum and the Zoology Museum, founded in 1811.

Back in Via Paladino, look out for the sumptuous Baroque interior of the college church (at No. 38), begun in 1564, and containing works by Solimena and Fanzago.

㉑ Corso Umberto I

Map 4 D5 & 7 C1 (10 D5/E4/F3). 🚌 E1, N1, N3, R2, 202. Ⓜ Università, Garibaldi.

This wide street, known to Neapolitans as the Rettifilo, connects the central railway station *(Stazione Centrale)* with the city centre. It was built in the late 19th century as part of the Urban Renewal Plan *(see pp30–31)*. The most important building on Corso Umberto I is the University of Naples, featuring an impressive Neo-Renaissance façade.

㉒ Cappella Pappacoda

Largo San Giovanni Maggiore. **Map** 7 B1 (9 C4). 🚌 E1, R2. Ⓜ Università. **Closed** to the public.

In the early 15th century Artusio Pappacoda, Grand Seneschal and councillor in the Angevin court, founded this small church. The original late Gothic doorway

Portal of Cappella Pappacoda

is the work of Antonio Baboccio (1351–1435), a sculptor, architect and goldsmith who also sculpted the main portal of the cathedral *(see pp86–7)*. The campanile is particularly interesting because of the colour contrast created by the different materials. The church is now deconsecrated and is used as the Great Hall by the nearby Istituto Universitario Orientale (Oriental Institute).

㉓ Santissima Annunziata

Via dell'Annunziata 34. **Map** 4 D4 (10 F3). 🚌 E2, N1, N3, R2, 202. Ⓜ Piazza Garibaldi. **Open** 8am–noon, 5–7:30pm Mon–Sat, 8am–1:30pm Sun. 🔆 ♿ 🌐 annunziatamaggiore.it

The Santa Casa dell'Annunziata was a charitable institution that existed as long ago as

The façade of the University in Corso Umberto I after expansion of the site

the early 1300s to offer help to abandoned children.

The church was destroyed by fire in 1757 and rebuilt by Luigi and Carlo Vanvitelli, who designed the cupola and one-nave interior with 44 Corinthian columns and three chapels on each side. Among the parts fortunately untouched by the fire is the sacristy, which features frescoes by Corenzio (1605) along with 16th-century inlaid wooden cupboards. To the left of the church, an impressive marble doorway leads to the former foundling hospital (now a pediatric hospital), where desperate mothers could leave unwanted babies anonymously.

Painting of the *Madonna Bruna* in Santa Maria del Carmine

㉔ Santa Maria del Carmine

Piazza del Carmine 2. **Map** 4 E5.
Tel 081 20 06 05. E2. Garibaldi.
Open 6:30am–12:30pm, 4–7:30pm
Mon–Sat; 6:30am–1:30pm,
4–7:30pm Sun & hols.
W santuariocarminemaggiore.it

Neapolitans are devoted to this church because of its many works of art, but in particular because of the *Madonna Bruna*, a 14th-century painting kept behind the altar. This famous effigy, the object of deeply felt veneration, is celebrated annually on 16 July at the feast of the Madonna del Carmine *(see p45)*.

Except for the cross dome in the presbytery, little remains of the original Angevin construction. Instead the

Piazza Mercato

Thanks to their position near the harbour, the churches of Sant'Eligio and Santa Maria del Carmine and the area around them became the focal point of commercial life in late 13th-century Angevin Naples. The lively market quarter around Piazza Mercato in the heart of Naples was also the setting for significant events in the city's history. In 1268, Corradino, the last Hohenstaufen king of Naples, was beheaded at the tender age of 16 in front of the Carmine church and the new Angevin rulers decreed that in future all executions were to be carried out in the square. In 1647

Piazza Mercato, with Santa Maria del Carmine

the uprising against the Spanish headed by Tommaso Aniello d'Amalfi, known as Masaniello *(see pp26–7)*, began here. Ten years on, the square was used for the graves of those who had died during the plague epidemic. But the most dramatic events occurred in 1799, when the short-lived, glorious Parthenopean Republic was crushed and all its leaders were executed in Piazza Mercato.

church displays typical 18th-century architectural forms both inside and out. The interior was decorated by Tagliacozzi Canale; the ceiling, destroyed in World War II, has been completely rebuilt in keeping with the original. To the left of the nave is the tomb of Corradino, Duke of Swabia, who was beheaded in 1268 in Piazza Mercato opposite the church *(see above)*. The medieval wooden crucifix placed in a tabernacle under the triumphal arch is also the object of devout worship. There are frescoes and canvases by Solimena in the wings of the transept. The 75-m (246-ft) campanile, completed by Fra Nuvolo in 1631, is the tallest in Naples.

㉕ Sant'Eligio Maggiore

Via Sant'Eligio. **Map** 4 D5 (10 F4).
E1, E2. **Open** 8:30am– 1pm daily.
Tel 081 553 84 29.

The history of Sant'Eligio has parallels with that of Santa Chiara *(see pp70–71)*. This church, the first to be founded by the Angevin dynasty in Naples, was destroyed in World War II and in the process of reconstruction none of the later Baroque additions was restored.

Go through the side doorway with the pointed arch to enter the austere Gothic three-nave interior with its impressive raised transept. The left-hand nave leads to a cross-vaulted area decorated with 14th-century frescoes by artists of the Giotto school. Outside, the Gothic archway and belltower date from the 15th century; the clock was added later.

The campanile of Santa Maria del Carmine (1631)

MATER·OIE

NVLLVS·T.Λ·DOΛ·FZ·SIΛ·SΛΛ·F·T·IN·HONORIS
ΛΛ·TRIVS·SΛCRE·QVODΛΛ·ΛΛVNΛTVΛ·ΛVLΛ
PRESVL·ΛPOSTOLICΛ·NVΛ·GOSTΛS·GΛΛDO·GOLVΛNE
HOC·OPVS·EXΛCTVΛ·ΛΛILLE·CVRRΛTIB·ΛNNIS

POTΛ·PΛ·RVTH·ΛSSISTΛΛGIΛ·PΛΛLΛ·GO
EXΛCOLVIT·POPISHΛTΛΛGIΛS·SVΛ·TIBVS
QVI·PVOGΛGOLVIT·IN·VITΛ·POS·ΛΛTΛ·PΛ
QVO·ΛΛΛTΛ·DΛTV·SΛPTΛ·IERΛV·ΛΛIOΛ

DECUMANO MAGGIORE

In the heart of Greco-Roman Naples, part of the ancient grid plan with three parallel east-west roads (Roman *decumani*), intersected at right angles by the north-south *cardines*, is present-day Via dei Tribunali. It was once called Decumano Maggiore (or Massimo) because it was such a vital part of the city structure. In the late 13th and early 14th centuries the area was significant for its Gothic religious architecture. Today, the churches of San Lorenzo, San Pietro a Maiella and especially the Duomo (cathedral), reveal this past. The Duomo is a stupendous blend of art and architectural styles from the 4th to 19th centuries. Outside the city walls, past 18th-century Piazza Dante, lies the Museo Archeologico Nazionale, home of one of the world's richest Classical archaeological collections.

Sights at a Glance

Historic Buildings
5 Palazzo Spinelli di Laurino
13 Pio Monte della Misericordia
14 Castel Capuano and
   Porta Capuana
20 Accademia delle Belle Arti

Churches
2 San Pietro a Maiella
3 Cappella Pontano
4 Santa Maria Maggiore
   della Pietrasanta
6 Santa Maria delle Anime
   del Purgatorio ad Arco
7 San Paolo Maggiore
8 San Lorenzo Maggiore
9 San Gregorio Armeno

10 Gerolamini
11 *Duomo pp86–7*
15 Santa Caterina a Formiello
17 Santa Maria di
   Donnaregina Nuova

Historic Streets and Squares
1 Piazza Bellini
18 Via Anticaglia
21 Piazza Dante

Spires
12 Guglia di San Gennaro

Museums
16 Museo MADRE
19 *Museo Archeologico
   Nazionale pp90–93*

Restaurants *pp190–91*
1 La Cantina di Via Sapienza
2 Mimì alla Ferrovia
3 Osteria da Carmela
4 Pizzeria i Decumani
5 Pizzeria di Matteo
6 Pizzeria Sorbillo

0 metres 500
0 yards 500

*See also Street Finder
maps 3, 4, 9 and 10*

◀ Fine statuary on the façade of the Duomo

For keys to symbols *see back flap*

Street-by-Street: Via dei Tribunali

Via dei Tribunali was named after Castel Capuano, visible in the distance at the end of this long avenue, when it became the home of the civil courts *(tribunali)* in the 1500s. One of the streets crossing the Decumano Maggiore is Via San Gregorio Armeno, among the loveliest streets in Old Naples, where art and handicrafts flourish. The craftsmen in San Gregorio Armeno still carve shepherds and other figures for the traditional Neapolitan nativity scenes *(see p43)*, just as they did four centuries ago – to the delight of visitors and Neapolitans alike.

❼ San Paolo Maggiore
The sacristy was frescoed by Solimena in 1689–90.

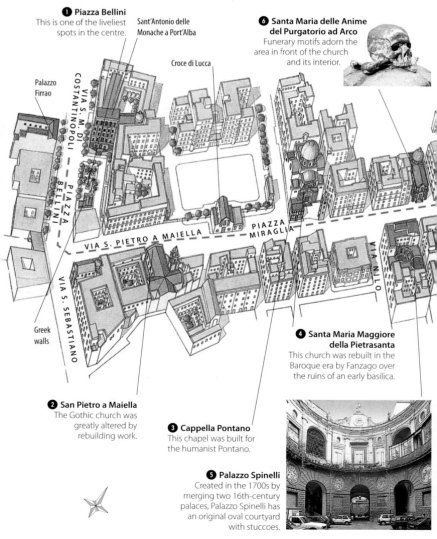

❶ Piazza Bellini
This is one of the liveliest spots in the centre.

Sant'Antonio delle Monache a Port'Alba

Croce di Lucca

❻ Santa Maria delle Anime del Purgatorio ad Arco
Funerary motifs adorn the area in front of the church and its interior.

Palazzo Firrao

VIA S. M. DI COSTANTINOPOLI

PIAZZA BELLINI

Greek walls

VIA S. SEBASTIANO

VIA S. PIETRO A MAIELLA

PIAZZA MIRAGLIA

VIA NILO

❹ Santa Maria Maggiore della Pietrasanta
This church was rebuilt in the Baroque era by Fanzago over the ruins of an early basilica.

❷ San Pietro a Maiella
The Gothic church was greatly altered by rebuilding work.

❸ Cappella Pontano
This chapel was built for the humanist Pontano.

❺ Palazzo Spinelli
Created in the 1700s by merging two 16th-century palaces, Palazzo Spinelli has an original oval courtyard with stuccoes.

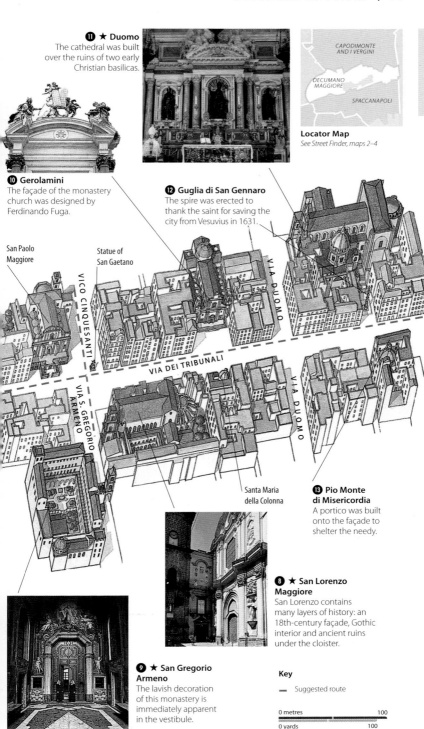

⑪ ★ Duomo
The cathedral was built over the ruins of two early Christian basilicas.

Locator Map
See Street Finder, maps 2–4

⑩ Gerolamini
The façade of the monastery church was designed by Ferdinando Fuga.

⑫ Guglia di San Gennaro
The spire was erected to thank the saint for saving the city from Vesuvius in 1631.

San Paolo Maggiore

Statue of San Gaetano

VICO CINQUESANTI

VIA DUOMO

VIA DEI TRIBUNALI

VIA S. GREGORIO ARMENO

VIA DUOMO

Santa Maria della Colonna

⑬ Pio Monte di Misericordia
A portico was built onto the façade to shelter the needy.

⑧ ★ San Lorenzo Maggiore
San Lorenzo contains many layers of history: an 18th-century façade, Gothic interior and ancient ruins under the cloister.

⑨ ★ San Gregorio Armeno
The lavish decoration of this monastery is immediately apparent in the vestibule.

Key

— Suggested route

| 0 metres | 100 |
| 0 yards | 100 |

❶ Piazza Bellini

Map 3 B5 (9 C3). E1, N3, R4, 201. Dante, Cavour-Museo. Montesanto.

This square, situated at the southern end of Via Santa Maria di Costantinopoli, is one of the most interesting places in Old Naples. The area now occupied by the piazza and street lay outside the city proper until the mid-16th century, when the viceroy Pedro de Toledo extended the city walls. The remains of part of the ancient Greek walls of *Neapolis* were brought to light in the piazza after excavations carried out in 1954. The walls are visible in the middle of the square, at the foot of the monument to the composer Vincenzo Bellini. Overlooking the square is the monastery of Sant'Antonio a Port'Alba, which incorporates the 15th-century Palazzo Conca. The square is well known as a hip, trendy area where students and artists linger. Intra Moenia (*see p199*), a café-bookstore that also runs its own publishing house, is especially popular.

❷ San Pietro a Maiella

Piazza Miraglia 393. **Map** 3 B5 (9 C3). **Tel** 081 45 50 26. E1, R4, 201. Dante, Cavour-Museo. Montesanto. **Open** 7:30am–1:30pm Mon–Sat, 7:30am–1pm Sun.

The founder of this church, the nobleman Pipino da Barletta, dedicated it to Pietro da Morrone, the hermit friar from Maiella who became Pope Celestine V in 1294. The original Gothic architecture, modified by the numerous additions over the centuries, was restored between 1888 and 1927. The restoration uncovered some 14th-century frescoes in two of the chapels. The removal of the Baroque decoration also revealed splendid gilded wooden

An outdoor café in Piazza Bellini

ceilings in the nave and transept with paintings by Mattia Preti (1656–61), regarded as among the most supreme examples of 17th-century Neapolitan painting.

Since 1826 the monastery (at No. 35) annexed to the church has housed one of Italy's music conservatoires.

❸ Cappella Pontano

Piazzetta Pietrasanta 16. **Map** 3 B5 (9 C3). E1, R4, 201. Dante, Cavour-Museo. Montesanto. **Open** 9am–1pm daily.

The famous humanist Giovanni Pontano, secretary to King Ferdinand of Aragon, commissioned this small, elegant chapel in 1492. Based on a design for a pagan temple, the harmonious proportions make it one of the most significant works produced in Renaissance Naples. The chapel contains a frescoed triptych by Francesco Cicino da Caiazzo – restored in 1792 – and a 15th-century pavement of coloured tiles, which is still well-preserved. The numerous Latin epigraphs were written by Giovanni Pontano himself.

Bust of Giovanni Pontano

❹ Santa Maria Maggiore della Pietrasanta

Piazzetta Pietrasanta. **Map** 3 B4. E1, R4, 201. Dante, Cavour-Museo. **Open** 9am–6:30pm Sun.

A church was first erected in this location in AD 566 by Bishop Pomponio; however, the majestic, centrally planned church that is visible today was built by Cosimo Fanzago in the 17th century. The campanile (*see p24*) belonged to the original basilica; it was built after the main building in the 10th century and is the sole example of early medieval architecture in Naples. In the Middle Ages the road was lower and passed under the bell tower arch. A wall of the ancient Greek city of *Neapolis* and a Roman villa lie directly underneath the church, as

The interior of Santa Maria Maggiore della Pietrasanta

does a 3 km- (2 mile-) long Roman aqueduct that was used as a bomb shelter during World War II.

❺ Palazzo Spinelli di Laurino

Via Tribunali 362. **Map** 3 B5 (9 C3). **Tel** 081 29 95 79. E1. Dante, Cavour-Museo. Montesanto. **Open** 8am–7pm Mon–Sat (courtyard only).

In the 18th century, the prominent local architect Ferdinando Sanfelice (1675–1748) carried out radical changes to this 16th-century palazzo. He also created the oval courtyard and the building beyond, where the chatter from the crowded Via dei Tribunali could be clearly heard by the dukes of Laurino. The double-flight staircase is another of Sanfelice's designs. Similar examples can be seen in the Palazzo Serra di Cassano (see p62), Palazzo dello Spagnolo and Palazzo Sanfelice (see p98).

❻ Santa Maria delle Anime del Purgatorio ad Arco

Via Tribunali 39. **Map** 3 B4 (9 C3). **Tel** 081 29 87 91. E1. Dante, Cavour-Museo. Montesanto. Church, Museum and Hypogeum: **Open** 10am–2pm Mon–Fri, 10am–5pm Sat. **W** purgatorioadarco.it

This church still belongs to the confraternity of the same name founded in 1604 to collect alms to pay for the masses for the souls of the dead. Evidence of the importance attached to worship of the dead in 17th-century Naples is shown by the many skulls, bones and other funerary motifs on and around the façade, and in the interior. The church has a single nave and lavish Baroque decoration. In the apse area there is a relief with a winged skull by Cosimo Fanzago, who also designed the church. Steps lead to the underground cathedral and a crypt of bones,

Interior of the church of Purgatorio ad Arco

including those of the virgin-bride Lucia, who died of consumption shortly before her wedding day in the 1700s.

❼ San Paolo Maggiore

Piazza San Gaetano. **Map** 3 C4 (10 D2). **Tel** 081 45 40 48. C57, E1, E2. Dante, Cavour-Museo. Montesanto. **Open** 9am–6pm Mon–Sat, 10am–6pm Sun. Crypt: **Open** 8–10am & 5–7pm daily.

In Greco-Roman Naples, present-day Piazza San Gaetano was the site of the Greek *Agora* and later, of the Roman Forum. The Romans built a Temple of the Dioscuri here, which was converted into a Christian basilica in the 8th century. This ancient church was then remodelled from 1583 to 1603 by Francesco Grimaldi. The new church, with a three-nave Latin cross plan, also incorporated the pronaos of the pagan temple, but only two Corinthian columns of the latter survived the 1688 earthquake.

In the richly decorated interior there are frescoes by Massimo Stanzione on the vault over the central nave. Sadly, they were damaged by water and bombardments during World War II. The Cappella Firrao, on the left side of the apse, has many 17th-century tombs, sculptures and frescoes. The marvellous paintings in the sacristy are by Francesco Solimena (1689–90). A stairway leads down to the crypt, which is the final resting place of San Gaetano, one of Naples' patron saints.

Façade of San Paolo Maggiore

Underneath the City

Underneath Naples there is another world to be explored, just as fascinating as the city above. Since its early days the city has been built out of material quarried from the ground – the local yellow tufa is excellent for building. Over the years, caves and tunnels were left in this way, and became catacombs, aqueducts, passageways, and escape and shelter areas during World War II bombing raids. The caves were extended to their current size during Spanish rule (see pp26–7), when it was

Tour of the tunnels beneath the streets of Naples

forbidden to import raw material for building houses and palazzi. Today you can descend into the bowels of Naples: on the left-hand side of San Paolo Maggiore is one of the entrances to *Napoli Sotterranea (see p221)*.

❽ San Lorenzo Maggiore

Via dei Tribunali 316. **Map** 3 C4
(10 D3). 🚌 E1. Ⓜ Dante, Cavour-
Museo. 🚇 Montesanto. Church: **Tel**
081 45 49 48. **Open** 7:30am–12:30pm,
5–7:30pm daily. 🏛 Excavations &
Museum: **Tel** 081 211 08 60. **Open**
9:30am–5:30pm daily. 🎟 🏛
🅦 sanlorenzomaggiore.na.it

The construction of one of
Naples' oldest and richest
monumental complexes began
in 1265, for Charles I of Anjou, on
the site of a 6th-century church
(see p39). The façade was totally
rebuilt by Sanfelice in 1742, but
the 14th-century portal and
original wooden doors are intact.
The single-nave Gothic interior
has an apse, designed by French
architects, with nine chapels
placed around the ambulatory.
Here is the tomb of Catherine
of Austria, a fine sculpture by
Tino da Camaino (c.1323) and,
in the sixth chapel from the
right, frescoes by a Neapolitan
pupil of Giotto. It was in this
church that Boccaccio first saw
the girl he celebrated in his
writings as Fiammetta.
  To the right of San Lorenzo is
the monastery, where you can
visit the cloister, the chapter-
house and the refectory, which,
from 1442, was the assembly
hall of the royal Parliament. It
also houses the Museo dell'
Opera, which has local artifacts
dating from the 3rd century BC
to the 19th century. The
cloister affords access to the
excavation site that has revealed

The Baroque interior of the church of San Gregorio Armeno

important remains of the Greco-
Roman city. These include a
macellum (market) and
evidence of other buildings.

❾ San Gregorio Armeno

Convent: Piazzetta San Gregorio
Armeno 1 Church: Via San Gregorio
Armeno 44. **Map** 3 C5 (10 D3).
Tel 081 552 01 86. 🚌 E1.
Ⓜ Dante, Cavour-Museo.
🚇 Montesanto. Convent, Church
and Cloister: **Open** 9:30am–noon
Mon–Sat, 9:30am–12:30pm Sun. 🎟

Located on the street known as
"Christmas Alley", where artisans
sell statuettes and scenery for the
presepe (Christmas crib; see p43),
San Gregorio was founded in the
8th century by a group of nuns
who had fled Byzantium with the
relics of St Gregory to escape
religious persecution. The

monastery was rebuilt in the
1500s and enlarged during the
following century. The campanile
was erected in 1716 on a
footbridge that connected two
parts of the complex. The
decoration of the sumptuous
Baroque interior – a "room of
Paradise on Earth", as Carlo
Celano wrote in his guide to
Naples – was designed in the
mid-18th century by Niccolò
Tagliacozzi Canale. Notable
works include the late
16th-century wooden ceiling,
the two organs and, above the
entrance, Luca Giordano's
frescoes of *The Embarkation,
Journey and Arrival of the
Armenian Nuns with the Relics
of St Gregory* (1671–84).
  There is a lovely fountain
in the cloister with a statue
of Christ and the Samaritan,
sculpted in 1733 (see p27).

❿ Gerolamini

Church: Piazza Gerolamini. Cloisters &
Gallery: Via Duomo 142. Cappella
dell'Assunta: Via Duomo 144 **Map** 3 C4
(10 D2). **Tel** 081 29 23 16. 🚌 C57, E1,
E2. Ⓜ Dante, Cavour-Museo.
🚇 Montesanto. Church, Cloisters &
Gallery: **Open** 8:30am–7pm Mon–Fri,
8:30am–2pm Sat & Sun. Library:
Closed to the public. 🖼

The monastery of the Gerolamini was founded in the late
16th century by the Oratorio di
San Filippo Neri congregation,
also called "dei Gerolamini"
because they came from San
Girolamo alla Carità in Rome.

Cloister of San Lorenzo Maggiore

The church was built in Tuscan Renaissance style; the interior was rebuilt in the early 1600s; and the façade was modified by Ferdinando Fuga in 1780. Luca Giordano, Pietro da Cortona and Guido Reni decorated the Baroque interior.

Alongside the church there are two cloisters. The first, designed by Giovanni Dosio, shares features with the cloister he created at the Certosa di San Martino (see pp112–15). There are fine paintings in the Quadreria (art gallery). The 60,000-volume library has 18th-century furnishings and decoration.

The cloister in the Gerolamini

⑪ Duomo

See pp86–7.

⑫ Guglia di San Gennaro

Piazza Riario Sforza. **Map** 3 C4 (10 E2). 🚌 C57, E1, E2. Ⓜ Dante, Cavour-Museo.

This sculpted marble spire is dedicated to San Gennaro, the patron saint of Naples, for having protected the city during the 1631 eruption of Vesuvius. The *guglia*, the oldest of the three spires in Naples, was designed by Cosimo Fanzago in 1636, the same artist who later worked on the Guglia di San Domenico (see p72). The bronze statue at the top of the spire was sculpted by Tommaso Montani. Behind the

Guglia di San Gennaro

The Seven Acts of Mercy, a masterpiece by Caravaggio

spire in the small square you can glimpse the stairway of the side entrance to the Duomo (see pp86–7) and, higher up, the dome of the Cappella di San Gennaro.

⑬ Pio Monte della Misericordia

Via Tribunali 253. **Map** 3 C4 (10 E2). **Tel** 081 44 69 44. 🚌 C57, E1, E2. Ⓜ Cavour- Museo, Garibaldi. Church & Gallery: **Open** 9am– 2:30pm Thu–Tue. 📷 🎫 by appt. 🌐 piomontedellamisericordia.it

Pio Monte is one of the most important charitable institutions in Naples. It was founded in 1601 to aid the poor and ill and to free the Christian slaves in the Ottoman Empire. The entire complex was designed by Francesco Antonio Picchiatti in the second half of the 17th century. After passing through the five-arch loggia (where pilgrims could shelter) decorated with sculptures by Andrea Falcone (1666–71), you enter the church. The eye is immediately drawn to the extraordinary altarpiece, *The Seven Acts of Mercy*, a masterpiece by Caravaggio (1571–1610), one of Italy's greatest artists. The art gallery on the first floor of the building houses the fine Pio Monte collection. Pio Monte is still active as a charitable institution today.

⑭ Castel Capuano and Porta Capuana

Piazza Enrico De Nicola and Via Concezio Muzy. **Map** 4 D4 (10 F2). 🚌 C57, E2. Ⓜ Garibaldi. Cappella Sommaria: **Open** in May, by appt; call 081 410 72 19 (tourist office).

A palace and fortress built by the Normans in 1165 to defend the nearby city gateway, Castel Capuano remained a royal residence for the Angevin and Aragonese rulers even after the construction of Castel Nuovo (see pp58–9). In 1540 Don Pedro de Toledo turned the castle into law courts, a function it maintains to this day. On the first floor is the huge frescoed Court of Appeal, which leads to the splendid Renaissance Cappella della Sommaria, decorated by the Spanish painter Pietro Roviale, also known as Pedro de Rubiales (1511–82).

A short distance away from the courts stands the gateway of Porta Capuana, where the ancient road to Capua entered the city. Although much older in origin, its present appearance is the result of late 15th-century reconstruction by the Italian architect and sculptor Giuliano da Maiano. The two towers, which are named Honour and Virtue, enclose the marble arch, repeating the pattern established in the Arco di Trionfo in Castel Nuovo.

The marble arch of Porta Capuana, rebuilt in the 1400s

⓫ Duomo

This great cathedral was built for Charles I of Anjou in the late 1200s–early 1300s. The church incorporated older Christian buildings and has been altered substantially over the centuries. The left-hand nave leads to the early medieval basilica of Santa Restituta, radically changed in the 17th century, and the San Giovanni in Fonte baptistry. The Cappella Minutolo has retained its original Gothic structure and decoration; the mosaic pavement and 13th-century frescoes are by Montano d'Arezzo. The Crypt of the Succorpo was built under the apse in the 1500s to house the relics of San Gennaro, kept until then in the Montevergine sanctuary. In the early 1600s the Cappella di San Gennaro was erected once the plague of 1527 had ended.

★ **Baptistry**
This is the oldest baptistry in the Western world, built around AD 550. The mosaics date from the same period.

★ **Santa Restituta**
The structure of the early Christian basilica was changed in the Angevin period and its decoration was replaced in the late 1600s. In the last chapel on the left is the beautiful mosaic Madonna and Saints Gennaro and Restituta, executed by Lello da Orvieto in 1322.

KEY

① **The middle portal** bears two 14th-century lions and Tino da Camaino's *Virgin and Child* in the lunette.

② **The underground archaeological area**, currently closed for restoration, reveals layers of buildings from three successive periods: Greek, Roman and early Middle Ages.

③ **A terrace**, accessible by elevator from the sacristy, offers breathtaking city views.

④ **Over 100 ancient columns** are used as facing for the nave pillars.

⑤ **Cappella Minutolo**

⑥ **Guglia di San Gennaro** (see p85)

Font
The basin is made of Egyptian basalt. The right-hand nave also has Greek sculptures and a 14th-century episcopal throne.

c.450 The Santa Restituta and Santa Stefania basilicas built	**1300** Duomo built on the site of the two basilicas	**1497** Work begins on crypt to house relics of San Gennaro	**1876** The façade is rebuilt in Neo-Gothic style	
400	**1000**	**1300**	**1600**	**1900**
c.550 The San Giovanni in Fonte baptistry added to Santa Restituta	**1349** An earthquake destroys the façade of the Duomo	**1621** Old ceiling replaced by present-day one in gilded wood	**1969** Digs begin in archaeological area	
		1608–37 Cappella di San Gennaro erected		

The Crypt of the Succorpo was
decorated by Tommaso Malvito
and his assistants. San Gennaro's
remains are kept here.

Miracle of the Blood

On the Saturday preceding the first Sunday
in May and on 19 September *(see p44 and
p46)*, the blood of San Gennaro, kept in
two phials, turns to liquid. This ritual dates
from the late 1300s and in Naples is the
equivalent of an oracle: if the miracle does
not occur, catastrophes are imminent.

★ **Cappella di
San Gennaro**
The dome, with its
depiction of Paradise, was
frescoed by Lanfranco in
1641–3. The reliquary
bust of San Gennaro, a
masterpiece of Gothic
craftsmanship, is also here.

The monumental façade of Santa Maria di Donnaregina Nuova

⓯ Santa Caterina a Formiello

Piazza Enrico De Nicola 65. **Map** 4 D4 (10 F1). **Tel** 081 44 42 97. 🚌 C57, E2, 203. Ⓜ Garibaldi. **Open** 8:30am–12:30pm, 4:30–8pm daily; 9am–1:30pm public hols.

The dome of Santa Caterina a Formiello dominates the surrounding area. The church was called *formiello* because it was built next to *formali*, the ancient city aqueducts. The 16th-century building has delightful Baroque decoration in the interior. Luigi Garzi and Guglielmo Borremans executed the frescoes (1695–1709). The marble tombs of the Spinelli family are in the apse area.

⓰ Museo MADRE

Via Settembrini 79. **Map** 3 C4 (10 D1). **Tel** 081 19 31 30 16. 🚌 C57, E2, N4, 182, 203. Ⓜ Cavour-Museo. **Open** 10am–7:30pm Mon & Wed–Sat; 10am–8pm Sun. 🚫 (free Mon). 🖥 🎦 ♿ 🆆 madrenapoli.it

Opened in 2005, the Museo d'Arte Contemporanea Donna Regina Napoli (MADRE) houses a remarkable collection of works by artists such as Mimmo Paladino, Jeff Koons, Anish Kapoor, Jannis Kounellis

and Giulio Paolini among others. The first floor has a library and a children's area, while the third floor is used for temporary exhibitions. The museum often hosts special events such as cinema screenings, concerts and theatrical performances.

The back of the museum is also the entrance to the 8th-century church of Santa Maria di Donnaregina Vecchia, rebuilt in 1293 at the request of Marie of Hungary, wife of Charles II of Anjou. The church, with a single nave ending in a pentagonal apse, contains the marble tomb of the queen, sculpted by Tino da Camaino in 1325–6.

⓱ Santa Maria di Donnaregina Nuova

Largo Donnaregina 7. **Map** 3 C4 (10 D1). **Tel** 081 557 13 65. 🚌 C57, E1, E2. Ⓜ Cavour-Museo. **Open** 9:30am–4:30pm Mon, Wed–Sat; 9:30am–2pm Sun. 🚫 🆆 museodiocesanonapoli.it

The single-nave interior of this Baroque church built in the early 1600s for the Poor Clares is splendidly decorated in multi-coloured marble. Fine frescoes by Francesco Solimena (1657–1747) can be admired in the nuns' choir. The second floor houses the Diocesan Museum of Naples, which boasts two hallways of paintings, including *St Paul's Landing in Pozzuoli* by Giovanni Lanfranco (1582–1647). Other artists featured along these corridors include Vaccaro, De Matteis and several Neapolitan painters from the 16th to the 19th centuries. Between the two hallways, a lookout point provides breathtaking views of the church.

⓲ Via Anticaglia

Map 3 C4 (10 D2). 🚌 C57, E1, E2. Ⓜ Cavour-Museo.

The third, northernmost *decumanus* (east–west major road) in Greco-Roman Naples today has four official sections (Via Sapienza, Via Pisanelli, Via Anticaglia and Via Santi Apostoli), as does Spaccanapoli, the lower *decumanus (see p65)*.

The elegant interior of the pharmacy in the Ospedale degli Incurabili

Foro Carolino, present-day Piazza Dante, the 18th-century palace and hemicycle designed by Luigi Vanvitelli

The name "Anticaglia", meaning ruins, derives from the remains of the brick walls of a Roman building in this stretch of the street. These walls connected the ancient theatre, on the left as you go towards Via Santa Maria di Costantinopoli, and the bath-house on the opposite side of the street. The theatre, where Emperor Nero is known to have acted, had a seating capacity of about 8,000. Nearby was the *odeion*, or ancient roofed theatre, used for concerts and poetry readings.

On the corner of Via Duomo and the third *decumanus*, there is a fine marble and piperno double stairway – from here you can visit the atrium of the church of San Giuseppe dei Ruffi, which was added in the early 18th century. Once past the Roman ruins, a right-hand turn at Via Armanni takes you to the Ospedale degli Incurabili. Inside is the unusual *Farmacia* (pharmacy) with about 400 brightly coloured majolica vases on shelves of inlaid wood – a positive art gallery of Neapolitan ceramics. However, visits are allowed only during the month of May for the "Maggio dei Monumenti" *(see p44)*.

⑲ Museo Archeologico Nazionale

See pp90–93.

⑳ Accademia delle Belle Arti

Via Vincenzo Bellini 36. **Map** 3 B4 (9 B2). **Tel** 081 44 18 88. E1, N3, N8, R4, 201. Cavour-Museo. **Open** 10am–2pm Tue–Thu & Sat; 2–6pm Fri.
W accademiadinapoli.it

Architect Errico Alvino transformed the 18th-century convent of San Giovanni delle Monache into the Academy of Fine Arts in the 1840s. The Neo-Renaissance style throughout reflects the prevailing fashion of the time and a broad staircase with plaster casts of ancient sculptures leads to the first floor. The building contains

The Accademia delle Belle Arti staircase

important collection of modern painting, especially works by 19th-century Neapolitan and southern Italian artists.

㉑ Piazza Dante

Map 3 A5 (9 B3). C63, N3, N8, R4, 201. Montesanto. Dante.

Until the 1700s this square lay outside the city walls and was used as a marketplace, hence the name Largo del Mercatello (Market Square).

In the second half of the 18th century it took on its present form and was renamed Foro Carolino by Charles III, King Charles of Bourbon and ruler of Naples from 1735 to 1759, who commissioned the new layout. The semicircular façade with its colossal columns was designed by architect-of-the-day Luigi Vanvitelli as a setting for the king's statue, which was intended for the central niche but was never sculpted. The 26 figures on the cornice are allegories of the sovereign's qualities.

Following the unification of Italy, a statue of Dante was placed in the middle of the square, and the square was renamed again. The square is now lined with book shops all the way up to Via Port'Alba and Port'Alba, the gateway built in 1625 to connect the city with outlying districts.

⑲ Museo Archeologico Nazionale

This building, housing one of the world's most important archaeological museums, started life in the late 1500s as the home of the royal cavalry and was rebuilt in the early 17th century as the seat of Naples university. In 1777, when Ferdinand IV transferred the university to the former monastery of Gesù Vecchio *(see p76)*, the building was again adapted to house the Real Museo Borbonico and library. In 1860 it became public property. Restoration and reorganization of exhibits still continue in the museum.

Blue Vase
This wine vessel found in a Pompeii tomb was made with the so-called glass-cameo technique: a layer of opaque white paste was placed over coloured glass and then engraved with decorative motifs.

Bust of "Seneca"
Found in the Villa dei Papiri *(see p148)* in Herculaneum, this 1st-century BC bronze head was long thought to represent the philosopher Seneca the Elder. Today, however, its identity is less certain.

★ **The Battle of Alexander**
The splendid mosaic from the House of the Faun in Pompeii *(see p154)* depicts Alexander the Great's battle against the Persian emperor Darius III (333 BC).

The Secret Cabinet
The erotic works from Pompeii and Herculaneum housed here caused embarrassment at the time of the Bourbons.

Key to Floorplan
- ☐ Basement
- ☐ Ground floor
- ☐ Mezzanine
- ☐ First floor
- ☐ Non-exhibition space

Sacrifice of Iphigenia

In this Pompeiian fresco, Iphigenia, daughter of Agamemnon, is about to be sacrificed to Artemis, who saves her by taking a deer instead.

VISITORS' CHECKLIST

Practical Information
Pza Museo 19. **Map** 3 B4 (9 B1).
Tel 081 442 21 49.
Open 9am–7:30pm Wed–Mon.
Closed 1 Jan, 1 May, 25 Dec.
🖼 ♿ 🖼 🎥

Transport
Ⓜ Cavour-Museo. 🚌 CS, C51, C52, E1, R1 and others.

Spring Fresco

This fresco removed from the Villa Ariana in the Campo Varano is a masterpiece of grace and elegance; the female figure is rendered with soft, delicate colours.

Stairs down to
Egyptian Collection

★ Farnese Hercules

Made by Glykon of Athens, this statue is an enlarged copy of a sculpture by the Greek master Lysippus. Napoleon is said to have regretted leaving it behind when he removed his booty from Italy in 1797.

Entrance

★ Farnese Bull

Excavated in the Baths of Caracalla in Rome, this is the largest sculptural group to have survived from antiquity (c.200 BC). It shows the punishment of Dirce who, having ill-treated Antiope, was tied to an enraged bull by the latter's sons. The Farnese Bull hall is currently undergoing restoration.

Exploring the Museo Archeologico

The real Museo Borbonico, as the museum was known, held the Farnese Collection of paintings, ancient artifacts and books, and archaeological finds from sites in Campania and Southern Italy. In 1925 the books were moved to the Palazzo Reale *(see pp54–5)* and in 1957 the Farnese Collection paintings were returned to Capodimonte *(see pp102–5)*. The remaining material consisted of ancient finds, and the museum became the Archaeological Museum.

The impressive Farnese Collection and sculpture from Herculaneum, Pompeii and other Campanian cities can be seen on the ground floor, the mezzanine level, and the first floor. Pompeiian mosaics, on the mezzanine level, and domestic items, weapons and murals, on the first floor, show daily life in the ancient cities. A lower ground floor level houses the Egyptian Collection. The arrangement aims to display the exhibits in context.

Funerary stela of the scribe Huy

These were the intermediaries between men and gods. The limestone funerary stela of Huy (1320–1200 BC) retains some of its original colouring.

As well as human and animal mummies, the Egyptian section includes Canopic vases, containers for the internal organs of the deceased with lids in the shape of animal heads. The collection of *shabti* comprises wood, stone and faience statuettes representing workers for the deceased in the afterlife.

Sculpture

The fine collection of Greco-Roman sculpture consists mostly of works found in excavations around Vesuvius and the Phlegraean Fields, as well as the treasures from the Farnese Collection. The sculptures – most of which are the only existing Roman copies of lost Greek originals – are displayed on the ground floor. Among the numerous fine works are the statues of *Harmodios and Aristogeiton*, or the "tyrannicides", young Athenians who killed the 6th-century BC tyrant, Hipparchos, and the bronze and alabaster *Artemis of Ephesos*, whose breasts symbolize fertility. The *Doryphoros* carrying a spear is a copy of a famous Greek original, as is the impressive *Farnese Hercules*. The *Farnese Atlas*, holding up the world, is a Hellenistic statue, while the huge *Dioscuri* statues, discovered in the Roman baths of Baia *(see p141)*, and the *Farnese Flora* are copies by Roman sculptors.

The Farnese Flora

Cameo with Dionysus and satyr

Incised Gems

This precious collection, begun by Cosimo de' Medici, contains Greek, Roman and Renaissance gems. The highlight is the veined sardonyx *Farnese Cup*, a large and beautiful cameo carved in Egypt around the 2nd and 1st centuries BC. Another stunning agate and sardonyx cameo shows the infant Dionysus playing with a satyr.

The Egyptian Collection

Valuable works of Egyptian art from the Ancient Kingdom (2700–2200 BC) to the Roman age are exhibited here. The black basalt *Farnese Naophorous* represents a kneeling official.

Mosaics

The majority of the mosaics on display in the museum come from Pompeii, Stabiae, Herculaneum and Boscoreale and date from the 2nd century BC to AD 79. The realistic images, such as the female portraits from Pompeii, are particularly fascinating. Among the many pavement mosaics

Mosaic of a female from Pompeii

made of tiny tesserae and often derived from Greek paintings, is *La Fattucchiera* (the Sorceress). This interesting example of the Hellenistic tradition depicts a scene from *Synaristoi*, a comedy by the Greek playwright Aristophanes. Another masterpiece is the *Battle of Alexander* found at Pompeii. This large, detailed mosaic was based on a Hellenistic painting and depicts Alexander the Great leading his cavalry against Darius III, the Persian Emperor, seen fleeing in his chariot.

Some rooms in the museum have reconstructions of large mosaic paved floors.

Villa dei Papiri

This villa in Herculaneum *(see p148)*, still partly buried today, was an art gallery in its own right. The rich array of artworks found here during the excavations in 1750–61 are exceptional: this ancient private collection has been handed down to us intact. A map of the villa shows where every object was found.

Among the pieces on display are life-size statues and small sculptures in marble and bronze, such as the *Dancing Faun* which greeted visitors in the atrium of the villa. Most of the pieces were inspired by Greek figurative art. A vast library of around 1,800 papyrus scrolls was also found in the villa. An apparatus used to unroll the charred scrolls is on display. The original scrolls are now kept in the Biblioteca Nazionale *(see p55)*.

Salone della Meridiana

When the building was being reorganized and fitted out as a museum in the late 18th century, the architects had the idea of adding an observatory. A large sundial *(meridiana)*, decorated with the signs of the zodiac, was created for the spacious hall which had originally been destined to be the Bourbon library (Biblioteca Borbonica).

The plans of the observatory, however, were scrapped in favour of a different location *(see p101)*, and as originally planned, the Salone della Meridiana was opened to the public in 1804 as a library. Its beautiful ceiling fresco, painted by Neapolitan artist Pietro Bardellino in 1781, is among the most impressive in all Europe.

Ancient Frescoes

Most of the frescoes in the collection were removed from buildings in cities buried by the eruptions of Vesuvius, and assembled here from the mid-1700s onwards. The most important came from the Basilica in Herculaneum (such as the painting of *Achilles and Chiron*). Others were taken from the Villa di Fannio Sinistore at Boscoreale, where one wall was decorated with illusionistic architectural perspective, and from the extensive landed property of Julia Felix in Pompeii. The frieze from her house, with a still life of apples and grapes and scenes from the forum, gives a fascinating glimpse of everyday life in a 1st-century AD city.

Statue of a faun, Villa dei Papiri

The famous fresco *Achilles and Chiron* from Herculaneum

There are also numerous fragments of frescoes which depict landscapes, portraits and mythological scenes and characters, such as the *Sacrifice of Iphigenia*. These show the variety and quality of Roman painting from this period.

Temple of Isis

The paintings, sculptures and furnishings from the Temple of Isis in Pompeii are presented in such a way as to recreate the sanctuary as it appeared to the first archaeologists in 1764. The *Portrait of Io at Canopos* was uncovered on 18 November of the same year in the presence of King Ferdinand IV, and shows the nymph Io being welcomed to Egypt by Isis. The marble head of the goddess, to whom the temple was dedicated, dates from the 1st century AD.

Head of Isis

Model of Pompeii

The Model of Pompeii

Paper, cork and wood were all used in the making of this extensive scale model of the Pompeii excavations. The archaeologist Giuseppe Fiorelli had the original idea and the model was constructed in various stages between 1861 to 1879. The extraordinarily exact reproduction of every detail found in the ruins (including paintings and mosaics done in watercolour), make this an extremely important historical document. In some cases, when detailed records of Pompeiian decoration are needed, this model is the only useful source that remains.

CAPODIMONTE AND I VERGINI

Although the Spanish viceroys had forbidden construction outside the city walls, from the 17th century onwards suburban development continued. In the early 19th century, building began in the northern suburbs. The avenue leading to the Capodimonte palace, now the home of one of Europe's most important museums, was created as an extension of Via Toledo. The square next to the Museo Archeologico was redesigned and Via Foria, on which the Botanic Garden and, from 1751, the huge Albergo dei Poveri were being built, was widened. The old Sanità, Vergini and Fontanelle districts are a lively working quarter in which visitors need to exercise caution. On the streets leading to the early Christian cemeteries, tenements alternate with historic churches and buildings.

Sights at a Glance

Churches and Cemeteries
④ San Gennaro Catacombs
⑤ Santa Maria della Sanità and San Gaudioso Catacombs
⑥ Cimitero delle Fontanelle
⑦ San Giovanni a Carbonara
⑧ Santi Apostoli
⑨ Santa Maria degli Angeli alle Croci

Historic Buildings
② Palazzo dello Spagnolo
③ Palazzo Sanfelice
⑪ Albergo dei Poveri
⑫ Torre del Palasciano
⑭ Osservatorio Astronomico

Historic Gate
① Porta San Gennaro

Museums and Galleries
⑬ *Museo Nazionale and Park of Capodimonte pp102–5*

Parks and Gardens
⑩ Orto Botanico

☐ Restaurants *p190*
1 Cantina del Gallo
2 Pizzeria Starita

See also Street Finder maps 3, 4, 9 and 10

0 metres		500
0 yards		500

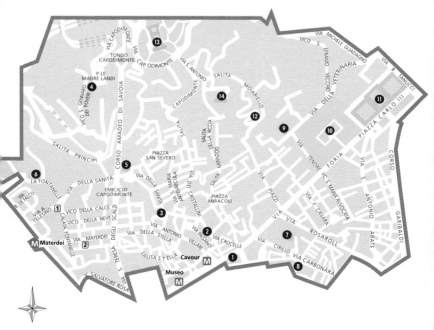

◀ Palazzo Reale Capodimonte, home of the Museo Nazionale

For keys to symbols *see back flap*

Street-by-Street: North of the Ancient Walls

The area north of the city walls has been used for burials and worship of the dead since it was first inhabited. A visit to the catacombs (which were underground cemeteries and not hiding places), first created in the early Christian era, is an unforgettable experience. The area outside the walls was also used to dump rubbish. The district known today as Via San Giovanni a Carbonara was once called the Fosso Carbonario (literally, "coal ditch"), and this is how the street and the beautiful 14th-century church acquired their current names.

The church of Santa Maria dai Vergini, built in the 14th century, was badly damaged in World War II.

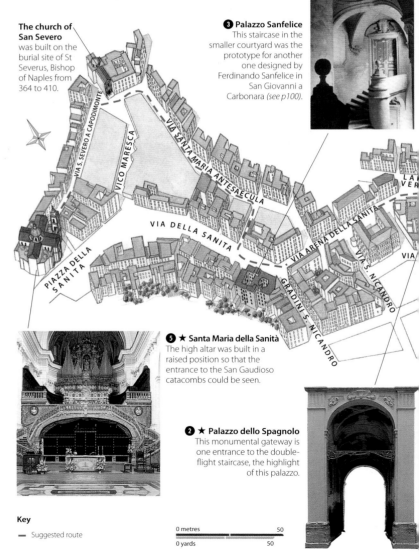

The church of San Severo was built on the burial site of St Severus, Bishop of Naples from 364 to 410.

❸ Palazzo Sanfelice
This staircase in the smaller courtyard was the prototype for another one designed by Ferdinando Sanfelice in San Giovanni a Carbonara (see p100).

❺ ★ Santa Maria della Sanità
The high altar was built in a raised position so that the entrance to the San Gaudioso catacombs could be seen.

❷ ★ Palazzo dello Spagnolo
This monumental gateway is one entrance to the double-flight staircase, the highlight of this palazzo.

Key

— Suggested route

0 metres   50
0 yards   50

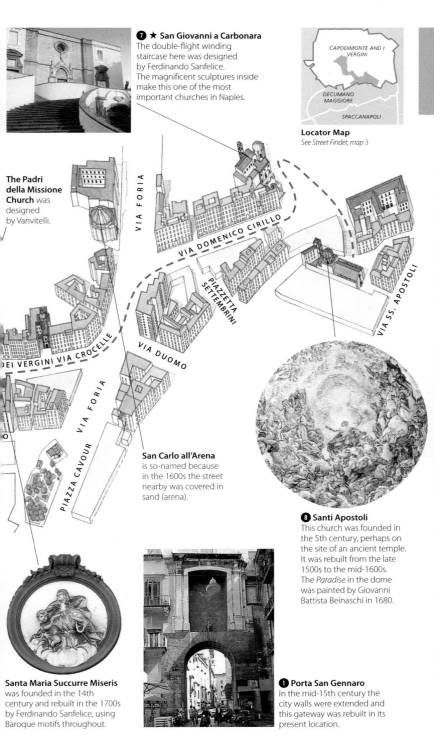

❼ ★ San Giovanni a Carbonara
The double-flight winding staircase here was designed by Ferdinando Sanfelice. The magnificent sculptures inside make this one of the most important churches in Naples.

Locator Map
See Street Finder, map 3

CAPODIMONTE AND I VERGINI

DECUMANO MAGGIORE

SPACCANAPOLI

The Padri della Missione Church was designed by Vanvitelli.

VIA FORIA

VIA DOMENICO CIRILLO

PIAZZETTA SETTEMBRINI

VIA S.S. APOSTOLI

DEI VERGINI VIA CROCELLE

VIA DUOMO

VIA FORIA

PIAZZA CAVOUR

San Carlo all'Arena
is so-named because in the 1600s the street nearby was covered in sand (arena).

❽ Santi Apostoli
This church was founded in the 5th century, perhaps on the site of an ancient temple. It was rebuilt from the late 1500s to the mid-1600s. The *Paradise* in the dome was painted by Giovanni Battista Beinaschi in 1680.

Santa Maria Succurre Miseris
was founded in the 14th century and rebuilt in the 1700s by Ferdinando Sanfelice, using Baroque motifs throughout.

❶ Porta San Gennaro
In the mid-15th century the city walls were extended and this gateway was rebuilt in its present location.

The double-flight staircase in Palazzo dello Spagnolo

❶ Porta San Gennaro

Map 3 C3 (10 D1). 🚌 C51, C52, E1, 182, 184, 201, 203. Ⓜ Cavour-Museo.

This gateway was named after San Gennaro, the patron saint of Naples, because it marked the beginning of the street that leads to the catacombs where he was buried. After the plague of 1656, Mattia Preti painted a fresco on each city gate as an *ex voto* from those who survived. Porta San Gennaro is the only one that still has traces of the artist's work. On the inner façade is a bust of San Gaetano with a dedication and the date – 1658.

❷ Palazzo dello Spagnolo

Via Vergini 19. **Map** 3 B3 (9 C1). 🚌 C51, C52, E1, 182, 184, 201, 203. Ⓜ Cavour-Museo. **Open** courtyard only.

This palace, built in 1738 for the Marquis Nicola Moscati, is said to have been designed by Ferdinando Sanfelice (1675–1748). The architect's name does not appear in any of the notary deeds; however, since Sanfelice built his own palazzo just a few blocks away, it is likely that he consulted and advised on this building too.

Indeed, once through the majestic doorway of the Palazzo dello Spagnolo, you will notice a feature taken from Palazzo Sanfelice: the double-flight external staircase, which effectively separates the main courtyard from the smaller one.

Moscati ran into massive debt during the construction and was forced to sell the building to the Marquis of Livardi. In 1813, the Spanish nobleman Tommaso Atienza bought the property, which has since been called the "Palace of the Spaniard".

❸ Palazzo Sanfelice

Via Sanità 2–6. **Map** 3 B3. 🚌 C51, C52. Ⓜ Cavour-Museo. **Open** courtyard only.

The famous Neapolitan architect Ferdinando Sanfelice (1675–1748) built this large palazzo for his own family from 1723–28. Despite being in a very dilapidated state now, the building was once considered to be one of the finest *palazzi* in Naples. It was here that Sanfelice first created the unusual external staircase that was subsequently adopted, with some variations, in the Palazzo dello Spagnolo. This type of strikingly original staircase became Sanfelice's trademark. His contemporaries likened the design to a large bird with outspread wings, and it became known as a stair *ad ali di falco* – a "falcon's wing" staircase.

The best way to grasp the beauty of the design is to walk up the steps. On the far side of the second courtyard (at Via Sanità No. 2), which has unfortunately lost its original decoration, there is yet another elliptical staircase.

The palazzo's dilapidated splendour has attracted film makers over the years. The comedy *Questi Fantasmi* (1950) by Neapolitan writer Eduardo de Filippo and the 2011 remake of the Oscar-nominated classic *Four Days in Naples* (1962) were both shot here.

❹ San Gennaro Catacombs

Via Tondo di Capodimonte 13. **Map** 3 A1. **Tel** 081 744 37 14. 🚌 C63, C67, N4, N8, R4, 178. ⏱ 10am–5pm Mon–Sat, 10am–1pm Sun (tours every hour; book in advance). 🅿 🌐 **catacombedinapoli.it**

The original nucleus of this large subterranean cemetery may have been the tomb of a pagan aristocrat donated in the 2nd century to the Christian community. The catacombs grew in importance in the 3rd century after acquiring the tomb of Sant'Agrippino, but it was as the burial site of the saint, bishop and martyr Gennaro, brought here in the 5th century, that they became famous. The cemetery also housed the tombs of Neapolitan bishops up to the 11th century. The vast size and two-level layout of this holy site distinguish it from other catacombs of the same era, making it the most important complex in Southern Italy. Remains of 2nd- to 10th-century mosaics and frescoes (including the oldest known portrayal of San Gennaro, dating from the 5th century) adorn the catacombs' walls. Don't miss the Bishops' Crypt on the upper floor and the Sant'Agrippino Oratory and baptistry on the lower level. The basilica of San Gennaro extra Moenia was erected over the catacombs in the 5th century but greatly modified in the 11th century and in 1932.

Fresco of Saint Gennaro and Saint Peter, San Gennaro Catacombs

Central nave of Santa Maria della Sanità

❺ Santa Maria della Sanità and San Gaudioso Catacombs

Piazza Sanità 14. **Map** 3 A2.
Tel 081 744 37 14. 🚌 C51, C52, R4.
Open 10am–1pm daily.
🎫 Catacombs: 🕐 every hour
10am–1pm daily. 🗺
w catacombedinapoli.it

The heart of the working-class Sanità quarter is the basilica of Santa Maria. Confusingly, the church is also known as the church of San Vincenzo because it houses a much revered image of the popular saint, known locally as *'o munacone* (the big monk). Designed by Fra Nuvolo, the church was built on a Greek cross plan in 1603–13, with 24 columns supporting one central dome and 12 lateral domes (a reference to Christ and the Apostles). The central tiled dome is overlooked by the 19th-century Ponte della Sanità, linking the city centre to Capodimonte.

Inside, the main altar was raised to allow worshippers to see the space that serves as a kind of atrium for the underground cemetery. The entrance to the catacombs can be clearly seen.

Tradition has it that in 452, the African bishop Settimio Celio Gaudioso died in exile in Naples, and was buried in the Sanità valley. The catacombs grew up around his tomb and were named after him. The many corridors still bear traces of frescoes and mosaics (4th–6th centuries AD). Later, the Dominicans added their own burial methods and macabre artistic sense to the crypt. They would drain the blood from the deceased, propping the corpses on seats that are still in evidence. After removing the head and burying the body elsewhere, they would embed the skull into the tufa stone.

The morbid tours are an hour long. Call ahead for an English-speaking guide.

❻ Cimitero delle Fontanelle

Via Fontanelle 80. **Map** 3 A3. **Tel** 338 965 22 88. 🚌 C51, C52. **Open** 10am–5pm daily (last adm: 4:30pm). 🎫 Book through local tour company such as **w** insolitaguida.it

A walk along Via Fontanelle, through a poor area that is more like a country village than a city district, leads to the church of Maria Santissima del Carmine. Tours sometimes run to the huge rock-hewn caverns on the hill of Materdei, location of the Fontanelle cemetery (*cimitero*), which was named after the numerous fresh-water springs that flowed through the area during ancient times.

Thousands who died during the plague of 1656 were interred anonymously in the caves. The ossuary continued to be used as the final resting place of the very poor and those unable to pay for a dignified church burial. The last to be interred here were the victims of the 1836 cholera epidemic.

Some people may find the place upsetting, as did the tourist played by Ingrid Bergman in Rossellini's film *Viaggio in Italia* (1954), which made the cemetery famous. Controversy over "adoptions" of skulls to bring good luck has made this a sensitive site.

The ossuary of the Fontanelle Cemetery

Cappella Caracciolo di Vico, San Giovanni a Carbonara

❼ San Giovanni a Carbonara

Via San G a Carbonara 5. **Map** 3 C3. **Tel** 081 29 58 73. C57, E1, E2, 203. Cavour-Museo. **Open** 8am–noon, 4:30–8pm daily.

The imaginative double-flight staircase designed by Ferdinando Sanfelice in the early 1700s leads to the 14th-century Chapel of Santa Monica. Left of the chapel is the doorway to San Giovanni a Carbonara. Founded in 1343 by Augustinian monks, this church was restored and enlarged at the end of the century by King Ladislas to make it a worthy burial site for the Angevin rulers.

When the king died in 1414, his tomb (see p24), the work of anonymous Tuscan and Lombard sculptors was erected at the request of his sister, Joan II, who succeeded him to the throne. The grandiose funerary monument, with seated statues of Ladislas and Joan, dominates the single-nave interior. Through a small doorway beneath the monument is the circular Cappella Caracciolo del Sole, built in 1427 and paved with coloured Tuscan tiles. Behind the altar is the tomb of Ser Gianni Caracciolo, Joan's lover and Grand Seneschal at the court, who died in 1432.

To the left of the presbytery is the harmonious Cappella Caracciolo di Vico, built in the Renaissance style in 1517 by Giovan Tommaso Malvito following a design by Bramante. Another work by Malvito is the richly decorated tomb of the Miroballo family opposite the entrance of the church.

❽ Santi Apostoli

Largo SS Apostoli. **Map** 3 C4 (10 E1). C57, E2, 203. Cavour-Museo. **Open** 9am–noon, 5–8pm daily.

To reach the church of Santi Apostoli you have to go along a short stretch of Via Pisanelli, which turns into Via Anticaglia (see p88). The church was founded in the 5th century and restructured at the beginning of the 17th century by Francesco Grimaldi (1610) and, after 1627, by Giovanni Conforto. The church is best known for a wonderful fresco cycle by Giovanni Lanfranco (1638–46). This masterpiece influenced artistic development in Naples. The artist also frescoed the cupola of the Cappella del Tesoro di San Gennaro (see pp86–7).

❾ Santa Maria degli Angeli alle Croci

Via Veterinaria 2. **Map** 3 C2. **Tel** 081 44 07 56. 12. Cavour-Museo. **Open** 8–11am, 5–7:15pm Mon–Sat; 8–11am Sun.

The name of this church refers to the Stations of the Cross, once marked by wooden crosses (croci) alongside the ascent to the church. Santa Maria was founded at the end of the 16th century by Franciscans and rebuilt in 1638 by Cosimo Fanzago. The façade is simply decorated with white and grey marble.

The white and grey marble façade of Santa Maria degli Angeli alle Croci

This plain design was a daring shift from the usually lavish architecture of Neapolitan Baroque. The interior houses a magnificent marble pulpit sculpted by Cosimo Fanzago. The eagle supporting it symbolizes St John the Evangelist. The extraordinary bas-relief of the dead Christ on the altar was sculpted by Carlo Fanzago, Cosimo's son.

Greenery in the Orto Botanico

❿ Orto Botanico

Via Foria 223. **Map** 4 D2. **Tel** 081 442 15 28 or 081 253 39 37. 12, 182, 184, 201, 203. Cavour-Museo. **Open** 9am–1:30pm Mon–Fri (May: also Sun).

Established in 1807 by Joseph Bonaparte, the "Royal Plant Garden" is today one of the leading Italian botanical gardens for the high quality of its collections as well as its sheer size, covering 12 hectares (30 acres). It has a rich stock of tree and shrub specimens from all latitudes and examples of many plant species, as well as several glasshouses with varying climatic conditions. The temperate house is an early 19th-century Neo-Classical building. The collections of citrus trees, desert plants and tree ferns are particularly interesting. A walk along the paths of this green oasis, in the heart of one of the busiest areas in Naples, can make a very pleasant break from the city. Ring the bell at the gate, and the custodian will let you in.

⓫ Albergo dei Poveri

Piazza Carlo III. **Map** 4 E1. **Tel** 081 795 11 11. 🚌 N4, 12, 201, 202, 540.

The enormous building visible today is only one-fifth of the large-scale complex that King Charles wanted to build to provide a refuge for "the poor of the entire kingdom". Construction of the "Hotel of the Poor" began in 1751 according to a design by Ferdinando Fuga. Work continued until 1829. In reality, the building was hated by the poor, including orphans, who were compelled to live and work there, without hope of leaving. In 1981 a wing of the building collapsed as a result of earthquake damage. After many years in a state of neglect, restoration work is now under way.

⓬ Torre del Palasciano

Salita Moiariello 65. **Map** 3 C1. 🚌 C63, C66. **Closed** to the public.

Located just behind the observatory, and inspired by the Palazzo della Signoria in Florence, this dwelling was commissioned and owned by the physician and surgeon Ferdinando Palasciano (1815–91). He became famous for providing medical care to the wounded of both sides in Messina during the popular

The Neo-Classical façade of the Osservatorio Astronomico

revolts of 1848. For this serious act of insubordination, Palasciano was sentenced to be executed. The intervention of King Ferdinand II of Bourbon spared his life, and Palasciano's sentence was commuted to one year in prison. His case attracted a great deal of international attention, providing the starting point for the Geneva Convention of 1864, which in turn led to the creation of the Red Cross.

The architect Antonio Cipolla (1822–74) directed the construction work, and the building was completed in 1868. The grounds once included a temple, two gardens and an orchard for fruit trees. Today the area, on the hill of Capodimonte, provides a pleasant walk with great views of the city.

The Florentine-style Torre del Palasciano

⓭ Museo Nazionale and Park of Capodimonte

See pp102–5.

⓮ Osservatorio Astronomico

Salita Moiariello 16. **Map** 3 B1. 🚌 C63, C66. Observatory: **Tel** 081 557 51 11. 📅 twice a month (8:30–11pm); call for more detailed information. Museum: **Tel** 081 557 54 35. **Open** Mon–Sat. 📅 10am–4pm (book in advance). 🌐 **na.astro.it**

Situated in a large park on top of the hill of Miradois, 150 m (490 ft) above sea level, the observatory benefits from a splendid vantage point, with fine panoramic views of the city and the bay. Founded in 1819 by Ferdinand IV, this was the first scientific facility of its kind in Europe. The Bourbon court had always been keenly interested in astronomic studies, and it was King Charles who established the first university chair of astronomy in Naples in 1735. The observatory was originally planned for the Museo Archeologico, and in fact construction of a new observatory began there in 1791 *(see p93)*, but the project was discarded. A few years later the elegant Neo-Classical building that now houses the observatory was built by the Gasse brothers. Today part of the observatory is occupied by a museum with a fine collection of clocks, telescopes and old scientific instruments.

⑬ Museo Nazionale and Park of Capodimonte

From the beginning Capodimonte was intended to be both a royal palace and a museum because Charles of Bourbon wanted to create a home for the works of art he had inherited from his mother Elizabeth Farnese. Construction began in 1738 under architect Antonio Medrano, but the palace was only completed a century later, despite the fact that a large part of the Farnese Collection had been on display there since 1759. The collection was dispersed after the French occupation in 1799 *(see p29)*, but following the Bourbon restoration in 1815, it was enlarged considerably.

In 1860 Capodimonte became the property of the House of Savoy and was the residence of the Dukes of Aosta until 1947. The museum was opened to the public again in 1957.

Pietà
This painting by Annibale Carracci, which dates from around 1600, drew inspiration from Michelangelo and is one of the masterpieces of Carracci's monumental style.

The Park of Capodimonte

Charles of Bourbon was drawn to Capodimonte because of hunting, his favourite pastime, and he decided to build an important hunting lodge here. The first section of this large park (over 120 hectares/300 acres), with numerous ancient trees, was laid out by Ferdinando Sanfelice in 1742 into five broad radiating roads, lined with holm-oaks. The buildings used for various court activities can be found in the woods.

The rooms in the Royal Apartments on the first floor reveal the two-fold function as royal palace and museum that Capodimonte fulfilled from the outset.

Ferdinand IV at Capodimonte by Antonio Joli

Key

- ☐ Farnese Gallery
- ☐ Borgia Collection
- ☐ De Ciccio Porcelain Collection
- ☐ Farnese and Bourbon Armoury
- ☐ Maria Amalia's Porcelain Parlour
- ☐ Royal Apartments
- ☐ Non-exhibition space

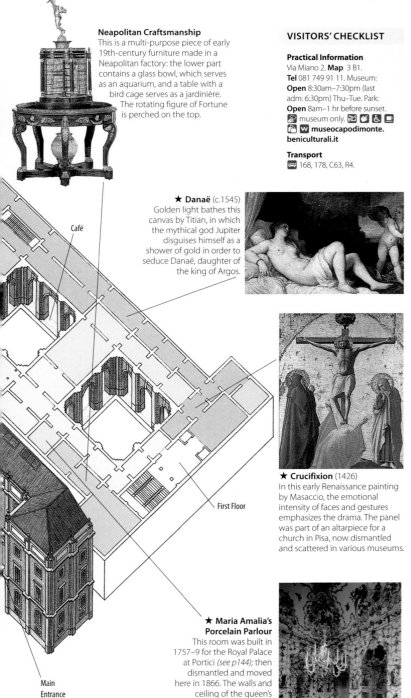

Neapolitan Craftsmanship
This is a multi-purpose piece of early 19th-century furniture made in a Neapolitan factory: the lower part contains a glass bowl, which serves as an aquarium, and a table with a bird cage serves as a jardinière. The rotating figure of Fortune is perched on the top.

Café

★ **Danaë** (c.1545)
Golden light bathes this canvas by Titian, in which the mythical god Jupiter disguises himself as a shower of gold in order to seduce Danaë, daughter of the king of Argos.

First Floor

★ **Crucifixion** (1426)
In this early Renaissance painting by Masaccio, the emotional intensity of faces and gestures emphasizes the drama. The panel was part of an altarpiece for a church in Pisa, now dismantled and scattered in various museums.

Main Entrance

★ **Maria Amalia's Porcelain Parlour**
This room was built in 1757–9 for the Royal Palace at Portici *(see p144);* then dismantled and moved here in 1866. The walls and ceiling of the queen's parlour are tiled with about 3,000 pieces of finest Capodimonte porcelain.

Exploring the Museo di Capodimonte

The Farnese Collection, which is the core of the Art Gallery, features the major Italian and European schools of painting from the 15th to the 17th centuries. When the Real Museo (now the Museo Archeologico Nazionale, *see pp90–93*) was created in Palazzo degli Studi in the early 1800s, the paintings were transferred from Capodimonte but they were returned in 1957, along with other works purchased since the 19th century by the Bourbon rulers and the Italian government. The first floor is devoted to the Farnese Collection and the Royal Apartments, while 13th- to 18th-century Neapolitan paintings and sculpture are on the second floor, and 19th-century art is on the third floor. The second and third floors also have a fine collection of modern and contemporary works.

Antea (1531–5) by Parmigianino

Paintings from the 13th to the 16th Centuries

The Farnese Collection did not focus on medieval works, so that paintings from this period are later purchases or come from churches in the Naples region. For example, the beautiful *Santa Maria de Flumine* (c.1290) came from a church of the same name in Amalfi. The most important 14th-century painting is the large altarpiece *St Louis of Toulouse Crowning Robert of Anjou King of Naples,* painted by Simone Martini in 1317 on the occasion of the canonization of St Louis of Toulouse (*see pp24–5*).

The 15th century is also represented by a superb canvas – Masaccio's *Crucifixion,* actually the upper part of a dismantled polyptych taken from the church of the Carmine in Pisa. The other panels are in Pisa, London, Berlin and Malibu.

Transfiguration by Giovanni Bellini

Giovanni Bellini's masterpiece, *Transfiguration* (c.1480–85), has been considered one of the gems of the Farnese Collection since the 1600s. The *Tavola Strozzi* panel is an extraordinary "snapshot" of 15th-century Naples.

The focal point of the 16th-century paintings are the splendid Titians: *Portrait of Pope Paul III, Pope Paul III with His Grandchildren* and *Danaë (see p103),* which exemplify the Venetian genius's masterly use of colour. Artists from the region of Emilia Romagna, the home of the Farnese family, are well represented. Major works are

Correggio's masterpiece *Mystic Marriage of St Catherine* and the *Antea* by Parmigianino, a portrait of a young woman with elegant dress and a marten stole. An important group of canvases by the Carraccis includes Annibale Carracci's *Pietà,* inspired by the strong sculptural forms of Michelangelo, and his large allegorical work, *Hercules at the Crossroads,* in which the mythical hero has to choose between pleasure and virtue.

Paintings from the 17th to the 20th Centuries

Among the 17th-century works in the museum, Bartolomeo Schedoni's *Charity* (1611) is one of the most famous, and is greatly admired for its expressive intensity. The myth of *Atalanta and Hippomenes* is depicted in Guido Reni's canvas, which the Bourbon rulers bought in 1802 because they lacked a major work by the Bolognese master.

The astounding *Flagellation of Christ* by Caravaggio was painted in stages from 1607 to 1609–10, and hung in San Domenico Maggiore until its move to Capodimonte. It is regarded as the linchpin of all 17th-century Neapolitan painting, which is represented here by many leading artists, such as Battistello Caracciolo, Luca Giordano and Mattia Preti. No less astounding is Artemisia Gentileschi's painting of *Judith and Holofernes,* a subject

The *Tavola Strozzi*, a representation of 15th-century Naples (detail)

CAPODIMONTE AND I VERGINI | **105**

she made her own. The artist, who favoured rather violent themes, was an exceptionally gifted painter and remarkably independent for a woman of her times.

Portrait of Ferdinand IV as a Youth was painted by the German artist Anton Raphael Mengs in 1759; the young king, whose luxurious clothes are rendered in great detail, was nine at the time. In addition, there are some fine landscapes by Ferdinand IV's court painter, Jakob-Philipp Hackert.

Capodimonte also has a large body of 19th-century Neapolitan paintings, including works by Anton Pitloo, the Dutch painter who settled in Naples, and Giacinto Gigante. Don't miss the latter's famous painting of the Cappella del Tesoro in the Duomo. Among the modern works is a copy of Andy Warhol's *Mount Vesuvius (see p32)*, painted in 1985 for an exhibition at the museum in the same year.

Judith and Holofernes by Artemisia Gentileschi (1597–1651)

The Collection of Drawings and Prints

Among the museum's huge inheritance there are about 2,500 drawings and watercolours and 22,000 prints and engravings. One of the most famous works is a cartoon (a preparatory drawing made with charcoal or chalk) made by Michelangelo around 1546. It was drawn for part of the fresco of *The Crucifixion of St Peter* in the Cappella Paolina

Francesco Solimena's *Study of a Young Man's Face* (1728)

in the Vatican. Perforations (which can still be seen) were made with a needle, and powder was sprinkled over the holes to transfer the lines to the wall where the fresco was to be painted.

Solimena's *Study of a Young Man's Face* is a charming study for a later painting. Another important cartoon is Raphael's *Moses before the Burning Bush*, a preparatory drawing for a detail of a fresco in the Stanza di Eliodoro in the Vatican.

The Decorative Arts

The major section in the fine Decorative Arts collection is the armoury, which has about 4,000 weapons and is one of the most important of its kind. Many of the objects here come from the Naples Royal Arms Factory, founded in 1734

by Charles III. There are also over 4,000 ceramic pieces in this part of the museum, including the De Ciccio majolica collection and examples of the superb porcelain manufactured in Naples at the instigation of Charles III. A fine example of this craftsmanship is Queen Maria Amalia's Porcelain Parlour *(see p103)*.

Other decorative arts include objects made of ivory, amber and rock crystal, as well as medallions, semi-precious stones and other pieces such as the 17th-century gilded silver table trophy of Diana by Jacob Miller.

Diana on a Deer, table trophy

The Royal Porcelain Factory

King Charles of Bourbon promoted and fostered the manufacture of decorated porcelain in Naples. The "soft-paste" porcelain, produced with the aid of leading chemists and mineralogists in the Kingdom of Naples, allowed the Real Fabbrica to vie with top European manufacturers such as Meissen. A new pavilion for the Royal Factory was opened in the royal park of Capodimonte in 1743, and the fame of Neapolitan porcelain continued to grow. By 1759, when the king returned to Spain, the factory had become so important to him that he had it dismantled and took it, as well as its staff, with him. The factory was reopened in 1771 by Ferdinand, and production of top-quality pieces began again. Today the Royal Factory is the home of the Institute for the Porcelain and Ceramics industry.

The Biscuit Vendor (1750–51)

VOMERO

In 1885 the Town Council of Naples approved a plan for a new district to be developed "in the rise between Castel Sant'Elmo, the village of Vomero and Antignano", which, once completed, would accommodate 30,000 inhabitants. So began the story of the district of Vomero, which soon became famous for its scenic beauty and healthy climate. These qualities have since been partly ruined (especially since World War II) by chaotic, uncontrolled property development with total disregard for the natural surroundings. Yet, some interesting areas are preserved. At the top of the hill is one of the most important monuments in Naples, the Certosa di San Martino, with its splendid Baroque church, fine museum and the elegant residence called the Quarto del Priore.

Sights at a Glance

Historic Buildings
4 Castel Sant'Elmo
5 Certosa di San Martino pp112–15

Parks and Gardens
2 Villa La Floridiana

Streets and Squares
1 Via Scarlatti
6 Pedamentina
7 Via Luigi Sanfelice

Museums and Galleries
3 Museo Nazionale della Ceramica Duca di Martina

☐ **Restaurants** p192
1 Friggitoria Vomero
2 Osteria Donna Teresa

See also Street Finder
map 2

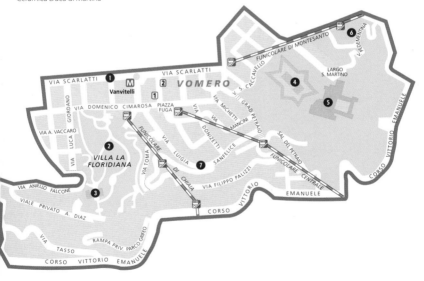

 The grand stairway and façade of Villa La Floridiana

For keys to symbols see back flap

Street-by-Street: Vomero

Take one of the funicular railway lines up the hill to Vomero for fine views of the city centre and the Bay of Naples. Art-lovers will find that Neapolitan masters are well represented in the museums of the Certosa di San Martino and Villa Floridiana (the Duca di Martina). Meanwhile, a walk along the atmospheric streets in the heart of the district reveals an eclectic range of shops and goods, including the Caffè Scarlatti in Via Scarlatti, selling excellent coffee and delectable cakes. In Via Luigia Sanfelice is the villa of the Neapolitan comic Eduardo Scarpetta.

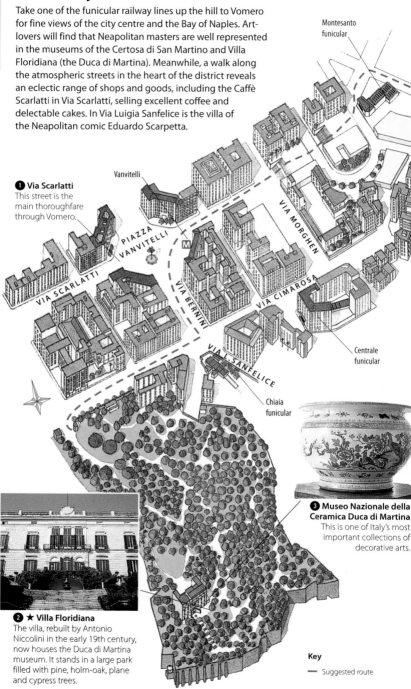

Montesanto funicular

Vanvitelli

❶ Via Scarlatti
This street is the main thoroughfare through Vomero.

PIAZZA VANVITELLI

VIA MORGHEN

VIA SCARLATTI

VIA BERNINI

VIA CIMAROSA

VIA L. SANFELICE

Centrale funicular

Chiaia funicular

❸ Museo Nazionale della Ceramica Duca di Martina
This is one of Italy's most important collections of decorative arts.

❷ ★ Villa Floridiana
The villa, rebuilt by Antonio Niccolini in the early 19th century, now houses the Duca di Martina museum. It stands in a large park filled with pine, holm-oak, plane and cypress trees.

Key

— Suggested route

For hotels and restaurants in this area see p183 and p191

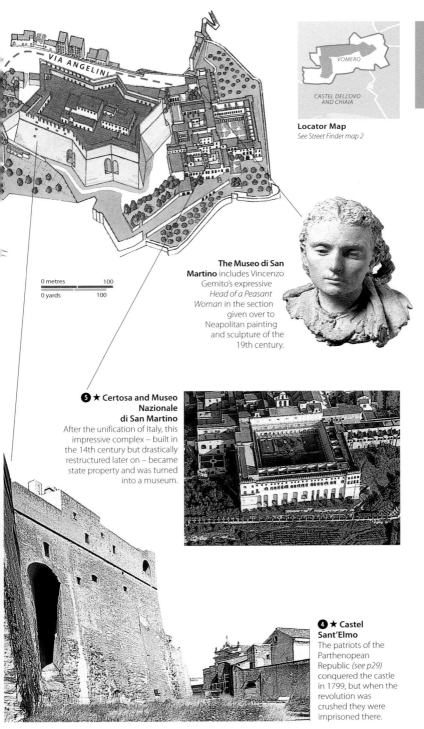

VIA ANGELINI

Locator Map
See Street Finder map 2

VOMERO

CASTEL DELL'OVO
AND CHIAIA

0 metres 100
0 yards 100

The Museo di San Martino includes Vincenzo Gemito's expressive *Head of a Peasant Woman* in the section given over to Neapolitan painting and sculpture of the 19th century.

❺ ★ **Certosa and Museo Nazionale di San Martino**
After the unification of Italy, this impressive complex – built in the 14th century but drastically restructured later on – became state property and was turned into a museum.

❹ ★ **Castel Sant'Elmo**
The patriots of the Parthenopean Republic *(see p29)* conquered the castle in 1799, but when the revolution was crushed they were imprisoned there.

For keys to symbols *see back flap*

❶ Via Scarlatti

Map 2 D5. 🚇 Centrale: Piazza Fuga; Chiaia: Via Cimarosa. Ⓜ Vanvitelli. 🚌 C31, V1, 128.

The most elegant street in Vomero is lined with tall plane trees and descends from Piazza Vanvitelli towards Via Cilea. Closed to traffic, Via Scarlatti is the perfect place for a pleasant walk interrupted by the odd break for shopping. If you lift your gaze above the line of shops you will note the striking contrast between the 19th-century buildings and those constructed in the last 30 years in the wave of property development that has radically altered the face of Vomero.

❷ Villa La Floridiana

Via Domenico Cimarosa 77, Via A Falcone 171. **Map** 2 D5. **Tel** 081 578 84 18. 🚌 V1, 128. 🚇 Centrale: Piazza Fuga; Chiaia: Via Cimarosa. Ⓜ Vanvitelli. Villa: **Open** 8:30am–2pm daily (last adm: 1:15pm). Park: **Open** 8:30am–1 hr before sunset daily.

In 1817 Ferdinand I acquired an estate on the Vomero hill as a present for his second wife Lucia Migliaccio, the Duchess of Floridia, whom he had married shortly after the death of Maria Carolina of Austria. The estate, which was named La Floridiana in honour of the duchess, included a park with

Looking across the Floridiana park

a magnificent view of the city. There were two buildings on the property. The Villa Floridiana was rebuilt as a summer residence in the Neo-Classical style by Antonio Niccolini in 1817–19. The Italian government purchased the villa in 1919, and it now houses the Duca di Martina Ceramics Museum *(see below)*. There was also a "Pompeian" coffee-house, later called Villa Lucia, also designed by Niccolini, which became private property.

❸ Museo Nazionale della Ceramica Duca di Martina

Villa Floridiana, Via Domenico Cimarosa 77, Via Aniello Falcone 171. **Map** 2 D5. **Tel** 081 578 84 18. 🚇 Centrale: Piazza Fuga; Chiaia: Via Cimarosa. Ⓜ Vanvitelli. 🚌 V1, 128. ⏰ 8:30am–2pm Wed–Mon (last adm: 1:15pm). 🅿 🖾 ♿ 🌐 **polomusealecampania. beniculturali.it**

Placido de Sangro, the Duke of Martina and member of an illustrious noble family, was an avid, passionate collector of decorative art objects, especially porcelain and ceramics. When he died in 1891, his valuable collection of about 6,000 pieces was inherited by his grandson Placido, who donated them to the city of Naples in 1911.

Since 1927 Villa La Floridiana has been the home of the Duca di Martina National Ceramics Museum, where curators aim to reproduce as closely as possible the arrangement and spirit of the collections in the De Sangro residence. The pleasant and unusual atmosphere of a home-cum-museum has remained unchanged, despite additions and later donations.

The porcelain pieces come from the most important Italian and other European factories, while the collection of Oriental art – consisting mostly of 18th- and 19th-century porcelain – is one of the best in Italy.

Interior of the Duca di Martina ceramics museum

The museum also contains 15th-century ivory pieces, majolica, Limoges enamel, leather and tortoiseshell objects and drawings by 17th- and 18th-century Neapolitan artists, including Solimena, Giordano and De Matteis.

❹ Castel Sant'Elmo

Via Tito Angelini 22. **Map** 2 E5. **Tel** 081 229 44 31. 🚌 V1. 🚇 Montesanto: Via Morghen; Centrale: Piazzetta Fuga; Chiaia: Via Cimarosa. Ⓜ Vanvitelli. **Open** 8:30am–7:30pm Wed–Mon (last adm 6:30pm). 🅿 ♿ partial. 🌐 **polomusealecampania. beniculturali.it**

In the 1330s the Angevin rulers instigated a flurry of building on the Vomero hill west of Naples – the construction of the Certosa di San Martino and the enlarge-ment and reconstruction of the nearby fortified residence of Belforte, which had been inhabited by Charles I of Anjou's family since 1275.

In the 16th century Pedro Scriba, a leading military architect of the time, completely transformed the 14th-century castle into its present six-pointed star configuration.

Because of its strategic position, Castel Sant'Elmo under viceroy Pedro de Toledo became the focal point of the new defence system for Naples. For centuries it was used as a prison; among its illustrious "guests" were the great Renaissance philosopher Tommaso Campanella, the 1799 revolutionaries and patriots involved in the 19th-century Risorgimento.

The entrance bears Charles V's coat of arms and a fine epigraph. The complex, which also contains a large lecture hall, has been the venue for temporary exhibitions and cultural events since 1988. The castle walls offer a spectacular 360-degree view of Naples and the bay.

The interior of the magnificent Certosa di San Martino

❺ Certosa di San Martino

See pp112–15.

❻ Pedamentina

Map 2 F5. Montesanto: Via Morghen. V1.

The steps connecting Castel Sant'Elmo and the city sprawling below allow you to descend "towards the sea amidst the green slopes", as old guidebooks put it, even though the landscape has changed considerably in the meantime. The 414 steps from San Martino to Corso Vittorio Emanuele offer beautiful panoramic views that change at every stage. The views of

the bay are very rewarding, but be aware that the route passes by dilapidated buildings, slum housing and unsavoury neighbourhoods. Do not attempt this walk on your own and always be alert to potential dangers.

❼ Via Luigi Sanfelice

Map 2 D5 & 2 E5. Centrale: Piazza Fuga; Chiaia: Via Cimarosa. M Vanvitelli. E4.

Should you ask for the "Santarella", people will point to Via Luigi Sanfelice. The key to this riddle lies in a curve in the road where there is a villa with a curious nameplate: "Qui rido io" (this is where I laugh). This was the home, built in 1909, of the well-known Neapolitan author and comic actor Eduardo Scarpetta (the father of Eduardo De Filippo) *(see p41)*, whose best-known work is *Na santarella*. In Via Luigi Sanfelice and nearby Via Filippo Palizzi there are a number of elegant houses that are interesting examples of Neo-Renaissance or Art Nouveau styles.

QUI RIDO IO
SCARPETTA

Nameplate at the villa of comic actor and author Eduardo Scarpetta

From the "Ferrovia di Delizia" to the Funicular Railway

In 1875 the engineers Bruno and Ferraro designed a rail system to take passengers up the Vomero hill along the Chiaia and Montesanto slopes, using two funiculars, connected so that the ascent of one line caused the descent of the other. The "train of delights", as it was called, allowed travellers to admire stupendous views of the bay while crossing the hill, in those days a rural area. The initial scheme gradually evolved into two independent funicular railways which ran through a tunnel, providing a rapid and efficient means of transport between Vomero and the city centre. The Chiaia funicular was opened in 1889, Montesanto in 1891. In order to improve connections with what in the meantime had become the most rapidly expanding district in the city, the Centrale funicular was built in 1928. Centrale was the longest of the three; from its starting point in Via Toledo it reaches a point halfway between the other two. There is also a fourth line, the Mergellina funicular, which connects the seafront with Via Manzoni. The funiculars are reliable and fast, running approximately every ten minutes.

The present-day funicular railway

⑤ Certosa di San Martino

In 1325 Charles Duke of Calabria began construction of what is one of the richest monuments in Naples. The Carthusian monks were forward looking, and from the 16th to the 18th centuries the greatest artists of the time worked at the Certosa (charterhouse) of San Martino. The original look of San Martino was gradually altered by Mannerist and Baroque rebuilding. The most radical redecoration and enlargement was carried out by the architects Giovanni Antonio Dosio, at the end of the 16th century, and Cosimo Fanzago, who took over in 1623. The 17th and 18th centuries brought further changes.

The French deconsecrated the monastery in 1806, and since 1866 it has housed the San Martino museum, with displays of Neapolitan art and history.

Chiostro dei Procuratori
This cloister was built in the late 16th–early 17th century by Giovanni Antonio Dosio.

★ Quarto del Priore
The Prior's Residence was richly decorated and had a splendid panoramic view over the Bay of Naples (see p115).

1325 Construction begun under Charles of Anjou	**1578** Decoration and enlargement by Dosio and Conforto	**1631–56** Complex rebuilt and redecorated by Cosimo Fanzago **1807** The last monks forced to leave the monastery

Chain of the Order of the Two Sicilies

1400	1600	1800

1368 Consecration of the church	**1623** Cosimo Fanzago begins work on the Chiostro Grande	**1799** Monastery damaged during Parthenopean revolution	**1866** The Certosa becomes state property and part of it is turned into a museum

★ **Church and its Subsidiary Rooms**
Sumptuous Baroque decoration and alterations such as the large round windows in the façade were successfully incorporated into the original Gothic church.

Entrance

Central Nave
In 1580 Giovanni Antonio Dosio closed the aisles and built six side chapels. The vaults of the original 14th-century nave are still visible.

KEY

① The Prior's garden
② Navigation section
③ Nativity section
④ Historical section
⑤ 19th-century Neapolitan art
⑥ Monks' cemetery

★ **Chiostro Grande**
The main cloister, with its 64 marble columns, was designed by Giovanni Antonio Dosio at the end of the 16th century and later remodelled by Cosimo Fanzago. The latter also designed the seven corner marble doors supporting figures of Carthusian saints.

Exploring the Certosa di San Martino and the Museum

From the outset the Carthusian monks intended San Martino to be a storehouse for Neapolitan history and civilization. Accordingly, the collections document the rich and varied forms of artistic expression that thrived in Naples between the 15th and the 19th centuries: from paintings to coral jewellery, traditional crib scenes *(presepi)*, porcelain, sculpture and ivory carvings. There is also a fascinating collection of maps and a print library that contains over 8,000 pieces. One part of the museum is devoted to Neapolitan theatre. The minor arts section contains an interesting collection of glass from Venice and other European sources. In addition, the church, the Quarto del Priore (Prior's Residence), the cloister and the gardens contribute to making this one of the premier attractions in the city.

Detail of the inlaid wood panelling in the sacristy (1587–98)

The Church and its Subsidiary Rooms

In 1568, the prior Severo Turboli set up an elaborate plan for the complete restructuring of the San Martino charterhouse. The original Angevin church was enlarged and modernized and its Gothic structure almost completely disappeared under the multitude of frescoes, stucco-work and marbles produced by leading artists of the time.

The most radical changes to the building were carried out in the 17th century by architect and sculptor Cosimo Fanzago, who worked at San Martino from 1623 to 1656. He designed the interior of the church and its lavish decoration. Coloured marble adorns the nave and chapels, such as the Cappella di San Bruno. The rooms adjacent to the church are also richly ornamented. In the sacristy the panels of the beautiful inlaid walnut wardrobes contain 56 intarsia scenes with striking perspective effects (16th century). The fresco of *The Triumph of Judith* on the vault of the brightly lit Cappella del Tesoro Nuovo was painted by Luca Giordano in 1704.

Historical Section

These interesting rooms are dedicated to the history of the Kingdom of Naples. Paintings, furnishings, sculptures, medallions, arms and memorabilia recreate the key moments in the political, social and cultural history of Naples, from the Aragonese to the Bourbon dynasties. The importance of this valuable collection is exemplified in two famous works that combine histo-rical and artistic documentary significance: *The Revolt of Masaniello* (see pp26–7), painted in 1647,

The Cappella di San Bruno, designed by Cosimo Fanzago (1631)

Statue of Charles III of Spain (1754)

and *Piazza del Mercatello during the 1656 Plague*, both painted by Micco Spadaro. These dramatic compositions tell the story of two important events in the history of 17th-century Naples. They are also an accurate and useful representation of what the city looked like at that time.

Panorama of Naples Viewed from the Conocchia, by Giacinto Gigante

The Nativity Scenes

Only towards the end of the 19th century did the *presepe* or nativity scene start to be considered an artistic genre in its own right, worthy of a museum. This section of the San Martino museum has one of the most important public collections of its kind, with displays of entire nativity scenes as well as individual figures, such as Mary and Joseph, the Three Kings or the shepherds. Animals and accessories, such as the crib, are also displayed.

Among the most important nativity scenes is a creation by the Neapolitan playwright, Michele Cucinello. Many of the statuettes were executed

Blind Beggar with Cataracts by Giuseppe Sanmartino

by famous Neapolitan artists. *Blind Beggar with Cataracts* (c.1780), in the Perrone Collection, is by the artist Giuseppe Sanmartino, who sculpted the *Veiled Christ* in the Cappella Sansevero *(see p72)*.

Nineteenth-Century Neapolitan Art

This collection of paintings and sculpture also displays pieces that are significant from both an artistic and historical standpoint. The collection consists of purchases made by the Italian government but owes its strength primarily to donations of important private Neapolitan collections.

All the schools of painting that flourished in this area during the 19th century are represented here. A recurring theme was the Campania landscape, a favourite with local artists. The paintings usually depict a serene and beautiful landscape, such as in Giacinto Gigante's *Panorama of Naples Viewed from the Conocchia*. Among the pieces of sculpture, those by Vincenzo Gemito are not to be missed. *Il Malatiello* (The Sick Child) and *Testa della Popolana* (Head of a Peasant Woman) portray the expressive intensity characteristic of this artist's work.

The Quarto del Priore

Triptych by Jean Burdichon (c.1495) in the art gallery of the Quarto del Priore

The prior, the only individual who was allowed contact with the outside world, governed the workings of the monastery from his private apartments, otherwise known as the Quarto del Priore. This was a fabulous residence, rich with artistic treasures and opening onto lush gardens overlooking Naples and the sea.

Built in the 17th century and enlarged the following century, the luxurious quarters have undergone scrupulous restoration. Originally, this part of the complex was used to exhibit the rich art collection of the Carthusian monks. Following the restoration, an attempt has been made to re-create the Quarto del Priore as it was when inhabited by the prior, with paintings, sculpture, fabric and furniture adorning the various rooms.

The art collection and high-quality furnishings reflect the refinement and great artistic sensitivity of the Carthusian monks as well as their ability to keep abreast of the latest artistic and architectural developments. With its stunning decor, works of art and sculpture and stunning panoramic views over the city, the Quarto del Priore is one of the highlights of a visit to the Certosa di San Martino.

The Borgo Marinaro and Castel dell'Ovo

Sights at a Glance

Historic Buildings
2 Castel dell'Ovo

Historic Streets and Sites
1 Santa Lucia
3 Lungomare
4 Piazza dei Martiri
11 Mergellina

Museums and Galleries
7 Museo Diego Aragona Pignatelli
Cortes and Museo delle
Carrozze in Villa Pignatelli

Churches
8 Santa Maria in Portico
9 Santa Maria di Piedigrotta
12 Santa Maria del Partzo

Parks and Gardens
5 Villa Comunale
10 Parco Virgiliano

Aquarium
6 Stazione Zoologica

CASTEL DELL'OVO AND CHIAIA

The Chiaia area grew to its present extent in the 19th century, although there had been buildings along the seafront outside the city walls since the 16th century. In the late 18th century the construction of the Villa Reale (now called the Villa Comunale) along the Riviera di Chiaia changed the face of this part of Naples.

In the meantime, the city was becoming popular with tourists: 8,000 per year were reported by 1838 – a significant number of visitors for that time. In the second half of the 19th century, the development of the Amedeo quarter and the elegant streets that radiate from Piazza Amedeo made this the favourite residential area of the upper middle class. The Chiaia area also bears traces of the distant past: Castel dell'Ovo, the fortress jutting into the sea in front of Santa Lucia, and the oldest castle in Naples, and the Parco Vergiliano a Piedigrotta in Mergellina, said to be the place where the Roman poet Virgil was buried.

⬜ **Restaurants** *p190*

1 Antica Latteria
2 Ba-Bar Kitchen + Wine Bar
3 Caruso Roof Garden Restaurant
4 Enoteca Belledonne
5 Giappo Sushi Bar
6 Napoli Mia
7 La Scialuppa
8 La Taverna del Brigante
9 Trattoria Castel dell'Ovo
10 Umberto

| 0 metres | 250 |
| 0 yards | 250 |

See also Street Finder maps 5, 6 and 7

For keys to symbols *see back flap*

Street-by-Street: Lungomare

Besides being a pleasant way of spending the time, walking along the seafront is a tradition handed down over generations of Neapolitans. This is one of the city's most upscale districts, with five-star hotels and restaurants once frequented by A-list celebrities, such as Sophia Loren and Salvador Dalí. Mary Shelley also visited in 1818, and some speculate that her novel *Frankenstein* was conceived during her walks along the Lungomare. At the Villa Comunale you can combine a walk in the park with a visit to Europe's oldest aquarium. Nearby Villa Pignatelli has stupendous rooms with 19th-century furnishings and decoration.

❹ Piazza dei Martiri
A column flanked by four lion statues stands in the centre of this square.

❺ Villa Comunale
The kiosk, known as the Cassa Armonica or sound box, was built in the gardens during the 19th-century restoration of the villa.

VIA RIVIERA DI CHIAIA

DELLA

VIA FRANCESCO CARACCIO

Villa Pignatelli

❻ Stazione Zoologica
This aquarium was founded in 1872 as a centre for marine studies.

❽ Santa Maria in Portico
The church is built on a Latin cross plan with one nave, and its dome is covered with multi-coloured tiles.

Key

— Suggested route

❼ ★ Villa Pignatelli
Originally called Villa Acton, this house was modelled on an ancient Pompeiian design, with the side facing the sea consisting of a loggia supported by Doric columns.

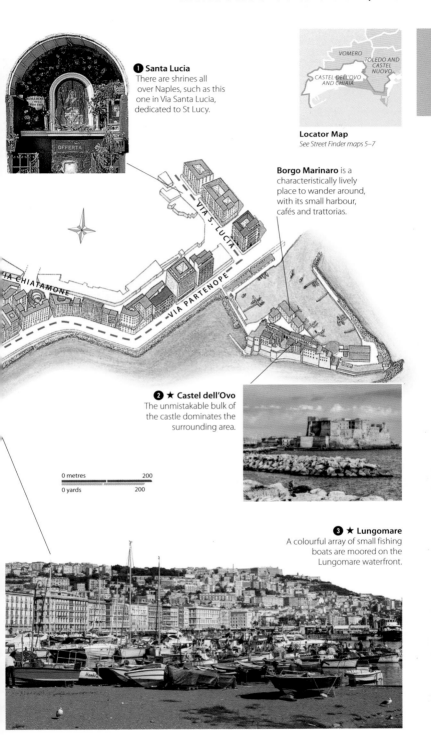

❶ Santa Lucia
There are shrines all over Naples, such as this one in Via Santa Lucia, dedicated to St Lucy.

Locator Map
See Street Finder maps 5–7

Borgo Marinaro is a characteristically lively place to wander around, with its small harbour, cafés and trattorias.

VIA S. LUCIA

VIA CHIATAMONE

VIA PARTENOPE

VOMERO

TOLEDO AND CASTEL NUOVO

CASTEL DELL'OVO AND CHIAIA

❷ ★ Castel dell'Ovo
The unmistakable bulk of the castle dominates the surrounding area.

| 0 metres | 200 |
| 0 yards | 200 |

❸ ★ Lungomare
A colourful array of small fishing boats are moored on the Lungomare waterfront.

❶ Santa Lucia

Map 7 A4. 🚌 C25, E6, N1, 128, 140.

One of the most famous streets in Naples, Santa Lucia exemplifies the city's striking contrasts. Luxury hotels that were built for the elite in the 19th century and imposing buildings for the regional government rub shoulders with the Pallonetto di Santa Lucia slum area where the poor eke out a living. This quarter is named after the church at the beginning of the street, Santa Lucia a Mare, whose history goes back to the 9th century. It has been rebuilt several times. Before you reach the seafront, on the right, you will see the tall rocky face of the hill of Pizzofalcone, the site of the oldest part of Naples (see p63).

The Immacolatella Fountain

❷ Castel dell'Ovo

Borgo Marinaro. **Map** 7 A5.
Tel 081 795 45 93. 🚌 C25, E6, N1, 128.
Open 8am–sunset Mon–Sat, 9am–2pm Sun & public hols.

The oldest castle in Naples is built on the islet of Megaris, once the site of a villa, Castrum Lucullanum, owned by the Roman patrician Lucius Licinius Lucullus. Later, in the 5th century, the villa was fortified, and the last Roman emperor, Romulus Augustulus, was exiled here. In 492, a community of monks founded the San Salvatore monastery, the only remaining part of which is the church. The oldest part of the castle dates from the 9th century.

Under the Norman, Hohenstaufen, Angevin and Aragonese rulers, the castle underwent continuous changes

Castel dell'Ovo with its tall tufa curtain walls

according to the requirements of each dynasty. The present appearance is the result of the rebuilding carried out after 1503, the year the fortress was almost destroyed during a siege by Ferdinand II of Spain.

Despite the rebuilding, there followed a period of decline that lasted until 1871, at which point the castle was so rundown that one Urban Renewal Plan proposed its demolition. Thorough restoration work was begun just over a century later in 1975, and succeeded in bringing the site back to life. It is now used for cultural events and there are great views from the ramparts.

Around the castle is the picturesque Borgo Marinaro quarter, built at the end of the 19th century for the fishermen of Santa Lucia. It is a popular place for visitors because of its restaurants, cafés and lively atmosphere.

❸ Lungomare

Map 5 & 6. 🚌 C12, C16, C18, C20, C24, N1, N2, 140. Ⓜ Mergellina.

A walk along the road skirting the coast from Santa Lucia to Mergellina is another experience not to be missed, with breathtaking views of the city and the bay. The first stretch of the seafront – which corresponds to Via Nazario Sauro and the pedestrianized Via Partenope – was built in the 19th century, as a result of reclamation along Via Santa Lucia and Via Chiatamone. The two ends of this long and pleasant seafront promenade are marked by two beautiful 17th-century fountains: the Immacolatella, which was built by Michelangelo Naccherino and Pietro Bernini in 1601, and the Sebeto fountain, which was the work of Cosimo Fanzago (1635–7).

The Legend of the Egg

Opinions vary as to the origin of the curious name given to Castel dell'Ovo, or Castle of the Egg, which first appears in 14th-century documents. One possible explanation is the shape of the castle. However, popular tradition has it that the name derives from a magic egg hidden in the castle which determined its fate and that of the entire city: as long as the egg remained intact, both would be protected from catastrophes. The magic spell was supposed to have been originally cast on the ancient egg by the Latin poet Virgil, who, according to medieval legends, possessed supernatural powers and the gift of divination.

The castle in the 1800s

❹ Piazza dei Martiri

Map 6 F2. 🚇 C24, E6.
🚇 Chiaia: Piazza Amedeo.

The Square of Martyrs is the heart of the "chic" commercial centre of Naples. Its focal point is the Monumento ai Martiri Napoletani designed by Errico Alvino in 1866–8, with four lions at the base symbolizing the anti-Bourbon uprisings of 1799, 1820, 1848 and 1860. Palazzo Calabritto (No. 30), built by Luigi and Carlo Vanvitelli, dominates the square on the seaward side. Palazzo Portanna (No. 58), built in the 18th century by Mario Gioffredo, was rebuilt by Antonio Niccolini for Lucia Migliaccio, the morganatic wife of Ferdinand IV.

Along the streets that radiate from the square, historic palazzi alternate with elegant shops and cafés. Among the Neo-Renaissance and Liberty-style buildings along Via Filangieri and Via dei Mille, Palazzo Mannajuolo (No. 36 Via Filangieri) is worth seeing for its beautiful inner staircase. In nearby Via Poerio and Via San Pasquale are the Lutheran and Anglican churches, founded in 1861–2.

19th-century statue at the Villa entrance

❺ Villa Comunale

Via Carracciolo, Riviera di Chiaia.
Map 6 E2. **Tel** 081 795 36 14.
🚇 C12, C18, C24, N1, 128, 140.
Open May–Oct: 7am–midnight daily; Nov–Apr: 7am–10pm daily.

The first design for this park area dates from 1697, during the rule of viceroy Luis de la Cerda, but it was Ferdinand IV who, almost a century later, asked architect Carlo Vanvitelli and landscape gardener Felice Abate to lay out the Real Passeggio di Chiaia as a public park.

The Villa Reale, later the Villa Comunale, was completed in 1781, and was enlarged in the following century. Among the pine, monkey puzzle, palm and eucalyptus trees there are 19th- and early 20th-century sculptures and several fountains, including the so-called *Paparelle*, which in 1825 replaced the famous *Farnese Bull* sculpture group, which is now in the Museo Archeologico *(see p91)*. The park, which extends from the Riviera di Chiaia to Via Caracciolo, also boasts the Neo-Classical Stazione Zoologica and the iron and glass kiosk known as the Cassa Armonica, designed in 1877 by Errico Alvino. Today the park hosts children's activities such as pony riding.

Façade of the Stazione Zoologica

❻ Stazione Zoologica

Villa Comunale. **Map** 6 E2. **Tel** 081 583 31 11. 🚇 C12, C18, C24, N1, 128, 140.
Open Mar–Oct: 9:30am–6:30pm Tue–Sun; Nov–Feb: 9:30am–5pm Tue–Sun.
🅿 ♿ 🆆 szn.it

This institute, run by the Consiglio Nazionale delle Ricerche (National Research Council), is one of the oldest and best known of its kind in the world. It was established in 1872–4 by the German scientist Anton Dohrn to study marine environments. The building, which was designed by Adolf von Hildebrandt, contains research labs, a small exhibition and the oldest aquarium in Europe, with specimens from the Bay of Naples.

The frescoes depicting marine and rural scenes in the reading room of the library were painted by Hans von Marées in 1873 and can be viewed by appointment.

Four lion statues support the Paparelle fountain in the Villa Comunale

❼ Museo Diego Aragona Pignatelli Cortes and Museo delle Carrozze in Villa Pignatelli

Riviera di Chiaia 200. **Map** 6 D2.
Tel 081 761 23 56. 🚌 C12, C18,
C24, N1, 128, 140. 🚊 Chiaia: Parco
Margherita. **Open** 8:30am–2pm Wed–
Mon (last adm: 1pm). 🛇 🛇

The Neo-Classical villa was built in 1825 by Pietro Valente for the illustrious Acton family. The Rothschilds became the new owners 20 years later and changed the furnishings and interior. Prince Diego Aragona Pignatelli Cortes then bought the villa, which is named after him, and in 1955 his grand-daughter donated it to the Italian state. The loveliest rooms are the red hall in Louis XVI style, the smoking room with leather-lined walls and the ballroom with its large mirrors and magnificent chandeliers. Villa Pignatelli is used for temporary exhibitions, concerts and other cultural events. A small building nearby is occupied by the **Museo delle Carrozze** (Carriage Museum), which has an interesting collection of 34 Italian, English and French coaches dating from the late 1800s to the early 1900s.

Façade of Santa Maria in Portico

Presbytery and apse of Santa Maria in Portico

❽ Santa Maria in Portico

Via Santa Maria in Portico 17. **Map** 6
D2. **Tel** 081 66 92 94. 🚌 C12, C18,
C24. 🚇 Amedeo. 🚊 Chiaia: Parco
Margherita. **Open** 8–11am, 4:30–
7pm daily. 🛉

In 1632 the Duchess of Gravina, Felice Maria Orsini, donated some of her property to the Padri Lucchesi della Madre di Dio congregation so they could build a monastery and church. The name "in Portico" refers to the Roman church of Santa Maria in Campitelli al Portico d'Ottavia, where the Padri Lucchesi came from. For years the façade in piperno stone was attributed to Cosimo Fanzago, but is now known to be the work of Arcangelo Guglielminelli who completed it in 1682. The interior is decorated with fine 18th-century canvases and stuccoes by late-Baroque artist Domenico Antonio Vaccaro (1678–1745), who also designed the high altar. There is a crib with 17th-century figures in the sacristy.

A short walk down nearby Via Piscicelli takes you to the **Chiesa dell'Ascensione a Chiaia**, with fine paintings by the prolific Neapolitan painter Luca Giordano (1634–1705), including an altarpiece of St Michael the Archangel. The 14th-century church was rebuilt in the 1600s by Cosimo Fanzago and the dome was reconstructed in 1767.

❾ Santa Maria di Piedigrotta

Piazza Piedigrotta 24. **Map** 5 B3.
Tel 081 66 97 61. 🚌 C4, C16, C24.
🚇 Mergellina. **Open** 8am–7pm Mon-
Sat, 8:30–10:30am, 12:30–7pm Sun & hols.
🛉 🌐 madonnadipiedigrotta.it

This church is mentioned in a letter written by Giovanni Boccaccio in Neapolitan dialect in 1339, in which he mentions the "Madonna de Pederotta". Much altered over the years, Santa Maria di Piedigrotta is commonly believed to have been built in 1353 to replace a church founded by fishermen in Mergellina. In the mid-1500s, it was rebuilt again, and this time the orientation of the church, which had faced a cave (*grotta*), was altered so that it would face the city. The present façade is the result of 19th-century restoration by Errico Alvino. Gaetano Gigante decorated the vault. Inside is the 15th-century wooden panel *Descent from the Cross*, by an unknown Neapolitan artist.

The church's great popular-ity is linked to a beautiful 14th-century wooden sculp-ture of the *Madonna and Child*, made by the Siena School, which dominates the church from a high tabernacle. The worship of the Piedigrotta Madonna culminates in the September feast (*see p46*). In the past, even the royal family took part in the solemn procession. Worshippers, however, did not appreciate the statue's restoration in 1976 to its original state, because the Virgin's large blue mantle and luminous halo were removed.

Fresco by Belisario Corenzio in Santa Maria di Piedigrotta

View of the Parco Virgiliano

⑩ Parco Virgiliano

Via Salita Grotta 20. **Map** 5 A2. C16, C24, N2. **M** Mergellina. **Open** 9am–1 hr before sunset.

Myth, legend, traces of the past and natural beauty, including panoramic views over the bay, are what make this park one of Naples' most intriguing sites. It officially became a park after restoration work in 1930. In 1939 a monument to the poet Giacomo Leopardi *(see p40)* was erected, and his remains were transferred here from Recanati, his home town in Le Marche.

The park is famous mostly because, according to legend, the poet Virgil is buried here. However, the so-called Tomb of Virgil is in fact an anonymous Roman funerary monument and has nothing to do with the great poet.

Another legend involving Virgil is that with a single gesture he created the *Crypta Neapolitana*, a tunnel about 700 m (2,300 ft) long; but this too is belied by historical facts: it was built by the Roman architect Cocceius in the 1st century BC to connect *Neapolis* and Puteoli. In the 1920s the tunnel caved in and is now inaccessible. The entrance, however, with its medieval frescoes and epigraphs, can still be seen from the park.

⑪ Mergellina

Map 5 B4. C16, C21, C24, N2, 140. Mergellina. **M** Mergellina.

The fishermen's quarter that developed over the inlet at the foot of Posillipo hill, and was hailed by poets and writers for its beauty, was a popular place for pleasure trips from the Angevin age onwards. The harmony of the landscape was broken by 19th-century land reclamation that extended the coastline further into the sea. However, Mergellina is still an enjoyable place for a leisurely stroll. The numerous cafés, called *chalet* by the locals, offer excellent ice cream and fresh fruit.

⑫ Santa Maria del Parto

Via Mergellina 96. **Map** 5 B4. **Tel** 081 66 46 27. C16, C21, C24, 140. Mergellina. **M** Mergellina. **Open** 8:30am–7pm Mon–Sat, 9–10am, 11:30–7pm Sun & hols; closes 6:30pm daily in winter.

The history of the church of Santa Maria del Parto is closely linked with the figure and works of Jacopo Sannazaro (1458–1530), the famous Neapolitan humanist and poet in the service of the Angevin court. The church was built in the 1520s, on the initiative of Sannazaro, on a plot of land donated by Frederick of Aragon and was named after one of the poet's works, *De Partu Virginis*. Behind the high altar is the tomb of the poet himself, a fine marble group sculpted by Giovanni Angelo Montorsoli and Francesco del Tadda in 1537, and probably designed by Sannazaro himself. Before leaving, don't forget to look at the "Mergellina devil" depicted in a wooden panel by Leonardo da Pistoia on the right-hand altar. The panel shows St Michael, who has just vanquished the devil – the devil has assumed the guise of a beautiful woman.

St Michael and the "Mergellina devil"

The small harbour of Mergellina, filled with fishing boats and pleasure craft

TWO GUIDED WALKS

Naples is a city of contradictions: on the one side there are narrow, labyrinthine streets in the historic centre, full of revving scooters and the pungent aroma from fish stores; on the other there are wide avenues lined with chic shops, frequented by bejewelled ladies in fur coats. These two walks explore both sides of Neapolitan life. The first moves from the military district of Pizzofalcone to the elegant shopping streets of the Chiaia region, offering a complete change of atmosphere with just the short ride down the Ponte di Chiaia lift. The second walk takes you from the Fascist-era buildings of Piazza Matteotti,

and then through the Montesanto district and the bustling Pignasecca market with its wide variety of food and clothing stalls crammed in between rows of discount houseware shops and *tripperie* (tripe shops). Day-to-day life is on constant display here – mothers and babies, hawkers and shoppers all mingle on the streets together. Montesanto also skirts a claustrophobic but characteristic grid of tiny streets you might wish to venture into for a true experience of local life, complete with wafting cooking odours and rows of laundry flapping from balconies in the breeze.

CHOOSING A WALK

The Two Walks
This map shows the location of the two guided walks in relation to the main sightseeing areas of Naples.

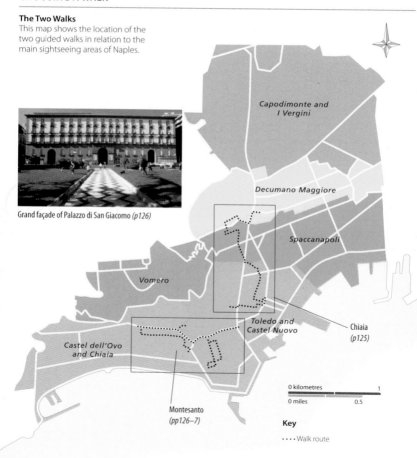

Grand façade of Palazzo di San Giacomo *(p126)*

Capodimonte and I Vergini

Decumano Maggiore

Spaccanapoli

Vomero

Toledo and Castel Nuovo

Chiaia *(p125)*

Castel dell'Ovo and Chiaia

Montesanto *(pp126–7)*

0 kilometres 1

0 miles 0.5

Key

···· Walk route

A 45-Minute Walk Through Chiaia

This walk balances hidden architectural gems with elegant window shopping as it winds its way through one of Naples most glamorous neighbourhoods.

② Via Chiaia as seen from the Ponte di Chiaia

Baroque Naples

Start at Piazza Trieste e Trento ① and head west on Via Chiaia to the lift under the 17th-century Ponte di Chiaia ② *(see p62)*. Take the lift up to Piazza Santa Maria degli Angeli for the church of the same name ③ *(see p62)*. This Baroque church was erected by Francesco Grimaldi in the early 17th century and boasts frescoes by Beinaschi. Head south on Via Monte di Dio and pop into the Palazzo Serra di Cassano ④ *(see p62)*, one of Naples' many hidden architectural treasures, particularly its spectacular staircase. At the end of Via Monte di Dio, turn right for a short walk to the Nunziatella ⑤ *(see p63)*, Italy's famous military academy. Founded in 1787, it takes its name from the nearby Annunziata, a Baroque church noted for its frescoes and paintings by Francesco de Mura as well as for its 17th- century crypts, the final resting places for the era's Neapolitan nobility.

Walk round the square until you are on back on Via Monte di Dio, turn right and then left onto Via Egiziaca a Pizzofalcone and left again on Via G. Serra, which will bring you back to the lift. Take the lift down again and continue west on Via Chiaia. Follow the curve of Via Santa Caterina to the church of Santa Maria della Mercede ⑥, built in the 17th century by the Spanish Mercedari fathers. Turn right on Via Filangieri, a street full of fashionable clothing stores. Gran Caffè Cimmino at No. 12 ⑦ is a good spot for a break.

Art and boutiques

Take the stairs on your right where Via Filangieri meets the elegant Via dei Mille, and walk up to Palazzo Cellamare ⑧ *(see p62)*, a Bourbon-era building once known for its royal revelries. Head back down to Via dei Mille and stroll past the Palazzo delle Arti Napoli, the contemporary art museum ⑨, to the church of Santa Teresa a Chiaia ⑩ with its two altarpieces by the Baroque painter Luca Giordano. Turn left onto Via Bausan, filled with Spanish restaurants. Turn left onto Via Santa Teresa a Chiaia ⑪ for window shopping at the high-class boutiques heading east. Passing through Piazza Rodinò ⑫, head down to Via Alabardieri to find the fine-dining restaurant and pizzeria Umberto ⑬, a long-time Chiaia favourite, then continue on to the Piazza dei Martiri ⑭, located in the chic heart of Naples.

④ The double staircase in Palazzo Serra di Cassano, decorated with white marble

0 metres 250
0 yards 250

Key

···· Walk route

Tips for Walkers

Starting point: Piazza Trieste e Trento.
Length: 2 km (1 mile).
Getting there: Bus E6 stops in front of Piazza Trieste e Trento, while 500 m (1640 ft) to the northeast is the Piazza Municipio metro stop.
Safety tips: Petty crime is a problem in Naples: leave valuables in a safe and carry cash in a money belt.

For keys to symbols *see back flap*

A 90-Minute Walk Through Montesanto

A visit to Naples would not be complete without a stroll through at least one of its fascinating open-air markets. This walk begins on the wide shopping street Via Toledo and winds its way past the imposing Fascist structures of Piazza Matteotti and through the Pignasecca in the Montesanto district. Though officially a *mercatino* (little market), the Pignasecca is a favourite among Neapolitans. In addition, several atmospheric churches here make for welcome havens from the jostling and haggling crowds.

⑭ Fish stall on Pignasecca

Renaissance to Fascism

Start the walk at the Funicolare Augusteo ①, then turn left onto Via Toledo (see p57) heading northwards. Turn right shortly afterwards onto Via Santa Brigida. The 17th-century church of Santa Brigida ② (see p60) will be ahead of you – its interior, particularly the paintings by Luca Giordano, is its real treasure. Just beyond to the right is an entrance to the Galleria Umberto I ③ (see p57). Built in 1887, this towering arcade features an impressive iron-and-glass roof and elegant painted marble. Cross Via Verde then turn left, right and then left into Via Vittorio Emanuele III and up to Piazza Municipio. Turn right onto Via Cervantes, home to the Palazzo San Giacomo with its church of San Giacomo degli Spagnoli ④ (see p60), erected in 1540 by Viceroy Pedro of Toledo. The church was built in typical Mannerist style, and behind the main altar stands Giovanni da Nola's magnificent High Renaissance marble monument to the viceroy. The palazzo has been Naples' municipal headquarters since the Italian Unification in 1861.

Continue along Via Cervantes until you reach Piazza Matteotti ⑤ and its circle of stark Fascist-era buildings. The Palazzo delle Poste e Telegrafi ⑥ (see p61) is the square's main attraction, the monumental edifice being an emblem of 1930s rationalist architecture. Take Via Battisti to Piazza Carità and the Istituto Nazionale Assicurazioni ⑦, erected in 1938. In front of the building stands the monument to Salvo d'Acquisto ⑧, the one-time Vice Brigadier of the *carabinieri* (the military arm of the Italian police) and a noted World War II hero. Born in Naples in 1920, d'Acquisto sacrificed himself to the Germans in 1943 in order to save the lives of 22 innocent Italians who were falsely accused of setting off a bomb that killed two German soldiers.

Art and Architecture

Across Via Toledo, still in Piazza Carità but along Via San Liborio, there are two striking 18th-century buildings, the Palazzo Mastelloni ⑨, with its fine staircase, and Palazzo Trabucco ⑩,

④ Nave of San Giacomo

⑨ Impressive double staircase of Palazzo Mastelloni

both built by Nicolò Tagliacozzi Canale, one of the three architects to renovate the beautiful Certosa of San Martino in Vomero (see pp112–15). Continue north on Via Toledo until you reach the church of San Nicolà alla Carità ⑪. The highlight here is the nave that features an enormous landscape painted over two centuries by several Neapolitan artists including Francesco Solimena and Alessio d'Elia. Turn back and walk 100 steps or so

to reach Via Pignasecca. This busy and lively street is a great place to watch animated locals as they haggle for goods. Stop for tasty, mostly fried snacks at Fiorenzano ⑫, then continue to the bustling Pignasecca *mercatino* in Piazza Pignasecca ⑬. Take the left fork onto Via Portamedina. On the right is the Ospedale Pelligrini, the courtyard of which hides the church of SS Trinità dei Pellegrini ⑭, built in the 16th century for religious pilgrims. Via Portamedina ends at Piazza Montesanto where the church of Santa Maria di Montesanto ⑮ stands. From the church, follow Via Montesanto and turn left onto Vico Spezzano. Turn right and walk along to the Palazzo Spinelli di Tarsia ⑯, one of Naples' largest and finest noble residential complexes, which now houses shops on the ground floor. It was built by the architect Domenico Antonio Vaccaro for the aristocratic Spinelli family in the 1700s. The Teatro Bracco is just across the street.

Lively piazzas

Head down Via Tarsia and turn left to Piazza Dante ⑰ (see p89). This square has been pedestrianized and now serves as a general meeting point for students, a rest spot for elderly Neapolitans, and an unofficial

Tips for Walkers

Starting point: Funicolare Centrale (Augusteo station).
Length: 3 km (2 miles).
Best time for walk: Start the walk in the morning when all the churches and markets are open.

Wide thoroughfare of Via Toledo

football arena for the young. The entrance to the Convitto Nazionale di Napoli Vittorio Emanuele II ⑱ can be seen on the eastern side of the square. The colonnade was designed by the architect Luigi Vanvitelli and now marks the western side of a boarding school. Follow the road round to the right to Port'Alba and spend an hour or so on this pedestrianized lane lined with bookshops and outdoor book stalls. At the end of this street is Antica Pizzeria Port'Alba ⑲, said to be the restaurant where pizza was invented in the 18th century. The walk ends at Piazza Bellini ⑳ (see p82), an ideal spot for a refreshing apéritif.

| 0 metres | 200 |
| 0 yards | 200 |

Key

···· Walk route

⑰ Imposing Piazza Dante, a popular meeting place

TWO TRIPS AROUND POSILLIPO

The peninsula that juts into the sea, separating the Bay of Naples from Pozzuoli, was called *Pausilypon* ("respite from pain") by the ancient Greeks, because of the great beauty of the site. As can be seen by the many ruins along the coast, in Roman times a huge settlement grew up along the westernmost edge of what is now called Posillipo, and was connected to the neighbouring Phlegraean Fields *(see pp140–43)*. Posillipo was occupied by religious communities and suburban villages during the Middle Ages, and became the favourite holiday resort of the Spanish aristocracy in the 17th century, when luxurious seaside villas and aristocratic palaces were built here. In the following century, the area began to decline, and it was only in the early 19th century that it regained its former popularity. This was partly as a result of improved access, thanks to the coastal road opened in 1812. From the 1950s on (during the era when Achille Lauro, *see pp32–3*, was mayor of Naples), the upper part of the hill between Via Orazio, Via Petrarca and Via Manzoni was overtaken by unregulated, unscrupulous property development that blighted the area. Fortunately, however, its historic beauty can still be enjoyed by visiting its luxurious villas and rambling gardens.

Sights at a Glance

① Palazzo Donn'Anna
② World War I Memorial
③ Capo Posillipo
④ Marechiaro
⑤ Santa Maria del Faro
⑥ Parco Virgiliano
⑦ Grotto di Seiano and Pausylipon

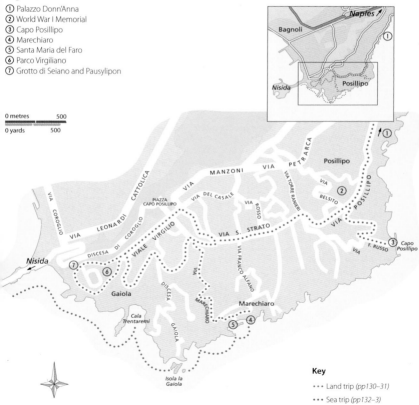

Key

••• Land trip *(pp130–31)*
••• Sea trip *(pp132–3)*

◀ Docked fishing boats at the village of Marechiaro

Posillipo by Land

If you decide to explore Posillipo by land, bear in mind that the complete itinerary shown here would make a very long walk. The best way to get around is, in the following order, by scooter, taxi (you are advised to agree on the fare beforehand), Citysightseeing Napoli tour bus *(see p221)*, bus (routes 140, C27, C31 and N2) or, least popular because of traffic and parking problems, a rented car. Many of the old villas, which are now privately owned, are hidden from view and only a few of them can be seen from the road. However, the views are stupendous and the routes down to Capo Posillipo and Marechiaro, though demanding, are very rewarding.

Palazzo Donn'Anna on the seafront

① Palazzo Donn'Anna

In 1637 the Spanish viceroy Ramiro Guzman, Duke of Medina, married the Neapolitan princess Anna Carafa. To celebrate, Don Ramiro asked the architect Cosimo Fanzago to build the large Palazzo Donn'Anna at the water's edge. Construction began in 1642, but the building was never completed and was never used by the couple. The viceroy returned to Spain in 1644 and

Donn'Anna died soon after. The palazzo was damaged during the 1647 uprising and again as a result of the 1688 earthquake. It was partly restored in the early 1700s but decades later it was still being described in tourist guides as a building in a state of total neglect.

Its air of mystery gave rise to the rumour that in its past the palace had been used by Queen Joan II for secret assignations with her lovers. Popular belief has it that after these men had served their purpose, they were thrown into the sea below the palace.

Palazzo Donn'Anna suffered further damage in the early 19th century when part of the façade was demolished to build the Via Posillipo. In 1870 attempts were made to turn it into a hotel, but the idea was abandoned.

Despite its tormented history and the damage wrought by time and neglect, the massive tufa palace with its cavernous vaults is still majestic, and one of the city's celebrated sights.

② World War I Memorial

From Piazza San Luigi it is clear to see how property development has spoilt the view of the hill. Beyond the piazza stands the Ara Votiva, or War Memorial, situated in a small park. The middle of the park is dominated by the large Egyptian-style mausoleum that Matteo Schilizzi began building in 1883 as a tomb for his brother Marco. This impressive monument was purchased and finished in 1923 by the Naples city council, in order to house the remains of soldiers who had died in World War I.

③ Capo Posillipo

After Piazza Salvatore di Giacomo, a square with a small garden in the middle, go down Via Ferdinando Russo towards the bay of Capo Posillipo and Villa Volpicelli, which gives the impression of a castle floating on the sea. Originally known as *Candia e Santacroce* villa, it was built in the 17th century. In 1881, the villa was bought by Raffaele Volpicelli, who set about restoring it and added romantic details such as the crenellated towers.

The Neapolitans call the area around the Villa Volpicelli the Riva Fiorita, or flowered shore. In the summer months, the little harbour, the beach and the cliff area opposite hum with life. Cafés and restaurants lend atmosphere to this area. To reach the fishing village of Marechiaro, return to Via Ferdinando Russo and turn left on to Via Posillipo until it becomes Via S Strato. Turn left onto Via Marechiaro.

The 17th-century Villa Volpicelli, built on the water's edge

A 1920s photograph of the Bay of Naples from Posillipo

④ Marechiaro

A famous song by the Neapolitan artist Salvatore di Giacomo says that this coastline is so romantic, even the fish make love in the moonlight. Going down Via Marechiaro by day, you will see elegant villas surrounded by greenery and beautiful panoramic views of the countryside.

Towards the sea is a small square with the remains of a Roman column from the so-called Temple of Fortune. Further down, in the pretty fishing village of Marechiaro, there are bars, cafés, restaurants and bathing facilities.

⑤ Santa Maria del Faro

This church, recorded in documents as far back as the 1300s, was probably built over the remains of an ancient Roman lighthouse (*faro* in Italian). It was restored by Sanfelice in the 18th century, but the façade dates from the 19th century. From here you can walk down the Calata del Ponticello, which brings you close to the sea.

⑥ Parco Virgiliano

After going back up Via Marechiaro, turn left on Via Coroglio, then left again down Viale Virgilio, and you will arrive at the beautiful Parco Virgiliano, also known as Parco della Rimembranza. It occupies the top of the hill overlooking the sea and offers a spectacular view from the Bay of Naples to Mount Vesuvius and the Sorrento peninsula on one side, and the Bay of Pozzuoli and the Phlegraean Fields on the other. Below are the island of Nisida, formed from an ancient volcanic crater, and the remains of the old ILVA steelworks (*see pp30–31*). At sunset, the views towards Ischia are stunning.

⑦ Grotto di Seiano and Pausylipon

In Roman times, a 770 m- (0.5 mile-) long grotto allowed access to a vast villa, perched high on a cliff. Known as *Pausylipon* ("respite from pain"), the villa included an amphi-theatre and a kitchen decorated with marble. The Bourbon kings discovered the ruins in the 1700s and repaired the tunnel to make it structurally sound again. Visits are by appointment only (call 081 575 44 65).

The Villas of Posillipo

The northern stretch of Via Posillipo is dominated by **Villa Doria D'Angri**, built in 1833 by Bartolomeo Grasso for Prince D'Angri and now the Istituto Santa Dorotea. Further down, on the seaward side, is 17th-century **Villa Quercia**, painted a typically Pompeiian red. A hunting lodge built by the Duke of Frisio in the 1700s was bought at the end of the 19th century by Count **Pavoncelli**, who gave the villa at No. 43 his name. **Villa Grottamarina** (No. 33) was the home of Maria Anna, sister of King Philip IV of Spain, in the 1630s. The French engineer Alfredo Cottreau built the **Villa Cottreau** (No. 35) in the late 1800s; several wings on different levels descend towards the sea. Pompeiian red is again the colour of the **Villa Bracale**

Villa Rosebery, now state property

(No. 37), whose original 17th-century structure is almost unrecognizable today. The pagoda-shaped **Villa Roccaromana** (No. 38a) was built in 1814 for Prince Caracciolo. **Villa d'Abro** (No. 46) was named after the nobleman Aslan d'Abro, who bought it in 1870 and had it restored in Neo-Romantic style. Beyond Capo Posillipo is **Villa Rosebery** (No. 26 Via Russo), the Neapolitan residence of the President of the Italian Republic. It was here, on 9 May 1946, that King Vittorio Emanuele II abdicated and the crown passed to his son Umberto. Adjacent to Villa Rosebery, and skirting the edge of the harbour, is **Villa Volpicelli** (*see p130*). The romantic castle-like building is where the popular soap opera *Un posta al sol (A Place in the Sun)* is filmed. At No. 27 Via Russo is the 17th-century **Villa Emma**, the summer residence of the German painter Jakob Philipp Hackert who depicted the excavations of Pompeii. Fringed palms give a tropical feel to the **Villa Gallotta**, built close to the water's edge.

Villa Gallotta

Viewing Posillipo from the Sea

From the sea, Naples and the bay can be viewed in all their splendour. To the west of the city, from Castel dell'Ovo north to Nisida and beyond, as far as the Phlegraean Fields, the coast is dotted with grottoes and inlets. Beyond Capo Posillipo you can see the fishing village of Marechiaro, Roman ruins, and the small islands of Gaiola and Nisida. Bars and bathing beaches lure visitors here in summer. In winter the dramatic coastline can still be admired from a hydrofoil or ferry on an excursion to Procida and Ischia *(see pp174–7)*.

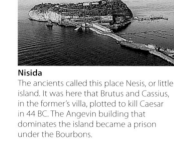

Nisida
The ancients called this place Nesis, or little island. It was here that Brutus and Cassius, in the former's villa, plotted to kill Caesar in 44 BC. The Angevin building that dominates the island became a prison under the Bourbons.

Cala di Trentaremi
The tufa cliffs of Cala di Trentaremi are reflected in the sea, which gleams blue and green. This cove is particularly sheltered and is a favourite with bathers.

KEY

① **Punta Pennata**

② **Harbour of Gaiola**

③ **Marinella Beach**, with its parks and lido, is one of the area's most popular resorts.

④ **Church of Santa Maria del Faro**

← Nisida

Gaiola
The presence of ruined ancient buildings between the tufa island of Gaiola and the village of Marechiaro has led scholars to suggest that a complete Roman city once existed here. The Gaiola Underwater Park offers snorkelling, diving and glass-bottom boat tours to catch a glimpse of the submerged ruins.

Parco Virgiliano
A well-equipped sports centre is one of the attractions in the park of Posillipo, on the Coroglio summit.

Marechiaro
The original name for the water by this fishing village was *Mare planum* (calm sea), which was translated literally in Italian as "Marepiano". With usage it became "Marechiaro", the name now used for the area as a whole. At weekends Neapolitans love to come and eat out here *(see p199)*.

DIRECTORY

Bagno Elena
Via Posillipo 14.
Tel 081 575 50 58.
W bagnoelena.it

Bagno Marechiaro
Calata Ponticello di
Marechiaro 31.
Tel 081 769 12 15.

Gaiola Underwater Park
Discesa Gaiola 27/28.
Tel 081 240 32 35.
W areamarinaprotettagaiola.it

Villa Fattorusso
Via Posillipo 68
Tel 344 190 68 58.
W villafattorusso.com

Villa Imperiale
Via Marechiaro 90.
Tel 081 575 43 44
W villaimperiale.eu

Palazzo degli Spiriti
The remains of the "palace of the spirits" are visible only from the sea. This name was given to the three-storey Roman ruins because of their mysterious appearance.

Swimming and Relaxing

If sightseeing in Naples in midsummer becomes too much, take a break at one of the *stabilimenti balneari* (bathing spots) along the Posillipo coast. Rent a deckchair and an umbrella and swim in the sea or the pool provided. Neapolitans started the habit in the 19th century at the **Bagno Elena**, which first opened in 1838. For those who prefer cliffs to sand, there is the **Villa Fattorusso**, with two seawater pools; **Bagno Marechiaro**, with its restaurant overlooking the waters of the bay; and the elegant **Villa Imperiale**.

The rocks at Posillipo

The remains of Pompeii, with Mount Vesuvius behind ▶

POMPEII AND THE AMALFI COAST

POMPEII AND THE AMALFI COAST

To the north of Naples, fertile plains sweep down to the town of Santa Maria Capua Vetere, home to one of the largest remaining Roman amphitheatres in Italy. The remote hinterland to the east is wild, mountainous and lonely country. To the south is the breathtaking Amalfi coast and the dramatic seaboard of the Cilento. Buried Roman towns and Greek ruins reveal the region's ancient history.

From the 17th century onwards Naples was an increasingly crowded and often tormented metropolis. By contrast, the countryside around the city managed to retain its charm and attracted visitors, especially foreigners, many of whom made Campania their home. "A brief sojourn in Naples", the German historian Gregorovius wrote in the mid-1800s, "is enough to demonstrate that not all life is concentrated in the city but flows mightily into the surroundings".

Today, a visit to Pompeii, buried by an erupting Vesuvius in AD 79, is a high priority for tourists, but this was not always so. Travellers on the Grand Tour in the 1600s and early 1700s preferred the volcanic phenomena of the Solfatara crater and the Phlegraean Fields to the west of Naples. Even in the late 18th century Goethe described the area around Paestum, southeast of Naples, as "anything but picturesque", populated by "buffaloes that look like hippopotami, with wild, bloodshot eyes". Only when the first archaeological digs unearthed the remains of Paestum and the buried cities around Mount Vesuvius, did a tour of the ancient ruins become popular.

The beautiful colour, light and atmosphere found on the islands of Capri and Ischia, and the Sorrento peninsula began to interest landscape painters in the 19th century. The southern flank of the peninsula – the Amalfi coast – remained isolated, and regarded by many as barren, until the mid-1960s, when it attracted visitors in search of an alternative, remote lifestyle. Ironically, the Amalfi coast has since become a very popular holiday area.

The Temple of Ceres in Paestum, south of Naples, was built around 500 BC

◄ Precipitous coast of the resort-island of Capri

Exploring the Coast

The main centre from which to explore Campania is Naples itself, well situated in the middle of the bay. Road and rail links are generally good in the region, with both state railways (FS) and privately run lines serving a variety of destinations. The Circumvesuviana railway connects all the sights in the area of Vesuvius, including Pompeii. The islands in the bay are accessible by hydro-foil (half an hour) or ferry (one hour) from Mergellina and Beverello. Services also run from Sorrento, Positano, Amalfi and Salerno.

Castello Aragonese in Ischia

Sights at a Glance

1. Bagnoli
2. Pozzuoli
3. Baia and Bacoli
4. Cumae
5. Portici and the Vesuvian Villas
6. Torre Annunziata
7. Torre del Greco
8. Mount Vesuvius
9. Herculaneum
10. Pompeii
11. The Sorrento Peninsula
12. Sorrento
14. The Amalfi Coast
15. Paestum
16. Caserta
17. Capri
18. Ischia
19. Procida

Tours

13. Along the Sorrento Coast

Key

▬▬ Motorway
▬▬ Major road
▬▬ Secondary road
∷∷∷ Minor road
▬ Scenic road
╍╍ Main railway
╌╌ Minor railway
△ Summit

0 kilometres   20
0 miles   20

The Phlegraean Fields at Cumae

For hotels and restaurants in this region see pp183–5 and pp192–7

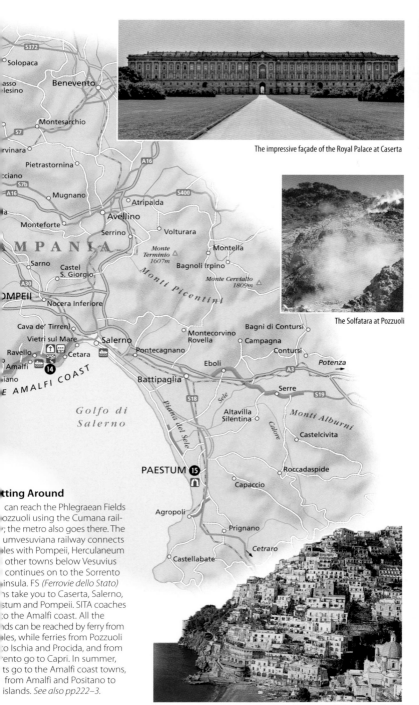

The impressive façade of the Royal Palace at Caserta

The Solfatara at Pozzuoli

CAMPANIA

Benevento
Solopaca
S372
asso
lesino
Montesarchio
S7
rvinara
Pietrastornina
S57b
cciano
A16
Mugnano
Atripalda
A16
Monteforte
Avellino
Serrino
Volturara
Monte Terminio 1607m
Montella
Sarno
Castel S. Giorgio
Bagnoli Irpino
A30
Monte Cerviallo 1809m
OMPEII
Nocera Inferiore
Monti Picentini
Cava de' Tirreni
Montecorvino Rovella
Bagni di Contursi
Vietri sul Mare
Campagna
Salerno
Ravello
Pontecagnano
Contursi
Cetara
Amalfi
Eboli
Potenza
iano
Battipaglia
A3
E AMALFI COAST
Serre
S18
S19
Golfo di Salerno
Altavilla Silentina
Monti Alburni
Castelcivita
PAESTUM **15**
Roccadaspide
Capaccio
Agropoli
Prignano
Cetraro
Castellabate

Getting Around

can reach the Phlegraean Fields
ozzuoli using the Cumana rail-
; the metro also goes there. The
umvesuviana railway connects
les with Pompeii, Herculaneum
other towns below Vesuvius
continues on to the Sorrento
insula. FS (*Ferrovie dello Stato*)
s take you to Caserta, Salerno,
stum and Pompeii. SITA coaches
o the Amalfi coast. All the
ds can be reached by ferry from
les, while ferries from Pozzuoli
o Ischia and Procida, and from
rento go to Capri. In summer,
s go to the Amalfi coast towns,
from Amalfi and Positano to
islands. *See also pp222–3.*

The village of Positano perched on the Amalfi coast

For keys to symbols *see back flap*

❶ Bagnoli

Road map B3. 🚌 C1, C14, R7.
Ⓜ Bagnoli. 🚊 Cumana: Bagnoli.

The area west of Naples, beyond Posillipo, is called "de' Bagnoli" because of the fumaroles and hot springs there. Though its pretty natural setting is blighted by the sprawling old derelict steel mill (*see pp30–31*), significant revitalization projects are in the works.

Nearby, the **Museo del Mare di Napoli** covers Italy's proud maritime history through collections of model ships and navigation equipment.

The *macellum* at Pozzuoli, commonly known as the Temple of Serapis

🏛 Museo del Mare di Napoli
Via di Pozzuoli 5. **Tel** 081 1936 19 67.
Open 8am–1pm, 2–6pm Mon–Fri,
9am–2pm Sun. 🚫 Ⓦ **museodel marenapoli.it**

❷ Pozzuoli

Road Map B3. 🔼 82,000.
ℹ Azienda Autonoma di Soggiorno e Turismo, Via G Matteotti 1/A.
Tel 081 526 14 81. **Open** 9am–3pm Mon–Fri. 🚌 Garibaldi: M1B.
Ⓜ Pozzuoli. 🚊 Cumana: Pozzuoli. 🛥 to Ischia & Procida.
Ⓦ **infocampiflegrei.it**

Around the 7th century BC, the Greek colony of Dicearchia was founded on this site overlooking the port. By 194 BC Roman Puteoli was a flourishing trade centre with luxurious villas. The town later became the Rione Terra quarter.

Evacuated in 1970 due to volcanic activity and neglected for decades, the area has since received a great deal of archaeological attention, most notably in the Roman temple complex under the San Procolo cathedral. The amphitheatre, one of Italy's most ancient, shows how important the city once was.

🏛 La Cattedrale San Procolo Martire
Largo Sedile di Porto. **Tel** 388 101 97 12. **Open** 10am–noon, 5:30–7:30pm Sat; 10am–1pm, 5:30–7:30pm Sun 📷 (by appt)
Ⓦ **cattedralepozzuoli.it**

🏛 Anfiteatro Flavio
Corso Terracciano 75. **Tel** 848 800 288 07. **Open** 9am–one hr before sunset Wed–Mon. 🚫

The amphitheatre, the third largest of the Roman world, had a seating capacity of 40,000. The underground area was used for caged animals and the equipment to lift them up to the arena, as well as a sophisticated drainage system to collect rainwater.

🏛 Tempio di Serapide
Piazza Serapide. 🚫
The so-called Temple of Serapis (2nd century AD), actually the *macellum* or food market, is all that remains of the ancient port district.

The excavated remains of the Anfiteatro Flavio at Pozzuoli

For hotels and restaurants in this region see pp183–5 and pp192–7

Solfatara in Pozzuoli, known as *Forum Vulcani* in ancient times

Solfatara

Via Solfatara 161. **Tel** 081 526 23 41.
Open Apr–Oct: 8:30am–7pm daily;
Nov–Mar: 8:30am–4:30pm daily.
solfatara.it

A dormant volcano, the Solfatara features a mud lake bubbling at 160° (320° F) and two fumaroles belching sulphur fumes. Vulcan, the Roman god of fire, was thought to have his workshop here, and the Solfatara is also believed to have been the inspiration for Virgil's description of the underworld in *The Aeneid*. The Romans, whose ruins are scattered across the western side of the area, harnessed the therapeutic waters and created mineral baths. Today hi-tech equipment tracks the movements of the earth's crust.

❾ Baia and Bacoli

Road Map B3. 27,000.
Cumana: Lucrino, Fusaro.

Along the coast between Pozzuoli and Capo Miseno there are many places that were well known in antiquity. Baia boasted sumptuous Roman villas with terraces overlooking the sea, famous therapeutic springs (still in use in the Middle Ages) and an Aragonese castle, now an archaeological museum.

Bacoli lies along the coast and runs into the modern town of Miseno, which developed over the site of the Roman town of Bauli. At the time of the Emperor Augustus, the port of Miseno was connected to Lake Miseno in the interior. The port was planned so as to avoid silting from volcanic movement, and replaced Porto

Giulio *(see p143)*, the head-quarters of the Roman navy. The Arco Felice, which in the 1st century AD was the gate-way to Cumae *(see pp142–3)*, stands on the peninsula protecting the Bay of Pozzuoli.

Beaches and clubs make this area a summer favourite.

Casina Vanvitelliana del Fusaro

Via Fusaro 162, Baia. **Tel** 081 868 70 80.
Cumana: Fusaro. **Open** summer:
3–7pm Sat, 11am–7pm Sun.
parcovanvitelliano.it

In 1794 Vanvitelli built a hunting lodge for Ferdinand IV on an island in Lake Fusaro, linked to the shore by an arched wooden bridge. This is the only non-volcanic lake in the area.

🏛 Parco Archeologico di Baia

Via Sella di Baia 22, Bacoli.
Tel 081 868 75 92. Cumana:
Fusaro. **Open** 9am–one hr before sunset Tue–Sun. only Sat & Sun

The large domes at this site are the remains of a spa that included baths named after Venus and Mercury and the so-called Temple of Diana.

This monumental complex was built from the late 2nd century–

The Bath of Mercury at Baia

early 1st century BC, on two levels, with terraced land descending to the sea. Some of the park lies underwater, but guided dives are available *(see p211)*.

The site is now used to exhibit excavation finds from the Phlegraean Fields area.

🏛 Museo Archeologico dei Campi Flegrei

Via Castello 39, Baia. **Tel** 081 523 37 97.
Cumana: Fusaro. **Open** 9am–2:30pm Tue–Sun (May–Sep: to 7pm). only Sat & Sun

The Castello di Baia was once an Aragonese fortress. It was totally rebuilt in the 1600s.

View of the city of Baia, with the Roman ruins in the foreground

It is now an Archaeological Museum, with finds from the Phlegraean Fields (Campi Flegrei). Also on display are the Roman plaster casts of Greek statues found in Baia. From the northwest tower you can see the reconstructed Sacello degli Augustali, used for worship of the emperor, found near the Forum at Miseno. The zone is now partly underwater.

Hall in the Museo Archeologico

🏛 Piscina Mirabilis

Via Piscina Mirabile 63, Bacoli. **Tel** 081 523 31 99. **Open** 9am–1:30pm, 2:30–4:30pm Tue–Sun; call ahead for appointment. 🏛 donation.

This enormous reservoir, divided into five longitudinal sections supported by pillars, collected water from the River Serino via the Roman aqueduct and supplied it to the fleet at Miseno.

🏛 Capo Miseno

A windy, narrow stretch of road leads through a dark tunnel to the dramatic peak of Capo Miseno. Pliny the Younger watched the eruption of Vesuvius from this hill. This is also where the Roman Imperial Navy had its headquarters. You can park here and hike up a trail leading to some stunning views of Naples.

The Piscina Mirabilis at Bacoli

The tufa corridor in the Sibyl's Cave

❹ Cumae

Road map B3. 🚇 Cumana: Fusaro. 🚌 EAVBUS: from Piazza Garibaldi, from Fusaro (10 mins to Cumae).

Founded in the 8th century BC, probably by Greeks stationed on Ischia, Cumae is one of the oldest colonies of Magna Graecia. A powerful port for centuries, Cumae resisted the Etruscans but succumbed to the Romans in the 3rd century BC and became a Roman colony. A village grew up over the ruins of the upper city in the 5th–6th centuries but was utterly destroyed by the Saracens in 915. The ancient settlement has not yet been completely excavated.

The best-known areas are the **acropolis** on the rise to the northwest and the **necropolis** on the plain. The acropolis walls, partly rebuilt, and two huge temples are well preserved. The Temple of Apollo lies on the lower terrace, the Temple of Jupiter on the upper one; both were rebuilt in the age of Augustus and the pre-Christian era. At the foot of the acropolis is the entrance to the so-called Sibyl's Cave.

The lower city, inhabited at a later period, is still being excavated and studied. There is a forum, various baths and an amphitheatre. There are also the remains of different epochs: the Samnite-age forum conceals the more ancient agora, or Greek city centre. A sanctuary dedicated to Isis, destroyed with the rise of Christianity, has also been discovered in the port area.

Archaeological Park

Acropolis

Temple of Jupiter

🏛 Archaeological Park

Via Acropoli. **Tel** 081 804 04 30. **Open** 9am–dusk, Tue–Sun.

🏛 Temple of Apollo

Most of the finds from the Temple of Apollo date from the Roman era, when a terrace overlooking the city was added. In the early Christian period the temple was turned into a basilica and burial pits were hewn out of the ancient foundations.

🏛 Sibyl's Cave

According to myth, this was the place to find the Cumaean Sibyl, the oracle consulted by Aeneas. The tufa passageway, trapezoid in section, is illuminated by narrow fissures

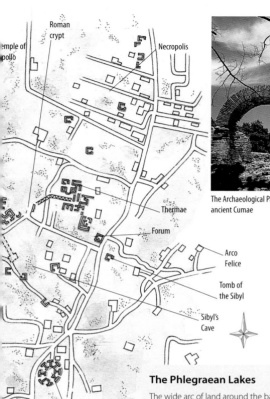

Roman
crypt

Necropolis

Temple of
Apollo

Thermae

Forum

Arco
Felice

Tomb of
the Sibyl

Sibyl's
Cave

Amphitheatre

↓ To the station

0 metres   500
0 yards   500

The Archaeological Park, the site of the excavations revealing
ancient Cumae

🏛 Temple of Jupiter

This ancient sanctuary became an early Christian church and the remains of the altar and baptistry are still visible today.

🏛 Roman Crypt

The part that is visible is the last stretch of a long tunnel that begins at Via Sacra and goes through the hill of Cumae.

The Phlegraean Lakes

The wide arc of land around the bay of Pozzuoli has been known for centuries as the Campi Flegrei, or Burning Fields, because of its constant volcanic activity. Mud still bubbles from the clay bed of the Solfatara and in places the ground is still hot. Over time some of the Phlegraean craters have become lakes. **Lake Averno**, in ancient times thought to be the entrance to hell, owes its name (a-ornon in Greek: "without birds") to the once-suffocating vapours. At the end of the 1st century BC, its almost sacred character declined after the construction of Porto Giulio, a system of channels that connected the sea and the lakes. Ships first reached the outer port in **Lake Lucrino** and then the inner basin of Lake Averno, connected to Cumae by the tunnel through Monte Grillo. The port was abandoned when it silted up and trade was transferred to Miseno. Lake Lucrino again became a pleasure area. Its extent was greatly reduced by the 1538 eruption that created **Monte Nuovo**.

and ends in a vaulted chamber. Despite its undoubted fascination, there is no proof of the tunnel ever having had a religious function. It seems more likely that the tunnel was part of a network of underground routes used for military purposes. The complex system includes the Roman crypt and the Grotto of Cocceius, which connected Cumae to Lake Averno.

Lake Averno

❾ Portici and the Vesuvian Villas

Road Map C3. �· 55,000. 🚇
🚊 Circumvesuviana: Via Libertà, Bellavista, Miglio d'Oro. 🚌 city buses.
ℹ️ Fondazione Ente Ville Vesuviane, Villa Campolieto, Corso Resina 283, Ercolano. **Tel** 081 732 21 34. **Open** 10am–1pm Tue–Sun (3–8pm spring & summer). 🌐 villevesuviane.net

The coast east of the city, up to the foot of Mount Vesuvius, has always been dotted with rural estates, owned by the nobility but used for agriculture as much as rural retreats. The luxurious villas now known as the Ville Vesuviane were built in the early 1700s, when the value of land in the area rose because of the interest in local archaeological excavations. Prince d'Elboeuf, who discovered Herculaneum in 1709, built a villa here. A few decades later, after the building of the Royal Palace at Portici, these villas grew in number, and the road between Resina and Torre del Greco became known as the **Miglio d'Oro**, or Golden Mile. The presence of the Bourbon palace and the location of these villas, with fine views of, and often access to, the countryside and sea, made this area a favourite resort among the aristocracy. A port was built here in 1773.

The Royal Palace in Portici

There are 122 villas in all, but only a few can be visited. Some are well worth a stop, if only to see the decorations on the façade or the magnificent gardens that have survived massive urbanization.

🏛 Reggia di Portici
Via Università 100, Portici. Orto Botanico: **Tel** 081 775 51 36.
Open by appt. Herculanense Museum: **Tel** 081 253 20 16. **Open** by appt.

The Royal Palace (reggia) was built between 1738 and 1742 in the centre of a splendid park at the foothills of Vesuvius and overlooking the sea. Two villas had previously occupied the site, and a road still crosses the large inner courtyard, continuing towards Herculaneum. On the site are botanical gardens and the Herculanense Museum, which houses copies of sculptures found in Herculaneum;

the originals are in the museum at Capodimonte (see pp104–5).

The palace did not have a mooring, so the sovereigns bought the Villa d'Elboeuf for this purpose. Designed by Ferdinando Sanfelice, the villa incorporates some splendid stucco-work and a magnificent circular staircase. The villa was separated from the sea by the Naples–Portici railway (see p29) in 1839.

In 1873, the Royal Palace and its park became the home of the Faculty of Agriculture of the University of Naples. Every March, it hosts an antiques fair.

🏛 Villa Campolieto
Corso Resina 283, Ercolano. **Tel** 081 732 21 34. **Open** 10am–1pm Tue–Sun. 🎭
Built in 1755–75 first by Gioffredo and then by Vanvitelli, this is the only Vesuvian villa that has been completely restored. A monumental staircase links the ground floor and upper floor. Vanvitelli's elegant portico hosts the Festival delle Ville Vesuviane (see p45) each summer, and the villa sometimes stages events.

🏛 Villa Favorita
Corso Resina 291, Ercolano. **Tel** 081 739 39 61. **Open** 10am–1pm Tue–Sun (park only).

This villa, set in an extensive park, was designed by Ferdinando Fuga in 1768 as a royal residence. Ferdinand IV decorated it with paintings, silk from San Leucio (see p169) and a mosaic removed from the Villa Jovis in Capri (see p173). His son Leopold supervised the layout of the stables and the park, which can be accessed from Via Gabriele D'Annunzio.

🏛 Villa Ruggiero
Via Alessandro Rossi 40, Ercolano. **Tel** 081 732 21 34. **Open** 10am–1pm Tue–Sun.

Built in the first half of the 18th century, this villa has been owned by the Ruggiero family since 1863. It was occupied all year round, not just in the summer, as the rich agricultural land shows. The barn is now used for exhibitions.

Vanvitelli's curved portico in Villa Campolieto

For hotels and restaurants in this region see pp182–5 and pp192–7

❻ Torre Annunziata

Road Map C3. ⛰ 51,000. ℹ Pro Loco Ufficio Informazioni Turistiche: Via Sepolcri 16. **Tel** 081 862 31 63. 🚇 Circumvesuviana: Torre Annunziata.

The town was built over the ruins of ancient Oplontis, which was destroyed in the eruption of Vesuvius in AD 79. Its name derives from a watchtower here *(torre)* built to warn the populace of any imminent Saracen raids, and a chapel consecrated to the Annunziata (the Virgin Mary), around which the town grew up.

In the 18th century Charles III founded an arms factory here, designed by a pupil of Vanvitelli and finished by Ferdinando Fuga. In the late 1700s and early 1800s Torre Annunziata became a centre for pasta production. Towards the sea are the spas, Terme Vesuviane Nunziante, named after the general who discovered the ruins of a Roman baths complex here in 1831. He was responsible for the present-day structure, which is still in operation.

❒ Oplontis Excavations

Via Sepolcri 1. **Tel** 081 857 53 47. **Open** Apr–Oct: 8:30am–7:30pm daily (last adm 6pm); Nov–Mar: 8:30am–5pm daily (last adm 3:30pm). **Closed** 1 Jan, 1 May, 25 Dec. 🅿

The excavation area includes the villas of Craxus and Poppaea (the latter was Nero's second wife), which were buried during the AD 79 eruption of Vesuvius. Brought to light in 1964, the complex reflects the elegant taste of its owners. As well as gardens and porticoes, the private baths of the house can also be seen, complete with *calidarium* (the hot room) and *tepidarium* (the warm room), and a swimming pool, a full 60 m (197 ft) in length. Also interesting are the 1st century BC–1st century AD wall paintings. These depict still lifes or scenes combining architecture and figures, in some cases with illusionistic effects around the doorways or windows. Many amphoras were found in the rooms of the Villa of Craxus, which were used as storerooms or shops.

Harbour at Torre Annunziata

❼ Torre del Greco

Road Map C3. ⛰ 88,000. ℹ Via Procida 2a. **Tel** 081 881 46 76. 🚇 Circumvesuviana: Torre del Greco.

The name derives from a watchtower built by Frederick II and from the vineyards which produce wine from a grape variety called Greco. Torre del Greco is mainly known for its fine coral manufacture. The old town, rebuilt several times after the various eruptions of Vesuvius, lines the coast, while the newer districts, with villas surrounded by gardens, lie on the slopes of the volcano itself. Don't miss Palazzo Vallelonga in Via Vittorio Emanuele and the Camaldoli alla Torre monastery, both 18th-century buildings. The poet Giacomo Leopardi lived in the Villa delle Ginestre (on a road crossing Via Nazionale) and wrote his last poems there, including *La Ginestra* (The Broom).

The imperial villa of Poppaea Sabina at Torre Annunziata

The Red Gold at Torre del Greco

By the 15th century the main trade in Torre del Greco was coral fishing. Over the centuries the town became a collection point for coral, and other coastal towns followed suit. The first factories were established by foreigners during the course of the 1800s and the Bourbon rulers then set up their own. Local designs were at first inspired by classical models, and subsequently influenced by the Art Nouveau style. As well as coral, there are mother-of-pearl, turtle shell and ivory pieces. The *coralline* boats that went out to collect the coral have been modernized and re-equipped, but today most of the raw material comes from Japan. Admirers of "red gold" can visit the numerous workshops in town or the Coral Museum (open 9am–1pm Mon–Sat) at No. 6 Piazza Palomba.

Carved piece of coral

❽ Mount Vesuvius

In ancient times Vesuvius was simply "the mountain", covered with vegetation and vines. The first person to understand its volcanic nature was the Greek geographer, Strabo (AD 19), who suggested that its rocks had been burned by fire. In AD 79 an almighty eruption smothered the cities on its foothills and greatly altered the surrounding landscape. Ash and debris showered Pompeii, and Herculaneum was buried by a landslide of thick mud. Pliny the Younger recorded the cloud of black smoke that rose "like an umbrella pine" from the mountain. His uncle, Pliny the Elder, was suffocated by the gaseous vapours that engulfed the area. Today, the volcano inspires both fear and fascination and it is constantly monitored for activity.

Vineyards
The land around volcanoes, rich in alkali and phosphorus, is extremely fertile. On the slopes of Vesuvius, the grapes grown make *Lacrima Christi*, once considered one of Italy's best wines.

History of the Volcano

These sections show the changes in the structure of Vesuvius following the most significant eruptions, from prehistoric times to the formation of the present-day cone.

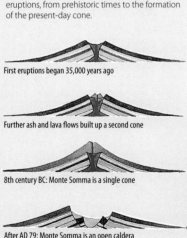

First eruptions began 35,000 years ago

Further ash and lava flows built up a second cone

8th century BC: Monte Somma is a single cone

After AD 79: Monte Somma is an open caldera

Today's cone, Vesuvius, formed in the old caldera

Vesuvius Observatory
The observatory on the slopes of Vesuvius was built by Ferdinand II in 1841–5. The Neo-Classical building has a well-stocked library and an interesting collection of minerals. There is a splendid panoramic view from the square. Today it is only used as a base for recording data; the research section has been transferred to Naples.

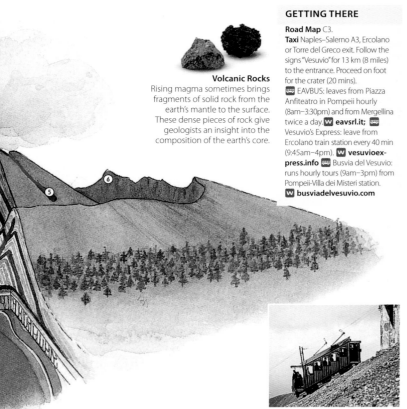

Volcanic Rocks

Rising magma sometimes brings fragments of solid rock from the earth's mantle to the surface. These dense pieces of rock give geologists an insight into the composition of the earth's core.

GETTING THERE

Road Map C3.

Taxi Naples–Salerno A3, Ercolano or Torre del Greco exit. Follow the signs "Vesuvio" for 13 km (8 miles) to the entrance. Proceed on foot for the crater (20 mins).

🚌 EAVBUS: leaves from Piazza Anfiteatro in Pompeii hourly (8am–3:30pm) and from Mergellina twice a day. **W** **eavsrl.it;** 🚌 Vesuvio's Express: leave from Ercolano train station every 40 min (9:45am–4pm). **W** **vesuvioexpress.info** 🚌 Busvia del Vesuvio: runs hourly tours (9am–3pm) from Pompeii-Villa dei Misteri station. **W** **busviadelvesuvio.com**

The Funicular

The funicular dates from 1880. Two cars took visitors up to an altitude of 1180 m (3,870 ft) above sea level. After a series of accidents, however, the funicular was taken out of service in 1944.

KEY

① **Magma** (molten rock from the earth's mantle) wells upwards and forms a reservoir beneath the earth's surface.

② **Layers of lava**

③ **Layers of ash** alternate with lava flow and settle on the sides of the volcano. Gradually these layers build up the cone.

④ **Crater summit**

⑤ **Lava flows**

⑥ **Monte Somma** contains the ancient volcano crater, which was created by successive eruptions. The crater is 200m (655 ft) deep and has a diameter of 600 m (1,970 ft).

⑦ **The main conduit** for magma, which is pushed up to the surface.

1694 Another eruption, with lava flow from the crater	**1794** Torre del Greco destroyed	**1906** Another eruption: the crater widens by 300 m (985 ft)	**1933** A series of shocks shows the volcano is active once again. Lava appears on 3 June
1600	**1700**	**1800**	**1900**
1631 On 16 December the lava claims 600 victims. Naples is saved and thanks San Gennaro by building the Guglia in Piazza Sforza (see p85)	**1767** The lava reaches San Giorgio a Cremano and approaches Naples	**1880** The funicular opens to the public	**1944** After a final violent explosion, the trail of smoke disappears

❾ Herculaneum

Ancient Herakleion fell under Greek influence around the 5th century BC and then under Samnite rule. In 89 BC the town became part of the Roman Empire, a residential *municipium* and resort. The town's quiet existence was brought to an abrupt halt in AD 79, when the eruption of Vesuvius that buried Pompeii covered Herculaneum with a deep layer of lava and mud.

Excavations began in the 18th century, and uncovered Roman houses built around a rectangular plan. Perhaps the best known is the Villa dei Papiri, the inspiration for the J Paul Getty museum in Malibu, Los Angeles. Sculptures found in the villa are now in the Museo Archeologico Nazionale *(see pp90–93)*.

★ House of the Neptune and Amphitrite Mosaic
This mosaic is in the summer dining room. The building and a shop, with wooden shelves for amphoras, are among the best preserved.

★ Trellis House
A characteristic example of an inexpensive Roman multi-family dwelling, the Trellis House has wood and reed laths in the original crude tufa and lime masonry.

House with the Mosaic Atrium
This house has a famous mosaic floor with geometric patterns, as well as living rooms, and a portico and terrace facing the sea.

Villa dei Papiri

★ House of the Stags
The name derives from the beautifully sculpted groups of stags found here. The house is one of the more elaborate: the inner porticoed garden connects the northern section (entrance, indoor triclinium and smaller rooms) to the southern side, which has bedrooms and an arbour with a sea view.

House of the Bicentenary
This patrician residence, excavated 200 years after digging began, had mosaic floors and wall paintings.

VISITORS' CHECKLIST

Practical Information
Road Map C3. **Tel** 081 732 43 38.
Open Apr–Oct: 8:30am–7:30pm;
Nov–Mar: 8:30am–5pm.
🏛 Villa dei Papiri: **Closed** to the public. 🆆 **pompeiisites.org**

Transport
🚆 Portici-Ercolano. 🚌 Circum-vesuviana: Ercolano-Scavi.

Entrance

KEY

① **The House of the Gem** is named after a cameo portrait from the era of Claudius that was found here.

② **The city baths**, built in 10 BC, are divided into two sections. The one for men is larger and decorated, and includes a gymnasium; the women's section is smaller and better preserved.

③ **Decumanus Maximus**

④ **Decumanus Inferiore**

⑤ **The House of Telephus** contains a 1st-century BC relief narrating the myth of Achilles and Telephus.

0 metres   50
0 yards   50

The Excavation Area
The site of ancient Herculaneum is well below the level of the modern town. The area is still being excavated. The restored Villa dei Papiri contains frescoes, mosaics and the skeleton of a horse, but is closed to visitors.

⓾ Pompeii

An earthquake in AD 62, which shook Pompeii and damaged some of its buildings, was merely a prelude to the tragic day in AD 79, when Vesuvius erupted, engulfing the city and its inhabitants with a terrible storm of cinders and ash. The remains of Pompeii were discovered by accident in the 1590s, but it was not until the 1750s that the site was seen as an archaeological treasure. The bodies of people were unearthed along with their houses, temples, works of art and everyday objects. The first archaeologists removed the most important finds, which became part of the royal collection and were then transferred to the Museo Archeologico Nazionale *(see pp90–93)*.

★ House of the Vettii
This is one of the most famous places in Pompeii *(see p154)*. It has rich wall decoration dating from the last Pompeiian period after AD 62. The array of themes includes Daedalus and Pasiphaë, shown here.

The Forum
Originally the market place, the Forum *(see p152)* became the focus for the most important civic functions, both political and religious.

Porta Marina entrance

Macellum
The macellum was the covered meat and fish market. Fronted by a portico with two moneychangers' kiosks, it opened onto the Forum near the weights and measures office and the Forum Holitorium vegetable market.

Fresco from the Lupanare

The Latin word *lupa* means prostitute, and this *lupanare* was the best-organized of Pompeii's many brothels. Here, the walls are decorated with erotic paintings and graffiti depicting this world and the services offered by prostitutes, including boys, to satisfy their clients and lovers.

VISITORS' CHECKLIST

Practical Information
Road Map D3. Entrances: Porta Marina, Piazza Anfiteatro, Piazza Esedra. **Tel** 081 857 53 47.
Open Apr–Oct: 8:30am–7:30pm (last adm: 6pm); Nov–Mar: 8:30am–5pm (last adm: 3:30pm).
🎧 📷 ℹ AAST, Via Sacra 1.
Tel 081 850 72 55.
Ⓦ pompeiisites.org

Transport
FS Pompei-Scavi.
🚊 Circumvesuviana: Pompei-Villa dei Misteri.

Plaster Casts

Since 1863, plaster cast techniques have enabled researchers to re-create body shapes. Many inhabitants were killed by the toxic fumes while engaged in everyday tasks.

The Archaeological Site

The illustration shows the western section of Pompeii. For a plan of the entire area see p155.

KEY

① **Temple of Venus** *(see p152)*

② **Basilica** *(see p152)*

③ **Forum** *(see p152)*

④ **Temple of Apollo** *(see p152)*

⑤ **House of the Faun** *(see p154)*

⑥ **The House of the Golden Cupids** is named after the delightful images in the bedroom. They are reproductions of the originals.

⑦ **Via dell'Abbondanza** was lined with private homes and shops selling a range of goods.

⑧ **The Great Theatre**, was built in the hollow of a hill for good acoustics *(see p152)*.

⑨ **The Temple of Isis**, built in the late 2nd century BC, has two niches holding statues of Egyptian gods.

⑩ **Small Theatre** *(see p153)*

⑪ **Gladiators' courtyard and barracks** *(see p153)*

★ Via dei Sepolcri

"Twenty steps wide, 500 long, the entire length still furrowed by the ancient carriage wheels, completely furnished with pavements like ours, and lined throughout, at left and right, with funerary monuments." This is how an awestruck Alexandre Dumas described Via dei Sepolcri, outside the northwest city wall, which was discovered in the first digs.

Exploring Pompeii

Thanks to its strategic position near the Sarno River, Pompeii was a centre of commerce for inland areas. The first town plan (6th century BC) was irregular but, from the 4th century BC on, building developed on a Greek-inspired grid plan. Slabs of old lava from Vesuvius were used to pave the roads. Large villas and houses of different periods and styles, made of brick, stone and cement and often richly decorated, offer an unparalleled view of ancient domestic architecture *(see pp154–5)*. Furthermore, the streets, workshops and public areas are in an excellent state of preservation. Finds such as furnishings, tools, jewellery and even food and drink reveal how the people of Pompeii lived, from the ruling class down to the slaves.

The Forum viewed from the Temple of Apollo

Pompeii, her temple was badly damaged in the earthquake of AD 62, then totally devastated by Vesuvius.

Forum Baths

Built after 80 BC, these well-preserved baths follow the traditional sequence from dressing room to *frigidarium* (cold room), then on to *tepidarium* (warm room) and *calidarium* (hot room). Mythological figures decorate the vaults of the warm room, and the hot room contains a mammoth marble basin. Most people would use the public baths for their ablutions.

The Basilica, Pompeii's ancient judicial seat opening onto the Forum

The Forum

The Forum, a rectangular paved area, was the centre of public life, and the oldest part of Pompeii, built on the highest spot. Arranged around it are a number of important administrative and religious institutions. To the south is the Basilica, or law court, while opposite are the temples of Apollo, Jupiter and Vespasian, and the Sanctuary of the Lari. The imposing Eumachia building was perhaps used by the wool merchants' guild or, more probably, for commercial transactions. On the other side of the Basilica is the site of the Temple of Venus. The goddess was the protectress of the city, but in tandem with the fate of

Theatres

The Great Theatre (2nd century BC) was rebuilt several times in its history and in modern times has again been used as the venue for summer cultural events. It was built to seat about 5,000 people. The quadrangular portico behind the stage, originally designed as a space for the audience to stroll in

The Forum, with Vesuvius in the background

The Great Theatre at Pompeii, first built between 200–150 BC

during intermissions, was turned into a barracks for the gladiators after AD 62. Skeletons, including one of a baby, have been excavated here.

Next door is the indoor theatre, or Small Theatre, used for music concerts. Behind this is the Temple of Isis, the goddess worshipped locally.

Via Stabiana

This avenue, passing through the Porta di Stabia, to the south, was a major thoroughfare used by carriages travelling between Pompeii and the port and coastal districts. On the west side of the avenue are the Stabian Baths. These are the most ancient in Pompeii – the original structure dates from the 4th century BC.

Near Porta Vesuvio it is possible to see the remains of an aqueduct. This channelled water from the Serino River aqueduct, built in the era of Augustus, into three conduits that served both private homes and public fountains. The aqueduct fell into disuse after being damaged by the earthquake of AD 62. On the street parallel to Via Stabiana are the remains of the most organized of Pompeii's many brothels. While other such places were mostly single rooms or the top floor of a shop, this *lupanare* features five rooms on the ground floor with stone beds as well as a latrine. Erotic frescoes and ancient graffiti line the walls.

An inn in Via dell'Abbondanza

Amphitheatre and Great Gymnasium

The Amphitheatre (80 BC) and the Augustan-era Great Gymnasium, with a swimming pool in the middle, are in an outlying area between the Nocera and Sarno gateways.

The amphitheatre, the oldest of its kind in existence, was used for gladiatorial combat and could hold 20,000 people. The stone tiers were separated into different sections for the various social classes. A cloth canopy *(velarium)* shaded spectators from the sun.

A public fountain in Via dell'Abbondanza

Via dell'Abbondanza

The excavations for this street lined with homes and shops end just to the left of the Amphitheatre. The buildings and contents present a vivid picture of everyday life, down to the cart tracks in the street. Well-preserved residences include the House of the Ceii *(see p154)* and the home belonging to Octavius Quartio *(see p155)*. You can visit the shop of Verecundus, who made felt and tanned hides; Stefano's well-preserved laundry, where urine was used as a cleaning agent; or the bakery run by Sotericus, where bread was baked but not sold retail. Among the inns, the most famous belonged to Asellina, whose obliging foreign waitresses are depicted in graffiti on the wall. Asellina's inn *(thermopolium)* still has the record of the proceeds of that fateful day in AD 79: 683 sesterces.

The Houses in Pompeii

Many large houses of great historical value and architectural interest are concentrated in the area between Via di Mercurio (the most elegant *cardo*, reserved for pedestrians, in the northwest of Pompeii) and Via Stabiana, and along Via dell' Abbondanza. Wealthy residents had houses with courtyards, living rooms and gardens (*see pp22–3*), often with decorated walls. A typical Pompeiian house was constructed around two open courts: the atrium, an Italic feature, and the colonnaded garden, a feature of Greek origin. The layout of suburban farmsteads was different; the Villa of the Mysteries is one of the most famous. Houses are occasionally closed; ask an official guide.

The lari shrine, House of the Vettii

House of the Vettii

The owners of the House of the Vettii were freedmen who had become rich merchants. The house's interior walls are adorned with splendid paintings and friezes featuring mythological themes. In the atrium of the more rustic part of the house is the altar of the lari – the deities who protected the place. This depicts the ancestral spirit of the *pater familias* with two lari and, below, a serpent.

On the north side of the house is a kitchen, with a small room decorated with erotic scenes, murals and tapestries.

House of the Faun

The name comes from a bronze statue in the middle of the *impluvium* (pond) in one of the atria. The original is in the Museo Archeologico Nazionale, as are many of the mosaics, including the famous *Battle of Alexander (see pp90–93)*. Built in the 2nd century BC, this is one of the largest private dwellings here.

House of the Tragic Poet

The entrance has a mosaic of a dog with a "beware of the dog" inscription, but many of its frescoes are in the Museo Archeologico. The name of the house derives from a mosaic showing a drama rehearsal.

Bronze statue, House of the Faun

House of the Ceii

The façade of this house bears a series of inscriptions that seem to indicate an electoral campaign programme. One of the messages is signed L Ceius Secundus, who is thought to have been the owner of the house at the time of the eruption. Behind the atrium, a richly decorated garden features a back wall frescoed with hunting scenes and fountains, giving the impression of a wider space. The sides are decorated with landscapes with an Egyptian flavour, a common style in the final years of Pompeii.

House of Venus

This house is named after the goddess of Love because of a fresco discovered there in 1952. Located on the back wall of the garden, it portrays Venus with two cherubs in a pink seashell. The atrium of the house was damaged by a bombardment on Pompeii in 1943.

Thermopolium

Ancient Pompeiians mostly consumed lunch outside the home, in a *thermopolium*. Such places usually had a long counter on the street side, with benches and terracotta receptacles for food. A colourful fresco adorns the back wall of this shop, which belonged to Vetuvius Placidus and which

The peristyle in the House of the Vettii

Plan of Pompeii

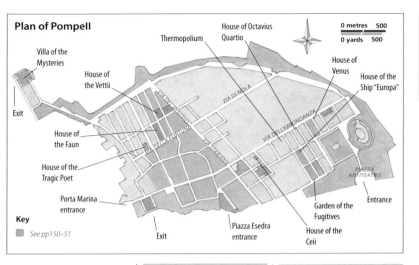

Villa of the Mysteries

House of the Vettii

Thermopolium

House of Octavius Quartio

House of Venus

House of the Ship "Europa"

Exit

House of the Faun

House of the Tragic Poet

Porta Marina entrance

Garden of the Fugitives

Entrance

House of the Ceii

Piazza Esedra entrance

Exit

Key

See pp150–51

VIA DEI SEPOLCRI
VIA DI NOLA
VIA DELL'ABBONDANZA
VIA DELLA FORTUNA
VIA STABIANA
PIAZZA ANFITEATRO

0 metres 500
0 yards 500

is also one of the best examples of a business owner's house annexed to the workplace. It has bedrooms, an atrium and an interesting garden *triclinium*, which is the room where Pompeiians would eat lying down on beds. This *triclinium* is decorated with a fresco of *The Rape of Europa*, where Jupiter appears as a bull.

Across the street is the **House of the Chaste Lovers**, which had a bakery with an annexed dining and living room. The structure also contains the fossilized bodies of the mules that were used to drive the millstone for grinding wheat.

House of Octavius Quartio

This house belonged to a man who had made his fortune thanks to the two *cauponae* (restaurants) at the front of the building. The atrium has a marble *impluvium* (a canal used to collect rain water) flanked by flower beds. Beyond the atrium is a vast garden that imitates an aristocratic country residence. A canal, whose borders are decorated with statuary, runs the length of the garden, interrupted only by a small temple in the middle. At one end of the garden is a frescoed nook with a double bed that was probably used for outdoor dining.

Garden of the Fugitives

Walking along the Via dei Sepolcri and just around the bend, you will come to a series of steps leading to an overview of the city and into a villa with a large vineyard. Against one wall, behind glass, are the plaster casts of some of the victims of the eruption. It was Giuseppe Fiorelli, director of the Pompeii digs from 1860 to 1875, who introduced the plaster cast method of preserving the bodies. Liquid plaster is poured into the cavity left in the bed of ashes by the gradual decomposition of the victim's body. As the plaster solidifies, it reproduces the body shape. This method is still used today.

Villa of the Mysteries

This large villa outside the city walls on Via dei Sepolcri was built in the early 2nd century BC. It was converted from an urban dwelling into an elegant country house. The architecture and paintings make it one of the most famous houses in Pompeii. It contains a well-known cycle of frescoes with 29 brightly coloured life-size figures against a red background, who represent a bride's initiation to the Dionysian mysteries or a postulant's initiation to the Orphic mysteries. Some scholars say this subject was depicted because the owner was a priestess of the Dionysian cult, which was widespread in Southern Italy.

Scene from the famous fresco cycle in the Villa of the Mysteries

⑪ The Sorrento Peninsula

The peninsula created by the Lattari hills rises steeply out of the sea and forms a boundary between the bays of Naples and Salerno. The softer northern side has been inhabited for centuries, and is dotted with ancient as well as modern villas. The coast between Vico Equense and Sorrento *(see pp158–9)* is especially built up, though spectacular views across the Bay of Naples abound. The rugged coastline is wilder and more precipitous on the southern side *(see pp162–5)* after Punta della Campanella, which was almost inaccessible by land until the 19th century. Today tourism is the most important industry but inland, olive groves and citrus trees are still tended and out of season many of the small coastal communities regain their fishing village atmosphere.

Vico Equense, perched on a clifftop

Castellammare di Stabia

Road map D3. 🚆 66,000.
🚉 Circumvesuviana: Castellammare.
ℹ️ Azienda di Cura, Soggiorno e Turismo: Castellammare di Stabia, Piazza Giacomo Matteotti, 34/35.
Tel 081 871 13 34. 🌐 stabiatourism.it

Castellammare was totally rebuilt in the 9th century along with the castle used to defend the most important of its many sources of therapeutic waters. In 1780, the Bourbon rulers established the royal shipyards at Castellammare di Stabia, and commercial shipbuilding remains the town's main industry today.

Ancient Stabiae, an agglomeration of villas and farmsteads, lies outside the modern town on the Varano plain. Stabiae was destroyed by the Vesuvius eruption of AD 79, and was only partly excavated in the 18th century. After World War II more ancient houses were found along the coast and in the interior. Many of these villas were richly decorated and placed in splendid scenic positions. The oldest is the **Villa di Arianna** on the Varano hill, with a 1st-century BC nucleus and 13 rooms overlooking the bay. **Villa San Marco**, 1 km (half a mile) away on the same site, has the remnants of a Roman swimming pool.

🏛 Villa di Arianna and Villa San Marco

Via Passeggiata Archeologica.
Tel 081 857 53 47.
Open 8:30am–7:30pm daily (Nov–Mar: to 5pm). Last adm: 90 mins before closing. **Closed** 1 Jan, 1 May, 25 Dec. 📷

🚡 Monte Faito

A cable car departing from the Circumvesuviana train station (May–Oct) takes visitors up to the wooded slopes of Monte Faito. From the cable-car station it is possible to climb even higher to the church of San Michele, 1,280 m (4,195 ft) above sea level.

Tour Around the Sorrento Peninsula

① Castellammare di Stabia
② Stabiae
③ Villa di Arianna & Villa San Marco
④ Monte Faito
⑤ Vico Equense
⑥ Sorrento *(pp158–9)*
⑦ Massa Lubrense
⑧ Punta della Campanella
⑨ Sant'Agata sui due Golfi

Gulf of Naples
(Golfo di Napoli)
Equa
Meta
Piano di Sorrento
S. Agnello
Termini
Nerano
Marina del Cantone
S145
S. Pietro
Moiano
Pimonte
S. Michele
Monti Lattari
S163
Positano
Agerola
Gulf of Salerno
(Golfo di Salerno)

0 kilometres   6
0 miles   3

Key
━━━ Suggested route

For keys to symbols *see back flap*

The picturesque village of Marina di Lobra, Massa Lubrense

Vico Equense

Road map C4. 22,000.
Circumvesuviana: Scraio, Vico Equense.
Via Filangieri 100. **Tel** 081 801 57 52.
vicoturismo.it

On a rocky spur with precipitous cliffs, this town of Etruscan origin, famous in antiquity for its wine, is now a tourist resort with popular bars and restaurants. With its steep antique streets, piazzas and castle, Vico Equense retains its independence from the coastal sprawl. The Vescovado quarter is built on a Roman street plan and has striking medieval buildings including **Castello Giusso**, which can be seen from the outside but is not open to the public.

The Gothic church of **Santissima Annunziata** was built in the 14th century. From the front of this former cathedral (reached by passing under the arch of the belltower) there is a sheer drop to the sea far below allowing for dramatic panoramas.

Local pizzerias claim to have invented *pizza a metro* (pizza by

Breathtaking views from Monte Faito

the metre) and Neapolitans come here to test their appetites, seeing what length they can eat.

Santissima Annunziata
Via Vescovado. **Open** 5–7pm Tue & Thu, 10am–noon Sun.

Massa Lubrense

Road map C4. 14,000.
Viale Filangieri 11. **Tel** 081 533 90 21. Fri. **massalubrense.it**

Massa is a market town and bathing resort on the western end of the peninsula. Its 16th-century church, **Santa Maria delle Grazie** dominates Piazza Largo Vescovado. Just below the square there are dazzling views across the sea to Capri *(see pp172–3)* and a steep path winds down past the tiled dome of **Santa Maria di Lobra** to the pretty village of **Marina di Lobra**, where a scattering of restaurants face the beach and fishing boats are left abandoned on the sand.

Punta della Campanella

Road map C4.

The coastline and turquoise waters around the south-westerly tip of the Sorrento Peninsula are protected as a maritime area. Wild and rocky, steep cliffs with improbably perched trees rise from small coves. A popular paved path leads from

Termini out to the point. Alternatively, ramblers can follow the ridge path from Nerano *(see p162)*.

Santa Maria delle Grazie, Massa Lubrense

Sant'Agata sui Due Golfi

Road map C4.

Perched inland with beautiful vistas north and south, Sant' Agata is famous for its two Michelin-starred restaurant, Don Alfonso 1890 *(see p197)*, and a favourite with Neapolitans. On a hill high above the town, with the most stunning views of all, is the vast 17th-century building of **Il Monastero del Deserto**, which was built as a Carmelite monastery. It is now inhabited by Benedictine nuns who occasionally open it up for visitors.

Il Monastero del Deserto
Tel 081 878 01 99. **Open** for mass *(phone ahead to check)*.

For hotels and restaurants in this region see pp183–5 and pp192–7

⑫ Sorrento

On the cliffs at the southern end of the Bay of Naples, Sorrento has been a popular resort town since the 1700s: Casanova and Goethe both stayed here as guests of the British envoy, Sir William Hamilton, and his wife Lady Hamilton. The town has ancient origins though and you can still distinguish the original Greek town plan in the centre of Sorrento to the west of Piazza Tasso, and just out of town there are Roman remains at Punta del Capo. In the summer the laid-back town fills with wandering tourists taking in the views or relaxing at cafés. Down at the water's edge both Marina Grande and Marina Piccola have small beaches but the town is dominated more by boats than by sand as ferries arrive and depart for the Amalfi Coast, Naples and the islands. Lemons, a reminder of the fertility of the surrounding countryside, also dominate, as both flavouring and decoration.

The Agruminato is owned by the town council and run by a local farm. Visitors can wander around the orchard and buy a variety of lemon-based products, as well as other liqueurs, including mandarin and liquorice.

🏛 Piazza Tasso

The hub of Sorrento, Piazza Tasso is also the most attractive part of town, with narrow streets following the layout of Roman Surrentum. The statue here is of Torquato Tasso, the 16th-century Renaissance poet who was born in the town. The square is also the popular starting and finishing place for the evening *passeggiata*, or stroll.

🌳 Villa Comunale

Open dawn–dusk.

One of Sorrento's most tranquil spots, the Villa Comunale is a thin stretch of tree-lined park overlooking Marina Piccola and the Bay of Naples beyond. The views are especially spectacular when the colours change at sunset, and it is easy to while away the time watching the comings and goings far below. Steps from the park lead down to the sea.

🏛 San Francesco

Piazza San Francesco 8–9.
Open 8:30am–9pm daily.

Vibrant bougainvillea flowers tumble down around the beautiful and peaceful

14th-century cloisters attached to the church of San Francesco. The architecture is a mixture of styles and periods: rounded arches on two sides and interlaced Arabic ones on the other two.

🏛 Museo Correale di Terranova

Via Correale 50. **Tel** 081 878 18 46. **Open** Apr–Oct: 9:30am–6:30pm Tue–Sat, 9:30am–1:30pm Sun; Nov–Mar: 9:30am–1:30pm Tue–Sun. **W** museocorreale.it

The Museo Correale di Terranova is Sorrento's most important museum. Housed in an ancient villa, the collections consist of 17th–19th-century objets d'art including furnishings, china, ceramics and glassware, as well as paintings by Neapolitan and international artists and local archaeological finds.

🍋 Cataldo Lemon Orchard

Corso Italia 267. **Tel** 081 878 18 88. **Open** 9am–7pm daily.
W igiardinidicataldo.it

Lemons are everywhere in Sorrento: the distinctively large, thick-skinned fruit hang outside shops, decorate ceramics and flavour the local tipple, limoncello. In the centre of town is a traditional citrus grove typical of the kind found all over the region.

Fresh fruit and vegetable stalls lining Sorrento's narrow streets

🏛 Sedile Dominova

Via P R Giuliani. **Closed** to the public.

The Sedile Dominova, in the piazza of the same name, is a 16th-century building once used as an assembly hall for the nobility. Its external frescoes, including the coats of arms of local families, can still be seen in its arches, though the building is now used as a working men's club.

🏛 Duomo

Corso Italia. **Tel** 081 878 22 48.
Open 8am–12:30pm, 4:30–9pm daily.

The Duomo is of ancient origin and was rebuilt in the 1400s and then remodelled several times. Its façade was reconstructed in the early 20th century. Inside the cathedral is the archbishop's marble throne, sculpted in 1537, and fine *intarsia*- (inlaid wood) decorated choir stalls.

Thriving citrus groves, Cataldo Lemon Orchard

For hotels and restaurants in this region see pp183–5 and pp192–7

The colourful harbour at Marina Grande

VISITORS' CHECKLIST

Practical Information
Road map C4. 18,000.
Azienda Autonoma di
Soggiorno Sorrento–Sant'Agnello,
Via de Maio 35. **Tel** 081 807 40 33.
Tue. **sorrentotourism.com**

Transport
Circumvesuviana: Sorrento.
Sita.
from & to Naples and Capri.

Museo Bottega della Tarsialignea

Palazzo Pomarici Santomasi, Via San Nicola 28. **Tel** 081 877 19 42. **Open** Apr–Oct: 10am–6:30pm daily; Nov–Mar: 10am–5pm daily. **Closed** public hols. **museomuta.it**

Sorrento's tradition of inlaying wood, instances of which can be seen in its cathedral, is on display at this private museum. The collection includes plenty of fine examples of the art, including furniture and natural and stained wooden objects from the 17th–20th century. Don't miss the impressively decorated ceilings in two of the rooms.

Marina Grande

Fishing boats bob gently in the calm water at picturesque Marina Grande, to the west of the town centre. The colourful, if somewhat shabby houses that face the waterfront add to its charm. Nearby, the deep waters at Marina Piccola make for a hectic port. Boats leave here for Naples, Capri, and in summer for the Amalfi Coast. Both harbours have small stretches of sand, most of which you must pay to access.

Bagno della Regina Giovanna

Punta del Capo descent (Calata). West of the town, a cobbled lane leads from Capo di Sorrento down to Punta del Capo, where you can visit the so-called Bagno della Regina Giovanna, Roman ruins of what was probably the home of the wealthy citizen, Pollius Felix. Close to the water, the archaeological site is surrounded by trees, and the sea enters a small, rocky cove through an arch, making it a sheltered swimming spot. Above, Roman walls and the remains of an under-floor heating system are all that is left of the ancient villa.

Marina di Puolo

Beyond Punta del Capo a path and a road descend to Marina di Puolo, a small, secluded cove and one of the best beaches in the area. Sunbathers share the sand and pebbles with small boats and a row of pretty fishermen's cottages line the beach.

Sorrento

For keys to symbols *see back flap*

⓭ Along the Sorrento Coast

The best way to take in all the beauty of the bay is by sea – to discover the isolated beaches, villages perched on the hillsides and ancient watchtowers. From Amalfi, Sorrento and Capri you can rent a launch or a slow *gozzo* boat. In the summer the major centres offer organized excursions on larger boats with a guide, but you cannot stop where you like. A favourite excursion is from the Amalfi coast to Capri (or vice versa), an all-day trip with an evening meal at one of the coastal restaurants; the return in the moonlight is an unforgettable experience.

Sorrento Peninsula
An enjoyable way of seeing the coast from the sea is to take a fast motorboat and travel the full length of the Sorrento coastline, rounding Campanella point.

Punta della Campanella
An ancient temple of Minerva stood on this rocky cliff; before then the site was possibly dedicated to the cult of the Sirens, after whom Sorrento, or Surrentum, may have been named. A paved path leads here from Termini *(see p157)*.

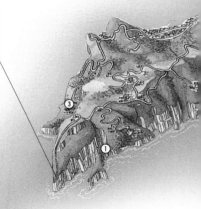

Capri
The island of Capri *(see pp172–3)* is also associated with the Sirens: the promontory of Marina Piccola is called Scoglio delle Sirene. Those who want to stroll on the "blue island" can alight here, otherwise take a boat trip around the island, or simply stop for lunch at one of the many restaurants along the coast *(see pp193–4)*.

0 kilometres 4

0 miles 2

VISITORS' CHECKLIST

Transport
At **Positano** you can hire a boat
from **Lucibello** on the large beach:
Tel 089 87 50 32. **W** **lucibello.it**
At **Capri**, from **Capri Sea Service**:
Via Cristoforo Colombo 64.
Tel 081 837 87 81.
W **capriseaservice.com**

KEY

① **Marina del Cantone** is an
excellent place to stop for lunch:
the local speciality is pasta with
courgettes. The small Recommone
restaurant in the nearby cove is
also good.

② **Isca** is a small island just offshore,
where the Neapolitan actor and
playwright Eduardo De Filippo *(see
p41)* lived. The house now belongs to
his son Luca.

③ **Marina di Massa Lubrense**, a
picturesque fishing harbour, is now
a popular resort.

④ **Sorrento**

Positano

The square, pastel-coloured houses of
Positano *(see pp162–3)* cling to the steep
slopes of Monte Sant'Angelo a tre Pizzi and
Monte Comune overlooking the sea. Lush
gardens and bougainvillea fill the terraces
of these charming houses. This is one of the
most popular resorts on the Amalfi coast,
famous for its bright, patterned textiles.

The Li Galli Archipelago
These islands, known as the Sirenuse until the 19th century, were once considered to be the home of the
mythical Sirens who lured sailors onto the rocks. The clear water between the three crags, Gallo Lungo,
La Rotonda and Castelluccia, makes swimming irresistible.

⑭ The Amalfi Coast

Suspended between sea, sky and earth, state road 163, which twists and turns along the full length of the Amalfi coast, offers stunning views at every corner. Until the 19th century, this stretch of the "divine coast" was isolated and could only be reached by going up difficult mountain paths on mules. By the early 1900s, this very isolation had become the main appeal and the coast began to attract travellers, artists and writers. Visitors of all kinds were drawn to steep-stepped Positano, clinging to tall cliffs; Amalfi with its glorious past as a marine republic; and Ravello, which Wagner chose as "the magic garden of Klingsor", the setting for his opera *Parsifal*. The limestone islands called Li Galli, southwest of Positano, are traditionally the home of the Sirens made famous by Homer in his accounts of the trials of Odysseus. Exploring by boat *(see pp160–61)* enables you to appreciate this astonishing coast at closer quarters.

The steep rise of homes in Positano

Nerano
Road Map C4. 🚌 Sita.

The first stop on the Amalfi coast road is the quiet village of Nerano, administratively part of Massa Lubrense. The road to Nerano goes upwards from Sorrento and cuts across the end of the peninsula near the small village of **Termini**. The sea sparkles in the distance, and the panoramic views are stunning. You can even see Capri and the rocky islands of Li Galli *(see p161)*.

Nerano is perched on a ridge; below is the beach and the town of **Marina del Cantone**, popular mostly because of its small seafront restaurants, some supported by stilts. Walkers can descend on foot among the olive trees to the bay of **Ieranto**.

Positano
Road Map D4. 🔼 4,000. 🚌 Sita. 🚢 from Capri, Naples, Salerno, Amalfi & Sorrento. 🛈 AAST, Via del Saracino 4. **Tel** 089 87 50 67. 🌐 aziendaturismopositano.it

In 1953 John Steinbeck wrote that Positano "...bites deep. It is a dream place that isn't quite real when you are there and becomes beckoningly real after you have gone". The town climbs the hill in steps, with the oldest houses in the upper part of Positano, either faded red or pink, decorated with Baroque stuccoes. The traffic-free street going down to the sea, Via Pasitea, penetrates the atmospheric heart of town with its narrow stepped alleys, houses with vaulted roofs, terraces and tiny gardens that defy the rock. The brightly coloured articles

Positano is famous for – such as cloth bags and beachwear – on display inside and outside the many shops, blend well with the pastel-coloured houses, and the local craftsmen are only too happy to make sandals for you while you wait.

Near the beach is the small church of Santa Maria dell' Assunta, whose cupola is covered with yellow, blue and green majolica tiles. The descent ends at Marina Grande, a pebble beach used by fishing boats, lined with bars and restaurants.

If you want to go to inlets inaccessible by land, or to the little islands of **Li Galli**, or take a trip along the coast, boats are always available. If you prefer to go on foot, you can always swim at Ciumicello, Arienzo or take the easy path to Fornillo beach, with its two watchtowers. There are also craggy grottoes in the inlets, including La Porta, where

View from the clifftop town of Ravello, overlooking the Bay of Salerno

For hotels and restaurants in this region see pp183–5 and pp192–7

there are Palaeolithic and Mesolithic ruins.

Positano can get very busy with day trippers. To escape the tourist hordes and stretch your legs, make the steep ascent to **Montepertuso**, from where a splendid scenic path leads to the quiet mountain village of **Nocelle**, a pleasant place to pause for lunch.

The coast at Praiano

Praiano

Road map D4. 🏔 2,000. 🚌 Sita. This fishing village is perched on the ridge of Monte Sant'Angelo and stretches towards Capo Sottile. The church of San Luca, with 16th-century paintings by Giovan Bernardo Lama, lies in the upper part. In an inlet just outside Praiano is **Marina di Praia**, a small beach surrounded by fishermen's houses. On the road from Positano there are more delightful beaches; just before Praiano is **Vettica Maggiore** and further on, Conca dei Marini. The views are splendid from the terraced square of Vettica Maggiore, by the church of San Gennaro. Before you reach Amalfi, the road widens into an open space where you can go down (by lift) to the **Emerald Grotto**, where stalagmites and stalactites merge to form great columns in the emerald-green water.

🔆 Emerald Grotto

State road 163, km 264 (via lift or stairs); boat from Amalfi or Praiano. **Open** daily (weather permitting). 🔆

Amalfi

Road map D4. 🏔 6,000. 🚌 Sita. ℹ️ AAST, Corso Repubbliche Marinare 27. **Tel** 089 87 11 07. 🇼 **amalfitouristoffice.it**

Tucked in between mountains and sea, Amalfi is a perennial favourite with visitors for its scenic beauty and original architecture. It also has a glorious history as a powerful maritime republic – in the 11th century Amalfi was a rival to the ports of Venice and Genoa.

Little remains to show for the colourful trading history of this small town, whose inhabitants once numbered 60,000. Amalfi's cathedral, the **Duomo di Sant'Andrea**, founded in the 9th century, was rebuilt in Romanesque style in the 11th century and then altered several times. The façade and atrium date from the late 1800s, but the carved bronze doors were cast in Constantinople around the year 1000, and the campanile (1276) is decorated with Arabic-style interlaced arches typical of southern Italian Romanesque. Left of the porch, the Chiostro del Paradiso (Paradise cloister) was built in around 1266 as a cemetery for

Buildings stacked along the Amalfi Coast

prominent citizens. The garden is surrounded by an ornate colonnade with interlaced arches supported by paired columns and with fragments of sculpture from different periods. Near Piazza Duomo is the Arsenal; you can still see the ruins of two naves and the vault. Heading inland from Amalfi, you can visit the Valle dei Mulini (Valley of the Mills), famous for its traditional paper production and the **Museo della Carta** or Paper Museum.

🔆 Duomo di Sant'Andrea

Piazza Duomo. **Open** daily. Mar–Oct: 7:30am–7pm; Nov–Feb: 9–11:30am, 4:30–7pm.

🏛 Museo della Carta

Via delle Cartiere. **Tel** 089 830 45 61. **Open** Mar–Oct: 10am–6:30pm Tue–Sun; Nov–Feb: 10:30am–3:30pm Tue, Wed & Fri–Sun. 🇼 **museodellacarta.it**

Piazza Duomo in Amalfi and the wide steps leading to the cathedral

Ravello

Road map D4. 🏛 2,500. 🚌 Sita.
🚌 AAST, Via Roma 18 bis. **Tel** 089 85
70 96. 🌐 ravellotime.it

Ravello's history is entwined
with that of Amalfi: the former
became part of the Duchy of
Amalfi in the 9th century. The
period of greatest splendour
was the 13th century, when
trade with Sicily and the Orient
was at its height. Somewhat off
the beaten track, Ravello is for
those who love peace and
quiet and stupendous coastal
views. However, it does liven
up for the Ravello Festival
hosted during July and August.
The **Duomo** is dedicated to San
Pantaleone, the town's patron
saint, whose blood is kept here.
The church dates from 1086
and its bronze doors from
1179. Inside is a splendid
raised pulpit, the work of
Niccolò di Bartolomeo da
Foggia in 1272. The twisted
columns, patterned with
mosaics, rest on sculpted lions.

Walking around the town,
Moorish details are evident
in the buildings, in the inner
courtyards and gardens and
the many churches. The narrow
streets and pathways offer
occasional, often unexpected,
glimpses of marvellous
coastal views. Two of Ravello's
architectural highlights are
Villa Rufolo and Villa Cimbrone.

The view from the terrace at Villa Cimbrone

Villa Rufolo, originally built for
the Rufolo family, is a mixture
of 13th- and 14th-century
constructions. It was remodelled in the 19th century by
a Scottish enthusiast, who
preserved the Arabic elements.
It is famed for its courtyard
with double arches and even
more for its tropical gardens,
which inspired Wagner's
Parsifal. The annual Ravello
Festival stages concerts here.

On Via San Francesco, which
takes you to Villa Cimbrone, are
the churches of San Francesco,
of Gothic origin but rebuilt in
the 18th century, and Santa
Chiara, the only one on the
coast that has retained its
gynaeceum (women's gallery).

Villa Cimbrone was built in
the late 1800s by the English-
man Lord Grimthorpe. A range
of ancient architectural
elements were incorporated

in the house. From the villa's
clifftop terrace there is a spellbinding view of the coast to
Punta Licosa and the Paestum
plain. Villa Cimbrone is now
a small hotel *(see p196)*.

Another place well worth
visiting is the church of San
Giovanni del Toro, in the square
of the same name, with its three
tall semicircular apses and
beautifully decorated domes.

🏛 **Duomo**
Piazza Duomo. **Tel** 089 85 83 11.
🌐 chiesaravello.it
Open 9am–noon, 5:30–7pm daily.

🏛 **Villa Rufolo**
Piazza Duomo. **Tel** 089 85 76 21.
Open Apr–Oct: 9am–8pm; Nov–Mar:
9am–4pm. 🔲 🌐 villarufolo.it

🏛 **Villa Cimbrone**
Via Santa Chiara 26. **Tel** 089 85 74 59.
Open 9am–sunset. 🔲
🌐 villacimbrone.com

The ornamental garden of the picturesque Villa Rufolo

For hotels and restaurants in this region see pp183–5 and pp192–7

Maiori, Minori and Cetara

Road map D4 & E4. ⚇ Maiori: 5,600;
Minori: 2,800; Cetara: 2,500. 🚌 Sita.
ℹ️ Maiori: AAST, Corso Regina 73.
🆆 **aziendaturismo-maiori.it**
Cetara: Pro Loco, Corso Garibaldi 15.
🆆 **prolococetara.it**

Ancient *Reginna Minori* and
Maiori are now two popular
seaside resorts with a long and
noble history. **Minori**, where
the Amalfi Maritime Republic
arsenals were situated, dates
back to Roman times. Near
the seafront is the basilica
of Santa Trofimena, built in
the 12th–13th centuries and
then rebuilt in the 1800s. The
church houses the relics of
the ancient patron saint of the
town, Santa Trofimena, in an
elaborate altar in the crypt.

Maiori is like an amphitheatre at the end of the
Tramonti valley. It was
founded in the 9th century
but is today a modern town,
rebuilt after a flood in 1954.
The fine beaches and good
bathing facilities have made it
one of the most visited towns
on the coast. The 18th-century
campanile on 12th-century
Santa Maria a Mare towers
over the Maior stream.

After the lovely beach
of Erchie, **Cetara** was the
easternmost possession of
Amalfi. At the end of the 9th
century it was also a stronghold for the Saracens, who
anchored their ships at Cala di
Fuenti cove. The name perhaps
derives from the Latin *cetaria*,
or tuna-fishing net; the fish,
salted and sold in ceramic
pots, is a typical local product.

A characteristic ceramics shop in Vietri sul Mare

Vietri Sul Mare

Road map: E4. ⚇ 8,600. 🚌 Sita.
ℹ️ Pro Loco, Via O Costabile 4.
🆆 **prolocovietrisulmare.it**

The majolica-decorated
dome and bell tower of San
Giovanni Battista (begun
in the 11th century)
have almost come to
symbolize this town
overlooking the Bay
of Salerno. Vietri sul
Mare is famous as a
seaside resort and
especially for its
ceramics. Cooking
utensils, plates, vases
and tiles have been made
here since the 1400s. In the
mid-18th century, Vietri
became known as the
majolica-makers' district, a
suburb of the Cava de' Tirreni

Majolica plate
made in Vietri

(see below). The most original
items made were the very
popular tiles painted with
religious subjects. You can
still see these tiles in streets,
private homes and churches.
Today you can find
ceramics of all kinds,
catering for all tastes.
The green donkey
used as the logo
on pieces by local
artisans is a relatively
recent invention,
inspired by the
German artist Richard
Doelker in 1922.

The **Museo della Ceramica**
(Ceramics Museum) features
local items from the 1600s
to the present.

🏛️ Museo della Ceramica

Raito di Vietri sul Mare. **Tel** 089 21 18
35. **Open** Jun–Sep: 9am–6pm
Tue–Sun; Oct–May: 9am–3pm
Tue–Sun.

Cava De' Tirreni

Road map E4. ⚇ 54,000. 🚌 Sita.
Lying in a valley in the interior,
Cava de' Tirreni is the only
town in Southern Italy to have
streets lined with porticoes.
Go and see the 11th-century
abbey of Santissima Trinità and
the old Scacciaventi quarter,
whose winding streets block
the wind (*scacciaventi* means
"wind-chaser").

Vietri sul Mare, with the dome and campanile of San Giovanni

⓯ Paestum

Ancient Poseidonia, founded along the Sele River by Greek colonists from Sybaris around 600 BC, became the Roman colony of Paestum in 273 BC. The town began to decline in the 1st century BC due to malaria. Seismic disturbance and deforestation (the local pines made excellent raw material for building ships) had gradually turned the area into marshland. The inhabitants tried to combat the rising water level; they raised their streets and homes, or went to live on higher ground. It was at this time that the Temple of Hera was made into a church by the converted population. Eventually, however, Paestum was abandoned for the nearby town of Capaccio.

The ancient site of Paestum was first unearthed in the 18th century during the building of a road, but most of it remained undiscovered until the 1950s.

★ Temple of Ceres
This temple was built around 500 BC and dedicated to Athena. For centuries, until a votive offering was found nearby, it had been attributed to Ceres.

Temple of Neptune
The name of this temple has been a subject of debate. It was probably dedicated to Apollo or Zeus, but it is commonly known as the Temple of Neptune. Built in 450 BC, it is one of the most complete Greek temples in Europe.

The Three Temples at Paestum

These plans compare the structure of the 3 main temples at Paestum. The Temple of Hera (6th century BC) has 9 front columns, 18 side columns and 2 aisles divided by a row of columns. The Temple of Ceres (6th century BC) has 6 fluted columns at the front, 13 lateral ones and an un-divided *cella*. The largest, Temple of Neptune (5th century BC), has 6 front columns, 14 side ones and its *cella* is divided into 3 aisles by 2 rows of 2-tier columns.

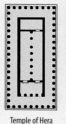

Temple of Hera

Temple of Ceres

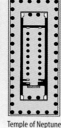

Temple of Neptune

| 0 metres | 100 |
| 0 yards | 100 |

Metope with Dancing Girls
This metope (decorative panel, which is part of a freize), on display in the Paestum Museum, comes from one of the two temples in the sanctuary of Hera Argiva at the mouth of the Sele River. Founded by the first colonists, the complex was discovered in 1934–40 after almost two centuries of searching.

VISITORS' CHECKLIST

Practical Information
Road Map F5. Via Magna Grecia.
Tel 082 881 10 23.
Site: **Open** 8:30am–1 hr before sunset. Museum: **Open** 8:30am–6:30pm daily. **Closed** 1st & 3rd Mon of month. 🅿 ℹ AAST, Via Magna Grecia 887. **Tel** 082 881 10 61. 🅦 **infopaestum.it**; 🅦 **paestumsites.it**

Transport
🆑 Napoli–Salerno: Paestum.

★ Tomb of the Diver
The frescoed slab of the Tomb of the Diver, which dates from about 480 BC, was discovered in 1968 about 1 km (half a mile) from Paestum. The image of the diver on the lid symbolizes the passage to the afterlife. More unique examples of Greek funerary art can be seen in the site's museum.

★ Temple of Hera, the "Basilica"
The absence of religious features led the first archaeologists to believe this was a civic building, when in fact it is the oldest temple in Paestum, built around 530 BC.

KEY

① **Forum**

② **Paestum Museum**

③ **The amphitheatre** (1st century BC–1st century AD) has only been partly excavated.

④ **Baths**

Antonio Joli, The Temples of Paestum (1758)
Temple ruins had a profound effect on local landscape painters, who often used them in their art. Antonio Joli's painting shows the Basilica, the Temple of Neptune and, beyond, the Temple of Ceres.

The Great Waterfall fountain in the Gardens of Royal Palace, Caserta

⑯ Caserta

Road map C1. ⊠ 77,000. 🚌 ATC.
🚆 Caserta. *i* Ente Provinciale
per il Turismo, Palazzo Reale.
Tel 0823 32 11 37. 🖥 **eptcaserta.it**

Caserta was once known as
the village of La Torre, named
after a medieval tower of the
Acquaviva d'Aragona family. It
was only from the mid-1700s,
when Charles of Bourbon
chose the plain at the foot
of the Tifatini mountains as
the site for his new centre of
administration, that the town
began to flourish and expand. It
was at this time that it took the
name of the nearby medieval
village of Caserta Vecchia.

Present-day Caserta is a
modern agricultural town
that was largely rebuilt in the
1950s. A few older buildings
remain, such as the church
and monastery of Sant'Agostino
in Via Mazzini and the former
residence of the Acquaviva
d'Aragona family in Piazza
Vanvitelli. However, the main
reason to visit Caserta is the
Royal Palace *(see pp170–71)*.
Conceived by King Charles as
the heart of his new administrative centre, the palace
was to be a leading European
court, modelled on Versailles
and linked to the capital and
other cities by radial roads and
protected by the fortress at
Capua. This plan to move power
away from the capital city was
influenced by the apparent
vulnerability of the Palazzo
Reale on the Naples seafront

(see pp54–5), a fact that came to
light in 1742 when the English
fleet had threatened to attack.
Once this danger had passed,
however, attention was turned
to the style of the palace. The
king summoned Luigi Vanvitelli,
technical adviser at the Vatican,
to draw up designs.

The palace and the new city
were begun in 1752. When
Charles became king of Spain
and returned to Madrid in 1759,
construction on the Royal Palace
languished. Supervision of the
costly works was handed over
to his son Ferdinand IV and, in
particular, his minister Tanucci.
The new king concentrated
on the magnificent park and
bothered little about the
unfinished palace. Some further
work was carried out, but as the
two semicircular buildings at the
entrance to the grounds illustrate,
these were poor substitutes
for the splendid buildings
proposed in Vanvitelli's
original designs.

Environs
🚌 Caserta Vecchia
Road map C1.

The fascination of Caserta
Vecchia, 10 km (6 miles) along
a winding road northeast of
Caserta, does not lie in the
individual monuments but
the town itself, which has a
remarkably well-preserved
medieval character. This small
hilltop town was probably
founded by the Lombards in
the 8th century and then
came under Norman rule.
When Charles III designed
his new palace, activity
in this lively community
moved into the new town
in the plains. Caserta Vecchia
revolves around the main
square where the cathedral
of San Michele stands.

Nearby is the Gothic
church of Annunziata, with
a marble portal opening
onto a 17th-century portico.
On the eastern side of the
village are the ruins of a 13th-
century castle, dominated
by a 30-m (98-ft) turret.

🏛 Cathedral of San Michele
Piazza del Vescovado 1. **Tel** 0823 37
13 18. **Open** 9am–1pm, 3:30–6pm
daily (to 10:30pm summer).

The cathedral in Caserta Vecchia
was completed in 1153. The
faded yellow and grey tufa
façade is simple, with three
marble portals. Columns on
the triangular tympanum
above the middle portal
are supported by lions. The
14th-century dome has the
interlaced Arabic arches often
seen on Romanesque buildings
in Southern Italy. The interior of

Caserta Vecchia, dominated by the Cathedral of San Michele

the church is lined with irregular columns and stunning majolica tiles. A starlit sky is represented in the dome, with grey stone for the night and white marble stars. To the right of the cathedral stands the dark stone bell tower, added a century later, with an archway over the road.

🏛 Belvedere Reale di San Leucio

Road map C2. Casino del Belvedere: Via del Setificio 7. **Tel** 0823 27 31 51. **Open** 9am–5pm Wed–Mon by appt. 📷 Sat & Sun.

This area, 3 km (2 miles) northwest of Caserta, was purchased by Charles of Bourbon in 1750. Five years later, Ferdinand IV built a royal lodge here, the Casino di Belvedere. In 1789, he ordered an existing building to be made into a silk factory to be used by the local artisans. All that remains of the ambitious project are the workmen's dwellings and the royal lodge, which was also the residence of the silk factory management.

Fresco at Basilica Benedettina di San Michele Arcangelo

🏛 Basilica Benedettina di San Michele Arcangelo

Via Luigi Baia. **Open** 9am–5pm Mon–Fri, 9am–12:30pm & 3–6pm Sat & Sun by appt; call 0823 96 08 17. 📷

This small Romanesque church lies 10 km (6 miles) northwest of Caserta. Built on the ruins of an ancient temple to Diana, Roman goddess of the forest, it was reconstructed in 1073. Many features of the temple were incorporated into the church, such as the delicate Corinthian columns on the portico and the church floor. Inside, a cycle of 11th-century frescoes, painted in Byzantine style by artists from the School of Montecassino, depict stories from the Bible.

The Ideal Village of San Leucio

The picturesque town of San Leucio

San Leucio was founded in 1789 by Ferdinand IV as a village for workers at the local silk factory. The aim of this social experiment was to create a community dedicated to the pursuit of happiness instead of personal profit. The community had its own laws, attributed to the king but in fact written by Antonio Planelli. These were based on reason and morality, included compulsory education, equal inheritance rights for men and women (who, however, had to marry within the community), the abolition of the dowry and medical assistance for the aged and disabled. The 1799 revolution brought about the end of the most ambitious project of the founders, the creation of an entire model city, Ferdinandopoli, although the designs survive. San Leucio is famous for its silk manufacture and the articles produced here are still very much in demand.

🏛 Roman Amphitheatre

Piazza Adriano, Santa Maria Capua Vetere. **Tel** 0823 79 88 64. **Open** 9am–1 hr before sunset Tue–Sun. 📷

The amphitheatre at Santa Maria Capua Vetere, 6 km (4 miles) west of Caserta, dates from the 1st century BC. Second in size only to the Colosseum in Rome, it once had four storeys and subterranean passageways where wild animals were kept in cages. A museum houses artifacts and displays a life-size reproduction of the gladiatorial fights. A short drive away is an underground sanctuary dedicated to the god Mithras. It features a 1st-century BC fresco of Mithras slaying a bull.

🏛 Ponti della Valle

This viaduct, 2 km (1 mile) from Maddaloni, is over 500 m (1640 ft) long and is supported by three arches. It was built between 1753 and 1762 by Vanvitelli to bring water to the Royal Palace at Caserta.

Ruins of the amphitheatre at Santa Maria Capua Vetere

Royal Palace of Caserta

In his memoirs, the architect Vanvitelli says it was the king who designed the Royal Palace. This may have been adulation, or perhaps Charles of Bourbon knew what he wanted – to emulate his favourite models, the Buen Retiro in Madrid and Versailles in France. Vanvitelli drew inspiration from the former for this quadrangular, 1,200-room structure, which was completed 72 years after the architect's death, in 1845. The lower ground floor houses a museum, with photos and exhibits relating to the palace and Caserta culture.

First floor

★ Eighteenth-century Royal Apartments
The Halberdiers Hall connects the upper vestibule and the 18th-century Royal Apartments. The ceiling is adorned by Domenico Mondo's fresco *The Triumph of the Bourbon Arms* (1785).

★ Throne Room
This is one of the large 19th-century salons – in contrast with the smaller 18th-century rooms – in the palace. It was decorated by Gaetano Genovese in 1844–5 and was once filled with elegant French furniture.

Main Entrance

The Upper Vestibule is a grand, imposing space, with its marble-lined walls and an inlaid floor.

For hotels and restaurants in this region see pp183–5 and pp192–7

Great Staircase
The staircase is positioned to one side so as not to interrupt the splendid view of the park from the main doorway.

VISITORS' CHECKLIST

Practical Information
Road Map C1. Via Douhet 22.
Tel 0823 44 80 84. Apartments:
Open 8:30am–7:30pm Wed–Mon.
Park: **Open** 8:30am–7pm (3:30pm winter). 🗓 🅿 ♿ 🆆 **reggia dicaserta.beniculturali.it**

Key (Upper floor)

- 18th-century Royal Apartments
- 19th-century Royal Apartments
- *Terraemotus* exhibition
- Cappella Palatina
- Biblioteca Palatina
- Art Gallery
- Non-exhibition space

Art Gallery
Among the portraits in the Art Gallery is that of Maria Carolina, Ferdinand IV's wife, who occupied four elaborate rooms in the 18th-century apartments.

★ Court Theatre
The theatre is on the ground floor. The rear of the stage could be opened to the air, creating a natural backdrop.

The Park

Luigi Vanvitelli designed this famous park, one of the last examples of the fashion for a regimented garden in the Baroque style. The long central axis is designed on descending levels, creating a remarkable effect with pools and fountains ornamented with splendid sculptures. The play of flowing water culminates in the **Grande Cascata** waterfall, almost 80 m (260 ft) high, also known as the Fountain of Diana and Actaeon.

Next to this is the English Garden, perhaps the first of its kind in Italy. The idea was suggested to Queen Maria Carolina by her friend Lord Hamilton and landscaping work began in 1786.

Flowing water with fountains and waterfalls, the park's central feature

⑰ Capri

Set at the southern end of the Bay of Naples, this small, rugged island has a long history of alluring well-heeled visitors. Roman emperors Augustus and Tiberius enjoyed lengthy stays, the latter ruling for the last decade of his life from his luxurious villa on Capri. In the 19th century, Capri became popular with Grand Tour travellers, ushering in the arrival of foreign politicians, artists and intellectuals. The island remains a tourist mecca, and while it can swell with hordes of day-trippers at peak times, particularly during July and August, its nostalgic charm and stunning natural beauty make it worth the visit.

The Grotta Azzurra, one of the most iconic attractions on Capri

Capri

🏘 8,000. 𝑖 AAST, Via Marina Grande, Piazza Umberto I.
Tel 081 837 06 86.

Straddling the eastern part of the island, the town of Capri is where most excursions around the island begin. The funicular from the harbour in Marina Grande lands you in the heart of the old town, focused around Piazza Umberto I. Known more commonly as the "Piazzetta", the famous square is surrounded by cafés and restaurants, and dominated by the Baroque dome of Santo Stefano. A prime people-watching venue, it is packed both day and night during the summer, with café tables spread from end to end, as locals down espressos while sharing gossip and visitors from far and wide sip cocktails while taking in the scene. The narrow alleys around the piazza are also a delight to explore. Stroll along Via Camerelle, Capri's answer to New York's Fifth Avenue, for luxury brand shopping.

Anacapri

🏘 7,000. 𝑖 AAST, Via Orlandi 59.
Tel 081 837 15 24.

On the slopes of Monte Solaro lies the island's second town, Anacapri. A refreshing contrast to the pomp of Capri town, its relatively quiet lanes and piazzas feature churches, museums and artisanal shops. The bus from Capri stops at Piazza Vittoria, just below the chairlift that carries visitors up Monte Solaro (see p177), the summit of which offers an excellent vantage point for taking in the entire island. A pleasant walking path from the top brings you back to Piazza Vittoria, which also marks the beginning of Via Giuseppe Orlandi, a long lane dotted with artisanal workshops and the **Casa Rossa**, which has the original Roman statues found in the Grotta Azzurra. Opposite Piazza Vittoria is **Villa San Michele**, a museum housed in the remarkable former home of Swedish physician Axel Munthe.

Grotta Azzurra

🏛 Casa Rossa

Via Giuseppe Orlandi 78.
Tel 081 838 21 93. **Open** Apr & May: 10am–5pm Tue–Sun; Jun–Sep: 10am–1:30pm, 5:30–8pm Tue–Sun; Oct: 10am–4pm Tue–Sun. 📷

🏛 Villa San Michele

Viale Axel Munthe 34.
Tel 081 837 14 01. **Open** Mar: 9am–4:30pm daily; Apr & Oct: 9am–5pm daily; May–Sep: 9am–6pm daily; Nov–Feb: 9am–3:30pm daily. 📷

Marina Grande

𝑖 AAST, Banchina del Porto.
Tel 081 837 06 34.

The colourful village of Marina Grande is Capri's main harbour and the arrival point for ferries and hydrofoils from the mainland. Many visitors pass through without stopping, hopping on the old funicular to Capri, or taking a boat tour of the Grotta Azzurra (Blue Grotto), one of the island's most popular sights. This large sea cave is illuminated by an incredible, other-worldly blue light, created by sunlight that streams through the small entrance and is then reflected from the bottom of the sea. (Note that the grotto can close during high tide or rough seas.) Aside from

The town of Anacapri as seen from Monte Solaro

The lively Piazza Umberto I in the town of Capri

0 metres 1000
0 yards 1000

Anacapri

Marina Grande

Capri

Villa Jovis

I Faraglioni

Certosa di San Giacomo

Marina Piccola

Giardini di Augusto

Fishing boats docked at the harbour of Marina Grande

being a great launching point, Marina Grande has a few offerings of its own: excellent seafood restaurants, Roman and Byzantine ruins and the island's largest public beach. From the harbour, near the hydrofoil ticket office, a shuttle boat transfers visitors to Bagni Tiberio, a private beach beside the scattered ruins of Palazzo a Mare, which was once one of Capri's largest imperial villas.

Villa Jovis

Via A Maiuri. **Open** 9am–1 hr before sunset daily.

This retreat built by Emperor Tiberius stands on the mountain named after him, the dramatic setting chosen for its seclusion. Excavations at the site have unearthed baths, apartments, cisterns and "Tiberius's Drop", from which the emperor's victims were supposedly thrown into the sea. The ruins also include the remains of a tower once used to communicate with the mainland.

Certosa di San Giacomo

Certosa di San Giacomo: Viale della Certosa. **Tel** 081 837 6218 (AACST). **Open** 9am–2pm Tue–Sun (also 5–8pm summer).

The Certosa di San Giacomo, a monastery just south of Capri town, is the island's most impressive medieval complex. Founded in 1371, it was expanded by Certosini monks throughout the 16th and 17th centuries and later converted into a prison and barracks. It is now partly occupied by the Karl Wilhelm Diefenbach Museum, in which the German painter's representations of Capri are displayed along with other historical objects.

Marina Piccola

Occupying a picturesque bay dotted with yachts, the laid-back Marina Piccola has bars and restaurants pressed along the water and a few spits of sand wedged between rocky outcrops. It's a great spot for swimming and sunbathing, with views of I Faraglioni, the rock formations soaring up to 109 m (360 ft) out of the sea. Via Mulo, winding down the slope from Capri's Via Roma, offers a shortcut to the town. Though rarely open these days due to renovations, the famous Via Krupp, built by German industrialist Alfred Krupp in 1902, offers a more scenic path from Capri to Marina Piccola, in a series of hairpin bends that make a vertiginous descent to the sea. Even when closed, the path is worth glimpsing from the pleasant **Giardini di Augusto** (Gardens of Augustus).

Giardini di Augusto

Via Matteotti. **Open** 9am–7:30pm daily (Mar–Nov: to 5:30pm).

The I Faraglioni rock formations tower high from the sea

⑱ Ischia

A low-key alternative to its upscale neighbour, Capri, the green and rugged volcanic island of Ischia, centred around the dormant volcano of Mount Epomeo, abounds with natural charm. Visitors will find something different on each coast, from beaches to steep hills, busy nightlife or quiet seclusion. With more than 100 hot springs, the island has also given rise to a thriving wellness industry. Ischia's history stretches back to the 8th century, when it was founded by the same Greek traders who are believed to have established Cumae on the mainland *(see pp142–3)*. Repeated attacks in the early 1300s forced people to take refuge on the small offshore island, which the Aragonese later turned into a castle.

The iconic white church Santa Maria del Soccorso in Forio

Ischia

🏛 20,000. 🚢 🚢 from Naples, Pozzuoli & Procida. ℹ AAST, Via Sogliuzzo 72, Ischia Porto.
Tel 081 507 42 11.
W **infoischiaprocida.it**

The island's largest and busiest town is set on its northeast corner, serving as the main port for ferries and hydrofoils linking Naples, Pozzuoli and Procida. Although the town is roughly divided into Ischia Porto and Ischia Ponte, locals know both parts of the town simply as "Ischia". Beyond the port, Ischia Porto has a flush of luxury hotels and an upscale shopping district along Corso Vittorio Colonna, while Ischia Ponte to the east contains the bulk of the town's attractions. These include a charming main street along the harbour that hosts a lively *passeggiata* (evening stroll), the Roman-style Pilastri aqueduct built in the 16th and 17th centuries

and, just across a 15th-century causeway, the medieval Castello Aragonese, which dominates the view out to sea.

Castello Aragonese

Ischia Ponte. **Tel** 081 99 19 59.
Open 9am–sunset daily.
W **castelloaragoneseischia.com**

This island castle is Ischia's most iconic landmark, towering over the pretty bay of Cartaromana. The fortress traces its history back to the Greeks, although many others have left their mark, including the Romans, Arabs, Angevins and Bourbons, the latter having used the castle as a prison. It is connected to Ischia Ponte by a narrow bridge, and within the fortified walls are gardens, frescoed catacombs and cathedrals. A variety of architectural styles are represented, from the Angevin cathedral of the Assunta to the hexagonal church of San Pietro a Pantaniello.

Forio

🏛 18,000.

Set on the west coast of Ischia, Forio is the island's second largest town, known for its magnificent gardens and iconic church, the Santa Maria del Soccorso. The English composer Sir William Walton lived to the north of the town at the now-famous **Giardini la Mortella** (Mortella Gardens). His wife, Lady Susana Walton, spent half a century cultivating the lush gardens, which contain a dazzling array of exotic flora. To the south of the town is the beautiful Citara beach. Nearby, there are a number of excellent thermal spa options.

🌿 Giardini la Mortella

Via F Calise 39. **Open** Apr–Nov: 9am–2 hrs before sunset Tue, Thu, Sat & Sun.

Giardini la Mortella

Forio

Citara beach

Castello Aragonese stands tall over the the bay of Cartaromana

For hotels and restaurants in this region see pp183–5 and pp192–7

Sant'Angelo
🏠 1,250.

At the southern end of the
island is the picturesque town
of Sant'Angelo, its small marina
and pleasantly pedestrianized
centre spread beneath vertical
cliffs. Originally a humble
fishing village, it is now known
for its thermal parks, great
beaches and coastal views.
Several beaches in both
directions offer pretty views
of the town, the most famous
among them being Maronti
beach, one of Ischia's largest,
with access along a steep and
winding road from Sant'Angelo.
From here, as well as the town,
taxi boats can be hired to take
visitors to coves otherwise
inaccessible by land. Between
Maronti and Sant'Angelo is a
smaller beach, Le Fumarole,
boasting volcanic steam jets

The habourside of the idyllic spa town Casamicciola Terme

that warm the sand – so much
so that the locals sometimes
use it for cooking food.

Casamicciola Terme
🏠 8,000. 🚌 🚌 from Naples,
Pozzuoli & Procida.

Set on the northern coast
between Lacco Ameno and
Ischia Porto, the spa town of

The resort village of Sant'Angelo

Casamicciola Terme has
attracted visitors since
Roman times. While an
earthquake in 1883
caused considerable
damage to the town,
it has retained some
of its Art Nouveau
architecture, and today
the atmosphere is
decidedly chic, with
plenty of glamorous
villas, gardens and
yachts around the
pretty marina. The

town's adjacent port connects
it to Naples and Pozzuoli,
serving as an alternative arrival
point to Ischia Porto.

Lacco Ameno
🏠 4,700.

The smallest of Ischia's main
towns, Lacco Ameno lies to the
west of Casamicciola on the
northern side of the island. Its
charming main square is named
after the town's patron saint,
Santa Restituta. There are several
good beaches and thermal spas
around the town, most notably
San Montano beach, with
shallow water in a protected
cove. Just up from the beach is
the **Negombo Giardini Termali**
(Negombo Thermal Gardens),
one of Ischia's very best. Off the
main pier from the centre of
town is the Fungo di Lacco
Ameno, a prominent mushroom-
shaped rock that reportedly
marks where Greek colonists
first landed. The town also has
several museums, including the
Museo di Pithecusae, where
items from the Greek settlement
are displayed, and the **Museo
di Santa Restituta**, which
illustrates island life as it was
in Greek and Roman times.

🔲 **Negombo Giardini Termali**
San Montano Bay. **Open** late Apr–
mid-Oct: 8:30am–7pm daily.

🏛 **Museo di Pithecusae**
Corso A Rizzoli. **Open** 9:30am–
1pm, 3–7pm (4–8pm summer)
Tue–Sun.

🏛 **Museo di Santa Restituta**
Piazza Santa Restituta.
Open 9:30am–12:30pm, 4–6pm
(5–7pm summer) daily.
Closed Sun noon.

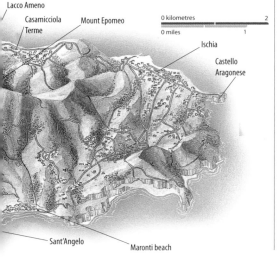

⑩ Procida

Road map A3. 🏛 11,000.
🚢 from Naples & Pozzuoli. 🛈 Pro
Loco: Piazza S Antonio 6. **Tel** 081 010
07 24. AACST, Via Sogliuzzo 72, Ischia.
Tel 081 507 42 11.
Ⓦ **prolocodiprocida.it**

Much smaller than Capri and Ischia and also much less affected by tourism, the third island in the Bay of Naples is a favourite with those who love the simplicity and traditions of the local culture. This is the enchanting world that author Elsa Morante, recollecting her many visits here, evoked in *Isola di Arturo* (Arthur's Island). Procida's economy is sustained not only by tourism but, to a large extent, by the money its emigrants send back home to their families.

Deeply rooted local traditions are evident in the various festivals; for example, the Good Friday procession *(see p44)* that descends to the modern port from so-called Terra Murata – the rise dominated by the Abbey of San Michele – or the Graziella celebration that takes place in the port in mid-August.

The multi-coloured houses resting against the tufa rock make the island architecture one of the most distinctive in the region. Unique to the island are the vaulted buildings; originally built as winter boat shelters and later enlarged, acquiring among other things façades with arches and half-arches that frame the doors and windows, terraces, loggias and long external staircases. You can see this type of architecture, albeit in a partially modernized version, on your arrival in Procida in Marina Grande near the area

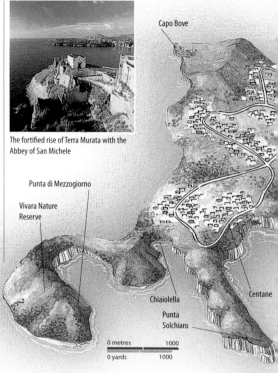

The fortified rise of Terra Murata with the Abbey of San Michele

Capo Bove

Punta di Mezzogiorno

Vivara Nature Reserve

Chiaiolella

Punta Solchiaro

Centane

0 metres   1000
0 yards   1000

Pastel-coloured buildings lining Marina Grande

For hotels and restaurants in this region see pp183–5 and pp192–7

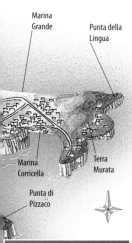

Typical Procida architecture

Walking on the Islands

While Procida is almost flat – the highest point, Terra Murata, is 91 m (300 ft) above sea level – Capri and Ischia are steep-sided. On Capri (see pp172–3), the path connecting Monte Solaro (589 m, 1930 ft)) to Anacapri is delightful and practicable even for lazy visitors, though there is always the option of the chairlift. Walkers will be well rewarded by the striking view and the 14th-century Santa Maria di Cetrella monastery on Marina Piccola (a detour halfway up). Experienced hikers come back down by the "Passetiello" path which includes a stretch directly above the sea and leads to Capri.

The highest mountain in the bay is the extinct Epomeo volcano (788 m, 2580 ft) on Ischia (see pp174–5). A climb up the cone traditionally starts at night from Fontana so as to admire the view at dawn. The view takes in the island itself, the Bay of Naples and the Tyrrhenian coast up to Roccamonfina and the Pontine Islands. A rough dirt track leads to the church of San Nicola (1459) and the adjoining monastery, both hewn out of the tufa rock. On your way down you can choose the road to Forio or Casamicciola.

Looking out over Capri from the Monte Solaro chairlift

built up in the 17th and 18th centuries, and at the small, popular Chiaiolella port on the other side of the island. The Abbey of San Michele, dominating Terra Murata, dates back to 1026, though it has since been rebuilt. Marina Corricella, at the foot of Terra Murata, has been virtually untouched by modern times; the soil is very fertile and the gardens here are filled with lemon trees.

Procida also has many splendid beaches, including Ciraccio, across the western shore and dotted with snack stands; Chiaia, on the southeastern cove; and Pozzo Vecchio, made famous by the film *Il Postino* (1994), which was filmed there.

🏛 **Abbey of San Michele**
Via Terra Murata 89.
Tel 081 896 76 12.
Open 10am–12:45pm, 3–5pm Tue–Sat, 10am–12:45pm Sun & Mon.
🌐 abbaziasanmicheleprocida.it

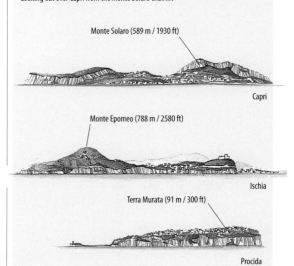

Monte Solaro (589 m / 1930 ft)

Capri

Monte Epomeo (788 m / 2580 ft)

Ischia

Terra Murata (91 m / 300 ft)

Procida

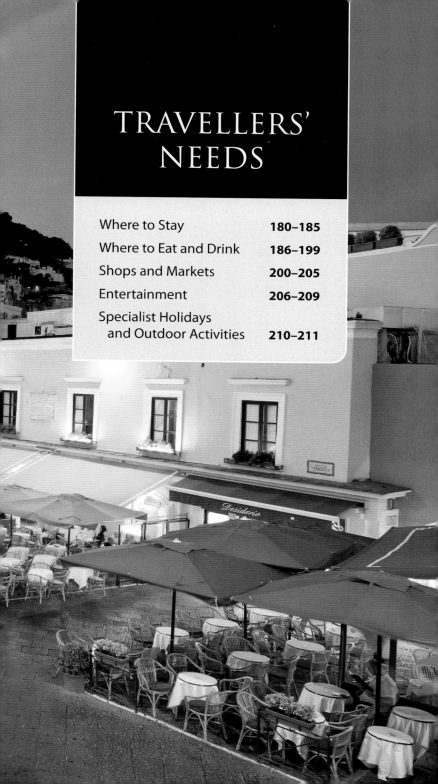

TRAVELLERS' NEEDS

WHERE TO STAY

The fascination and enchantment of Naples and the surrounding countryside have drawn visitors here for many centuries. Kings and queens, revolutionaries in exile, poets, writers and composers are among the host of celebrities who have wintered at the foot of Mount Vesuvius since the 18th century. Naples offers a wide range of accommodation options, both in terms of style and budget, from simple B&Bs to grand luxury hotels with infinity pools and magnificent views along the coast. In traditional holidaying areas – along the Amalfi coastline, around Sorrento and on the islands – expect accommodation rates to be higher, especially during peak seasons. This section and the lists of hotels on pages 182–5 will help you make your choice.

Prices and Grading

Italian hotels are classified by a star-rating system, from one, the lowest, to five stars. Prices including taxes are displayed inside each room. Breakfast may not be included, and if not can be an expensive item compared with a coffee and croissant in the nearest local bar. It is always worth asking about discounts, particularly off season, and it is often possible to negotiate special rates for groups or longer stays. On average, single rooms cost two-thirds of the double room rate. In holiday-resort areas prices differ steeply between low and high season; during the peak summer months minimum night stays or half-board may be required.

Booking and Paying

You should book well in advance if you have special requests such as a room with a good view. During July and August, the peak holiday season, hotels along the coast and on the islands get very full, so once

Precipitous terraced gardens and infinity pool, Monastero Santa Rosa *(p184)*

again you must book ahead of time. Naples can also get busy, particularly if there are special events scheduled, and advance booking is recommended. If you do need to find a hotel on arrival, the local tourist offices can advise you.

When booking, you will probably be asked to pay a deposit, which can be done by credit card. When you arrive at your hotel, the reception will ask for your passport; this is to register travellers with the police, a legal formality. By law, the hotel must give you a receipt when you check out.

Where to Look

EPT, the Italian Tourist Board, *(see p215)* publishes lists of hotels, *pensioni* and camp sites. You can also make inquiries at the **Associazione degli Albergatori Napoletani** (Neapolitan Hotel Owners' Association). To stay in the countryside in a private home or on a farm, a great option for families, try the **Agriturist** website. Alternatively, to rent an apartment or home in Naples check Airbnb (airbnb.com).

Budget Accommodation

Naples has a growing selection of hostels. One of the best is **Hostel of the Sun**, opposite the Molo Beverello ferry terminal. Hostelling International operates several hostels in the region, with discounts for members of the YHA (Youth Hostel Association) *(see p215)*.

Lobby of Hotel Amleto, near the ruins of Pompeii *(p184)*

◄ Piazza Umberto, on the island of Capri

Camping

Camp sites, usually open from April to October, are indicated by small brown road signs. **Vulcano Solfatara** can be reached by the Naples metro (Pozzuoli stop). It has bungalows with 2–4 beds, as well as a restaurant, swimming pool and a mini-market. Along the coast, at Meta di Sorrento, is **Bleu Village**, while Sorrento offers **Nube d'Argento**, in the middle of an orange grove, and **Santa Fortunata Campogaio**, overlooking the sea. On Ischia, try **Eurocamping dei Pini**, about 1 km (half a mile) from the centre, or **Mirage**, on Maronti beach. **Punta Serra** is a good camp site on Procida.

Recommended Hotels

The accommodation options featured in this guide – listed by area and then by price – have been selected across a wide price range for their excellent facilities and unique appeal. They have been divided into a number of categories to help you make the best choices for your trip.

Luxury hotels provide five-star service and facilities, most with stunning rooms, panoramic views and award-winning restaurants. You should expect impeccable service at these establishments.

Historic hotels can make for an atmospheric stay. They are set in historically significant buildings, whether a former monastery or a palazzo that once belonged to an aristocratic family.

Bay of Salerno views from the deckchairs on Casa Angelina's terrace *(see p185)*

Boutique hotels place an emphasis on smart design. They generally offer the same facilities and services as larger hotels, but in a more intimate setting.

Character hotels are independent places that may be family run. Although some are in interesting buildings, the emphasis may not be on historic authenticity, with rooms furnished in contemporary style.

B&Bs offer all the features of a hotel in a more familial setting, with an emphasis on service and comfort. They are excellent options for the budget-minded traveller and those seeking accommodation with character.

Entries labelled DK Choice are outstanding in some way. They might offer exceptional value for money, particularly good service or a romantic ambience. Whatever the reason, a DK Choice will provide an especially memorable stay.

Refined decor at one of Italy's best hotels, the Caruso *(see p185)*

DIRECTORY

Where to Look

Agriturist
Ⓦ agriturist.it

Associazione degli Albergatori Napoletani
Piazza Carità 32. **Tel** 081 552 02 05.
Ⓦ napleshotels.na.it

Budget Accommodation

Hi Hostels
Ⓦ hihostels.com

Hostel of the Sun
Via Melisurgo 15. **Tel** 081 420 63 93. Ⓦ hostelnapoli.com

Camping

Bleu Village
Via Carracciolo 199 (Meta di Sorrento). **Tel** 081 878 65 57.
Ⓦ bleuvillage.com

Eurocamping dei Pini
Via delle Ginestre 28 (Ischia). **Tel** 081 98 20 69.
Ⓦ ischia.it/camping

Mirage
Spiaggia dei Maronti (Barano d'Ischia). **Tel** 081 99 05 51.
Ⓦ campingmirage.it

Nube d'Argento
Via Capo 21 (Sorrento). **Tel** 081 878 13 44. Ⓦ nubedargento.com

Punta Serra
Via Serra 3 (Procida). **Tel** 081 896 95 19.
Ⓦ campingserra.altervista.org

Santa Fortunata Campogaio
Via Capo 39 (Sorrento). **Tel** 081 807 35 79. Ⓦ santafortunata.eu

Vulcano Solfatara
Via Solfatara 161 (Pozzuoli).
Ⓦ solfatara.it

Where to Stay

Naples

Toledo and Castel Nuovo

DK Choice

Cappella Vecchia 11 €
B&B **Map** 6 F2
Vicolo Santa Maria A Cappella Vecchia 11, 80121
Tel 081 240 51 17
W cappellavecchia11.it
This friendly B&B is set in an elegant neighbourhood and offers a welcoming stay in brightly decorated rooms. It is within easy walking distance of the trendy restaurants and shops of Chiaia, as well as bustling Piazza Plebiscito, the historic district sights and the waterfront. Service is helpful and friendly, and Wi-Fi is free.

Covo degli Angioini €
B&B **Map** 7 B2
Via Melisurgo 44, 80133
Tel 081 014 02 38
W covodegliangioini.it
This well appointed B&B has stylish and comfortable rooms. Conveniently located near to Castel Nuovo and the port, it is ideal for ferry trips across to Capri.

Chiaja Hotel de Charme €€
Boutique **Map** 6 F2
Via Chiaia 216, 80121
Tel 081 41 55 55
W chiaiahotel.com
Set on the first floor of a historic palazzo, on pedestrian-only Via Chiaia, this intimate hotel is close to Piazza Plebiscito. It offers wonderful Italian hospitality.

An elegantly furnished bedroom at San Francesco al Monte *(see p183)*

DK Choice

La Ciliegina Lifestyle Hotel
Boutique €€
 Map 7 A2
Via Paolo Emilio Imbriani 30, 80133
Tel 081 197 1 88 00
W cilieginahotel.it
This stylish hotel is dedicated to excellent service, with bright, Mediterranean-themed rooms. Relax on the multilevel terrace (with Jacuzzi and sun beds), which offers views of the glass dome of Galleria Umberto I, historic sights and even Vesuvius.

Hotel Palazzo Alabardieri €€
Historic **Map** 6 F2
Via Alabardieri 38, 80121
Tel 081 41 52 78
W palazzoalabardieri.it
Housed near Piazza dei Martiri in a former convent, this elegant hotel offers a comfortable stay.

Mercure Angioino €€
Character **Map** 7 B2
Via Depretis 123, 80133
Tel 081 491 01 11
W mercure.com
Located near the port, this hotel is a perfect base for ferry trips, and has a clean, modern design, plus a lovely rooftop terrace.

Spaccanapoli

Grand Hotel Europa €
Character **Map** 4 F4
Corso Meridionale 14, 80134
Tel 081 26 75 11
W grandhoteleuropa.com
Conveniently near Napoli Centrale train station, this hotel offers a variety of rooms decorated with a modern take on classic Neapolitan style.

I Visconti €
B&B **Map** 3 A5
Via Pasquale Scura 77, 80134
Tel 081 552 91 24
W napolibandb.it
Set on the second floor of a palazzo, this B&B is comfortably appointed. Charming terrace.

Decumani Hotel de Charme €€
Boutique **Map** 9 C4
Via San Giovanni Maggiore Pignatelli 15, 80134
Tel 081 551 81 88
W decumani.com
Located in an elegant 17th-century building, this boutique hotel boasts stunning features, luxuriously appointed rooms and attentive service.

Palazzo Decumani €€
Boutique **Map** 3 C5
Via del Grande Archivio 8, 80138
Tel 081 420 13 79
W palazzodecumani.com
This contemporary hotel has period features and offers a stylish and urban stay in Naples' historic centre.

UNA €€
Business **Map** 4 E5
Piazza Garibaldi 9/10, 80142
Tel 081 563 69 01
W unahotels.it
A good choice for business travellers. Close to Napoli Centrale train station. Clean and functional rooms with a rooftop terrace.

Decumano Maggiore

L'Alloggio dei Vassalli €
B&B **Map** 9 B5
Via Donnalbina 56, 80134
Tel 081 551 51 18
W bandbnapoli.it
This appealing B&B in a historic palazzo has wooden beams, antique furniture, smart rooms and is right next to a spa.

Belle Arti Resort €
B&B **Map** 3 B4
Via S. Maria di Costantinopoli 27, 80138
Tel 081 557 10 62
W belleartiresort.com
Located in a 17th-century building, this B&B has a refined style bringing together historic frescoes and modern design.

Donna Regina €
B&B **Map** 3 C3
Via Luigi Settembrini 80, 80139
Tel 081 44 67 99
W discovernaples.net
This B&B overlooks two churches and is filled with both heirlooms and modern art, the owner being a painter and collector.

Costantinopoli 104 €€
Boutique **Map** 3 B4
Via S. Maria di Costantinopoli 104, 80138
Tel 081 557 10 35
W costantinopoli104.it
This Art Nouveau villa has stylish rooms, a courtyard and garden, with a sun terrace and small pool.

Port Alba Relais €€
B&B **Map** 3 B5
Via Port'Alba 33, 80134
Tel *081 564 51 71*
w portalbarelais.com
With views of Piazza Dante from its
smart rooms, this B&B is near the
National Archaeological Museum.

Capodimonte and I Vergini

Casa d'Anna €€
B&B **Map** 3 B3
Via dei Cristallini 138, 80137
Tel *081 44 66 11*
w casadanna.it
A beautifully furnished B&B
with gorgeous artworks and a
Mediterranean roof garden.

Palazzo Caracciolo €€
Boutique **Map** 4 D3
Via Carbonara 112, 80139
Tel *081 016 01 11*
w accorhotels.com
Once the regal home of the
aristocratic Caracciolo family, this
hotel promises an elegant stay.

Vomero

DK Choice

San Francesco al Monte €€
Historic **Map** 2 F5
*Corso Vittorio Emanuele 328,
80135*
Tel *081 423 91 11*
w sanfrancescoalmonte.it
Once a Franciscan monastery,
this hotel is nestled on the
hillside just below Castel
Sant'Elmo with views over the
city and Bay of Naples from the
rooftop garden and pool. The
rooms – formerly monks' cells –
are beautifully decorated and
have luxurious bathrooms.

Grand Hotel Parker's €€€
Luxury **Map** 5 C1
Corso Vittorio Emanuele 135, 80121
Tel *081 761 24 74*
w grandhotelparkers.it
With fine views from its hillside
location, this luxurious hotel
boasts elegant rooms.

Castel dell'Ovo and Chiaia

Excelsior €€
Luxury **Map** 7 A4
Via Partenope 48, 80121
Tel *081 764 01 11*
w excelsior.it
Sitting along the waterfront with
views of Castel dell'Ovo and
Vesuvius, this hotel boasts fine
rooms with elegant decor.

A plush bedroom suite at the Grand Hotel Vesuvio

Hotel Micalò €€
Boutique **Map** 5 C2
Riviera di Chiaia 88, 80122
Tel *081 761 71 31*
w micalo.it
Decorated with contemporary
art by local artists, this hotel has
stylish and modern rooms.

Hotel Paradiso €€
Character **Map** 5 A4
Via Catullo 11, 80122
Tel *081 247 51 11*
w hotelparadisonapoli.it/
Rooms are spacious, elegant and
most feature a balcony. Wonderful
views from the rooftop bar.

DK Choice

Hotel Rex €€
Character **Map** 7 A4
Via Palepoli 12, 80132
Tel *081 764 93 89*
w hotel-rex.it
Just one street back from the
seafront and near the picturesque Borgo Marinaro and Castel
dell'Ovo, this hotel occupies
an Art Nouveau building with
spacious rooms, which are
decorated with paintings of
Naples. Excellent value for a
great location. No lift.

Miramare €€
Character **Map** 7 B4
Via Nazario Sauro 24, 80132
Tel *081 764 75 89*
w hotelmiramare.com
Furnished with antiques through-
out, Miramare offers wonderful
views of the sea and Vesuvius.

Palazzo Turchini €€
Boutique **Map** 7 B2
Via Medina 21/22, 80132
Tel *081 551 06 06*
w palazzoturchini.it
This venerable hotel, which
was formerly a 16th-century
orphanage, has good-sized
rooms and a rooftop terrace.

DK Choice

Grand Hotel Vesuvio €€€
Luxury **Map** 7 A4
Via Partenope 45, 80121
Tel *081 764 00 44*
w vesuvio.it
The icon of luxury in Naples,
the prestigious Grand Hotel
Vesuvio in Santa Lucia
overlooks Castel dell'Ovo and
the Bay of Naples, with views
of Vesuvius in the distance.
Decorated with antiques,
the rooms are sumptuous, and
many have either a balcony
or a terrace. The hotel also
features a spa, a gym and an
excellent rooftop restaurant
(see p190).

Pompeii and the Amalfi Coast

Amalfi

Albergo Lidomare €€
Character **Road Map** D4
Via Largo Piccolomini 9, 84010
Tel *089 87 13 32*
w lidomare.it
A welcoming, family-run
hotel with spacious rooms,
ceramic tiled floors and lovely
sea views, Albergo Lidomare
can be found on a quiet piazza
near the Duomo in the city's
historic centre.

Floridiana Hotel €€
Character **Road Map** D4
Salita Brancia 1, 84011
Tel *089 873 63 73*
w hotelfloridiana.it
A friendly hotel conveniently
located in the historic
centre of Amalfi. It has a
beautiful breakfast salon
lined with frescoes and
comfortable bedrooms
freshly decorated in blues
and yellows.

For more information on types of hotels *see p181*

DK Choice

Hotel Aurora   €€
Boutique   **Road Map** D4
Piazzale dei Protontini 7, 84011
Tel *089 87 12 09*
W aurora-hotel.it
Overlooking a rocky beach just
outside the port of Amalfi, this
family-run hotel is a pleasant
five-minutes' stroll along the
harbour from the historic
centre. This unique setting
offers private beach access
and fantastic views from the
spacious terrace lounge.

**Grand Hotel
Convento di Amalfi**   €€€
Historic   **Road Map** D4
Via Annunziatella 46, 84011
Tel *089 873 67 11*
W ghconventodiamalfi.com
Set in a beautifully remodelled
12th-century monastery clinging
to the cliffs above Amalfi, this
luxurious hotel has three excellent
restaurants and wonderful views.

Hotel Luna Convento   €€€
Historic   **Road Map** D4
Via Pantaleome Comite 33, 84011
Tel *089 87 10 02*
W lunahotel.it
Set in a 13th-century convent,
this hotel features a peaceful
cloister, beautiful rooms, a
seaside pool and great views.

Atrani

Palazzo Ferraioli   €€
Boutique   **Road Map** D4
Via Campo 16, 84010
Tel *089 87 26 52*
W palazzoferraioli.it
Tucked away in a picturesque
fishing village a short walk from
Amalfi, this hotel has bright,
contemporary decor.

Capri

Casa Mariantonia   €€
Boutique   **Road Map** B4
Via G. Orlandi 180, 80071 Anacapri
Tel *081 837 29 23*
W casamariantonia.com
Set amid citrus gardens, this is
a lovely spot to escape to. Stylish
rooms, a serene pool and an
excellent wine bar.

Villa Mimosa Resort   €€
B&B   **Road Map** B4
Via Nuova del Faro 48a, 80071 Anacapri
Tel *081 837 17 52*
W mimosacapri.com
This friendly B&B features terraces
off each room with delightful fur-
nishings, sea views and a garden.

Endless sea views from the lofty terrace at
Monastero Santa Rosa, Conca dei Marini

Grand Hotel Quisisana   €€€
Luxury   **Road Map** C4
Via Camerelle 2, 80073
Tel *081 837 07 88*
W quisisana.com
The reigning queen of luxury
offers a stunning pool and spa
and is located on Capri Town's
most fashionable street.

Hotel la Minerva   €€€
Boutique   **Road Map** C4
Via Occhio Marino 8, 80073
Tel *081 837 70 67*
W laminervacapri.com
This five-storey hotel offers flower-
filled terraces and sea views near
the scenic Punta Tragara.

J K Place Capri   €€€
Luxury   **Road Map** C4
*Via Provinciale Marina Grande 225,
80073*
Tel *081 838 40 01*
W jkcapri.com
This intimate hotel captures
Capri's refined charm with its
elegant rooms, attention to
detail and private villa setting.

Conca dei Marini

Monastero Santa Rosa   €€€
Historic   **Road Map** D4
Via Roma 2, 84010
Tel *089 832 11 99*
W monasterosantarosa.com
Clinging to the cliffside, this refur-
bished 17th-century monastery
offers luxury in one of the Amalfi
Coast's most spectacular settings.

Ischia

Hotel Villa Bianca   €
Character   **Road Map** A3
Via G. Mazzella 262, 80075, Forio
Tel *081 90 71 56*
W hotelvillabianca.com
This hotel offers traditional rooms
with colourful decor, within
walking distance of Citara beach.

DK Choice

Albergo Il Monastero   €€
Historic   **Road Map** A3
*Castello Aragonese, 80077, Ischia
Ponte*
Tel *081 99 24 35*
W albergoilmonastero.it
This hotel is set in a 16th-
century convent atop the
Aragonese Castle *(see p175)*.
The simple rooms reflect the
austerity of the remarkable
historic site. The sea-view
rooms showcase the island's
natural beauty.

Il Moresco Grand Hotel   €€€
Luxury   **Road Map** A3
*Via Emanuele Gianturco 16, 80077,
Ischia Porto*
Tel *081 98 13 55*
W ilmoresco.it
Guests at this luxury hotel can
enjoy a tranquil garden-setting
filled with thermal pools, as well
as access to a private beach.

Massa Lubrense

Relais Blu   €€€
Boutique   **Road Map** C4
Via Roncato 60, 80061
Tel *081 878 95 52*
W relaisblu.com
Practically at the tip of the Sorrento
Peninsula, the luxurious Relais pro-
vides spectacular views across the
sea from Capri to Ischia to Vesuvius.

Paestum

Hotel dei Templi   €€
Character   **Road Map** F5
Via Tavernelle 64, 84063
Tel *082 881 17 47*
W hoteldeitempli.it
Near the ancient site of Paestum,
this welcoming hotel offers a
rustic feel and views of the ruins.

Pompeii

Hotel Amleto   €
Character   **Road Map** D3
Via Bartolo Longo 10, 80045
Tel *081 863 10 04*
W hotelamleto.it
Walking distance from the ruins
of Pompeii, this family and
business-friendly hotel is a
convenient option.

Hotel Diana   €€
Character   **Road Map** D3
Vicolo San Abbondio 12, 80045
Tel *081 863 12 64*
W pompeihotel.com
A comfortable, simply furnished
place to stay with pleasant public
areas and a roof terrace.

Positano

Hotel California €€
Character **Road Map** D4
Via Cristoforo Colombo 141, 84017
Tel *089 87 53 82*
ⓦ hotelcaliforniapositano.it
Set in an 18th-century building, once occupied by a noble family. Rooms are large with sea views.

DK Choice

Miramare €€€
Character **Road Map** D4
Via Trara Genoino 27, 84017
Tel *089 87 50 02*
ⓦ miramarepositano.it
Surrounded by Positano's cascade of buildings, this small hotel captures the charms of the Amalfi Coast. It offers friendly service and sea-view balconies.

Le Sirenuse €€€
Luxury **Road Map** D4
Via Cristoforo Colombo 30, 84017
Tel *089 87 50 66*
ⓦ sirenuse.it
Said to be the finest hotel on the Amalfi Coast, Le Sirenuse boasts exquisite rooms and possibly the world's most glamorous pool.

Praiano

Hotel Margherita €€
Character **Road Map** D4
Via Umberto I, 70, 84010
Tel *089 87 46 28*
ⓦ hotelmargherita.info
A family home converted into a hotel with a pool, it is worth paying extra for a balcony and sea view.

Casa Angelina €€€
Luxury **Road Map** D4
Via Gennaro Capriglione 147, 84010
Tel *089 813 13 33*
ⓦ casangelina.com
This hotel features contemporary furnishings and sea views, and is close to several tourist spots.

Tramonto d'Oro €€€
Character **Road Map** D4
Via Gennaro Capriglione 119, 84010
Tel *089 87 49 55*
ⓦ tramontodoro.it
With a name meaning "golden sunset", this hotel offers spectacular views over Positano.

Procida

La Casa sul Mare €€
Character **Road Map** A3
Via Salita Castello 13, 80079
Tel *081 896 87 99*
ⓦ lacasasulmare.it
This harbour hotel, set inside a well-maintained 18th-century aristocratic building, has a sea balcony where breakfast is served. The hotel is close to Terra Murata and other tourist spots.

Ravello

Hotel Parsifal €€
Historic **Road Map** D4
Viale Gioacchino d'Anna 5, 84010
Tel *089 85 71 44*
ⓦ hotelparsifal.com
Set in a convent dating from 1288, this hotel offers friendly service and a beautiful, atmospheric setting.

Villa San Michele €€
Boutique **Road Map** D4
Via Carusiello 2, 84010
Tel *089 87 22 37*
ⓦ hotel-villasanmichele.it
Garden terraces cascade down to the sea at this beautiful villa with private sea access.

DK Choice

Hotel Caruso €€€
Luxury **Road Map** D4
Piazza San Giovanni del Toro 2, 84010
Tel *089 85 88 01*
ⓦ hotelcaruso.it
This hotel is considered one of the finest in the country, let alone on the Amalfi Coast. Escape to a tranquil and luxurious setting complete with gorgeous architectural details, sumptuous bedrooms, a spa and a stunning infinity pool overlooking the Bay of Salerno.

Palazzo Avino €€€
Luxury **Road Map** D4
Via San Giovanni del Toro 28, 84010
Tel *089 81 81 81*
ⓦ palazzoavino.com
This stunning hotel is set inside the former 12th-century Palazzo Sasso and was converted to a hotel in 1880. Picturesque architectural details with an elegant restaurant.

Salerno

B&B Verdi €
B&B **Road Map** E3
Via Indipendenza 5, 84121
Tel *345 341 63 72*
ⓦ bbverdi.it
Charming rooms and centrally located near the Teatro Verdi, historic centre and waterfront. Exceptional breakfast.

Sorrento

DK Choice

Il Roseto €€
B&B **Road Map** C4
Corso Italia 304, 80067
Tel *081 878 10 38*
ⓦ ilrosetosorrento.com
Feel at home at this tranquil B&B set in a lemon garden. Just a short stroll from the historic centre, Il Roseto is the perfect spot to relax after a day of sightseeing. Pool and free parking.

Grand Hotel Excelsior Vittoria €€€
Luxury **Road Map** C4
Piazza Tasso 34, 80067
Tel *081 877 71 11*
ⓦ exvitt.it
With the refined elegance of bygone days, this luxury hotel has beautiful grounds and a Michelin-starred restaurant. The bar and facilities such as jacuzzi and spa are the icing on the cake.

Vietri sul Mare

Hotel Lloyd's Baia €€
Character **Road Map** E4
Via Enrico de Marinis 2, 84019
Tel *089 763 31 11*
ⓦ lloydsbaiahotel.it
Built into the side of a cliff with a lift down to a private beach, this large hotel offers business facilities, family rooms and a comfortable stay.

Sun beds and parasols on the pool terrace at Casa Angelina, Praiano

For more information on types of hotels *see p181*

WHERE TO EAT AND DRINK

The region known to the Romans as *Campania felix* (happy country) revels in food, especially the fruit, vegetables and vines that grow in abundance on every available slope. Neapolitan cuisine is well known throughout the world, thanks to the emigrants who took pizza and pasta with them wherever they went. Neapolitans have never given up their passion for good food, and eating is a social occasion here – all important events are celebrated with huge meals that may last half a day. Key elements in Neapolitan cuisine are pasta, olive oil and tomatoes, but all along the coast and on the islands you'll find the freshest seafood and fish dishes, from simple pasta sauces to generous fish stews. This is also the home of ice cream, and delectable cakes and pastries.

Types of Restaurants and Bars

Naples and the outlying area offer a wide choice of restaurants, trattorias and bars to suit all budgets. A *ristorante* may be smarter (and more expensive) than a *trattoria*, which is generally much less formal. Every part of Campania has its own specialities and similar dishes may be interpreted in quite different ways from one location to another.

Many of the best restaurants in Naples are located in the seafront area with great views of the bay, while the city centre is the place to go for trattorias and pizzerias with typical Neapolitan food. Some pizzerias may offer pasta, meat and fish dishes as well as pizza, but don't be surprised if the most popular serve only pizza – and just a few varieties at that.

Trattorias are the best places to try genuine Neapolitan home cooking. They are usually family-run and small-scale, and many are located in central, popular areas. The interiors may be quite plain, with plastic tablecloths and paper napkins, and the menu will either be written on a blackboard or recited at your table by the waiter. In the Spaccanapoli and Decumano Maggiore districts there are many trattorias where you can eat well and enjoy house wine relatively cheaply.

At *tavole calde* (snack bars), first and second courses are economically priced. The food on sale at street stalls and *friggitorie* (for fried food) is often very good and includes local

La Caravella, serving top-quality seafood in Amalfi *(see p193)*

specialities such as *pizzelle* (fried pizzas) and *panzerotti* (potato croquettes). Bars usually offer filled rolls *(panini)* and sandwiches *(tramezzini)*, as well as cakes and pastries. Many bars also operate as *gelaterie*, with a tempting range of ice creams.

How Much to Pay

The average price for a full meal at a trattoria is about €20, and it can be as little as €8 in pizzerias. Restaurants generally cost from €25 upwards. *Vino sfuso*, or house wine, is often served in jugs and is inexpensive. Fresh fish is usually sold by weight, which can make calculating the cost of your meal difficult. You may find it can be quite expensive.

Opening Hours

Restaurants are generally open from 12:30 to 3pm and from 7:30 to 11pm, but this may vary somewhat, especially at weekends and in summer, when you can dine until fairly late. Family-run trattorias have more limited business hours and are usually closed on Sundays and in August, especially around Ferragosto (15 Aug), when many shops in Naples are closed for holidays. The restaurants in tourist centres on the islands and along the coast usually close in the winter and open around Easter.

Making Reservations and Paying

Restaurants and pizzerias tend to be very crowded on Saturday evening, so it's best to book in advance or arrive early. It is also

Views of the Faraglioni rock formations from Ristorante Il Geranio, Capri *(see p193)*

Stunning views of the Bay of Naples at the elegant Caruso Roof Garden Restaurant *(see p192)*

a good idea to book during the holiday season or on local feast days. Service charges are usually included in the menu prices, but it is customary to leave a tip of around five per cent. The larger restaurants accept major credit cards.

Reading the Menu

A typical Neapolitan menu begins with *antipasti*, which are so varied and interesting they make a meal in themselves: seafood salad, sautéed clams and mussels, or tomato, pepper and aubergine (eggplant) cooked in various different ways. The first course *(primo)* will depend on the season: spaghetti with seafood, aubergine baked in tomato sauce *(parmigiana di melanzane)* or a simple tomato, mozzarella and basil salad *(insalata caprese)* for lunch at the seaside; pasta and meat sauce or rice cake with meat and mushrooms *(sartù di riso)* for a heartier winter lunch. Among the main courses *(secondi)*, you can choose calamari or squid in tomato sauce, assorted fried fish *(fritto misto)* or grilled fish *(grigliata mista)*, or fried baby mozzarella, artichokes and potato or rice croquettes. Try the vegetable pies, the most famous of which is filled with endive cooked with pine nuts and capers. In the winter look out for another variety made with *friarielli* (a type of broccoli found only in Naples) sautéed

with sausage and *peperoncino* (hot chilli pepper).

Pizzerias

Naples is the original home of authentic pizza, freshly made and baked in wood-fired ovens. True pizza was originally a peasant dish, made very simply from dough spread with olive oil and tomatoes, and dating from the 18th century. Eaten in the poorer neighbourhoods of Naples, it was ignored by everyone else until Queen Margherita, wife of Umberto I, decided to try this famous dish. The pizza Margherita, with mozzarella and basil added to create the colours of the Italian flag – red, white and green – was invented in her honour. It is now found in every pizzeria around the world.

Neapolitan pizza chefs are famous for their creative flair,

and as well as classic pizzas like the Margherita and the Marinara, or Napoletana (with buffalo mozzarella, fresh tomatoes and basil), you may find they offer their own chef's special. Expect to wait for a table at many popular pizzerias.

Recommended Restaurants

Neapolitans have perfected the art of enjoying good food, a spirit you'll also find on the Amalfi Coast and the islands. Whether it's crafting lemon *gelato* with just the right balance of tart and sweet or passing down the secrets to creating the traditional Neapolitan pizza, there's passion and often generations of experience behind each dish. We've selected restaurants in Naples and surrounding areas for you to experience the best of Neapolitan cooking. Restaurants listed as Traditional Italian are where to go for local specialities while Modern Italian restaurants will often present regional dishes with a contemporary flair. Restaurants specializing in seafood have been indicated, but you will find seafood on offer at most restaurants in the area, especially in coastal settings. Finally, we've highlighted our DK Choice restaurants for their authentic and passionate presentation of traditional specialities – whether it's Pizza Napoletana or the perfect *sfogliatella (see p189)*.

Warm decor with ethnic details at Il Principe, Pompeii *(see p195)*

The Flavours of Naples and the Amalfi Coast

Juicy red tomatoes, creamy white *mozzarella di bufala* and fragrant green basil, topped with a swirl of olive oil – this is *caprese*, a classic Neapolitan *antipasto*. Its mix of intense flavours and vivid colours is characteristic of a cuisine that reflects the region's sunny Mediterranean climate. Dishes here are generally simple and rely for their success on the freshness that a ready supply of superb local ingredients – grains, pulses, vegetables, fruit, fish and olive oil – can deliver. In Naples' bustling streets, the enticing aromas of freshly picked lemons, fresh herbs and grilling fish mingle with the ever-present tang of sea salt.

Fresh herbs

Locals at one of the many freshly squeezed juice stalls in Naples

Naples

Neapolitan cuisine has always owed much to the brooding mass of Mount Vesuvius. The fertile volcanic soil on its lower slopes yields a bumper harvest of fruit and vegetables all year round. The superb local aubergines (eggplant), artichokes, fennel and courgettes (zucchini) are served cooked or preserved in oil or vinegar as *antipasti*. Traditionally, meat has been in short supply and meagre rations of lamb or kid were something to save for special occasions. For many, Sunday is still the day for preparing *braciole*, stuffed rolls of meat that are simmered for hours with wine and tomatoes.

The durum wheat used for pasta was first planted in the the region by the ancient Greeks, but the Neapolitans only became avid pasta-eaters after techniques for making it were introduced by the Sicilians several centuries later. The sunny climate proved perfect for making long strands of *maccheroni*, which were left out to dry in the streets. Spanish rule later brought peppers and tomatoes from

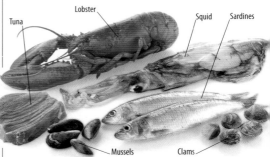

Lobster

Tuna

Squid   Sardines

Mussels   Clams

Superb seafood, caught along the coastline of southern Italy

Local Dishes and Specialities

Rich tomato sauces with herbs, onion and garlic are central to many dishes. Classic examples are *bistecca alla pizzaiola*, beef cooked with tomatoes, garlic and oregano, and *pollo alla cacciatora*, chicken braised in tomatoes, onions, rosemary and red peppers. *Spaghetti alla puttanesca* (literally, prostitute-style spaghetti) probably got its name because the tomato sauce with olives, anchovies and capers would have been quick for a busy, working woman to prepare. *Timballo di maccheroni*, a pie filled with macaroni, wild mushrooms and tomatoes, is a more elaborate local pasta dish. Neapolitans are also noted for being sweet-toothed. One traditional Easter treat – *pastiera napoletana* (candied fruits and ricotta cheese in a pastry case) – is now popular throughout Italy.

Ripe figs

Parmigiana di melanzane
Aubergines (eggplant) are layered with mozzarella, basil, tomato sauce and parmesan.

Making pizzas in an Amalfi restaurant

South America – and local pasta found its ideal partner. The most highly regarded of all local tomatoes is the strongly flavoured, plum-shaped San Marzano. Naples today is ringed by factories producing pasta and canned tomatoes for export, and the city is known the world over as the home of pasta, pizza and ice cream, or *gelati*.

The famous Neapolitan *gelati*, with three coloured layers, originated in the 19th century. Noted makers, such as Tortoni, used chocolate, cherries and pistachios to colour their creations.

Amalfi Coast and the Islands

The people of the Amalfi coast and its many islands have always depended on the daily catch. Buying fish fresh from the habour is still part of local life. Traditional recipes make the most of the readily available fresh anchovies, mackerel and sardines, as well as larger fish which are becoming increasingly rare in these waters. Fish stews are made from whatever is

Newly picked olives, ready for crushing to extract their oil

plentiful and *frutti di Mare*, such as clams, mussels, octopus, squid and cuttlefish, are served in dozens of ways, including with pasta.

Until the tourism boom of the 1960s, the islands were mainly home to peasant farmers. Dishes relied on whatever was to hand. A typical meal would be *coniglio all'ischitania* (rabbit stew with white wine, garlic, tomatoes and peppers).

All along the coast, bright yellow lemons grow on the steeply stepped terraces. Amalfi lemons are prized for their almost-sweet, tongue-tingling flavour and feature strongly in local desserts.

WHAT TO DRINK

Vesuvio wines The volcano's vines produce fruity reds and crisp white *Lachryma Christi*.

Fiano di Avellino and **Greco di Tufo wines** Both these dry whites are made from ancient Roman grape varieties.

Taurasi wine This powerful red is made from the local Anglianco grapes.

Ischia wines These include good quality reds, whites and sparkling varieties.

Capri wines Dry and white, these are good with seafood.

Limoncello This lemon liqueur is usually served at the end of a meal.

Pizza Napoletana This thin-crusted pizza is topped simply with tomato, garlic, oregano, basil and anchovies.

Pesce spada In Campania, Puglia and Sicily, swordfish steak is pan-fried or grilled with lemon and oregano.

Sfogliatella Paper-thin layers of pastry ooze with butter, sugar, cinnamon, orange peel and ricotta.

Where to Eat and Drink

Naples

Toledo and Castel Nuovo

Brandi €
Pizzeria **Map** 7 A3
Salita Sant'Anna di Palazzo 1–2, 80132
Tel *081 41 69 28* **Closed** *Mon*
One of the most historic pizzerias in Naples, Brandi lays claim to the invention of the famous pizza Margherita in 1780. Conveniently located near Galleria Umberto I and Via Toledo.

Il Gobbetto €
Traditional Italian **Map** 7 A2
Via Sergente Maggiore 8, 80132
Tel *081 251 24 35* **Closed** *Mon*
Small and friendly, this *osteria* is great for sampling Neapolitan specialities. You could dine solely on the abundant selection of *antipasti*, but don't miss the home-style pasta dishes, seafood main courses and traditional desserts.

DK Choice

Gran Caffè Gambrinus €
Café **Map** 7 A3
Piazza Trieste e Trento, 80132
Tel *081 41 75 82*
This prestigious, historic café has an elegant *belle époque* interior *(see p56)*. It was once a stylish literary café with regulars including Guy de Maupassant and Oscar Wilde. Try the *caffè alla nocciola*, a sumptuous espresso with hazelnut cream. Touristy and expensive, but fun.

Pintauro €
Pasticceria **Map** 7 A2
Via Toledo 275, 80134
Tel *081 41 73 39*
An excellent spot to sample both the *sfogliatella* and another Neapolitan classic – the *babà*, stop at this well-known neighbourhood *pasticceria* while shopping in Via Toledo.

La Sfogliatella Mary €
Pasticceria **Map** 7 A2
Via Toledo 66, 80134
Tel *081 40 22 18*
Located inside the elegant Galleria Umberto I, this little *pasticceria* is an excellent spot to sample the famous Neapolitan *sfogliatella*. Try both the crunchy *sfogliatella riccia* and *sfogliatella frolla*, made with short crust.

Trattoria da Nennella €
Traditional Italian **Map** 7 A2
Vico Lungo Teatro Nuovo 105, 80134
Tel *081 41 43 38*
This lively Neapolitan trattoria in Quartieri Spagnoli provides a true experience of home-cooking. The cooking here will change the way you think about pasta. First courses reflect the season – try the pasta Genovese if available.

Kukai Nibu €€
Japanese **Map** 7 A2
Via Carlo de Cesare 52, 80132
Tel *081 41 19 05*
One of the first sushi bars in Naples, this stylish restaurant offers a refreshing break from pizza and pasta. Modern decor with a glass wall separating the dining room from the kitchen means you can watch your sushi being freshly prepared.

Osteria Don Maccarone €€
Traditional Italian **Map** 6 F1
Via Gradoni di Chiaia 12, 80132
Tel *081 40 32 51* **Closed** *Mon*
This neighbourhood restaurant is popular for its traditional home-made dishes such as *pasta e fagioli* (pasta with beans), plus seafood, including *pasta con le vongole* (pasta with clams). Very small but with some seating outdoors as well.

Ristorante Amici Miei €€€
Traditional Italian **Map** 6 F2
Via Monte di Dio 77, 80132
Tel *081 764 60 63* **Closed** *Mon; Sun dinner; Jul & Aug*
A welcoming restaurant renowned for its excellent pasta and hearty meat dishes and with a very thorough wine list. A short stroll from Piazza del Plebiscito.

The modern interior of Kukai Nibu, one of Naples' first sushi bars

Price Guide
Prices are based on a three-course meal for one person, including tax and all service charges.

€ under €25
€€ €25 to €50
€€€ over €50

Spaccanapoli

DK Choice

L'Antica Pizzeria da Michele €
Pizzeria **Map** 10 F3
Via Cesare Sersale 1–3, 80139
Tel *081 553 92 04* **Closed** *Sun*
Perhaps the most legendary pizzeria in Naples, da Michele is the spot all pizza lovers must visit. The emphasis is on pizza purity with only two varieties served – the classic Margherita or the Marinara, which includes tomato, garlic, oregano and basil. Queues can be long.

Pizzeria Trianon da Ciro €
Pizzeria **Map** 10 F3
Via Pietro Colletta 44/46, 80139
Tel *081 553 94 26*
A Neapolitan pizza haven since 1923, this pizzeria is packed during lunch and dinner. One excellent pizza is topped with sausage and broccoli and shouldn't be missed.

Ecomesarà €€
Modern Italian **Map** 9 C4
Via S. Chiara 49, 80134
Tel *081 19 25 93 53* **Closed** *Mon*
Opened in 2011, this welcoming restaurant near Santa Chiara offers an inventive and sophisticated take on Neapolitan and southern Italian classics. Friendly setting and the freshest ingredients.

Osteria il Garum €€
Traditional Italian **Map** 9 B4
Piazza Monteoliveto 2, 80134
Tel *081 542 32 28*
Grab an outdoor table on the attractive piazza at this *osteria* serving traditional Neapolitan dishes with an innovative touch. Try the *linguine* with crab as a first course. Friendly service.

La Taverna dell'Arte €€
Traditional Italian **Map** 9 C4
Rampe San Giovanni Maggiore 1/a, 80134
Tel *081 552 75 58* **Closed** *Sun*
Dedicated to preserving the authentic flavours of Neapolitan cooking, this intimate restaurant features a lovely pergola for alfresco dining in the summer.

Sample delicious *antipasti* at Mimì alla Ferrovia

DK Choice

Palazzo Petrucci €€€
Modern Italian **Map** 5 A5
Via Posillipo 16/C, 80123
Tel 081 552 40 68 **Closed** *Mon lunch; Sun dinner*
Offering sweeping views of the Bay of Naples, from Mergellina to the beautiful Palazzo Donn'Anna (*see p130*), this Michelin-starred restaurant run by Neapolitan chef Lino Scarallo specializes in local dishes with a creative touch. The decor is stylish and minimal. Be sure to save room for the inventive and sumptuous desserts.

Decumano Maggiore

La Cantina di Via Sapienza €
Traditional Italian **Map** 9 C2
Via Sapienza 40, 80138
Tel 081 45 90 78 **Closed** *Sun; dinner daily*
An excellent lunch spot located just a short walk from the Museo Archeologico Nazionale, this eatery emphasises simple Neapolitan dishes and keeps the authentic flavours and traditions alive.

Pizzeria i Decumani €
Pizzeria **Map** 10 D3
Via dei Tribunali 58, 80138
Tel 081 557 13 09 **Closed** *Mon*
Popular among locals for its excellent pizza and convenient historic centre location, i Decumani offers a huge selection of pizzas – from traditional to dessert pizzas!

Pizzeria di Matteo €
Pizzeria **Map** 10 D2
Via dei Tribunali 94, 80138
Tel 081 45 52 62 **Closed** *Sun*
This classic pizzeria in the historic centre attracts large crowds, so expect a queue. While you wait, enjoy the tasty fried *antipasti*.

Pizzeria Sorbillo €
Pizzeria **Map** 9 C3
Via dei Tribunali 32, 80138
Tel 081 033 10 09 **Closed** *Sun*
This tiny eatery is one of Naples' best pizzerias, being run by the same family for three generations. The first-rate pizzas often draw a queue, but the service is prompt.

Mimì alla Ferrovia €€
Traditional Italian **Map** 4 E4
Via Alfonso d'Aragona 21, 80139
Tel 081 553 85 25 **Closed** *Sun*
Just off busy Piazza Garibaldi, this restaurant specializes in traditional Neapolitan *cucina povera* (simple cooking) and features notable *antipasti*, mozzarella and desserts.

Osteria da Carmela €€
Traditional Italian **Map** 9 B2
Via Conte di Ruvo 12, 80135
Tel 081 549 97 38 **Closed** *Sun; second half of Aug*
This traditional *osteria* is conveniently located near the Museo Archeologico Nazionale and is a welcoming choice for sampling Neapolitan specialities. Try the pasta with chickpeas or Genovese sauce (a beef and onion sauce).

Capodimonte and I Vergini

Cantina del Gallo €
Traditional Italian **Map** 3 A3
Via Alessandro Telesino 21, 80136
Tel 081 544 15 21 **Closed** *Sun dinner*
A rare blend of pizzeria and *osteria*, Cantina del Gallo in the Sanità district will satisfy many different tastes. Lovely home-style dishes, delicious pizza and warm atmosphere.

Pizzeria Starita €
Pizzeria **Map** 9 A1
Via Materdei 27–28, 80136
Tel 081 544 14 85 **Closed** *Sun lunch*
An excellent choice for traditional Neapolitan pizza with a touch of glamour, in the narrow streets of Materdei, Pizzeria Starita made cinema magic with Sophia Loren in the film *L'Oro di Napoli*.

Vomero

Friggitoria Vomero €
Traditional Italian **Map** 2 D5
Via Domenico Cimarosa 44, 80129
Tel 081 578 31 30 **Closed** *Sun*
Just a short walk from Castel Nuovo, Friggitoria Vomero is a particularly good spot to sample traditional street food typical of Naples. Try the fried pizza or the paper cone filled with a mix of local specialities.

Osteria Donna Teresa €€
Traditional Italian **Map** 2 D5
Via Michele Kerbaker 58, 80129
Tel 081 556 70 70 **Closed** *Sun*
Small and welcoming, this *osteria* brings simple, home cooking to the Vomero neighbourhood. Popular with limited seating so arrive early, especially for lunch.

Castel dell'Ovo and Chiaia

DK Choice

Ba-Bar Kitchen + Wine Bar €
Enoteca **Map** 6 E2
Via Bisignano 20, 80121
Tel 081 764 35 25 **Closed** *Mon*
Offering an impressive wine list and interesting menu to complement the drinks, this establishment is a delightful blend of bar and café with an artistic vibe. Perfect for soaking up the atmosphere of the trendy Chiaia district while meeting friends.

Enoteca Belledonne €
Enoteca **Map** 6 E2
Vico Belledonne a Chiaia 18, 80121
Tel 081 40 31 62
A great spot to sample local wines and experience the charm of exciting Chiaia. Extensive wine list along with irresistible *antipasti*.

DK Choice

La Taverna del Brigante €
Traditional Italian **Map** 6 D1
Via Giuseppe Martucci 75, 80121
Tel 081 066 41 85 **Closed** *Sun*
Offering an excellent selection of grilled vegetables and traditional Neapolitan meatballs, this eatery's specialities are listed on the house menu, which highlights the *cucina povera* dishes of Campania, such as pasta with beans or chickpeas, and lentils with spinach.

For more information on types of restaurants *see pp186–7*

Antica Latteria €€
Traditional Italian **Map** 6 F2
Vico II Alabardieri 30, 80100
Tel *081 012 87 75* **Closed** *Sun dinner*
Friendly and inviting, traditional
trattoria Antica Latteria is tucked
away on a narrow street. Try the
pasta e patate (pasta with potatoes)
for a unique and filling local dish.

Giappo Sushi Bar €€
Japanese **Map** 6 E2
Vico Belledonne a Chiaia 2, 80121
Tel *081 764 84 65* **Closed** *Sun lunch*
Excellent choice for international
flavours in the Chiaia district. Pick
from a variety of *bento* boxes
each with a different sushi or
sashimi combination, or choose
from a selection of fusion dishes.

La Scialuppa €€
Seafood **Map** 7 A5
Borgo Marinaro 4, 80132
Tel *081 764 53 33* **Closed** *Mon*
Situated on the waterfront in the
picturesque Borgo Marinaro, near
the Castel dell'Ovo, this romantic
restaurant specializes in freshly
caught seafood transformed into
simple, classic Neapolitan dishes.
Outdoor dining on terrace.

Trattoria Castel dell'Ovo €€
Traditional Italian **Map** 7 A5
Via Luculliana 28, 80132
Tel *081 764 63 52* **Closed** *Thu*
An affordable alternative in the
Borgo Marinaro, this restaurant
is a lovely spot to enjoy dinner
with beautiful views. The
spaghetti con le vongole (with
clams) is a Neapolitan speciality.

Umberto €€
Traditional Italian **Map** 6 F2
Via Alabardieri 30, 80121
Tel *081 41 85 55* **Closed** *Mon
lunch*
Enjoy Neapolitan pizza and local
specialities with a contemporary
twist in the heart of Chiaia.
Gluten-free options are available.

**Caruso Roof
Garden Restaurant** €€€
Traditional Italian **Map** 7 A4
Via Partenope 45, 80132
Tel *081 764 00 44* **Closed** *Mon*
Atop the Grand Hotel Vesuvio *(see
p182)*, the Caruso is one of the
city's most elegant dining choices
with spectacular views of the bay.
Consider dressing for the occasion.

Napoli Mia €€€
Modern Italian **Map** 6 E2
Riviera di Chiaia 269, 80121
Tel *081 552 22 66* **Closed** *Mon*
Bright and elegant, this restaurant
is set along the Lungomare in
Chiaia and offers modern takes on
Neapolitan classics. Excellent wine.

Posillipo & Mergellina

Chalet Ciro €€
Café **Map** 5 4B
Via Mergellina, 80122
Tel *081 66 99 28*
Located near the waterfront in
charming Mergellina, Chalet Ciro
is popular among locals for its
creamy *gelato* and large range of
pastries and desserts. Pretty
outdoor seating area.

Pizzeria la Notizia €
Pizzeria
*Via Michelangelo da Caravaggio
53, 80126*
Tel *081 714 21 55* **Closed** *lunch; Mon*
Master *pizzaiolo* Enzo Coccia
creates pizzas that many
Neapolitans consider the finest
in Naples. A little outside the
historic centre, but well worth
the trip.

Pompeii and the Amalfi Coast

Amalfi

Bar Royal €
Gelateria **Road Map** D4
Via Lorenzo d'Amalfi 10, 84011
Tel *089 87 19 82*
Just steps from Piazza Duomo in
the centre of Amalfi, this café is
noted for excellent *gelato*. Try
their flavour called *Passione degli
Dei* with lemon, strawberry and a
touch of champagne.

Gran Caffè €
Café **Road Map** D4
*Corso delle Repubbliche Marinare
37–8, 84011*
Tel *089 87 10 47*
With outdoor seating
overlooking the beach, this
café is an excellent spot for
drinks or a light lunch or dinner.
Beautiful sunset views and
lively night scene.

Pasticceria Pansa €
Pasticceria **Road Map** D4
Piazza Duomo 40, 84011
Tel *089 87 10 65* **Closed** *Tue*
A popular café and bakery dating
back to 1830, their candied citrus
dipped in chocolate is a must try.
Great spot for people watching.

L'Abside €€
Traditional Italian **Road Map** D4
Piazza dei Dogi 31, 84011
Tel *089 87 35 86* **Closed** *Sun*
Set on a charming and traffic-free
piazza, this wine bar and
restaurant is a perfect place for
people watching and enjoying
Amalfi's quieter side.

Traditional table settings at respected
Pizzeria la Notizia

Da Ciccio Cielo Mare e Terra €€
Traditional Italian **Road Map** D4
Via Giovanni Augustariccio 21, 84011
Tel *089 83 12 65* **Closed** *Tue*
With panoramic views of the
coastline, this restaurant offers
as the name suggests, regional
specialities from the sea
and land. The seafood is
particularly fine.

Da Maria €€
Pizzeria **Road Map** D4
Via Lorenzo d'Amalfi 14, 84011
Tel *089 87 18 80* **Closed** *Mon*
With an excellent central location
just off Piazza Duomo, this
pizzeria makes the best pizza
in Amalfi. The traditional wood-
fired oven makes all the
difference. There's also a full
restaurant menu available.

Lo Smeraldino €€
Traditional Italian **Road Map** D4
Piazzale dei Protontini 1, 84011
Tel *089 87 10 70* **Closed** *Wed
Sep–Jun*
With beautiful harbour views
from the terrace, this is a good
choice for a romantic lunch or
larger group gathering. Seafood
specialities and very good pizza.

Taverna Buonvicino €€
Traditional Italian **Road Map** D4
Largo San Maria Maggiore 1, 84011
Tel *089 873 63 85*
Offering excellent local cuisine,
this charming restaurant and
wine bar is set in a pretty and
secluded square down an alley
left of the Duomo.

Da Teresa €€
Seafood **Road Map** D4
*Via delle Sorgente 5, Spiaggia di
Santa Croce, Amalfi*
Tel *089 83 12 37* **Closed** *Nov–Apr*
This restaurant overlooks the
stunning Santa Croce beach just

west of Amalfi. The grilled fish is superb. Complimentary restaurant boat service available from the Pontile Il Faro in Amalfi.

Trattoria dei Cartari　€€
Traditional Italian　**Road Map** D4
Piazza dello Spirito Santo 5, 84011
Tel *089 87 21 31*　**Closed** *Mon*
A friendly restaurant located on Amalfi's main street. The seafood *antipasti* are fabulous as is the family recipe for Genovese, a pasta sauce made with beef and onions.

La Caravella　€€€
Modern Italian　**Road Map** D4
Via Matteo Camera 12, 84011
Tel *089 87 10 29*　**Closed** *Tue*
Renowned for its fresh fish, this elegant restaurant is formal but friendly. Decor is accented by a fine collection of ceramics by artisans from Vietri sul Mare.

Da Gemma　€€€
Traditional Italian　**Road Map** D4
Via Fra Gerardo Sasso 11, 84011
Tel *089 87 13 45*
This restaurant has a charming terrace overlooking Piazza Duomo. The menu features expertly presented seafood dishes and local specialities such as risotto with prawns and Amalfi Coast lemon. Reservations recommended.

DK Choice

Marina Grande　€€€
Modern Italian　**Road Map** D4
Viale della Regione 4, 84011
Tel *089 87 11 29*　**Closed** *Tue*
With picture postcard views overlooking Amalfi's main beach and harbour, this restaurant presents a carefully curated menu of local specialities revisited with a creative and contemporary flair. Enjoy fine dining with the casual elegance of a seaside setting. Private beach access and sunbeds available.

Atrani

Le Arcate　€€
Traditional Italian　**Road Map** D4
Largo Buonocore, 84010
Tel *089 87 13 67*　**Closed** *Mon*
This establishment is the perfect place to enjoy a romantic dining experience overlooking the sea at the charming village of Atrani next to Amalfi. Le Arcate specializes in seafood, but makes an excellent pizza as well. The preparation of the food is simple, although great attention is paid to the flavours.

Capri

DK Choice

Pasticceria Buonocore　€
Gelateria　**Road Map** C4
Via Vittorio Emanuele 35, 80073
Tel *081 837 81 25*　**Closed** *Tue*
You can find this *gelato* shop and *pasticceria* by following the heavenly scent that fills Via Vittorio Emanuele. The *gelato* is made with fresh fruit and ingredients. Save room for the pastries, especially the *caprilù* lemon and almond cookies invented here.

Pizzeria Aumm Aumm　€
Pizzeria　**Road Map** B4
Via Caprile 18, Anacapri, 80071
Tel *081 837 30 00*　**Closed** *Mon & lunch daily*
This excellent pizzeria boasts a traditional wood-fired oven and a peaceful, Anacapri setting. The large television screens make it a popular spot among locals and sports enthusiasts.

Buca di Bacco　€€
Traditional Italian　**Road Map** C4
Via Longano 35, 80073
Tel *081 837 07 23*　**Closed** *Mon*
Charming and intimate, with vaulted ceilings, this restaurant has a large menu with seafood, traditional Capri dishes and a wood-burning oven for fresh pizza.

La Fontelina　€€
Seafood　**Road Map** C4
Via Faraglioni, Capri 80073
Tel *081 837 08 45*　**Closed** *Nov–Mar; dinner*
Set on a rocky beach near the Faraglioni rocks, this restaurant is a little slice of heaven. After spending the morning on the beach, it's a perfect spot to linger over lunch.

Da Gelsomina alla Migliera　€€
Traditional Italian　**Road Map** B4
Via Migliera 72, 80071 Anacapri
Tel *081 837 14 99*　**Closed** *Jan & Feb; dinner: Oct–Apr*
Overlooking the sea, this eatery provides delicious home-cooked food, with house specialities including rabbit, chicken and ravioli capresi.

Pulalli Wine Bar　€€
Enoteca　**Road Map** C4
Piazza Umberto I 4, 80073
Tel *081 837 41 08*　**Closed** *Tue: Sep–Jul; Tues lunch: Aug*
This establishment has an extensive selection of wine with appetizers and substantial dining options. The best part, however, are the views afforded by the enviable location of the bar.

Da Paolino Lemon Trees　€€€
Traditional Italian　**Road Map** C4
Via Palazzo a Mare 11, Capri 80073
Tel *081 837 61 02*
A rustic, country-style restaurant with an enchanting dining area under lemon trees. Dedicated to authentic Caprese recipes with abundant *antipasti* and flavourful dishes as beautiful as the setting.

Ristorante Il Geranio　€€€
Traditional Italian　**Road Map** C4
Viale Giacomo Matteotti 8, Capri 80073
Tel *081 837 06 16*
With an outdoor terrace with views of the Faraglioni rocks, this restaurant is the perfect spot. The indoor seating area is equally lovely, and the seafood is presented with elegance.

Da Tonino　€€€
Traditional Italian　**Road Map** C4
Via Dentecala 15, 80073
Tel *081 837 67 18*　**Closed** *Mon*
Set on the path that leads to the Arco Naturale, this restaurant is a little out of the way but worth visiting for its superb cooking.

Dining in the citrus garden, Da Paolino Lemon Trees, Capri

For more information on types of restaurants *see pp186–7*

Villa Verde €€€
Traditional Italian **Road Map** C4
Via Sella Orta 6, Capri 80073
Tel *081 837 70 24*
Just off the main shopping streets in stylish Capri, this charming restaurant has a tucked-away terrace for outdoor dining. The menu highlights both seafood and meat, and the *antipasti* are excellent.

Cetara

Il Convento €€
Traditional Italian **Road Map** E4
Piazza San Francesco 16, 84010
Tel *089 26 10 39* **Closed** *Wed*
Set in a former convent right in the centre of the village, this restaurant and pizzeria is an excellent choice for larger groups or families. Seafood is Il Convento's speciality, but they also offer pizza, meat and vegetable based dishes.

San Pietro €€
Seafood **Road Map** E4
Piazza San Francesco 2, 84010
Tel *089 26 10 91* **Closed** *Tue*
Since Roman times this fishing village has been known for its *colatura di alici*, an infused fish oil, as well as its tuna fishing. San Pietro is a great choice to sample those traditions today.

Aquapazza €€€
Modern Italian **Road Map** E4
Corso Giuseppe Garibaldi 38, 84010
Tel *089 26 16 06* **Closed** *Mon*
The outdoor seating area at this elegant restaurant offers great views of the nearby boats dotted with colourful fishing boats. Local specialities are prepared with a light and modern touch.

Ischia

Bar Calise €
Café **Road Map** A3
Piazza degli Eroi, 80077
Tel *081 99 12 70*
A classic spot in Ischia Porto for coffee and something sweet, or after-dinner drinks. The fanciful interior is one of a kind. The large selection of desserts will please every palate.

Da Pasquale €
Pizzeria **Road Map** A4
Via S. Angelo 79, 80070
Tel *081 90 42 08* **Closed** *Dec–Mar; Tue*
Set in one of Ischia's most charming spots, this restaurant and pizzeria specializes in Neapolitan pizza made in a traditional wood-fired oven. Try the pizza with delicate zucchini flowers. A range of home-made desserts make for the perfect finish.

Pasticceria Dolce e la Vita €
Pasticceria **Road Map** A4
Via Nazario Sauro 10, 80070
Tel *081 99 91 20*
This noted *pasticceria* is famous for its creative take on sweets, sandwiches and other light fare, along with a thriving pastry section that will leave you spoiled for choice.

Al Pontile €€
Traditional Italian **Road Map** A3
Via Luigi Mazzella 15, 80077
Tel *081 98 34 92* **Closed** *Nov–Feb*
Set right beside the water with a great view of the Castello Aragonese, this simple, family-run seafood restaurant and café offers amazingly delicious seafood and homemade pasta.

Da Raffaele €€
Pizzeria **Road Map** A3
Via Roma 29, 80077
Tel *081 99 12 03*
Colourful and bright, this delightful restaurant and pizzeria is set along a popular shopping street in Ischia. Seafood is the main feature but pizza from the restaurant's wood-fired oven is also an excellent choice.

Enoteca la Stadera €€
Enoteca **Road Map** A4
Via Comandante Maddalena 15, 80070
Tel *081 99 98 93*
This small wine bar has a great selection of wines from Ischia and Campania, which are accompanied by a menu of locally produced *antipasti*, including cheeses and cured meats.

Da Coco €€€
Seafood **Road Map** A3
Piazzale Castello Aragonese 1, 80077
Tel *081 98 18 23*
With a remarkable location, very near the causeway leading to the

Bright, welcoming Da Raffaele in Ischia Ponte on the island of Ischia

tiny island of Castello Aragonese, this seafood restaurant serves ultra-fresh fish and excellent pasta in a picturesque setting.

Umberto a Mare €€€
Modern Italian **Road Map** A3
Via Soccorso 2, 80075
Tel *081 99 71 71*
This restaurant, sitting on the same rocky spit as Santa Maria del Soccorso, has uninterrupted views out to sea from the terrace and expansive windows in the dining room. Freshly caught seafood and an extensive wine list. Reservations recommended for one of the few outdoor tables.

Maiori

Pasticceria Napoli €
Pasticceria **Road Map** D4
Corso Regina 64, 84010
Tel *089 85 31 82* **Closed** *Tue*
Service is friendly and the pastries abundant at popular local bakery and café Pasticceria Napoli. Ideally located on Maiori's main street, stop in for a creamy cappuccino and a cornetto with a choice of fillings to start your day.

Nettuno €€
Traditional Italian **Road Map** D4
Via G. Capone 1, 84010
Tel *089 87 75 94*
Located right on the water-front, this restaurant is known for its fresh seafood and excellent pizza, all of which are served in abundant portions. Restaurant parking is also available, which makes Nettuno a convenient stop for those touring the Amalfi Coast.

Massa Lubrense

Relais Blu €€€
Modern Italian **Road Map** C4
Via Roncato 60, 80061
Tel *081 878 95 52* **Closed** *Mon*
Even if you're not staying at this charming boutique hotel *(see p184)* you can still enjoy its incomparable views across the sea to Capri from the hotel restaurant. The menu includes delicious seafood and regional specialities with a dash of modern creativity. Reservations recommended.

Minori

La Botte €
Traditional Italian **Road Map** D4
Via S. Maria Vetrana, 84010
Tel *089 87 78 93* **Closed** *Tue*
This restaurant and pizzeria is popular with locals who prefer splitting the very large pizzas. Try *nunderi*, a pasta dish of dumplings made with ricotta unique to Minori.

DK Choice

Sal de Riso €
Pasticceria **Road Map** D4
Via Roma 80, 84010
Tel 089 877 79 41 **Closed** *Sun*
Salvatore de Riso, an outstanding pastry chef known
throughout Italy, has set up a
bakery down near the waterfront.
All the sweet creations are made
on site or in Tramonti nearby.
Amalfi Coast lemons feature
prominently, but try the *gelato*,
liqueurs or the delicious *ricotta
e pera* (ricotta and pear) cake.

Il Giardiniello €€€
Traditional Italian **Road Map** D4
Corso Vittorio Emanuele 17, 84010
Tel 089 87 70 50
Enter through the lush garden
with pergola-sheltered tables
to find this family-run restaurant
just off Minori's central street.
Il Giardiniello specializes in
seafood but also features
wood-fired pizzas.

Nerano

Taverna del Capitano €€€
Modern Italian **Road Map** C4
*Piazza delle Sirene, Località Marina
del Cantone 10, 80061*
Tel 081 808 10 28 **Closed** *Nov–early
Mar; Mon & Tue: Oct–May*
Hidden away in the enchanting
Marina del Cantone, this
Michelin-starred restaurant
produces superb cuisine. Try the
spaghetti with zucchini, a Nerano
speciality. Unforgettable views.
Reservations recommended.

Paestum

Nettuno €€
Traditional Italian **Road Map** F5
*Via Nettuno 2, 84063 Capaccio
Paestum*
Tel 082 881 10 28 **Closed** *dinner*
This simple eatery offers some
excellent seafood, Paestum's own
mozzarella di bufala and views of
the ancient temple complex.
Located right next to the ruins,
but only open at lunchtime.

Pompeii

President €€€
Traditional Italian **Road Map** D3
Piazza Schettini 12, 80045
Tel 081 850 72 45
Skip the crowds around the
entrance to Pompeii and head for
gourmet dining at this Michelin-
starred restaurant nearby. Seafood
is the speciality here and a tasting
menu is available. Reservations
are recommended at weekends.

Rustically chic decor and casual, comfortable seating at Casa e Bottega in Positano

Il Principe €€€
Modern Italian **Road Map** D3
Piazza Bartolo Longo 8, 80045
Tel 081 850 55 66 **Closed** *Mon*
An elegant choice located
near to the ruins of ancient
Pompeii, this restaurant has
beautifully presented, traditional
Campania dishes produced
with a creative flair. Family-
run with attentive service.

Positano

La Brezza €
Café **Road Map** D4
Via del Brigantino 1, 84017
Tel 089 87 58 11
The perfect blend of wine bar
and Internet café, La Brezza has
an enviable position overlooking
Positano's Spiaggia Grande.
Ideal for a cappuccino in the
morning or an *aperitivo* as the
sun sets. Free Wi-Fi.

Da Adolfo €€
Seafood **Road Map** D4
Via Laurito 40, 84017
Tel 089 87 50 22
Accessible only by boat, the
delightful Da Adolfo sits on a tiny
beach near Positano. Dine on
freshly grilled fish, delicious
mussel soup and unmissable
mozzarella grilled on lemon
leaves, under the restaurant's
shady pergola.

Casa e Bottega €€
Traditional Italian **Road Map** D4
Viale Pasitea 100, 84017
Tel 089 87 52 25 **Closed** *Tue; dinner:
Nov–Mar*
A unique, stylish addition to
the Positano dining scene, this
cheery restaurant offers fresh,
light options, a juice bar, a
smoothie counter and healthy
choices for breakfast and lunch.
It is set inside a homeware shop,
so do not miss the interesting
items on display.

Mediterraneo €€
Traditional Italian **Road Map** D4
Viale Pasitea 236, 84017
Tel 089 812 28 28
This restaurant and art gallery has
a lovely outdoor seating area and
an air-conditioned indoor dining
room. Start with the zucchini
flowers stuffed with ricotta and
save room for dessert.

La Pergola €€
Traditional Italian **Road Map** D4
Via del Brigantino 35–7, 84017
Tel 089 81 14 61
Just steps from the beach, this
restaurant is the perfect choice
for a light meal, evening cocktails
or even a romantic dinner.

La Cambusa €€€
Seafood **Road Map** D4
Piazza Amerigo Vespucci 4, 84017
Tel 089 87 54 32
Sitting right at the base of
Positano's beautiful church with
its majolica-tiled dome, this
restaurant is the place to go for
delicate seafood and freshly-
caught fish. The terrace overlooks
Spiaggia Grande, the town's
main beach.

Chez Black €€€
Seafood **Road Map** D4
Via del Brigantino 19, 84017
Tel 089 87 50 36 **Closed** *Jan*
With tables just steps from the
beach, this is Positano's classic
dining address where you come
to see and be seen. The pasta with
sea urchins is a particular standout.

Max €€€
Modern Italian **Road Map** D4
Piazza dei Mulini 22, 84017
Tel 089 87 50 56
Set in a beautiful art gallery, this
chic restaurant has a terrace for
alfresco dining. Both meat and
seafood are highlighted on the
menu and all are finely presented.
Excellent wine list.

For more information on types of restaurants *see pp186–7*

DK Choice

Il Ritrovo €€€
Traditional Italian **Road Map** D4
Via Montepertuso 77, 84017
Tel *089 81 20 05*
High above Positano in the
scenic mountain village of
Montepertuso, this popular
restaurant has stunning views
and excellent food. Make a
reservation and arrange for the
shuttle bus to pick you up from
your Positano hotel.

Da Vincenzo €€€
Traditional Italian **Road Map** D4
Viale Pasitea 172, 84017
Tel *089 87 51 28* **Closed** *Tue dinner*
A vibrant restaurant setting with
home-cooked meals, generous
portions and dishes that use
seasonal ingredients. The
outdoor seating area is
surrounded by lively street life;
what it lacks in views it makes up
for in people-watching.

Praiano

DK Choice

Da Armandino €€
Seafood **Road Map** D4
Via Praia, 84010
Tel *089 87 40 87*
Located just steps from the
beach in Marina di Praia cove,
this family-run, friendly
restaurant is a casual spot
perfect for enjoying freshly
caught seafood and local wine.
Tables spill out onto a small,
peaceful piazza with views of
the sea. Try the risotto with
lemon and prawns.

La Brace €€
Traditional Italian **Road Map** D4
Via Gennaro Capriglione 146, 84010
Tel *089 87 42 26* **Closed** *Wed*
This establishment is a good
choice for families or groups
looking for a range of options –
excellent seafood, pasta and
meat, and wood-fired pizza,
which are their speciality. Fine
views of the sea and coastline
from the window-side tables.

Il Pirata €€€
Seafood **Road Map** D4
Via Terramare, 84010
Tel *089 87 43 77*
Overlooking the enchanting
Marina di Praia, this restaurant
has some of the most romantic views
on the coast, with some of the
best outdoor seating on the
balcony. Seafood is king and the
cave-like bar is truly unique.

Procida

Caracalè €€
Seafood **Road Map** A3
Via Marina di Corricella 62, 80079
Tel *081 896 91 92*
Dine outdoors just steps from
fishing boats bobbing in the
Marina Corricella. Seafood and fish
are presented with a fresh touch.

La Conchiglia €€
Seafood **Road Map** A3
Via Pizzaco 10, 80079
Tel *081 896 76 02*
This restaurant has a lovely view
across the bay to Marina Corricella
and is just steps from the beach.
Try the local speciality: *cappelletti*
filled with provolone and aubergine.

Girone €€
Seafood **Road Map** A3
*Lungomare C. Colombo 20, Marina
Chiaiolella, 80079*
Tel *081 896 73 67*
Set right on the beach at the port
of Chiaiolella, this restaurant
features seafood and also makes
a decent pizza. Lovely sunset views
make Girone a romantic dinner spot.

Ravello

Bar Calce €
Café **Road Map** D4
Via Roma 2, 84010
Tel *089 85 71 52*
Located next to the Duomo, with
outdoor dining in the piazza, this
café is a local institution, and noted
for its excellent pastries and coffee.
Sit inside or enjoy of the piazza
from one of the outdoor tables.

Cumpà Cosimo €€
Traditional Italian **Road Map** D4
Via Roma 44, 84010
Tel *089 85 71 56* **Closed** *Mon;
winter*
Carefully managed by owner Netta
Bottone, Cumpà Cosimo is a popular

Romantic dining at Garden in Ravello, with
views of the Bay of Salerno

trattoria near the Duomo. The
pasta and meat dishes are top notch
and the *crespolini* (filled crepes) are
an unmissable Ravello speciality.

Garden €€
Traditional Italian **Road Map** D4
Via Giovanni Boccaccio 4, 84010
Tel *089 85 72 26*
With views of the Bay of Salerno's
dramatic coastline, this restaurant
presents regional specialities
prepared with finesse. Try the
home-made ravioli or grilled fish.

Da Salvatore €€
Traditional Italian **Road Map** D4
Via della Repubblica 2, 84010
Tel *089 85 72 27* **Closed** *Mon*
This restaurant is a great choice
for seafood or pizza. It has friendly
staff and a terrace perched high
over the sea with a spectacularly
scenic view.

Il Flauto di Pan €€€
Modern Italian **Road Map** D4
Via Santa Chiara 26, 84010
Tel *089 85 74 59* **Closed** *lunch*
Tucked away in the gardens of
the Hotel Villa Cimbrone, this
exclusive Michelin-starred
restaurant offers a unique dining
experience and fresh interpretations of Mediterranean classics.
Reservations are required.

Rossellinis €€€
Modern Italian **Road Map** D4
Via San Giovanni del Toro 27, 84010
Tel *089 81 81 81* **Closed** *for lunch
Nov–Mar*
This gorgeous restaurant is set
in the romantic Palazzo Avino
high atop Ravello. Only the finest
ingredients are used, with special
care taken for food presentation.

Salerno

Hostaria Il Brigante €
Traditional Italian **Road Map** E3
Via Fratelli Linguiti 4
Tel *089 22 64 92*
This establishment is a cosy,
friendly favourite tucked above
the Duomo, with a changing hand-
written menu of both vegetarian
and seafood dishes, which are
prepared with utmost care.

Pasticceria Pantaleone €
Pasticceria **Road Map** E3
Via dei Mercanti 73–5, 84100
Tel *089 22 78 25* **Closed** *Tue;
Sun evening*
This eatery is a traditional and
much-loved *pasticceria* in the
heart of the historic district. One
of the specialities is the *scazzetta*,
a delightful cake of rum-soaked
sponge and cream, covered with
a strawberry glaze.

L'Antica Trattoria's pretty pergola-shaded terrace, Sorrento

Il Maestro del Gusto €€
Traditional Italian   **Road Map** E3
Corso Garibaldi 149–151, 84121
Tel *089 995 28 58*   **Closed** *lunch Mon–Fri*
This cosy restaurant in the city centre offers friendly service and local specialities. Reasonable prices and very nice wine selection.

Sant'Agata sui Due Golfi

Lo Stuzzichino €€
Traditional Italian   **Road Map** C4
Via Deserto 1/a, 80061
Tel *081 533 00 10*   **Closed** *Wed*
Run by the De Gregorio family, this friendly eatery focuses on Sorrento specialities and locally sourced ingredients. Gluten-free dishes are available on request. Large outdoor dining area.

Don Alfonso 1890 €€€
Modern Italian   **Road Map** C4
Corso Sant'Agata 11
Tel *081 878 00 26*   **Closed** *Mon: 16 Sep–14 Jun, Tue: 15 Jun–15 Sep*
Regional traditions combine with creative finesse in this two-Michelin-star restaurant run by one of Italy's finest chefs, Alfonso Iaccarino, along with his family. Reservations highly recommended.

Sorrento

Fauno €
Café   **Road Map** C4
Piazza Tasso 13–15, 80067
Tel *081 878 11 35*   **Closed** *Nov*
Find a seat and watch the world go by at the largest bar in Sorrento's central piazza. Vegetarian and gluten-free options available.

Mondo Bio Café €
Vegetarian   **Road Map** C4
Via degli Aranci 108–10, 80067
Tel *081 878 44 89*   **Closed** *Sun; Oct–Mar*
Part of an organic supermarket, this restaurant serves beautiful vegetarian dishes made with organic products. Simple but charming outdoor dining area.

Raki €
Gelateria   **Road Map** C4
Via San Cesareo 48, 80067
Tel *329 877 79 22*
Excellent *gelato* made with natural and fresh ingredients. Try the gelateria's unique flavour combinations as well as the traditional *limone* made with Sorrento lemons. The *granita* and milkshakes are also delicious. Gluten-free cones.

Aurora Light €€
Modern Italian   **Road Map** C4
Piazza Tasso 3–4, 80067
Tel *081 877 26 31*   **Closed** *Jan–Mar; Nov–Dec dinner*
A restaurant dedicated to fresh and seasonal dishes created to off-set delicate tastes with more powerful flavours, Aurora Light is a top choice for a simple and delicious meal. It is located right on Piazza Tasso.

Bagni Delfino €€
Seafood   **Road Map** C4
Via Marina Grande 216, 80067
Tel *081 878 20 38*   **Closed** *Nov–Mar*
This restaurant, with a beautiful setting in the colourful old harbour of Sorrento, offers traditional seafood specialities along with sunbeds for diners to recline on. Set on a dock jutting out from the Marina Grande.

Inn Bufalito €€
Traditional Italian   **Road Map** C4
Vico I Fuoro 21, 80067
Tel *081 365 69 75*   **Closed** *Nov–Feb; dinner*
Inn Bufalito is set in the historic centre and has a covered outdoor seating area. As the name implies, this restaurant specializes in *mozzarella di bufala*. You'll also find excellent quality meat, including signature buffalo, and traditional Italian home cooking.

DK Choice

Ristorante la Marinella €€
Traditional Italian **Road Map** C4
Piazzetta Marinella 1, 80065
Tel *081 807 56 74*   **Closed** *dinner & Mon*
This restaurant in the Sant'Agnello area marries stunning views overlooking the Bay of Naples with fresh and inventive dishes. The delectable food is distinguished by a creative and modern take on classic Neapolitan favourites. The most scenic time to visit is sunset.

Ristorante Sant'Antonino €€
Traditional Italian   **Road Map** C4
Via S. Maria delle Grazie 6, 80067
Tel *081 877 12 00*   **Closed** *winter;Wed*
A large restaurant with a veranda overlooking a garden with lemon and orange trees. Large selection of pasta, meat and seafood, as well as traditional pizza from a wood-fired oven.

Trattoria da Emilia €€
Traditional Italian   **Road Map** C4
Via Marina Grande 62, 80067
Tel *081 807 27 20*
This popular trattoria, in existence since 1947, is set right at the water's edge with a covered dining area overlooking the harbour. It serves excellent grilled fish and pasta with seafood, with a flair for big flavours that has not wavered over the decades.

L'Antica Trattoria €€€
Traditional Italian   **Road Map** C4
Via Padre Reginaldo Giuliani 33, 80067
Tel *081 807 10 82*
A Sorrento tradition since 1930, this appealing restaurant has indoor and outdoor seating, with delicious seafood and meat dishes featuring on the menu. The airy terrace is decorated with a colourful assortment of plants and flowers.

Ristorante il Buco €€€
Modern Italian   **Road Map** C4
2a Rampa Marina Piccola 5, 80067
Tel *081 878 23 54*   **Closed** *Wed*
Set in a wine cellar once used by monks, this elegant Michelin-starred restaurant offers the finest food from land and sea. It boasts an excellent wine list, and the attentive, friendly staff help keep the atmosphere informal.

For more information on types of restaurants *see pp186–7*

Light Meals and Snacks in Naples

Naples is full of bars, pastry shops, *rosticcerie*, and all kinds of places with stand-up counters where you can stop for a drink and a snack. It is an Italian habit to stop at a local bar to breakfast on a cappuccino and warm croissant, to pause for an apéritif before lunch or have a coffee in the afternoon. A quick and cheap meal can be bought at the numerous fast-food establishments that sell sandwiches, small pizzas and filled rolls, as well as prepared meals like pasta with different sauces, to eat on the spot or take away.

Bars and Cafés

In Naples, unlike most other European cities, the bars generally have only stand-up counters at which customers have a quick coffee. In bars and cafés where seating space is provided, there is usually an additional charge for service at the table. In the summer, however, all available outdoor space is packed with tables. Some of the cafés stay open until the early hours, and are equally popular with the young and the old. Many bars in Naples are also pastry shops (*pasticceria*), ice cream parlours (*gelateria*), quick self-service restaurants (*tavola calda*), or all these combined.

One historic Neapolitan café frequented by celebrities in the past is **Gran Caffè Gambrinus**, one of the most elegant bars in the centre (*see p56*). Here, a short distance from the Palazzo Reale, you can sit outside and admire the lovely Piazza del Plebiscito, which is closed to traffic. **Il Vero Bar del Professore** sits just to the north on Piazza Trieste e Trento, while further along in Galleria Umberto I is **Bar Brasiliano**, which offers coffee with a wide range of unusual twists. Another elegant café is **Caffetteria Bernini** in Vomero, which gets very busy in the evenings, especially at weekends. **Gran Caffè Cimmino** in Posillipo offers excellent coffee and pastries, as well as fine views of the bay.

The small and elegant **Antico Caffè Principe** in Piazza Municipio, which retains its original Art Deco interior, is a good place for breakfast in the city centre. **General Coffee** on Corso Garibaldi, with its spacious refreshment area, is popular with office workers during their breaks. For excellent coffee in Piazza Dante, try **Caffè Mexico**, and in Vomero, try **Caffè Scarlatti** or **Arx Café**, the latter situated near Castel Sant'Elmo. In the old city centre, **Bar Nilo** has courteous and friendly service, while **Caffeteria San Domenico** offers al fresco dining in Piazza San Domenico.

During the summer months, popular spots for night owls are the **Caffè dell'Epoca**, opposite the Academy of Art, and the cafés in Piazza Bellini: the **Intra Moenia** sells books and promotes cultural events. Just beside the cathedral, **Gran Caffè Duomo** does a nice *granita di caffè*.

Pastry Shops and Ice Cream Parlours

Neapolitan pastry shops, known throughout the world and descended from a centuries-old tradition, offer a number of specialities. Among these are the shortcrust or puff pastries called *sfogliatelle*, the *pastiera* eaten at Easter, *babà*, *zeppola di San Giuseppe* and seasonal Christmas pastries such as *rococò* and *struffoli* (pastry rings with honey and candied fruit).

A favourite spot for the locals, particularly on Sundays, is **Scaturchio** in Piazza San Domenico Maggiore, one of the best cafés in the historic centre. Also in Piazza San Domenico Maggiore, **Gran Caffè Aragonese** sells excellent pastries and sweets, as do **Licardo** and **Bellavia** in the Vomero and **Moccia** in the Chiaia district. The **Gran Bar Riviera**, opened in Chiaia in 1870, also offers many treats; the *tartufo* was invented here, a delectable *semifreddo* ice cream with chestnut cream filling. The best *sfogliatella* can be found at **Pintauro** on Via Toledo or **La Sfogliatella Mary** in the Galleria Umberto I. Good ice cream parlours are **La Scimmia** in Piazza Carità, the **Bilancione** in Posillipo, **Carraturo** near the railway station and **Soave** in Vomero.

The *chalets* on the seafront in the Mergellina area are legendary among Neapolitans. The most famous of these are **Remy Gelo**, with great ice creams and granita, and **Chalet Ciro**, specializing in home-made pastries and ice cream. People also come here for coffee or an apéritif. **Chiquito's**, on the Via Mergellina, was once a water vendor and is now famous for his fruit cups and exotic fruit shakes.

Take-Away Food

Founded in 1887 by Gaetano Cecere, the first Neapolitan fast-food establishment is aptly named **Vaco 'e presse** (I'm in a hurry). True to its founder's tradition, it still has marble furnishings and a quaint atmosphere. Rather than a burger bar, the locals usually prefer to drop in at a *tavola calda*, where they can eat a quick plate of pasta, or they buy a sandwich prepared in a delicatessen (*salumeria*), eat a local mozzarella or have hot snacks from a *rosticceria*. Excellent take-aways are **Friggittoria Vomero** in the Vomero area, where you can also buy tasty roast chicken, and **Friggi Friggi**, next to Piazzetta Nilo, offering a quick snack.

If you like street food, the stalls along Via Pignasecca, including **Tripperia Fiorenzano** are for you. The *rosticcerie*, such as **Elettroforno Giulia** in Posillipo, sell pizza by the slice as well as "crocché" (potato croquettes), *arancini di riso* (rice croquettes) and *saltimbocca* (veal). Many of these *rosticcerie* and *gastronomie*, such as **Rosticceria Magia** in Vomero, also sell roasted meats and other prepared foods to take away or eat on the go.

DIRECTORY

Toledo and Castel Nuovo

BARS AND CAFÉS

Antico Caffè Principe
Piazza Municipio 20.
Map 7 B2.

Bar Brasiliano
Galleria Umberto I, 78.
Map 7 A2.

General Coffee
Corso Garibaldi 378.
Map 4 E4.

Gran Caffè Gambrinus
Piazza Trieste e Trento 38.
Map 7 A3.

Il Vero Bar del Professore
Piazza Trieste e Trento 46
Map 7 A3

PASTRY SHOPS AND ICE CREAM PARLOURS

Pintauro
Via Toledo 275.
Map 7 A2.

La Scimmia
Piazza Carità 4.
Map 7 A1 (9 B5).

La Sfogliatella Mary
Via Toledo 66.
Map 7 A2.

TAKE-AWAY FOOD

Tripperia Fiorenzano
Via Pignasecca 14.
Map 7 A1 (9 A5).

Spaccanapoli

BARS AND CAFÉS

Bar Nilo
Via San Biagio dei Librai 129/130.
Map 3 C5 (10 D3).

Caffeteria San Domenico
Piazza San Domenico Maggiore 11.
Map 3 B5 (9 C3).

PASTRY SHOPS AND ICE CREAM PARLOURS

Gran Caffè Aragonese
Piazza San Domenico Maggiore 5/8.
Map 3 B5 (9 C3).

Scaturchio
Piazza San Domenico Maggiore 19.
Map 3 B5 (9 C3).

TAKE-AWAY FOOD

Friggi Friggi
Piazzetta Nilo 14.
Map 3 C5 (10 D3).

Decumano Maggiore

BARS AND CAFÉS

Caffè dell'Epoca
Via Constantinopoli 82.
Map 3 B5.

Caffè Mexico
Piazza Dante 86.
Map 3 A5 (9 B3).

Gran Caffè Duomo
Via Duomo 163.
Map 3 C4 (10 D2).

Intra Moenia
Piazza Bellini 70.
Map 3 B5 (9 C3).

PASTRY SHOPS AND ICE CREAM PARLOURS

Carraturo
Via Casanova 97.
Map 4 E3.

TAKE-AWAY FOOD

Vaco 'e Presse
Piazza Dante 87.
Map 3 A5 (9 B3).

Vomero

BARS AND CAFÉS

Arx Café
Via Tito Angelini 20c.
Map 2 E5.

Caffè Scarlatti
Via Scarlatti 183.
Map 2 D5.

Caffetteria Bernini
Piazza Fanzago 9.
Map 2 D4.

PASTRY SHOPS AND ICE CREAM PARLOURS

Bellavia
Via Luca Giordano 158.
Map 1 C4.

Licardo
Via Belvedere 178/180.
Map 1 B5.

Soave
Via Scarlatti 130.
Map 2 D5.

TAKE-AWAY FOOD

Friggitoria Vomero
Via Cimarosa 44.
Map 2 D5.

Rosticceria Magia
Piazza Fanzago 112/114.
Map 2 D4.

Castel dell'Ovo and Chiaia

PASTRY SHOPS AND ICE CREAM PARLOURS

Chalet Ciro
Via Caracciolo 1-2.
Map 5 B4.

Chiquito's
Via Mergellina (opposite the funicular).
Map 5 B3.

Gran Bar Riviera
Riviera di Chiaia 181.
Map 6 D2.

Moccia
Via San Pasquale a Chiaia 21/22.
Map 6 E2.

Remy Gelo
Via F Galiani 9.
Map 5 3C

Posillipo

BARS AND CAFÉS

Gran Caffè Cimmino
Via Petrarca 147.
Map 5 A4.

PASTRY SHOPS AND ICE CREAM PARLOURS

Bilancione
Via Posillipo 238/b.

TAKE-AWAY FOOD

Elettroforno Giulia
Piazza San Luigi 12/13.

SHOPS AND MARKETS

Shopping in Naples is an excellent way to explore the labyrinth of this fascinating city. Expensive boutiques line the main streets such as Via Toledo and Via Chiaia, where good quality, stylish clothes, shoes and jewellery can be bought. However, don't limit yourself to the fashionable areas, but wander around the alleyways in the old town to discover the small specialist shops and artisan workshops. Here it's possible to find authentic and handmade souvenirs.

These streets often bear the name of the trade practised there, such as Piazza degli Orefici (Goldsmiths' Square).

Perhaps the most enjoyable way to shop is to follow the example of most Neapolitans and buy from the numerous markets and stalls along the roadside. These *bancarelle* sell everything from clothes to kitchenware, and children's toys to jewellery. Common items are cheap seconds from the manufacturer or imitation designer labels.

Beautiful coral jewellery displayed in a shop window

Opening Hours

Shops are open from 10am to 2pm and from 4pm to 8pm. They are closed on Sundays and Monday morning in winter, Saturday afternoon and Sunday in summer. Food shops and markets are shut on Thursday afternoons. Before holiday periods like Christmas, many places are open on Sundays and extend their weekly opening hours. In summer most shops close for two weeks around 15 August (Ferragosto).

How to Pay

Major credit cards are accepted in most boutiques and department stores. Make sure you are given the receipt (*ricevuta fiscale*) for your purchase. By law the police can make a spot check outside the shop and if you are without a receipt, you may be fined. Artisans are not required to issue receipts.

Sales

From early July to early September and early January to mid-February, sales are held in Naples. You can find excellent bargains with discounts of up to 50 per cent and sometimes as much as 70 per cent. It is a good idea to check goods before you leave the shop as a refund is unlikely.

Fashion and Accessories

The exclusive shops are concentrated in Via dei Mille and Via Calabritto, in the elegant Chiaia district. Here the great fashion designers, such as **Emporio Armani**, **Prada** and **Mario Valentino**, have their stores. A jewellery shop, **Bulgari**, has also opened here. In Riviera di Chiaia, **Magazzini Marinella** sells ties that are worn by many VIPs. Fine accessories for men, such as silver cufflinks, are found at **Argenio**, while **Talarico** specializes in hand-carved umbrellas and canes.

At **Eddy Monetti** and **Deliberti** on Via dei Mille, the emphasis is on elegant and classical fashion. Clothes with an innovative touch are offered by **Barbaro** in Galleria Umberto I, while more avant-garde men's and women's wear is sold by **Maxi Ho. Livio De Simone**, who is a native of Naples, offers stylish clothes in bright Mediterranean colours, while **Amina Rubinacci** is known for her woollen and soft cashmere jumpers. Naples also has several **Max Mara** boutiques.

Clothing at somewhat more accessible prices is sold at **Stefanel** and **Motivi**. Young people have no lack of choice with clothes from the well-known **Benetton** outlets, as well as from **Mango**, which has a store on Via dei Mille, and **Zara** and **H&M**, which have stores on Via Toledo. The **Prénatal** chain caters for mothers-to-be and small children.

In the old centre between

High-end designer shops in Via Calabritto, Naples

Interior of the Colonnese bookshop in Via San Pietro a Majella

San Biagio dei Librai and Via degli Orefici there are many jewellers' and goldsmiths' shops. The age-old tradition of engraving and cameo work is still practised in many of these shops. **Ascione Coralli**, a coral and cameo atelier, is open by appointment. **Caso Agostino** has superb coral jewels, and other jewellery shops such as **Ventrella** stock original and attractive designs.

Department Stores and Shopping Centres

Most Neapolitans on the whole prefer the smaller, specialist shops, where the service is more personal. However, some of the department stores, in parti cular **Coin**, offer a good variety of products ranging from quality clothes, cosmetics and perfumes to household goods and crockery. If you are looking for those stores that specialize in household and kitchen goods, try the **Upim** and **Oviesse** chains of department stores, both of which are, as you would expect, generally cheaper and feature average-quality cosmetics, lingerie, household articles and clothes.

The shopping centres, **Galleria Vanvitelli** and the elegant **Galleria Scarlatti** can be found in the Vomero district of the city, and the extremely smart 19th-century

Galleria Umberto I, off Piazza Trieste e Trento, is an attractive arcade of numerous elegant shops.

Coin
Via Scarlatti 98/100.
Tel 081 578 01 11.

Galleria Scarlatti
Via Scarlatti 163.

Galleria Vanvitelli
Piazza Vanvitelli.

Oviesse
Via A Doria 40.
Tel 081 239 63 60.

Upim
Via Nicola Nisco 17.
Tel 081 41 75 20.

Art, Antiques and Interior Design

Naples is renowned for its many fascinating antique and second-hand shops. The best-known antique dealers can be found in Via Domenico Morelli: for instance,

Brandi and **La Florida** are specialists in 18th-century furniture and paintings. Shops that stock historic objects include **Antichità Gargiulo, Antichità Ciro Guarracino** and **Affaitati** in Via Costantinopoli. Old engravings, prints and lithographs, picture frames and other *objets d'art*, are on sale at **Bowinkel**, which has a shop in Santa Lucia and a gallery on Via Calabritto, near Piazza dei Martiri. Items such as rare books, prints and gouaches are sold at **Carlo Regina**, an antiquarian bookseller, while the **Colonnese** bookshop stocks traditional Neapolitan articles. **Maestranze Napoletane** sells exquisite antique marblework, as well as original marble objects made by the owner. Art galleries **Galleria Navarra, Lia Rumma** and **Studio Trisorio** often have interesting work on show.

The **Museum Shop** sells repro-ductions of famous pieces, as well as stylish T-shirts and stationery that make great souvenirs.

Leading interior design shops in the city include **Antica Galleria d'Arte**, in the

The traditional craft of making and restoring string instruments

Neapolitan second-hand dealer with goods on display in the street

Attractive display of traditional nativity scene dolls

Spaccanapoli area, and **Novelli**, featuring the latest styles in home furnishings. Avant-garde modern art pieces by local and foreign artists are available at **Galleria Raucci/Santamaria**, near Capodimonte.

Open-Air Markets

Street stalls and markets set up in the early morning and usually pack up after midday. Food stalls selling seasonal fruit and vegetables generally have fresher and less expensive produce than the shops. Clothes and household items will be cheap and, although they may not be designer quality, they are perfectly good. Bargaining is not usually done when buying food, but for clothes and other items try asking for a discount *(sconto)*.

Fiera Antiquaria Napoletana
Villa Comunale.
Open 8am–2pm third and fourth Sat & Sun of month. Antiques market: silverware, jewellery and ornaments.

Mercatino di Antignano
Porta Nolana & Piazza Principe Umberto. **Open** 7am–1:30pm Mon–Sat. Clothing, shoes, household articles, fabrics.

Mercatino della Pignasecca
Via Pignasecca. **Open** 8am–2pm & 4–8pm Mon–Sat. Mainly food.

Mercatino di Poggioreale
Via Nuova Poggioreale. **Open** 7am–1pm Thu–Sun. Shoes, clothes, antiques.

Handicrafts

The many workshops and second-hand shops in the historic centre offer a varied choice of articles, from the kitsch to the well-designed. In Via San Gregorio Armeno

Market at Porta Nolana

Mercatino della Torretta
Viale Gramsci. **Open** 9am–12:30pm Mon–Sat. Food and clothing.

Mercatino dell'Umberto
Via Vittorio Imbriani. **Open** 7am–2pm Mon–Sat. Clothes, shoes, music.

Mercato Contadino e Artigiano
Via Raffaele Ruggiero. **Open** 6am–2pm Sun. Food, clothing, crafts.

Mercato di Porta Nolana
Via S Cosmo. **Open** 8am–6pm Mon–Sat (8am–2pm Sun). Food, especially fish and seafood.

Mercato di Posillipo
Viale Virgilio. **Open** 7am–1pm Thu. Clothes, accessories, household articles.

is the workshop of the famous nativity scene artisan **Giuseppe Ferrigno**, while in Via San Biagio dei Librai is the **Ospedale delle Bambole** (hospital for dolls) where porcelain dolls, marionettes and puppets are repaired and restored. Nearby at **La Smorfia**, artisans make hand-crafted terracotta statuettes for nativity scenes and collectors. At the **Liuteria Calace**, they make and restore violins, violas, mandolins and lutes, while **Statuaria Sacra di Vincenzo Castaldo** sells religious articles and artifacts. **Nel Regno di Pulcinella** is a workshop dedicated entirely to the making of Neapolitan masks.

Elegant objects made from handmade Amalfi paper make **Legatoria Artigiana di Napoli** a fascinating place. If you are interested in ceramics, it is worth having a look at **Il Cantuccio della Ceramica**.

Food, Wine and Spirits

One of Naples' leading confectionaries is **La Botteghina**, offering a fantastic variety of local specialities along with lovely views. **Gay Odin** has the finest chocolate in Naples, including the delicious *Vesuvio* chocolate which is made with rum. The old-fashioned **Scaturchio** sells excellent cakes and sweets, as well as ice cream. A good selection of wines is to be found at both the **Enoteca Dante** and the **Enoteca Belledonne**.

The inviting entrance of the famous Scaturchio *pasticceria*

DIRECTORY

Fashion and Accessories

Amina Rubinacci
Via dei Mille 16.
Tel 081 41 30 48.

Argenio
Via Filangieri 15e.
Tel 081 41 80 35.

Ascione Coralli
Piazzetta Matilde Serao 19 (2nd floor).
Tel 081 42 11 11.
Open by appointment.

Barbaro
Galleria Umberto 44.
Tel 081 41 12 84.
One of many branches.

Benetton
Via Toledo 253–255.
Tel 081 42 63 72.

Bulgari
Via Filangieri 40.
Tel 081 40 95 51.

Caso Agostino
Piazza San Domenico Maggiore 16.
Tel 081 552 01 08.

Deliberti
Via dei Mille 65.
Tel 081 423 80 59.
One of many branches.

Eddy Monetti
Via dei Mille 45a/b/c.
Tel 081 40 70 64.

Emporio Armani
Piazza dei Martiri 61–62.
Tel 081 42 58 16.

H&M
Via Toledo 343.
Tel 063 283 24 05.

Livio De Simone
Via D Morelli 17.
Tel 081 764 38 27.

Magazzini Marinella
Via Riviera di Chiaia 287.
Tel 081 245 11 82.

Mango
Via dei Mille 62.
Tel 081 42 53 29.

Mario Valentino
Via Calabritto 10.
Tel 081 764 42 62.

Max Mara
Piazza Trieste e Trento 51.
Tel 081 40 62 42.

Maxi Ho
Via Nicola Nisco 20.
Tel 081 41 47 21.

Motivi
Via Toledo 157.
Tel 081 551 06 47.

Prada
Via Filangieri 26.
Tel 081 41 34 99.

Prénatal
Piazza F Cosimo 111.
Tel 081 229 54 12.
One of many branches.

Stefanel
Via dei Mille 57.
Tel 081 252 50 21.

Talarico
Via Toledo 329 (inside).
Tel 081 40 19 79.

Ventrella
Via C Poerio 11.
Tel 081 764 31 73.

Zara
Via Toledo 210–213.
Tel 081 423 80 60.

Art, Antiques and Interior Design

Affaitati
Via Costantinopoli 18.
Tel 081 44 44 27.

Antica Galleria d'Arte
Via B Croce 4.
Tel 081 551 70 36.

Antichità Ciro Guarracino
Via V Gaetani 26.
Tel 081 764 69 12.

Antichità Gargiulo
Via C Poerio 32.
Tel 081 764 38 54.

Bowinkel
Via Calabritto 1.
Tel 081 764 83 20.
Via S Lucia 25.
Tel 081 764 07 39.

Brandi
Via D Morelli 9–11.
Tel 081 764 38 82.

Casella
Via C Poerio 92e/f.
Tel 081 764 26 27.

Carlo Regina
Via Costantinopoli 51.
Tel 081 45 99 83.

Colonnese
Via S Pietro a Maiella 32/33. **Tel** 081 45 98 58.

La Florida
Via Merliani Giovanni 12.
Tel 081 556 97 21.

Galleria Navarra
Piazza dei Martiri 23.
Tel 081 764 35 95.

Galleria Raucci/ Santamaria
Corso Amedeo di Savoia 190.
Tel 081 744 36 45.

Lia Rumma
Via V Gaetani 12.
Tel 081 19 81 23 54.

Maestranze Napoletane
Via Conte di Ruvo 7/8.
Tel 081 544 88 36.

Museum Shop
Largo Corpo di Napoli 3.
Tel 081 360 42 28.
Ⓦ museum-shop.it

Novelli
Via Vetriera 20.
Tel 081 19 56 29 50.

Studio Trisorio
Riviera di Chiaia 215.
Tel 081 41 43 06.

Handicrafts

Il Cantuccio della Ceramica
Via B Croce 38 (inside).
Tel 081 552 58 57.

Giuseppe Ferrigno
Via S Gregorio Armeno 8.
Tel 081 552 31 48.

Legatoria Artigiana di Napoli
Via San Biagio dei Librai 39..
Tel 081 551 12 80.

Liuteria Calace
Via San Domenico Maggiore 9.
Tel 081 551 59 83.

Nel Regno di Pulcinella
Vico San Domenico Maggiore 9.
Tel 081 551 41 71.

Ospedale delle Bambole
Via S Biagio dei Librai 81.
Tel 081 20 30 67.

La Smorfia
Strada dell'Anticaglia 23.
Tel 081 29 38 12.

Statuaria Sacra di Vincenzo Castaldo
Via S Biagio dei Librai 76.
Tel 081 554 11 01.

Food, Wine and Spirits

La Botteghina
Via Orazio 106.
Tel 081 66 05 16.

Enoteca Belledonne
Vico Belledonne a Chiaia 18.
Tel 081 40 31 62.

Enoteca Dante
Piazza Dante 18.
Tel 081 549 96 89.

Gay Odin
Via Toledo 214.
Tel 800 20 00 30.
One of many branches.

Scaturchio
Piazza San Domenico Maggiore 19.
Tel 081 551 70 31.

Shops and Markets along the Coast

Every town and village in the region, from the islands to the coast, offers typical local handicrafts such as ceramics or glassware, as well as foods and wines associated with the history and culture of each place. Wandering through the narrow streets in these lovely seaside spots, you will discover all kinds of customs and crafts.

Fashion and Accessories

Besides shops with designer wear, there are still several old local fashion houses. You can find the top names in Italian and foreign fashion at places such as **Adario & Mario**, who have a shop at Sant'Agata sui due Golfi and another in Sorrento, or **Loro Piana** in Capri. **Capricci**, in Ischia, sells designer lingerie and swimwear. The shopping street in Capri, Via Camerelle, boasts the elegant **Amina Rubinacci** boutique, known for top-quality cashmere pullovers. Other cashmere luxuries are the speciality of **Le Farella**, also in Capri. Two top jewellers in Capri are **La Campanina** and **Chantecler**, both sited in Via Vittorio Emanuele, who stock precious stones in every colour as well as diamonds and coral necklaces of very fine quality.

Fashion styles in Positano are famous for their originality. Among the town's leading houses is **Maria Lampo**, who are well known for making their articles quickly (*lampo* meaning "in a flash"). Top designer wear as well as handmade patchwork clothing and quilts are sold at **Nadir**, while **La Bottega di Brunella** and **La Tartana** are distinguished for their fine fabrics and original patterns. For luxurious swimsuits, sarongs and kaftans, visit **Delfina** on Capri. For custom-made Capri pants, head for **La Parisienne** in Capri.

Sorrento, Positano and Capri are famous for their handmade sandals; to have a pair made especially for you, go to **Siniscalchi** in Sorrento, **Nana** in Positano, the imaginative **Canfora** in Capri or Antonio Viva's shop at Anacapri, aptly called **L'Arte del**

Sandalo Caprese. For the best in high fashion, **Mariorita**, Capri's luxury department store, stocks the finest Italian and international clothing brands and luxury goods.

Art and Handicrafts

By exploring the craftsmen's shops in the towns and villages outside Naples you can really get to know the heart of a place, and discover its cultural and artistic traditions.
The boats known as *gozzi* are built by the **Apreamare** company in Torre Annunziata, and are world-famous. The ancient tradition of marquetry in the Sorrento peninsula is carried on by craftsmen such as **Salvatore Gargiulo** and **Gargiulo & Jannuzzi**, the latter also offering ceramic crockery, pottery and embroidered lace in its three-floor shop a few steps from Piazza Tasso.

Vietri sul Mare is famous for its decorated ceramics; the **Ceramiche Artistiche Solimene** factory employs at least 40 craftsmen who, despite a large output, make fine handmade products. In Maiori, **Studio Fes** produces ceramic tableware and decorative tiles with geometric motifs. Other high-quality ceramics are produced by **Keramos d'Ischia** and **La Madonella Ceramiche** in Ischia and **Ceramiche d'Arte** in Ravello, while **La Bottega dell' Arte di Rubino** in Capri – thanks to the well-known ceramicist Sergio Rubini – now has over 200 outlets in the United States alone.

In Amalfi, visit the **Cartiera Amatruda** mill, where fine quality paper has been produced since the 15th century. As a souvenir of Capri there are the **Carthusia** perfumes, in several branches

around the island (you can also visit their laboratory at the branch on Via Matteotti (No. 2) in Capri).

Food, Wine and Liqueurs

Many fine dairy products such as cheese come from the area around Naples. In Sorrento you can visit the **Apreda** dairy and buy fresh plaits of *fiordilatte*, a type of mozzarella made from cow's milk, in the nearby shop. The **Fattoria Terranova**, in Massa Lubrense, is also worth a visit to stock up on olive oil, preserves and jams. For gourmets, **Capannina Piu'** in Capri offers a mouthwatering array of local food and wines, . as does **Anastasio Nicola**, in Amalfi, whose shop is filled with hanging hams, local cheeses, chocolate and more. For the sweet-toothed, Ischia's **Caffè Calise** has orange *sfogliatelle* and at Positano the **La Zagara** pastry shop has delicious fruit tarts called *crostate*. While in Amalfi, try the delightful lemon pastries at **Andrea Pansa**.

Some wine shops also sell local products such as jam, honey and spices: among them are **Piemme** at Sorrento and **Ischia Sapori** on Ischia. **Gusti e Delizie**, in Ravello, offers fine olive oils from across Italy. A good range of wine is on sale at **La Valle dei Mulini** in Amalfi. **Limoncello di Capri** is the most famous source of limoncello, or lemon-flavoured liqueur. **Profumi della Costiera** and **I Giardini di Ravello** also stock a good range.

Markets

There are numerous markets in the outlying areas. The most important in size and tradition is the second-hand market in Resina at Ercolano (Herculaneum), where you will find used clothes and accessories. It is half an hour from the central railway station in Naples: take the Circumvesuviana line and get off at Ercolano.

DIRECTORY

Fashion and Accessories

Adario & Mario
Via Nastro Azzurro 1–3
(Sant'Agata sui Due Golfi).
Tel 081 878 00 65.
Corso Italia 128 (Sorrento).
Tel 081 878 13 61.

Amina Rubinacci
Via V Emanuele 13
(Capri).
Tel 081 837 72 95.

L'Arte del Sandalo Caprese
Via G Orlandi 75
(Anacapri).
Tel 081 837 35 83.

La Bottega di Brunella
Via Pasitea 72 (Positano).
Tel 089 87 52 28.

La Campanina
Via V Emanuele 18 (Capri).
Tel 081 837 06 43.

Canfora
Via Camerelle 3 (Capri).
Tel 081 837 04 87.

Capricci
Via Roma 37 (Ischia Porto).
Tel 081 98 20 63.

Chantecler
Via V Emanuele II 51
(Capri).
Tel 081 837 05 44.

Delfina
Piazzetta Ignazio Cerio 10
(Capri).
Tel 081 837 55 26.

Le Farella
Via Fuorlovada 21c
(Capri).
Tel 081 837 52 43.

Loro Piana
Via Camerelle 51a–55
(Capri).
Tel 081 837 76 40.
One of two shops.

Maria Lampo
Via Pasitea 12–16
(Positano).
Tel 089 87 50 21.

Mariorita
Via Capodimonte 4/8/12
(Anacapri).
Tel 081 978 05 40.

Nadir
Via Pasitea 44 (Positano).
Tel 089 87 59 75.

Nana
Via Pasitea 164 (Positano).
Tel 089 81 16 16.

La Parisienne
Piazza Umberto 7 (Capri).
Tel 081 837 77 50.

Siniscalchi
Corso Italia 203 (Sorrento).
Tel 081 878 30 65. One of
two shops.

La Tartana
Via della Tartana
(Positano).
Tel 089 87 56 45.

Art and Handicrafts

Apreamare
Via Terragneta 72, Torre
Annunziata.
Tel 081 537 84 11.

La Bottega dell'Arte di Rubino
Via Catena 2–4 (Anacapri).
Tel 081 837 18 78.
W labottegadellartedi
rubino.com

Carmelina
Via Roma (Capri).

Carthusia
Viale Axel Munthe 26
(Anacapri).
Tel 081 837 36 68.
One of four shops.
W carthusia.it

Cartiera Amatruda
Via delle Cartiere 100
(Amalfi).
Tel 089 87 13 15.
W amatruda.it

Ceramiche d'Arte
Via Roma 22 (Ravello).
Tel 089 85 85 76.
W ceramichedarte.com

Ceramiche Artistiche Solimene
Via Madonna degli
Angeli 7 (Vietri sul Mare).
Tel 089 21 02 43.
W ceramicasolimene.it

Emporio Scialò
Corso Umberto I, 21
(Forio d'Ischia).
Tel 081 99 75 92.

Studio Fes
Via Roma 24, (Minori).
Tel 089 214 36 59.
W studiofes.com

Gargiulo & Jannuzzi
Viale Enrico Caruso 1
(Sorrento).
Tel 081 878 10 41.

Keramos d'Ischia
Via d'Aloisio 89,
Casamicciola Terme
(Ischia).
Tel 081 333 01 42.

La Madonella Ceramiche
Via Matteo Verde 32
(Forio d'Ischia).
Tel 081 98 92 38.

Salvatore Gargiulo
Via Fuoro 33 (Sorrento).
Tel 081 878 24 20.

Food, Wine and Liqueurs

Anastasio Nicola
Via Lorenzo d'Amalfi 36
(Amalfi).
Tel 089 87 10 07.

Andrea Pansa
Piazza Duomo 40
(Amalfi).
Tel 089 87 10 65.

Apreda
Via del Mare 20 (Sorrento).
Tel 081 878 13 34.
One of two shops.

Caffè Calise
Via A Sogliuzzo 69
(Ischia Porto).
Tel 081 99 12 70.

Capannina Piu'
Via delle Botteghe 34
(Capri).
Tel 081 837 88 99.

Fattoria Terranova
Via Pontone 10
(Sant'Agata sui Due Golfi).
Tel 081 553 02 34.

I Giardini di Ravello
Via Città 19 (Ravello).
Tel 089 87 22 64.

Gusti e Delizie
Via Roma 28–30
(Ravello).
Tel 089 85 78 02.

Ischia Sapori
Via Gianturco 1
(Ischia Porto).
Tel 081 98 44 82.

Limoncello di Capri
Via Roma 85
(Capri).
Tel 081 837 55 61.

Piemme
Via Gennaro Maresca
80/D (Piano di Sorrento).
Tel 081 532 21 99.

Profumi della Costiera
Via Trinità 37 (Ravello).
Tel 089 85 81 67.

La Valle dei Mulini
Via Lorenzo d'Amalfi 11
(Amalfi).
Tel 089 87 26 03.

La Zagara
Via dei Mulini 8/10
(Positano).
Tel 089 87 59 64.

ENTERTAINMENT

Naples knows how to entertain: demanding emperors, kings, residents and travellers have enjoyed its delights for over 2,000 years. Once a major European capital, Naples still revels in shows, games, banquets, and horse races, plus newer diversions like opera and football. Perhaps Italy's most energetic city, Naples buzzes with activity. The nightlife is dynamic, the cafés, nightspots and cultural venues are always open late, and just about every taste is catered for. Music and theatre performances take place throughout the year, bolstered by

some important international festivals in summertime, mostly held in the holiday resorts. For film buffs there are two main multiplexes as well as some arthouse cinemas. During the week people usually go to the cinema or out to eat; at weekends the piazzas are bustling with life, as it is customary for Neapolitans to meet up to have a drink before going on to nearby nightspots. Clubbers get going after midnight, perhaps winding down at dawn with coffee and a hot brioche at an all-night bar.

Night-time illuminations in a city that is happy to party until dawn

Information and Buying Tickets

Naples' daily newspaper *Il Mattino* has the most complete listings for the city, but the national newspapers also carry Naples listings in their local editions.

A monthly guide to events in Naples is published by the tourist office. Visit www.inaples.it to check it out online. Alternatively, pick up a copy of the magazine *Qui Napoli (see p215)*, or *Zero81*, which are available free from most tourist information offices and hotels.

Tickets for performances can generally be bought at the door on the day. They may be more difficult to obtain for operas at the San Carlo, popular shows at the Diana and Bellini, premieres and special events. The two main booking offices are **Concerteria** and **Box Office**.

Theatre, Opera and Dance

Naples is one of Italy's leading cities for theatre. It hosts international and national touring productions, as well as prestigious local companies. The main season is from October to May, though some theatres put on extra programmes and there are special events year-round.

Neapolitans are proud of their dialect, so don't be surprised if it features in some theatrical productions. **Teatro Sannazaro**, a 19th-century theatre staging traditional Neapolitan comedy, is the venue where Eleonora Duse, Eduardo Scarpetta and the De Filippo brothers starred. The **Mercadante**, home of Teatro Stabile di Napoli, sometimes stages plays by Eduardo De Filippo *(see p41)* in English.

Teatro Cilea, founded in the 1970s, focuses on traditional Neapolitan theatre. Italian classic drama and Neapolitan musicals

are on at the **Bellini**. **Teatro Trianon** bills itself as "the Theatre of Neapolitan Song". The **Augusteo** hosts musicals and concerts, while the **Totò** puts on variety shows, and the **Teatro Bracco** focuses on comedies.

The **Nuovo Teatro Sancarluccio** carries on a long tradition of avant garde performances, while more fringe and experimental theatre are on offer at **Galleria Toledo** and **Nuovo Teatro Nuovo**.

Teatro San Carlo *(see p41 and p57)* is one of Italy's top three opera houses. Its season runs from October through June and it also serves as the city's leading ballet venue, plus it hosts an important symphony season. A premiere here is a great social occasion. The San Carlo also stages performances designed to appeal to young people.

The highly ornate Teatro San Carlo, one of Italy's top venues for opera

Performance at a city music venue

Nightlife

La Movida is the Spanish term Neapolitans use to describe their moveable nightlife – snacks here, drinks there, live music somewhere else – in places that stay open until the small hours of the morning. *La Movida* shifts around according to what venues are popular or trendy at any particular time, but favourite streets in the Vomero neighbourhood are Via Giotto, Via Ruoppolo, Via Chiaia and Via Piccinni. Piazza dei Martiri sees plenty of action, and Piazza Bellini is also lively, with cultural associations that host a range of interesting exhibitions and events.

Intra Moenia *(see p82)* is a magnet in Piazza Bellini. It's a large bar-café-bookshop that appeals to a lefty intellectual crowd with its recorded fusion and jazz music. An alternative crowd that is into dance music favours **Kestè**, located near the Orientale University. There's a DJ and, at weekends, live jazz on a tiny stage.

Via Chiaia, a famously upmarket shopping area by day, attracts a similarly smart set in the evening. Multiple use is in vogue here, with several venues doubling up as bars in the day and as clubs at night. Head to **Chandelier** for the traditional evening *aperitivo* and stay on for a night of house, pop and R&B tunes. If your idea of an enjoyable evening is appreciating a fine wine in a relaxed environment, **Enoteca Belledonne** has an extensive list of Italian and international wines. Also in Chiaia are **Fusion Bar 66**, with its exotic Turkish feel and occasional live bossa nova acts, and longtime neighbourhood favourite **S'move**, a busy three-level bar where *aperitivo* is served from 7pm until 9pm.

Piazza Santa Maria la Nova draws a younger crowd to chug beer at its stands and cafés; however, it also plays host to the rather grown-up **Aret'a'palm**, a jazz and blues bar with a fine wine list.

Look out also for openings at contemporary art galleries clustered around **MADRE** (Museo d'Arte Contemporanea Donna Regina Napoli; *see p88*) and **PAN** (Palazzo delle Arti Napoli).

Naples is home to a famous symphony season at the **Teatro San Carlo**, while **Teatro Bellini** sometimes offers chamber music concerts.

Be aware that phone numbers for venues often change, so don't rely on them. A good hotel concierge should be able to provide up-to-the-minute advice – or you can simply head out, follow *La Movida* and see where it takes you.

Cinema

Most foreign films are dubbed into Italian; however, some movies are occasionally shown in their original language. If this is the case, newspaper listings will bear the words *versione originale* next to the show times. **Plaza Multisala** shows original version films on Tuesdays. Some foreign language institutes, such as the **Institut Français de Naples "Le Grenoble"**, also show films in their original language.

For around ten days in June, the **Napoli Film Festival** highlights international cinema. The **Filangieri Multisala** screens both mainstream and arthouse movies, while the **Modernissimo** and the **Plaza Multisala** have multiple screens and show childrens' films. For over two decades, **Artecinema**, an international festival of films on contemporary art, have been hosted by **Teatro San Carlo** and **Teatro Augusteo**.

Some cinemas in the city show new films for half price on Wednesdays. Summertime brings outdoor screenings in squares and at historic sites. Outside Naples there are also some drive-in cinemas *(see p208)*.

napoli film festival
Festival logo

Fireworks, a popular tradition in Naples and the Campania region

Water polo is a popular sport at the Piscina Scandone in Naples

Children's Entertainment

Edenlandia is the main amusement park in Naples, with over 200 attractions, including the World of Fables, Walt Disney favourites, models of sets from Disney stories and theme merry-go-rounds. It also has a flight simulator and 3D cinema. **Magic World** combines fun rides with a large water park featuring slides and pools. **Bowling Oltremare** has table tennis, football and virtual golf, as well as bowling.

Carousel at the Edenlandia funfair

Spectator Sports

Stadio San Paolo *(see p46)* hosts *calcio* (football), the sporting event that most fires the passion of Neapolitans. Usually games are held on Sundays and tickets always sell out quickly. Newer to Naples is *basket*: its basketball team is Azzurro Napoli.

The **Ippodromo di Agnano** race track lies in a splendid natural location. Every April it hosts the famous Gran Premio trotting races.

Canoe polo teams, active since the late 1980s, compete in the Coppa Italia di Canoa Polo; check *Il Mattino* sports section for information. If you are lucky enough to come across a

match, don't miss the chance to enjoy a unique experience.

Swimming, diving and, especially, water polo are extremely popular in Naples. All are practised at the **Piscina Scandone**, the city's public swimming pool.

Trotting races at Agnano

Outside Naples

Festivals celebrating classical music in the Amalfi Coast region are, in most instances, eagerly anticipated annual events. Because of their popularity, it is best to book tickets in advance. Concerts at the Estate Musicale Sorrentina, which are held in the cloister of the church

of San Francesco in Sorrento, are often in demand. The **Ravello Festival** *(see p45)*, which runs from early July until mid September, includes chamber music, orchestral concerts, film, dance and art exhibitions.

Lovers of classical music can also enjoy **Concerti al Tramonto**, a series of intimate sunset concerts each summer from June to August. They take place on the scenic terrace of Anacapri's Villa San Michele, which boasts sweeping views to the sea below.

Teatro Tasso stages the *Sorrento Musical*, a nostalgic performance depicting southern Italian life, and featuring classic Neapolitan songs and costumes. Aimed at tourists, this show offers a light evening of entertainment in a music hall setting.

Benevento, Santa Maria Capua Vetere and Caserta all have theatres staging a variety of plays and performances, and Pozzuoli and Caserta have drive-in cinemas.

The Phlegraean Fields area has many nightspots, bars and discos. South toward Licola, and on the Sorrento peninsula, the beach bars convert to beach discos on summer evenings. In Capri, after a stroll around La Piazzetta you could try **Number Two** for a night of energetic dancing. On Ischia, dancers at **Valentino** party until well into the night. It is open year round, though in winter only at weekends.

Chamber music above the Bay of Salerno, Ravello Festival

DIRECTORY

Information and Buying Tickets

Box Office
Galleria Umberto I 17.
Map 7 A2.
Tel 081 551 91 88.
W boxofficenapoli.it

eria
Via M Schipa 23.
Map 5 B2.
Tel 081 761 12 21.
W concerteria.it

Theatre, Opera and Dance

Galleria Toledo
Teatro Stabile
D'Innovazione,
Via Concezione a
Montecalvario 34.
Tel 081 42 58 24.
W galleriatoledo.info

Mercadante, Teatro Stabile
Piazza Municipio 64.
Map 7 B2.
Tel 081 551 33 96.
W teatrostabilenapoli.it

Nuovo Teatro Nuovo
Via Montecalvario 16.
Map 7 A1.
Tel 081 497 62 67.
W teatronuovo
napoli.it

Teatro Augusteo
Via Toledo 263 (Piazzetta
Duca d'Aosta).
Map 7 A1.
Tel 081 41 42 43.
W teatroaugusteo.it

Teatro Bellini
Via Conte di Ruvo 14.
Map 3 B4.
Tel 081 549 12 66.
W teatrobellini.it

Teatro Bracco
Via Tarsia 40.
Map 3 A5 (9 A3).
Tel 081 564 53 23.
W teatrobracco.it

Teatro Cilea
Via San Domenico 11.
Map 1 A5.
Tel 081. 714 15 01.
W teatrocilea.it

Teatro San Carlo
Via San Carlo 98f.
Map 7 A3.
Tel 081 797 23 31.
W teatrosancarlo.it

Nuovo Teatro Sancarluccio
Via San Pasquale a
Chiaia 49. **Map** 6 E2.
Tel 081 410 44 67
W nuovoteatrosan
carluccio.com

Teatro Sannazaro
Via Chiaia 157. **Map** 7 A3.
Tel 081 41 17 23.
W teatrosannazaro.it

Teatro Totò
Via Cavara 12. **Map** 4 D3.
Tel 081 564 75 25.
W teatrototo.it

Teatro Trianon
Piazza Calenda 9. **Map** 4
D5. **Tel** 081 225 82 85.
W www.teatrotrianon.
org

Nightlife

Aret'a'palm
Piazza Santa Maria La
Nova 14.
Map 7 B1 (9 C5).
Tel 339 848 6949.

Chandelier
Vico Belledonne a Chiaia
34–35.
Map 6 E2.
Tel 333 252 8177.

Enoteca Belledonne
Vico Belledonne a
Chiaia 18.
Map 6 E2.
Tel 081 40 31 62.

Fusion Bar 66
Via Bisignano 58.
Map 6 E2.
Tel 081 41 50 24.

Intra Moenia
Piazza Bellini 70.
Map 3 B5. **Tel** 081 29 09 88.

Kestè
Largo San Giovanni
Maggiore Pignatelli 26–7.
Map 7 B1.
Tel 081 193 609 32.

MADRE (Museo d'Arte Contemporanea Donna Regina Napoli)
Via L Settembrini 79.
Map 3 C3.
Tel 081 19 31 30 16.

PAN (Palazzo delle Arti Napoli)
Via dei Mille 60.
Map 6 E2.
Tel 081 795 86 05.

S'move
Vico dei Sospiri 10a.
Map 6 E2.
Tel 081 764 58 13.

Teatro Bellini
*See listing under Theatre,
Opera and Dance.*

Teatro San Carlo
*See listing under Theatre,
Opera and Dance.*

Cinema

Filangieri Multisala
Via Filangieri 43–7.
Map 6 F2.
Tel 081 251 24 08.

Institut Français de Naples "Le Grenoble"
Via Crispi 86.
Map 6 D2.
Tel 081 761 62 62.

Modernissimo
Via Cisterna dell'Olio 23.
Map 3 A5.
Tel 081 580 02 54.

Napoli Film Festival
Tel 081 423 81 27.
W napolifilmfestival.
com

Plaza Multisala
Via Kerbaker 85.
Map 2 D4.
Tel 081 556 35 55.

Teatro Augusteo
Via Toledo 263 (Piazzetta
Duca d'Aosta).
Map 7 A1.
Tel 081 41 42 43.
W teatroaugusteo.it

Children's Entertainment

Bowling Oltremare
Viale JF Kennedy.
Tel 081 62 44 44.
W bowlingoltremare.it

Edenlandia
Viale JF Kennedy.
Tel 081 239 40 90.

Magic World
Via S Nullo, Giugliano.
Tel 081 854 67 92.
W magicworld.it

Spectator Sports

Ippodromo di Agnano
Via R Ruggiero.
Tel 081 762 41 61.
W ippodromoagnano.it

Piscina Scandone
Viale Giochi del
Mediterraneo.
Tel 081 570 26 36.

Stadio San Paolo
Piazzale Tecchio
(Fuorigrotta).
W sscnapoli.it

Outside Naples

Number Two
Via Camerelle 1 (Capri).
Tel 081 837 79 00.

Concerti al Tramonto
Villa San Michele,
Viale Axel Munthe 34
(Anacapri)
W villasanmichele.eu

Ravello Festival
Tel 089 85 84 22.
W ravellofestival.com

Teatro Tasso
Piazza Sant'Antonio 25
(Sorrento).
Tel 081 80 755 25.
W teatrotasso.it

Valentino
Corso V Colonna
97 (Ischia).
Tel 081 98 25 69.

SPECIALIST HOLIDAYS AND OUTDOOR ACTIVITIES

Naples and the Amalfi Coast offer a variety of cultural and sporting activities as well as beautiful and arresting landscapes. You can learn to cook regional dishes and discover wines made from grapes unique to the area, some descended from those of Ancient Greece. Walks can be through small medieval towns, rolling hills, along dramatic cliff tops or over active volcanic terrain. Horse rides pass mountains, vineyards and ancient temples. Some of the world's most spectacular coastline beckons with its water sports and caves. Those interested in archaeology can join university projects at ancient sites. Alternatively, you can relax at thermal baths, the best of which are on the island of Ischia. Most guided activities are in Italian, unless noted otherwise.

Culinary Courses

Cookery courses are run close to Paestum (see pp166–7) by **Azienda Agrituristica Seliano**. The courses focus on cuisine derived from ancient Greek and Roman traditions and are held at Agriturismo Seliano, a working farm that can provide room and board. The farm raises buffalo, which produce milk for the best mozzarella. Courses usually last three to five days, but can be flexible.

Il Principe (see p195), a restaurant within walking distance of the ruins of Pompeii (see pp150–55), offers cookery lessons in ancient or modern Neapolitan cuisine. The ancient Roman recipes were devised in collaboration with the Archaeological Service of Pompeii. De Gustibus, a recipe booklet fine tuned by the restaurant's award-winning chef, describes how the Romans prepared their food. Courses taught by chef Gian Marco Carli are offered on request.

Pastafest, with tastings and demonstrations, is a five-day fair held in October in the pasta-making centre of Torre Annunziata (see p145).

Wine Courses and Tasting

Vitignoitalia is an annual wine trade show and tasting experience that began in 2005. For three days in late May participants visit wine makers, taste wines and enrol at sessions to learn more about single-varietal wines (those made from only one type of grape), most of which are from southern Italy.

Mastroberardino, a winery founded in 1878, has a joint project with the Archaeological Service of Pompeii to research the grapes and growing systems used in Pompeii at the time of the AD 79 eruption. It holds various wine tasting courses and tours of its cellar.

Feudi di San Gregorio is one of the region's larger wine makers and has a modern *cantina* (cellar) of architectural interest designed in 2002 by Hikaru Mori. It runs wine-tasting events and offers guest accommodation.

Walking and Horse Riding

Hiking through the glorious countryside is a popular activity. Free maps with suggested routes are available at EPT offices (see p215), which also have details of guided tours.

The Pozzuoli/Solfatara metro stop is recommended as a starting point for exploring Pozzuoli (see pp140–41). You can walk to the Temple of Serapis and then on to the Solfatara (see p141), with its volcanic phenomena such as fumaroles and bubbling mud.

The WWF runs the **Cratere degli Astroni** nature reserve on Vesuvius's crater. To get there take the Agnano exit on the *tangenziale* (bypass). Paths through the woods lead to stretches of water inhabited by herons and other birds. **Presidio Vulcano Vesuvio** leads guided tours in the park around Vesuvius and up to the crater.

Azienda Agrituristica Seliano in Paestum offers horse riding for experienced riders. It is also worth checking with tourist offices for equestrian centres and other *agriturismi* with horses.

Horse riding, an ideal way to appreciate the region's scenery

Treatment at one of the Amalfi Coast's spa resorts

Spa Holidays

The Amalfi Coast's thermal waters attracted the likes of the Roman emperor Tiberius. Unlike those in northern Italy, the region's spas draw few crowds and charge reasonable prices. Ischia has the best facilities. **Grand Hotel Punta Molino Terme** has a thermal pool and spa, as does **Giardini Poseidon Terme**. The Campania region offers the excellent **Terme di Agnano**. Thermal waters are also to be found at Lacco Ameno, Casamicciola Terme, Telesia near Benevento and Villamaina near Avellino. Many spas close in winter.

Water Sports and Excursions by Boat

Many Neapolitans head to Capri or Ischia on the ferry *(see p222)* for the day.

Scuba lessons and excursions are available at **Lucibello** and (in English as well as Italian) at the **Punta Campanella Diving Center**. For diving at Capri and Ischia, contact the **Capri Sea Service** and **Ischia Diving Center** respectively.

Naples' seafront clubs are reserved for members, but your hotel may be able to sponsor you as a guest. Many marinas offer sailing. Weekly yacht rentals (2–5 cabins), with or without a skipper, are available year-round at **Eva Mare** in Salerno. From March to October, **Amalfi Kayak** offers guided half-day and full-day tours from just outside Amalfi, along the rugged coastlines of the Sorrentine peninsula and Capri.

The **Centro Sub Campi Flegrei** offers regular dives as well as guided underwater excursions to the archaeological park of Baia *(see p141)*.

Archaeological Projects

From roughly April to October, the **Sanisera Archaeology Institute** runs week-long courses offering a chance to investigate Roman ruins submerged in Naples Bay.

Spelunking

Those who fancy having a go at cave exploring, otherwise known as spelunking, can experience it at the **Grotte dell' Angelo** (Angel Cave), a trek suitable for amateurs.

DIRECTORY

Culinary Courses

Azienda Agrituristica Seliano
Via Seliano, Paestum.
Tel 082 872 36 34.
W agriturismo
seliano.it

Pastafest
W pastafest.it

Il Principe
Piazza Bartolo Longo,
Pompeii.
Tel 081 850 55 66.
W ilprincipe.com

Wine Courses and Tasting

Feudi di San Gregorio
Loc Cerza Grossa,
Sorbo Serpico (Avellino).
Tel 082 598 66 86.
W feudi.it

Mastroberardino
Via Manfredi Altripalda
78/81 (Avellino).
Tel 082 561 41 11.
W mastroberardino.
com

Vitignoitalia
Tel 081 410 45 33.
W vitignoitalia.it

Walking and Horse Riding

Azienda Agrituristica Seliano
See Culinary Courses.

Cratere degli Astroni
Tel 081 558 37 20.
W crateredegliastroni.
org

Presidio Vulcano Vesuvio
Via S Vito 151, Ercolano.
Tel 081 777 57 20.
W guidevesuvio.it

Spa Holidays

Giardini Poseidon Terme
Via G Mazzella 87, Ischia.
Tel 081 908 71 11.
W giardiniposeidon.it

Grand Hotel Punta Molino Terme
Lungomare Cristoforo
Colombo 23, Ischia.
Tel 081 99 15 44.
W puntamolino.it

Terme di Agnano
Via Agnano Astroni 24,
Napoli.Tel 081 618 91 11.
W termediagnano.com

Water Sports and Excursions by Boat

Amalfi Kayak
Duoglio Beach, Via Mauro
Comite 41
Tel 338 36 29 520
W amalfikayak.com

Capri Sea Service
Via Cristoforo Colombo
64, Capri. Tel 081 837 87 81.
W capriseaservice.com

Punta Campanella Diving Center
Marina della Lobra, Via
Fontanelle 18, Massa
Lubrense. Tel 081 854 55 47.

Centro Sub Campi Flegrei
Via Miliscola 165, Pozzuoli.
Tel 081 853 15 63.
W centrosub
campiflegrei.it

Eva Mare
Via Porto 12, Salerno.
Tel 089 257 60 94.
W evamare.it

Ischia Diving Center
Via Iasolino 106, Ischia
Porto. Tel 081 98 18 52.
W ischiadiving.net

Lucibello
Via del Brigantino 9,
Positano. Tel 089 87 50 32.
W lucibello.it

Archaeological Projects

Sanisera Archaeological Institute
Tel 347 871 09 63
W archaeology.
institute

Spelunking

Grotte dell'Angelo
Petina or Polla exit from
A3, then SS19 and follow
signs to the cave.
Tel 097 539 70 37.
W grottedipertosa-
auletta.it

SURVIVAL GUIDE

PRACTICAL INFORMATION

Naples is a lively if somewhat chaotic city. It may seem bewildering at first, but after experiencing its vibrant street life and rich historic and artistic wealth, it is hard not to be won over by Naples' gritty charms. The city has undergone something of a rebirth, with more monuments open at regular hours and a reorganization of its major museums, making the most of their world-class collections. Improved facilities, an expanded metro and new pedestrian areas have revived public spaces, and cultural and social activities abound. The city has its frustrating aspects, such as crippling bureaucracy at banks and public offices, and it is wise to be on the lookout for petty crime, keeping money and valuables well out of view. However, with a few simple guidelines and some forward planning it's easy to make the most of this fascinating city and its remarkable treasures.

Castel Sant'Elmo, on Vomero hill

Immigration and Customs

European Union (EU) residents and visitors from the United States, Canada, Australia, New Zealand and Japan do not need a visa for stays of up to three months, but they must have one for a longer stay. Non-EU citizens must carry a valid passport with them at all times, while for EU citizens an ID card will suffice.

Non-EU citizens can bring in 200 cigarettes, 50 cigars, or 250 grams of tobacco; 1 litre of spirits or 2 litres of wine; and 50 grams of perfume. There is no limit for EU citizens. Non-EU citizens can also claim back sales tax (IVA) on purchases in excess of €155. For further details on customs allowances, contact your embassy or consulate.

Tourist Information

It is possible to organize your itinerary before your trip to Naples via the **ENIT** (Italian tourist board) office in your home country. Once in Italy, the network of local tourist offices known as **EPT** (Ente Provinciale per il Turismo) can provide useful information about accommodation, guided tours and excursions in Naples and the surrounding area. EPT offices can be found at key arrival points such as the airport and the main railway station, as well as in the city centre.

The **Azienda Autonoma di Soggiorno, Cura e Turismo** has offices in Naples and the main tourist resorts. They are good sources of information and will provide free maps and guide books. Smaller towns will also have an information office, called a Pro Loco, often based in the town hall.

Travel Safety Advice

Visitors can get up-to-date travel safety information from the **Foreign and Commonwealth Office** in the UK, the **State Department** in the US and the **Department of Foreign Affairs and Trade** in Australia.

Opening Hours and Admission Prices

Shops in Naples tend to be open 8:30am–1pm and 4:30–8:30pm Monday to Saturday. In the centre, however, many stay open throughout the day. Museums and archaeological sites alternate their closing days between Tuesdays and Wednesdays; smaller museums close on Mondays, while church opening hours vary depending on staff schedules and availability. Always check opening times before visiting.

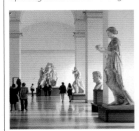

Museo Archeologico Nazionale

Entrance to most sights is free for EU citizens under the age of 18 or over 65, and half-price for those aged 18–25 (with ID). Churches are generally free but may charge for some areas. The Campania Artecard (www.campaniartecard.it) offers entrance and discounts on sites and includes public transport.

Travellers with Special Needs

Naples can be a challenge for travellers with disabilities. Progress is being made, but cobbled streets, chaotic traffic and limited parking make movement difficult for visitors in wheelchairs, the partially sighted or those with hearing impairments. The website **Turismo Accessible** has information on accessible hotels, restaurants, monuments and churches in the city. It is wise to call the establishments you plan to visit in advance to check for accessibility.

Steep hillsides and stone steps make travelling in a wheelchair rather difficult on the Amalfi Coast. The centre and waterfront of Amalfi town are the most wheelchair-friendly areas here. Local tourist offices have information on accessible public transport and accommodation. If you need assistance when travelling by train, contact customer services at the **Stazione Centrale** 24 hours before your train's departure.

Student Travellers

Travellers aged 18–25 can obtain discounted transport and entry to sites and museums in Naples and beyond when purchasing either the Naples or Campania Youth Artecard *(see p221)*.

Hostelling International operates several hostels in the region for members of YHA (Youth Hostel Association), offering discounts to members (€26 membership fee payable online or at any participating hostel). There are also plenty of hostels to be found on hostelworld.com.

Listings Information

The free monthly magazine *Qui Napoli*, available from most hotels and information offices, lists events in and around Naples. Each issue has up-to-date information in Italian and English on local exhibitions, theatre performances and concerts. More detailed

information on lectures, seminars, sports and entertainment can be found in the national magazines or in the relevant supplements of newspapers. *Il Mattino*, Naples' daily newspaper, lists museum opening hours and events, as well as ferry and train schedules.

Italian Time

Italy is 1 hour ahead of Greenwich Mean Time (2 hours ahead in the summer). London is therefore 1 hour behind Italian time and New York 6 hours behind; Tokyo is 8 hours ahead, and Sydney 10 hours ahead.

Responsible Tourism

Visitors can help preserve the beauty of this area by respecting the environment and supporting local businesses. Buying local foods and wines helps farming communities throughout the region. In Naples, shop at the open-air markets *(see p202)*, including the daily Mercatino della Pignasecca, near Via Toledo. Outside of the city, visit **Tenuta Vannulo**, a certified organic water-buffalo farm promoting sustainable agriculture. Take a tour of the mozzarella factory or relax in the café serving buffalo-milk products.

The ethos of **ICNOS Adventures** is explained by the full version of its name (Italian Culture, Nature, Outdoor, Sustainability). This tour operator specializes in non-damaging tourism that preserves the cultural heritage and natural beauty of the Amalfi Coast and Campania.

DIRECTORY

Tourist Information

Azienda Autonoma di Soggiorno, Cura e Turismo Naples
Via Marino Turchi 16.
Map 7 A4. **Tel** 081 245 74 75.
Piazza del Gesù Nuovo. **Map** 9 B4.
Tel 081 551 27 01.
Via San Carlo 9. **Map** 7 A3.
Tel 081 40 23 94. **w** inaples.it

Sorrento
Via Luigi De Maio 35.
Tel 081 807 40 33.
w sorrentotourism.com

ENIT
United Kingdom
Tel 020 7408 1254.
w italiantouristboard.co.uk
United States
Tel 212 245 56 18.
w italiantourism.com

EPT
Piazza dei Martiri 58. **Map** 6 F2.
Tel 081 410 72 19/ 405 311.
w eptnapoli.info

Travel Safety Advice

Australia (Department of Foreign Affairs and Trade) **w** dfat.gov.au, smartraveller.gov.au

United Kingdom (Foreign and Commonwealth Office)
w gov.uk/foreign-travel-advice

United States (Department of State) **w** travel.state.gov

Travellers with Special Needs

Stazione Centrale (Customer Services)
Tel 081 567 29 91.

Turismo Accessibile
w turismoaccessibile.org

Student Travellers

Hostelling International (HI)
w hihostels.com

Responsible Tourism

ICNOS Adventures
Via Mazzini 107, Vietri sul Mare.
Map 2 F3. **Tel** 089 21 24 89.
w icnosadventures.com

Tenuta Vannulo
Via G Galilei 10, Capaccio Scalo, Salerno. **Tel** 0828 72 78 94.
w vannulo.it

Fruit and vegetables on display at one of Naples' many open-air markets

Security and Public Services

While most areas outside Naples do not pose particular problems, petty crime is quite widespread in the city itself. However, by taking a few simple precautions, you will be able to protect yourself from pickpockets and purse-snatchers. Don't wear valuable jewellery or watches; handbags are easy targets, so hold on to them tightly, and carry your money in your pockets or in a money belt. If possible, keep cameras and video cameras hidden from sight. It's best to be wary in Naples, but don't let apprehension ruin your trip.

Officers of the *polizia*

Police and Security

In Naples there are several types of police force, each one serving a particular role. The state police, or *polizia*, wear blue uniforms and handle most crimes. The military-trained *carabinieri* wear black uniforms with red-striped trousers. They deal with offences ranging from organized crime to traffic violations, and they also conduct random security checks. The *vigili urbani* are the municipal traffic police, dealing with traffic and parking offences. Officers from any of these forces will be of assistance in an emergency.

What to Be Aware of

Do not carry large sums of money on you while walking around the city; leave it in your hotel safe. Make photocopies of vital documents like passports, or at least make a note of the number. Report any loss or theft to the police; lost or stolen credit cards and traveller's cheques should be immediately

reported to the issuing bank. If you are travelling by car, always park in supervised car parks, and do not leave items visible inside the vehicle. In crowded public areas or on public transport, be on your guard against pickpockets; purse-snatchers on mopeds prefer to take jewels and handbags from strolling pedestrians. The train station is best avoided at night, and it is not advisable to walk around alone after dark.

In an Emergency

For any police or medical emergency service, including ambulances, dial 113 *(Soccorso Pubblico di Emergenza)*. The *carabinieri* emergency number is 112. To call an ambulance, dial 118. For the *Vigili del Fuoco* (fire brigade), dial 115; and for roadside assistance *(Soccorso Stradale)*, dial 116.

Medical Matters

EU nationals with a European Health Insurance Card (EHIC; www.ehic.org.uk) receive reduced or free medical care, although you may find you first have to pay for the medical attention and reclaim the money later. Not all treatments are covered by the card, so it is a good idea to arrange medical cover before travelling. Non-EU citizens should try to arrive in Italy with comprehensive medical insurance.

If you should need urgent medical assistance, call the **Pronto Soccorso** (casualty department) of the nearest hospital. All pharmacies have a list of branches open at night and on public holidays *(farmacia di turno)* posted on their door. The **Farmacia Alma Salus** is open all night every night from 8pm.

Banks and Bureaux de Change

Opening hours for banks are usually 8:30am–1:20pm Monday to Friday; some are also open 2:45–3:45pm. Identification, such as a passport, is required for any transaction. Banks often offer the best exchange rates, but you can also exchange currency at post offices or private exchange offices. Larger hotels will also offer this service, often at a slightly higher rate.

Currency

The Italian currency is the euro. Euro banknotes have seven denominations. The €5 note (grey in colour) is the smallest, followed by the €10 note (pink), €20 note (blue), €50 note (orange), €100 note (green), €200 note (yellow) and €500 note (purple). The euro has eight coin denominations: €1 and €2; 50 cents, 20 cents, 10 cents, 5 cents, 2 cents and 1 cent. The €2 and €1 coins are both silver and gold in colour. The 50-, 20- and 10-cent coins are gold. The 5-, 2- and 1-cent coins are bronze.

Euro notes

Debit and Credit Cards

Major credit cards such as **VISA**, **MasterCard**, **American Express** and **Diners Club** are accepted by most larger businesses and restaurants. However, since some smaller restaurants, shops and bars do not take credit cards, it is advisable to carry some cash with you. Credit and debit cards are the most convenient way to access euros, and you can use either at ATMs (*Bancomat*), which display the logos of the cards they accept. Note that you may be charged for using your debit or credit card at some ATMs; check with your bank for more information. To avoid the inconvenience of international transactions blocking your card, contact your bank before travelling, and alert them to your travel dates and destinations.

A public telephone on the street

Public Telephones

The widespread use of mobile phones in Italy means that many Naples' payphones have been neglected or vandalized. Most of them require a phonecard (*scheda*), which can be purchased from tobacconists, newsagents or bars. Some phone boxes also take credit cards, but be wary: some unscrupulous companies stick official-looking 0800 numbers on public phone boxes and charge high rates for international calls. To be on the safe side, use an international calling card, also available at tobacconists or newsagents.

International call shops all over the city offer competitive rates for international calls, while making calls from hotel telephones can be very expensive. For the international

operator, and to have your calls charged to your home phone bill, dial 170.

The area code for Naples is 081. Note that in Italy you always need to dial the area code before the number, even when making a call within the same town or city.

Mobile Phones

Travelling with, or even acquiring, a mobile phone (*telefonino*) in Italy is easy. If your mobile is a GSM, dual- or tri-band phone, check if it can be unlocked. If so, consider purchasing an Italian SIM card (about €10), which gives you an Italian mobile number and access to a pre-paid service. Visit a **Vodafone**, **TIM** or **Wind** store and ask for a *SIM prepagato* (pre-paid SIM).

Internet

Many Internet cafés in Naples are located around the train station and on the side streets west of Via Toledo. Access costs from €2 to €5 per hour. Many hotels in the city and the surrounding areas include Internet access in their rates. Call ahead for details. Cafés and bars offering a Wi-Fi service to their customers are also on the increase. If you are travelling with your laptop and need frequent mobile Internet connection, you can purchase an Internet key (*chiavetta*) at mobile phone shops like Vodafone, TIM or Wind.

Post Offices

Post offices in Naples are open from 8:30am to 1:15pm Monday to Friday, 8:30am to noon Saturday and until noon on the last day of the month. The main office, **Posta Centrale**, is open from 8:20am to 7:05pm Monday to Friday (to 12:35pm on Saturdays). Post office branches are located all over the city, in the railway stations and at Capodichino airport. Stamps can be bought at tobacconists (*tabacchi*), as well as in the post office itself.

DIRECTORY

Police and Security

Ambulance
Tel 118.

Fire
Tel 115.

General Emergencies
Tel 113 or 112.

Police (Carabinieri)
Tel 112.

Police Headquarters
Via Medina 75.
Map 7 B1.
Tel 081 794 11 11.

Traffic Police
Tel 081 595 41 11.

Medical Matters

Farmacia Alma Salus
Piazza Dante 71.
Map 9 B3.
Tel 081 549 93 36.

Pronto Soccorso Ospedale Cardarelli
Via Cardarelli 9.
Tel 081 747 11 11.

Ospedale dei Pellegrini
Via Portamedina 41.
Map 9 A4.
Tel 081 254 21 11.

Ospedale San Paolo
Via Terracina 219.
Tel 081 254 82 11.

Credit Cards and Traveller's Cheques

MasterCard/VISA
Tel 800 819 014.

American Express
Tel 067 22 82 or 800 91 49 12.

Diners Club
Tel 800 86 40 64.

Mobile Phones

TIM
W tim.it

Vodafone
W vodafone.it

Wind
W wind.it

Post Offices

Posta Centrale
Piazza Matteotti.
Map 7 B1.
Tel 081 428 98 14.
W poste.it

TRAVEL INFORMATION

Naples' only airport is Capodichino, which is conveniently close to the city and used for domestic, European and charter flights; the nearest intercontinental airport is located in Rome, to the north. The fastest means of reaching Naples by land is by train, since there are few long-distance coach connections with European cities, and driving is far from ideal because of traffic problems and parking restrictions. The city also has a large maritime passenger terminal with ferry connections to the various islands in the Bay of Naples. Moving within the city and its surrounding area is getting easier as Naples is working to improve its metro system and to create an efficient transport network. Three underground lines, buses and funiculars link all the main sights in the city of Naples itself.

Check-in desks at Capodichino airport, Naples

Arriving by Air

Daily flights to Naples from London, Paris, Frankfurt and Munich are operated by the Italian state airline **Alitalia** and foreign carriers such as **Air France** and **British Airways**. **Meridiana** flies domestic routes and also connects Naples to many European cities, plus Russia and the Middle East. Numerous budget and charter airlines also offer flights to Naples; these include **easyJet**, which has direct flights from London and Paris. **Gesac**, the airport authority, has a website with a useful facility for finding flights into Naples from foreign cities.

Naples' Capodichino airport is small, even though it is the only international airport in the region. Travellers from outside Europe will probably transfer to a connecting flight to Naples in Rome.

To get from the airport to the city centre, take the Alibus, which stops at Piazza Garibaldi and Piazza Municipio, and is run by the **Azienda Napoletana Mobilità (ANM)**. Piazza Municipio is within walking distance of Molo Beverello (see 219), where you can take ferries to the islands. From Napoli Centrale, you can pick up the Circumvesuviana railway (see pp222–3) to travel to Pompeii and the coast. Alternatively, buses operated by **Curreri** run direct from the airport to Pompeii, Castellammare and Sorrento and elsewhere. Every 90 minutes a **ATC** bus travels to Caserta.

If you want to travel by taxi, make sure you go to the airport's official rank and that the meter is on. There are set tariffs for journeys such as the one from the airport to Piazza Garibaldi (€16); these should be clearly displayed. The trip lasts about 20 minutes.

Arriving by Train

Most trains in Italy are run by state-owned **Trenitalia**. There are three main railway stations in Naples: **Napoli Centrale**, in Piazza Garibaldi; **Mergellina**, on the seafront; and **Campi Flegrei**, at Fuorigrotta. Napoli Centrale is also the main interchange for the city's public transport systems. Access to the Circumvesuviana (see pp222–3) is from inside the station, while the square in front of the station contains the main terminal for city, suburban and long-distance buses, as well as access to the underground (metropolitana).

The Frecciarossa and privately run **Italo** are high-speed services that run between Rome (Roma Termini) and Naples (Napoli Centrale), with a travel time of just 1 hour and 10 minutes. Other train services running several times each hour include the Eurostar (ES) trains, the InterCity (IC) trains and the regional services, which are generally very slow. Salerno is a convenient station for reaching the Amalfi Coast.

The elegant Campi Flegrei railway station

Heavy traffic in Naples city centre

Arriving by Car

Should you decide to travel to Naples by car, be prepared for stressful driving conditions, heavy traffic congestion and parking difficulties. A car may be convenient for visiting other towns in the region, but in Naples itself it is wise to use the public transport system or walk.

The **Automobile Club d'Italia (ACI)** provides road maps and a towing and repair service to its members and members of affiliated foreign associations. Tolls are charged on the *autostrada* (motorway) and can be paid in cash or with a magnetic Viacard, which can be purchased from tobacconists (*tabaccai*) or at an ACI agency. Emergency telephones can be found at regular intervals along the motorway.

The A1 motorway exits into the highway that runs through Naples (*Tangenziale–A56*), which then takes you quickly to the centre of the city and out to the Phlegraean Fields, including Pozzuoli and Cumae. For the coastal resorts, follow signs for the A3 *autostrada*, signposted Salerno; then take the SS145 into Sorrento. The SS163 runs the length of the Amalfi coastline.

Arriving by Boat

The main maritime passenger terminal used by cruise ships that come into Naples while touring the Mediterranean is the Molo Angioino, located opposite Piazza Municipio.

Ferries and hydrofoils for connections to the various islands in the Bay of Naples and the Sorrento Peninsula depart from the adjacent Molo Beverello *(see also pp222–3)*.

The **Tirrenia** ship line provides direct connections between Naples and several ports in Sardinia and Sicily. **Siremar** operates the route from Naples to the Aeolian Islands, off the northeast coast of Sicily. **SNAV** and **AliLauro** run high-speed hydrofoil services to and from the Aeolian Islands, Ponza and Ventotene. Be aware that some of these routes operate only in the summer months.

Passenger ferry at the Naples seaport

DIRECTORY

Getting Around Naples

Naples' transport system is slowly improving, but the main thoroughfares in this densely populated city are often blocked with traffic. Driving is not recommended, while travelling by bus or tram can be a slow affair at busy times, and taxis can be expensive when traffic is heavy. It will often be faster to travel around the centre on foot. The funicular railways offer a convenient link to the Vomero district. The main central squares have display panels that indicate the main bus, tram and metro stops.

Green Travel

The main focus in Naples is on improving and expanding the public transport network, which is run by **Azienda Napoletana Mobilità (ANM)**. While this goes on, green initiatives are not a priority. However, using the public transport system is a great way to travel in an environmentally friendly way.

The city centre and many of the key sights are easily accessible on foot or by public transport, so there is no need to rent a car. Although bus and tram services in Naples can be slow due to traffic, they are far-reaching.

Many popular destinations outside Naples – including Pompeii and Herculaneum, Mount Vesuvius, the Amalfi Coast, the Sorrento Peninsula and the islands in the Bay of Naples – can be easily reached by train, bus or ferry.

City Railways

Naples' rail system is confusing because many non-connecting lines run through the city. Construction of a comprehensive metro (Metropolitana) system, for years delayed by lack of funds and archaeological finds, has made significant progress, opening metro stops in the city centre.

There are three main metro lines. **MetroNapoli** runs Linea 1, or the hill metro (Collinare), which connects Piazza Garibaldi, Piazza Municipio and Piazza Dante as well as Vormero and beyond. From Garibaldi, the first and last

departures are at 6:20am and 11pm, respectively (extending to 1:30am on Friday and Saturday), with departures every 8 minutes. MetroNapoli also runs the short Linea 6, which links the Fuorigrotta area with Mergellina.

Trenitalia *(see p219)* runs Linea 2, which goes from Gianturco to Pozzuoli, with stops at Piazza Garibaldi, Piazza Cavour (where it intersects Linea 1), Montesanto, Piazza Amedeo, Mergellina, Campi Flegrei and Bagnoli. It runs from 5:45am to 10:45pm, with departures every 10–20 minutes.

There are also three above-ground railway lines: the Cumana and Circumflegrea, each heading through the city and into the Phlegraen Fields, and the Circumvesuviana, which runs from Porta Nolana around the Bay of Naples to Sorrento *(see p222).*

Modern funicular at a station

Funicular Railways

There are four funicular routes in Naples, all run by MetroNapoli. Funicolare Centrale, Funicolare di Montesanto and Funicolare di Chiaia connect the city centre with the Vomero district. The fourth funicular, Mergellina, links the seafront area (Via Mergellina) with Via Manzoni. The funiculars are reliable and fast, and they run every 10 minutes from 6:30am until 10pm. The Centrale and Chiaia lines operate until 12:30am at weekends.

Buses and Trams

In Naples, bus and tram journeys take time because of the heavy traffic; in addition, these means of transport are often crowded. Be aware of pickpockets, and keep your valuables tucked away. The bus and tram networks are run by the ANM. The red bus lines R1, R2 and R4 pass by key sights in

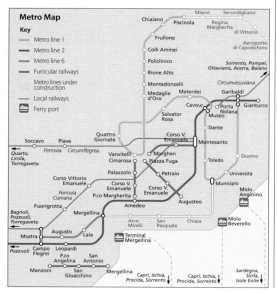

Metro Map

Key

- ▦ Metro line 1
- ▬ Metro line 2
- ▬ Metro line 6
- ▬ Funicular railways
- ▭ Metro lines under construction
- ─ Local railways
- 🚢 Ferry port

the city centre; they run every 10 minutes from 5:30am to 11:30pm. The electric buses E1 and E3 (7:30am–6:20pm, about half-hourly) serve the old town and the Quartieri Spagnoli.

Tickets and Fares

Naples' transport network runs under the integrated UnicoCampania system (www.unicocampania.it), whereby one ticket is valid for all local buses, trams, funiculars, the *metropolitana* and the Cumana, Circumvesuviana (within Naples) and Circumflegrea train lines. Available from stations, newsagents and tobacconists, a single "TIC" ticket (€1.50) is valid for 90 minutes. An all-day ticket is €4.50, a weekly ticket is €15.80, and a monthly ticket is €42. Validate your ticket before departure by stamping it in a machine. If you change to a different form of transport within your 90-minute journey, you must revalidate it.

Both the Napoli and Campania Artecard (www.campaniartecard.it) are popular passes including both transport and select museums..

Walking

Pedestrianized areas allow visitors to enjoy Naples in relative peace and quiet. For traffic-free shopping, head to Via Chiaia, Via Toledo and Via Scarlatti, in the Vomero area. Via Partenope and part of Via Caracciolo are also closed to traffic, enabling you to stroll the Lungomare seafront from Castel dell'Ovo to Mergellina. However, be very careful crossing the road elsewhere: drivers often ignore traffic lights and zebra crossings, and fast-moving scooters appear from nowhere.

Walking down an alley in Naples' historic centre

Guided Tours

Citysightseeing Napoli runs a hop-on, hop-off service with four routes: three covering the main city sights, and one along the Bay to Posillipo. The main stop is outside Castel Nuovo.

Visits to underground Naples are organized by **LAES La Napoli Sotterranea** (Thu, Sat, Sun and hols) and **Napoli Sotterranea** (daily). For a good introduction to Naples, hire a local tour guide via the tourist information offices *(see p215)* or by inquiring at your hotel reception desk.

Taxis

If you take a taxi, make sure it is from an official rank. The meter should read €3.50 at the start of the ride. The minimum fare is €4.50 on weekdays from 7am to 10pm, outside of which an extra €1.50 is added, and rides from the airport to Piazza Garibaldi cost €16, to Municipio €19 and to Vomero €23. There is an extra charge of €0.50 for each item of luggage.

You can find taxis in the official ranks at the train and metro stations, and in the main squares.

Driving and Parking

Traffic in Naples is a challenge even for experienced drivers, and parking is a problem. Designated parking areas are marked with blue lines and cost €1–2 per hour, with a maximum stay of 1 or 2 hours. For cheaper parking, head to **Parcheggio Brin**, a multilevel parking garage that is connected to the city centre by bus lines. Avoid areas with yellow lines; they are reserved for residents.

Scooter and Moped Hire

Mopeds and scooters can be hired at some car-hire agencies *(see p223)* or at **Rent Sprint**, which specializes in scooters. **Penisola Rent** is a convenient starting point for exploring the Sorrento Peninsula and Amalfi coast by scooter.

DIRECTORY

Green Travel

Azienda Napoletana Mobilità (ANM)
Tel 800 639 525 or 081 763 11 11.
W anm.it

City Railways

MetroNapoli
Tel 800 63 95 25.
W anm.it

Guided Tours

Citysightseeing Napoli
Tel 081 551 72 79.
W napoli.city-sightseeing.it

LAES La Napoli Sotterranea
Tel 081 40 02 56.
W lanapolisotterranea.it

Napoli Sotterranea
Tel 081 29 69 44.
W napolisotterranea.org

Taxis

Napoli
Tel 081 88 88.

La Partenope
Tel 081 01 01.

Driving and Parking

Centro Direzionale di Napoli
Viale della Costituzione 82.

Grilli
Via G Ferraris 40. **Map** 4 F5.
Tel 081 26 43 44.

Mergellina
Via Mergellina 112. **Map** 5 B4.

Parcheggio Brin
Via B Brin. **Tel** 081 763 28 55.

Supergarage
Via Shelley 11. **Map** 7 A2.

Turistico
Via A De Gasperi 14. **Map** 7 B2.
Tel 081 552 54 42.

Scooter and Moped Hire

Penisola Rent
Corso Italia 259, Sorrento.
Tel 081 877 46 64.
W penisolarent.com

Rent Sprint
Via Santa Lucia 36. **Map** 7 A4.
Tel 081 764 34 52.
W rentsprint.it

Travelling Outside Naples

Even if you are based in Naples, it is not difficult to reach ancient sites such as the Phlegraean Fields, Pompeii and Herculaneum, the towns on the Amalfi Coast (Amalfi, Positano and Ravello) and the enchanting islands of Capri, Ischia and Procida. Most places are easily accessible by local train, bus or ferry, and excursions are organized by bigger hotels and local travel agents.

A Circumvesuviana train from Naples to Sorrento

Local Trains

The **Circumvesuviana** commuter train service (run by EAV Campania) connects Naples with various towns around Mount Vesuvius (including ancient Pompeii and Herculaneum) and those on the Sorrento Peninsula. All stop beneath the Piazza Garibaldi station, though you are more likely to get a seat by boarding at the terminus, Porta Nolana, just southwest of Piazza Garibaldi.

The Circumvesuviana has six routes: San Giorgio–Napoli–Via Centro Direzionale; Napoli–Sorrento; Napoli–Pompei–Poggiomarino; Napoli–Ottaviano–Sarno; Napoli–Pomigliano–Acerra; and Napoli–Nola–Baiano. There are three types of train: the *accelerato* (ACC), which stops at all stations en route; the *diretto* (DIR), stopping only at the main ones; and the *direttissimo* (DD), stopping at even fewer stations. The new Campania Express runs four times daily from March to October, connecting Porta Nolana and Garibaldi to Sorrento in just 50 minutes. Services run from 6am to 10pm (to midnight in summer on the Napoli–Sorrento line), with trains departing roughly every 20 minutes.

You may want to avoid travelling late at night, because trains are infrequent and there are fewer people around. At all times, be sure to stay alert for pickpockets.

EAV has also recently re-opened the Funivia di Monte Faito, a cableway starting from Castellammare di Stabia on the Circumvesuviana line. This takes you up to the top of Monte Faito, which is one of the most scenic viewpoints overlooking the Bay of Naples *(see p156)*, Mount Vesuvius and the islands of Capri, Ischia and Procida.

To reach the various towns on the Phlegraean Fields and the coast, take the **Ferrovia Cumana**, while the **Ferrovia Circumflegrea** serves the region's interior. The main station for both Cumana and Circumflegrea is located in Piazza Montesanto (near Piazza

Dante and Via Toledo), and the service is fast and efficient. The Cumana service runs from 5:21am to 10:30pm, with departures every 10 minutes for Bagnoli and every 20 minutes for Pozzuoli.

For the Circumflegrea line, departures are every 20 minutes (5:12am– 9:43pm). Several trains per day stop at Cumae and Lido Fusaro.

Another useful train is the one departing every half-hour from Napoli Centrale to Caserta *(see pp168–71)*.

Jets and Ferries

Various shipping lines offer frequent high-speed jet crossings from Naples to the islands in the bay. The Sorrento Peninsula and the towns of Positano and Amalfi can also be reached by boat. In Naples, most companies operate from Molo Beverello *(see p219)*. From the port of Pozzuoli, the crossing to Procida and Ischia is shorter and cheaper; you can also take your car on board, but check on available space beforehand. The **Caremar** line operates a ferry to Procida, Ischia and Capri that departs from the Molo Beverello, and to Procida and Ischia from Pozzuoli. **Medmar** runs ferries from Calata Porta di Massa (north of Molo Beverello) and from Pozzuoli to Ischia. Also from Molo Beverello, **SNAV** runs ferries and hydrofoils to Procida, Ischia and Capri, and Alilauro runs ferries to Ischia and Sorrento. Jets run by **Navigazione Libera del Golfo** depart from Molo Beverello for Capri, Sorrento and the Amalfi Coast. For daily departures, check the local newspaper *Il Mattino* or visit the local tourist office.

Circumvesuviana

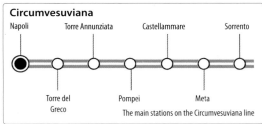

The main stations on the Circumvesuviana line

One of Sita's distinctive blue coaches

Travelling by Coach

You can also reach towns and resorts in the region by coach. Local companies depart from the coach terminus in Piazza Garibaldi or from Capodichino airport.

The bus company **ATC** serves the town of Caserta, with departures every 30 minutes on weekdays and every 15 minutes on Sundays and public holidays. **ANM** and **EAV** buses cover the towns in the Phlegraean Fields area (Baia and Bacoli), while the blue **Sita** coaches travel to various towns and resorts on the Sorrento Peninsula, the tourist sites on the Amalfi Coast (Amalfi, Maiori, Minori, Positano, Ravello and others) and Salerno. The main Sita terminus is located in the central Via Pisanelli, near Piazza Municipio. There are two departures daily.

Car Hire

Hiring a car in Italy is quite expensive. In addition, driving in Naples is a highly stressful experience and not recommended. However, if you are determined to drive, it is wise to make reservations prior to your arrival. The main international car hire companies, such as **Hertz** and **AVIS**, have desks at Naples' airport.

While public transport is the best option in Naples, reaching the Amalfi Coast by train or coach can be inconvenient and tiresome, especially after a long flight. Drivers find the Amalfi Coast road a thrill and a challenge. Contact your hotel to make sure parking is available. Be aware that you must be over

the age of 21 to rent a car. You will be asked to supply a credit card number as a deposit.

Rules of the Road

Driving in Naples requires strong nerves. Always stay alert, especially for scooters, which will zip past you at breakneck speed. Drive on the right, and give way to traffic from the right. Seat belts are compulsory for all passengers. Motorcyclists must wear helmets. Heavy fines are levied for using a mobile phone while driving. Headlights must be turned on even during the day on motorways and outside built-up areas. The speed limit in urban areas is 50 km/h (30 mph); outside urban areas it is 110 km/h (70 mph) on dual carriageways and 90 km/h (56 mph) on other secondary roads. On motorways the limit is 130 km/h (80 mph) for vehicles over 1100cc, 110 km/h (70 mph) for those under 1100cc.

The dramatic Vallone di Furore bridge, on the Amalfi Coast

DIRECTORY

Local Trains

EAV (Ente Autonomo Volturno)
Corso Garibaldi 387. **Map** 4 E4.
Tel 800 211 138.
W eavsrl.it

Jets and Ferries

AliLauro
Molo Beverello. **Map** 7 B3.
Tel 081 497 22 38.
W alilauro.it

Caremar
Molo Beverello and Pozzuoli.
Map 7 B3. **Tel** 081 18 96 66 90.
W caremar.it

Medmar
Calata Porta di Massa.
Tel 081 333 44 11.
W medmargroup.it

Navigazione Libera del Golfo
Molo Beverello.
Tel 081 552 07 63.
W navlib.it

SNAV
Molo Beverello.
Tel 081 428 55 55.
W snav.it

Travelling by Coach

ATC
Tel 082 396 90 57
W atcbus.it

Sita
Via Pisanelli 3–7. **Map** 3 B4 & 9 C2.
Tel 089 386 67 11.
W fsbusitalia.it (North),
W sitasudtrasporti.it (South)

Car Hire

AVIS
Piazza Garibaldi 92.
Map 4 E4.
Capodichino Airport.
Tel 081 780 57 90.
W avisautonoleggio.it

Hertz
Corso Arnaldo Lucci, 171 (Napoli Centrale station). **Tel** 081 202 860.
Capodichino Airport.
Tel 081 231 12 00.
W hertz.it

NAPLES STREET FINDER

The page grid superimposed on the *Area by Area* map below shows which parts of Naples are covered by this Street Finder. The map references given for the restaurants, hotels and sights in Naples refer to the maps in this section. Central Naples has been enlarged on map pages 9 and 10 to make it easier to read. Sights in

this area will have both map references. A complete index of the street names and major sights in the city follows on pages 226–9. The key on the opposite page shows the scales of the maps and explains the symbols. All the main sights in the city are clearly indicated in pink so they are easy to find.

0 metres 500
0 yards 500

3

Capodimonte and I Vergini

1

2

9

Decumano Maggiore

Spaccanapoli

Vomero

7

5

6

Toledo and Castel Nuovo

Castel dell'Ovo and Chiaia

How to Use the Maps

The first number corresponds to the Street Finder map.

❸ Gesù Nuovo

Piazza del Gesù Nuovo. **Map** 3 B5 (9 B4). **Tel** 081 551 86 13. **Open** 7am–12:30pm, 4–7:30pm daily.

The letters and numbers form the map coordinates. Letters are along the top, numbers are down the sides.

The map continues on page 7 of the Street Finder.

Key to Street Finder

- Major sight
- Place of interest
- Railway station
- M Metro station
- Bus stop
- Ferry boarding point
- Funicular station
- *i* Tourist information
- Hospital with casualty unit
- Police station
- Church
- Pedestrian street
- Railway line
- Funicular line

Scale of maps 1–8

0 metres	200
0 yards	200

1:11,100

Scale of maps 9–10

0 metres	125
0 yards	125

1:7,300

View of the centre of Naples

Street Finder Index

Map references in brackets refer to enlarged map section

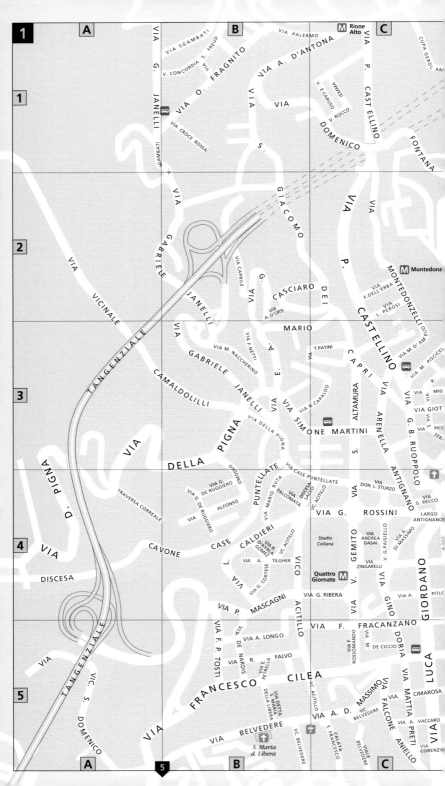

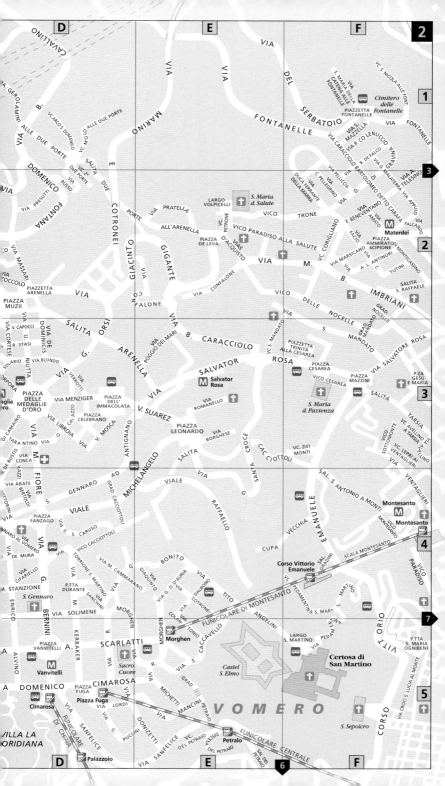

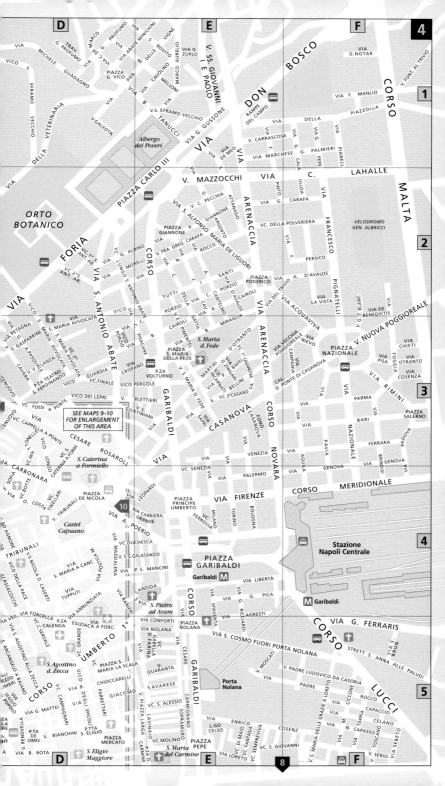

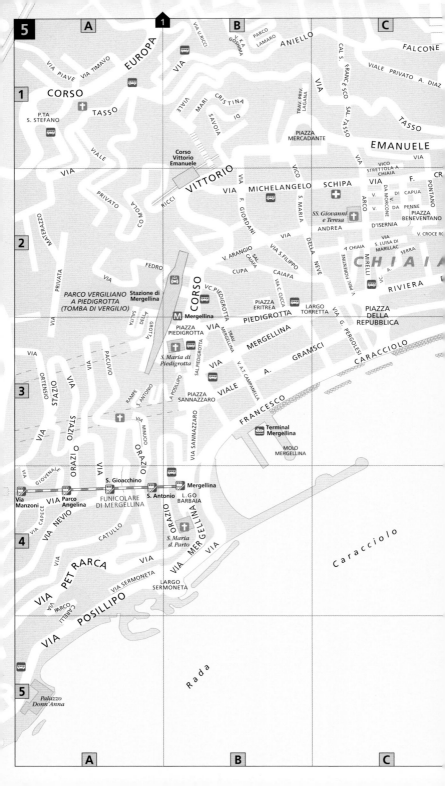

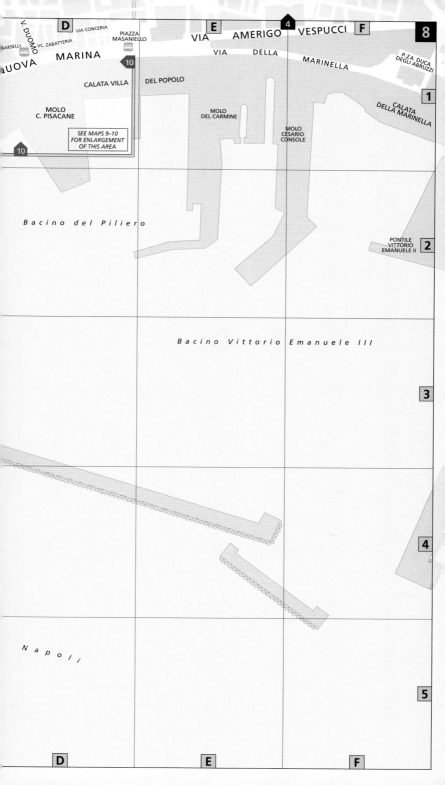

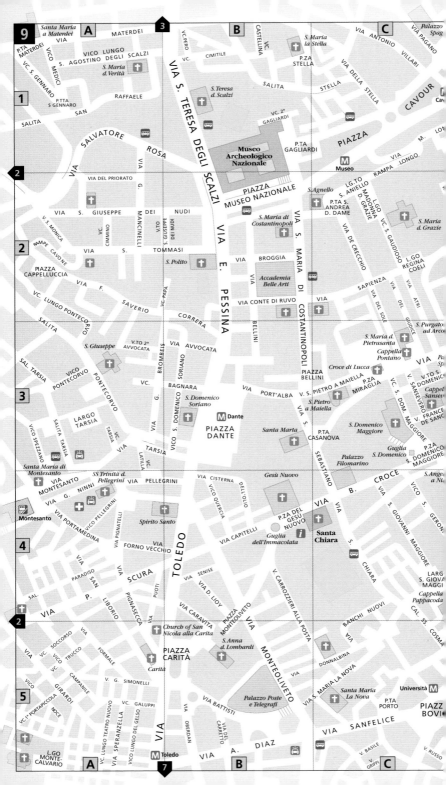

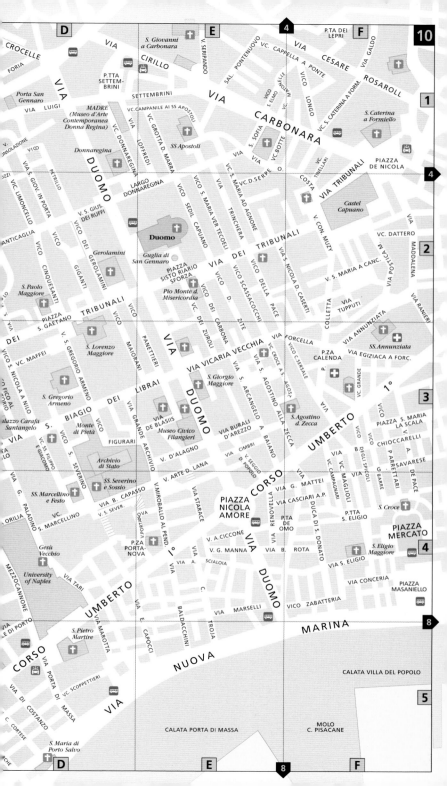

General Index

Acknowledgments

Dorling Kindersley would like to thank the following people whose contributions and assistance have made the preparation of this book possible: Guido Bevilacqua, Luigi Consiglio, Diana Georgiacodis, Costantino Pantano, Adriana Sandrini Maione. Dorling Kindersley would also like to thank all the museums and tourist information offices, too numerous to mention individually, for their assistance and kind permission to photograph at their establishments.

Editorial and Design Assistance

Ashwin Adimari, Gillian Allen, Riccardo Baldini, Claire Baranowski, Marta Bescos, Hilary Bird, Julie Bond, Cooling Brown, Nick Bruno, Imogen Corke, Michelle Crane, Felicity Crowe, Vivien Crump, Emer FitzGerald, Anna Freiberger, Swati Handoo, Annette Jacobs, Zafar-ul-Islam Khan, Kathryn Lane, Felicity Laughton, Jude Ledger, Hayley Maher, Nicola Malone, Georgina Matthews, Ferdie McDonald, Jane Oliver-Jedrzejak, Scarlett O'Hara, Giorgio Padovani, Catherine Palmi, Katie Parla, Adrian Potts, Alessandra Pugliese, Akshay Rana, Lucy Richards, Ellen Root, Sands Publishing Solutions, Sargasso, Ankita Sharma, Meredith Smith, Priyanka Thakur, Laura Thayer, Julie Thompson, Conrad Van Dyk, Ingrid Vienings, Dora Whitaker.

Additional Contributors

Sima Belmar, Judy Edelhoff, Julius Honnor, Leonie Loudon, Barbara Zaragoza.

Additional Photography

Demetrio Carrasco, Nigel Hicks, Ian O'Leary, Rough Guides/ Karen Trist, Barbara Zaragoza.

Picture Credits

Key: a = above; b = below/bottom; c = centre; f = far; l = left; r = right; t = top.

Every effort has been made to trace the copyright holders. The publisher apologizes for any unintentional omissions and would be pleased, in such cases, to add an acknowledgment in future editions. All the photographs reproduced in this book are from the Overseas S.r.l. Milano picture library except for the following:

123RF.com: dogstock 166cl; freeartist 174bl; Eddy Galeotti 118tr; Brenda Kean 172bl; Joseph Morelli 140b; Adriano Rubino 174tr; Eugene Sergeev 175tr. **4Corners Images:** SIME/ Mastrorillo Massimo 202tl; SIME / Paolo Giocoso 64. **Alamy Images:** AA World Library 188cl; Age fotostock 153tl; Boris Karpinski 202c; CuboImages srl 46cra; 57cl; CuboImages srl/ Alfio Giannotti 220cr; culliganphoto 89t, 127br; Richard Cummins 78; Adam Eastland 48-49, 158bl; Peter Forsberg 215bl; Christopher Griffin 223tl; Peter Horree 217cl; Svetlana Hristova 94; Lonely Planet Images/Dallas Stribley 216cla; NAfoto 44c; Pacific Press 208tl; Pangea Images 159tl; Photovoyager 163br; Ferdinando Piezzi 169tr; REDA &CO srl 30-31c, 43c; Rolf Richardson 157t; Vittorio Sciosia 207br; Stock Italia 14bl; UKraft 13br; Universal Images Group / DeAgostini 42tr, 116t. **Hotel Amleto House:** 180bl. **L'Antica Trattoria:** Virtual Trends SRL 197br. **Associazione Culturale Archivio Parisio, Naples:** 28br, 30c, 30clb, 31tl, 32bc, 59cl, 133c,139cra, 147cr. **AWL Images:**

Hemis 50, 134-135; Francesco Iacobelli 2-3, 178-179. **Belmond Hotels:** Hotel Caruso 181bl. **Ristorante La Caravella:** 186ca. **Casa Angelina:** 181tr, 185br. **Casa e Bottega:** 195tr. **Circumvesuviana srl:** 222cla. **Corbis:** The Art Archive/ Alfredo Dagli Orti 8-9; Jonathan Blair 31bl. **Il Dagherrotipo:** Roberto Della Noce 32- 33c, 124clb, 126bl, 127tl,158cr. **Da Paolino restaurant:** 193br. **Dreamstime.com:** Adeliepenguin 14br, 15tc; Alexchered 173cl, 173br; Antonio Amato 36cl, 168tl; Leonid Andronov 119cr; Danilo Ascione 35clb; Jennifer Barrow 15br; Vincenzo De Bernardo 128; Richard Billingham 121b; Elenaphotos 46bl, 119b; Fedecandoniphoto 137b; Evgeniy Fesenko 61br, 127cra; Francosant 12tr, 13bl, 35cra; Freesurf69 13tr, 162tr; Janos Gaspar 164b; Guillohmz 160tr; Hpdenecke 163cl; Iaceo 172tr; Francesco Riccardo Iacomino 160br; Ivanbastien 175cl; Kalman89, 225bl; Vladimir Korostyshevskiy 111tr; Lachris77 12bl, 34, 35crb, 58clb; Katherine Loveless 36tr; Rosario Manzo 106; Microstock77 11tr; Joseph Morelli 139tr; Mornok Nok 35bc; Photogolfer 57br, 69tl, 81tc, 162b; Picture-makersllc 163tr; Rinofelino 61t; Sailorr 14tr; Sarra22 35cl; Schalk62 212-213; Tanialerro 157bl; Yanta 11ca, 136; Yuliia Yurasova 35cla. **Garden Restaurant, Ravello:** 196tr. **Ristorante Il Geranio:** 186br. **Getty Images:** AFP/Stringer 218cla; DEA / A. DAGLI ORTI 169cl; De Agostini / L. Romano 1c; Richard Ellis 214cl; Picavet 221bl. **Giuseppe Avallone, Naples:** 25cr, 27cr, 33cr, 35bl, 37tl, 39tl, 42cl, 42br, 45cl, 45br, 59cr, 67tl, 80tr, 81bc, 93bc, 96br, 132(all images), 138br, 138cl, 139br, 144cl, 148cl, 161b, 164tr, 165tr, 165bl, 173tl, 176bl, 201cr, 206cl. **Grand Hotel Punta Molino:** 211tl. **Grazia Neri:** Toty Ruggeri 207tl; M. Sestini fotogiornalismo/M. Tramonte 33br; Francesco Vignali 157cr. **Hotel San Francesco al Monte:** 182bl. **Stockphoto.com:** Peeter Viisimaa 42cl. **Kukai Nibu:** 190bc. **LAES - Napoli e la città sotterranea:** 83br. **Lonely Planet Images:** Stephen Saks 223bc. **Marka, Milan:** Danilo Donadoni 126tr; D. Donati 66bc; L. Sechi 219cr. **Mimi alla Ferrovia:** 191tr. **Mimmo Jodice, Naples:** 44ca, 72bc, 84tr, 100bc. Monastero Santa Rosa: 180cra, 184tc. **Image Courtesy of Naples Botanical Garden, University of Study II, Italy:** G. Sibilio 100cra. **Napoli Film Festival:** 207cr. **Newimage s.r.l:** Ronaldo Fabrini 210br. **Luciano Pedicini, Naples:** 25tc, 72c, 73tr, 75ca, 85t, 88br, 156tr, 166tr, 167cb, 167cra, 167tc, 170bl, 171cr. **Photolibrary:** Tommaso Di Girolamo 214cr. **Pizzeria La Notizia 53:** 192tr. **Prestige Hotels:** Caruso Roof Garden Restaurant / Grand Hotel Vesuvio 187tl ; Grand Hotel Vesuvio 183tr. **Il Principe:** 187br. Da Raffaele 194bc. **Reuters:** Str Old 87bc. **Scala Group S.P.A:** 76tl, 90bc. **Rex Features:** REX / Photoservice Electa / Universal Images Group 103br. **Robert Harding Picture Library:** Petra Wallner 173tr. **SuperStock:** Cubo Images 200br; DeAgostini 63br; Hemis.fr 219tl.

Front Endpapers: **4Corners:** Paolo Giocoso / SIME (br). **Alamy Images:** Richard Cummins (fbr); Universal Images Group / DeAgostini (bl); Svetlana Hristova (tr). **AWL Images:** Hemis (bc). **Dreamstime.com:** Rosario Manzo (cla); Yanta (tc).

Sheet Map Cover: **4Corners:** SIME/Manfred Bortoli.

Jacket: **Front and spine - 4Corners:** SIME/Manfred Bortoli.

All other Pictures Dorling Kindersley. See www.dkimages.com for further information.

Phrase Book

In Emergency

Help!	Aiuto!	eye-**yoo**-toh
Stop!	Fermo!	**fair**-moh
Call a doctor.	Chiama un medico.	kee-**ah**-mah oon **meh**-dee-koh
Call an ambulance.	Chiama un' ambulanza.	kee-**ah**-mah oon am-boo-**lan**-tsa
Call the police.	Chiama la polizia.	kee-**ah**-mah lah pol-ee-**tsee**-ah
Call the fire brigade.	Chiama i pompieri.	kee-**ah**-mah ee pom-pee-**air**-ee
Where is the telephone?	Dov'è il telefono?	dov-**eh** eel tel-**leh**-foh-noh?
The nearest hospital?	L'ospedale più vicino?	loss-peh-**dah**-leh pee-**oo** vee-**chee**-noh?

Communication Essentials

Yes/No	Sì/No	see/noh
Please	Per favore	pair fah-**vor**-eh
Thank you	Grazie	**grah**-tsee-eh
Excuse me	Mi scusi	mee **skoo**-zee
Hello	Buon giorno	bwon **jor**-noh
Goodbye	Arrivederci	ah-ree-veh-**dair**-chee
Good evening	Buona sera	**bwon**-ah **sair**-ah
morning	la mattina	lah mah-**tee**-nah
afternoon	il pomeriggio	eel poh-meh-**ree**-joh
evening	la sera	lah **sair**-ah
yesterday	ieri	ee-**air**-ee
today	oggi	**oh**-jee
tomorrow	domani	doh-**mah**-nee
here	qui	kwee
there	là, lì	lah, lee
What?	Che?	keh?
When?	Quando?	**kwan**-doh?
Why?	Perchè?	pair-**keh**?
Where?	Dove?	**doh**-veh?

Useful Phrases

How are you?	Come sta?	**koh**-meh stah?
Very well, thank you.	Molto bene, grazie.	**moll**-toh beh-neh **grah**-tsee-**eh**
Pleased to meet you.	Piacere di conoscerla.	pee-ah-**chair**-eh dee coh-**noh**-shair-lah
See you later.	A più tardi.	ah pee-**oo** tar-dee
That's fine.	Va bene.	va **beh**-neh
Where is/are ...?	Dov'è/Dove sono...?	dov-**eh**/doveh **soh**-noh?
How long does it take to get to ...?	Quanto tempo ci vuole per andare a ...?	**kwan**-toh **tem**-poh chee voo-**oh**-leh pair an-**dar**-eh a ...?
How do I get to ...?	Come faccio per arrivare a ...?	**koh**-meh **fah**-choh pair arri-**var**-eh ah ...?
Do you speak English?	Parla inglese?	**par**-lah een-**gleh**-zeh?
I don't understand.	Non capisco.	non ka-**pee**-skoh
Could you speak more slowly, please?	Può parlare più lentamente, per favore?	pwoh par-**lah**-reh pee-**oo** len-ta-**men**-teh pair fah-**vor**-eh?
I'm sorry.	Mi dispiace.	mee dee-spee-**ah**-cheh

Useful Words

big	grande	**gran**-deh
small	piccolo	**pee**-koh-loh
hot	caldo	**kal**-doh
cold	freddo	**fred**-doh
good	buono	**bwoh**-noh
bad	cattivo	kat-**tee**-voh
enough	basta	**bas**-tah
well	bene	**beh**-neh
open	aperto	ah-**pair**-toh
closed	chiuso	kee-**oo**-zoh
left	a sinistra	ah see-**nee**-strah
right	a destra	ah **dess**-trah
straight on	sempre dritto	**sem**-preh **dree**-toh
near	vicino	vee-**chee**-noh
far	lontano	lon-**tah**-noh
up	su	soo
down	giù	joo
early	presto	**press**-toh
late	tardi	**tar**-dee
entrance	entrata	en-**trah**-tah
exit	uscita	oo-**shee**-ta
toilet	il bagno	eel **gah**-bee-**net**-toh
free, unoccupied	libero	**lee**-bair-oh
free, no charge	gratuito	grah-**too**-ee-toh

Making a Telephone Call

I'd like to place a long-distance call.	Vorrei fare una interurbana.	vor-**ray far**-eh oona in-tair-oor-**bah**-nah
I'd like to make a reverse-charge call.	Vorrei fare una telefonata a carico del destinatario.	vor-**ray far**-eh oona teh-leh-fon-**ah**-tah ah **kar**-ee-koh dell dess-tee-nah-**tar**-ree-oh
Could I speak to...?	Potrei parlare con...	po-tray par-**lah**-reh con
I'll try again later.	Ritelefono più tardi.	ree-teh-**leh**-foh-noh pee-oo **tar**-dee
Can I leave a message?	Posso lasciare un messaggio?	**poss**-oh lash-**ah**-reh oon mess-**sah**-joh?
Hold on.	Un attimo, per favore.	oon **ah**-tee-moh, pair fah-**vor**-eh
Could you speak up a little please?	Può parlare più forte?	pwoh par-**lah**-reh pee-oo for-teh?
local call	telefonata locale	te-leh-fon-**ah**-tah loh-cah-leh

Shopping

How much does this cost?	Quant'è, per favore?	kwan-**teh** pair fah-**vor**-eh?
I would like ...	Vorrei ...	vor-**ray**...
Do you have ...?	Avete ...?	ah-**veh**-teh... ?
I'm just looking.	Sto soltanto guardando.	stoh sol-**tan**-toh gwar-**dan**-doh
Do you take credit cards?	Accettate le carte di credito?	ah-chet-**tah**-teh leh **kar**-teh dee **creh**-dee-toh?
What time do you open/close?	A che ora apre/ chiude?	ah keh or-ah **ah**-preh/kee-**oo**-deh?
this one	questo	**kweh**-stoh
that one	quello	**kwell**-oh
expensive	caro	**kar**-oh
cheap	economico	ah bwon **pret**-soh
size, clothes	la taglia	lah **tah**-lee-ah
size, shoes	il numero	eel **noo**-mair-oh
white	bianco	bee-**ang**-koh
black	nero	**neh**-roh
red	rosso	**ross**-oh
yellow	giallo	**jal**-loh
green	verde	**vair**-deh
blue	azzurro	ah-**tsee**-roh

Types of Shop

antique	l'antiquario	lan-tee-**kwah**-ree-oh
bakery	il forno/ il panificio	eel **forn**-oh/ eel pan-ee-**fee**-choh
bank	la banca	lah **bang**-kah
bookshop	la libreria	lah lee-breh-**ree**-ah
butcher	la macelleria	lah mah-chell-eh-**ree**-ah
cake shop	la pasticceria	lah pas-tee-chair-**ee**-ah
chemist	la farmacia	lah far-mah-**chee**-ah
delicatessen	la salumeria	lah sah-loo-meh-**ree**-ah
department store	il grande magazzino	eel **gran**-deh mag-gad-**zee**-noh
fishmonger	il pescivendolo	eel pesh-ee-**ven**-doh-loh
florist	il fioraio	eel fee-or-**eye**-oh
greengrocer	il fruttivendolo	eel froo-tee-**ven**-doh-loh
grocery	l'alimentari	lah-lee-men-**tah**-ree
hairdresser	il parrucchiere	eel par-oo-kee-**air**-eh
ice cream parlour	la gelateria	lah jel-lah-tair-**ree**-ah
market	il mercato	eel mair-**kah**-toh
newsstand	l'edicola	leh-**dee**-koh-lah
post office	l'ufficio postale	loo-**fee**-choh pos-**tah**-leh
shoe shop	il negozio di scarpe	eel neh-**goh**-tsioh deh **skar**-peh
supermarket	il supermercato	eel su-pair-mair-**kah**-toh
tobacconist	il tabaccaio	eel tah-bak-**eye**-oh
travel agency	l'agenzia di viaggi	lah-jen-**tsee**-ah dee vee-ad-jee

Sightseeing

church	la pinacoteca	lah peena-koh-**teh**-kah
bus stop	la fermata dell'autobus	lah fair-**mah**-tah dell **ow**-toh-booss
church	la chiesa/ la basilica	lah kee-**eh**-zah/ lah bah-**seel**-i-kah
closed for holidays	chiuso per le ferie	kee-**oo**-zoh pair leh **fair**-ee-eh
garden	il giardino	eel jar-**dee**-no
library	la biblioteca	lah beeb-lee-oh-**teh**-kah
museum	il museo	eel moo-**zeh**-oh
railway station	la stazione	lah stah-tsee-**oh**-neh
tourist information	l'ufficio turistico	loo-**fee**-choh too-**ree**-stee-koh

Staying in a Hotel

Do you have a vacant rooms?	**Avete delle camere libere?**	ah-**veh**-teh deleh **kah**-mair-eh **lee**-bair-eh?
double room	**una camera doppia**	oona **kah**-mair-ah **doh**-pee-ah
with double bed	**con letto matrimoniale**	kon **let**-toh mah-tree-moh-nee-**ah**-leh
twin room	**una camera con due letti**	oona **kah**-mair-ah kon **doo**-eh **let**-tee
single room	**una camera singola**	oona **kah**-mair-ah **sing**-goh-lah
room with a bath, shower	**una camera con bagno, con doccia**	oona **kah**-mair-ah kon **ban**-yoh, kon **dot**-chah
porter	**il facchino**	eel fah-**kee**-noh
key	**la chiave**	lah kee-**ah**-veh
I have a reservation.	**Ho prenotato.**	oh preh-noh-**tah**-toh

Eating Out

Have you got a table for …?	**Avete una tavola per … ?**	ah-**veh**-teh oona **tah**-voh-lah pair … ?
I'd like to reserve a table.	**Vorrei riservare una tavola.**	vor-**ray** ree-sair-**vah**-reh oona **tah**-voh-lah
breakfast	**colazione**	koh-lah-tsee-**oh**-neh
lunch	**pranzo**	**pran**-tsoh
dinner	**cena**	**cheh**-nah
The bill, please.	**Il conto, per favore.**	eel **kon**-toh pair **fah**-vor-eh
I am a vegetarian.	**Sono vegetariano/a.**	**soh**-noh veh-jeh-tar-ee-**ah**-noh/nah
waitress	**cameriera**	kah-mair-ee-**air**-a
waiter	**cameriere**	kah-mair-ee-**air**-eh
fixed price menu	**il menù a prezzo fisso**	eel meh-**noo** a **pret**-soh **fee**-soh
dish of the day	**piatto del giorno**	pee-ah-toh dell **jor**-no
starter	**antipasto**	an-tee-**pass**-toh
first course	**il primo**	eel **pree**-moh
main course	**il secondo**	eel seh-**kon**-doh
vegetables	**il contorno**	eel kon-**tor**-noh
dessert	**il dolce**	eel **doll**-cheh
cover charge	**il coperto**	eel koh-**pair**-toh
wine list	**la lista dei vini**	lah **lee**-stah day **vee**-nee
rare	**al sangue**	al **sang**-gweh
medium	**al puntino**	al poon-**tee**-noh
well done	**ben cotto**	ben **kot**-toh
glass	**il bicchiere**	eel bee-kee-**air**-eh
bottle	**la bottiglia**	lah bot-**teel**-yah
knife	**il coltello**	eel kol-**tell**-oh
fork	**la forchetta**	lah for-**ket**-tah
spoon	**il cucchiaio**	eel koo-kee-**eye**-oh

Menu Decoder

l'acqua gassata/naturale	**lah**-kwah mee-nair-**ah**-leh gah-**zah**-tah/ nah-too-rah-leh	mineral water fizzy/still
aceto	ah-**cheh**-toh	vinegar
aglio	**al**-ee-oh	garlic
l'agnello	lah-**niell**-oh	lamb
al forno	al **for**-noh	baked/roasted
alla griglia	ah-lah **greel**-yah	grilled
l'aragosta	lah-rah-**goss**-tah	lobster
arrosto	ar-**ross**-toh	roast
basilico	bah-**zee**-lee-koh	basil
la birra	lah **beer**-rah	beer
la bistecca	lah bee-**stek**-kah	steak
il brodo	eel **broh**-doh	broth
il burro	eel **boor**-oh	butter
il caffè	eel kah-**feh**	coffee
i calamari	ee kah-lah-**mah**-ree	squid
i carciofi	ee kar-**choff**-ee	artichokes
la carne	la **kar**-neh	meat
la cipolla	la chip-**oh**-lah	onion
i contorni	ee kon-**tor**-nee	vegetables
le cozze	leh **coh**-tzeh	mussels
i fagioli	ee fah-**joh**-lee	beans
il fegato	eel **fay**-gah-toh	liver
il finocchio	eel fee-**nok**-ee-oh	fennel
il formaggio	eel for-**mad**-joh	cheese
le fragole	leh **frah**-goh-leh	strawberries
il fritto misto	eel free-toh **mees**-toh	mixed fried dish
la frutta	la **froot**-tah	fruit
frutti di mare	**froo**-tee dee mah-reh	seafood
i funghi	ee **foon**-ghee	mushrooms
i gamberi	ee **gam**-bair-ee	prawns
il gelato	eel jeh-**lah**-toh	ice cream
l'insalata	leen-sah-lah-tah	salad
il latte	eel **laht**-teh	milk

lesso	**less**-oh	boiled
la melanzana	lah meh-lan-**tsah**-nah	aubergine
la minestra	lah mee-**ness**-trah	soup
l'olio	loh-lee-oh	oil
il pane	eel **pah**-neh	bread
le patate	leh pah-**tah**-teh	potatoes
le patatine fritte	leh pah-tah-**teen**-eh **free**-teh	chips
il pepe	eel **peh**-peh	pepper
la pesca	lah **pess**-kah	peach
il pesce	eel **pesh**-eh	fish
il polipo	eel **poh**-lee-poh	octopus
il pollo	eel **poll**-oh	chicken
il pomodoro	eel poh-moh-**dor**-oh	tomato
il prosciutto cotto/crudo	eel pro-**shoo**-toh **kot**-toh/**kroo**-doh	ham cooked/cured
il riso	eel **ree**-zoh	rice
il sale	eel **sah**-leh	salt
la salsiccia	lah sal-**see**-chah	sausage
le seppie	leh **sep**-pee-eh	cuttlefish
secco	**sek**-koh	dry
la sogliola	lah **soll**-yoh-lah	sole
i spinaci	ee spee-**nah**-chee	spinach
succo d'arancia/ di limone	**soo**-koh dah-**ran**-chah/ dee leh-**moh**-neh	orange/lemon juice
il tè	eel **teh**	tea
la tisana	lah tee-**zah**-nah	herbal tea
il tonno	eel **ton**-noh	tuna
la torta	lah **tor**-tah	cake/tart
l'uovo	loo-**oh**-voh	egg
vino bianco	**vee**-noh bee-**ang**-koh	white wine
vino rosso	**vee**-noh **ross**-oh	red wine
il vitello	eel vee-**tell**-oh	veal
le vongole	leh von-goh-leh	clams
lo zucchero	loh **zoo**-kair-oh	sugar
le zucchine	leh dzu-**kee**-nee	courgette
la zuppa	lah **tsoo**-pah	soup

Numbers

1	**uno**	**oo**-noh
2	**due**	**doo**-eh
3	**tre**	**treh**
4	**quattro**	**kwat**-roh
5	**cinque**	**ching**-kweh
6	**sei**	**say**-ee
7	**sette**	**set**-teh
8	**otto**	**ot**-toh
9	**nove**	**noh**-veh
10	**dieci**	dee-**eh**-chee
11	**undici**	**oon**-dee-chee
12	**dodici**	**doh**-dee-chee
13	**tredici**	**tray**-dee-chee
14	**quattordici**	kwat-**tor**-dee-chee
15	**quindici**	**kwin**-dee-chee
16	**sedici**	**say**-dee-chee
17	**diciassette**	dee-chah-**set**-teh
18	**diciotto**	dee-**chot**-toh
19	**diciannove**	dee-chah-**noh**-veh
20	**venti**	**ven**-tee
30	**trenta**	**tren**-tah
40	**quaranta**	kwah-**ran**-tah
50	**cinquanta**	ching-**kwan**-tah
60	**sessanta**	sess-**an**-tah
70	**settanta**	set-**tan**-tah
80	**ottanta**	ot-**tan**-tah
90	**novanta**	noh-**van**-tah
100	**cento**	**chen**-toh
1,000	**mille**	**mee**-leh
2,000	**duemila**	**doo**-eh **mee**-lah
5,000	**cinquemila**	**ching**-kweh **mee**-lah
1,000,000	**un milione**	oon meel-**yoh**-neh

Time

one minute	**un minuto**	oon mee-**noo**-toh
one hour	**un'ora**	oon **or**-ah
half an hour	**mezz'ora**	medz-**or**-ah
a day	**un giorno**	oon **jor**-noh
a week	**una settimana**	oona set-tee-**mah**-nah
Monday	**lunedì**	loo-neh-**dee**
Tuesday	**martedì**	mar-teh-**dee**
Wednesday	**mercoledì**	mair-koh-leh-**dee**
Thursday	**giovedì**	joh-veh-**dee**
Friday	**venerdì**	ven-air-**dee**
Saturday	**sabato**	**sah**-bah-toh
Sunday	**domenica**	doh-**meh**-nee-kah

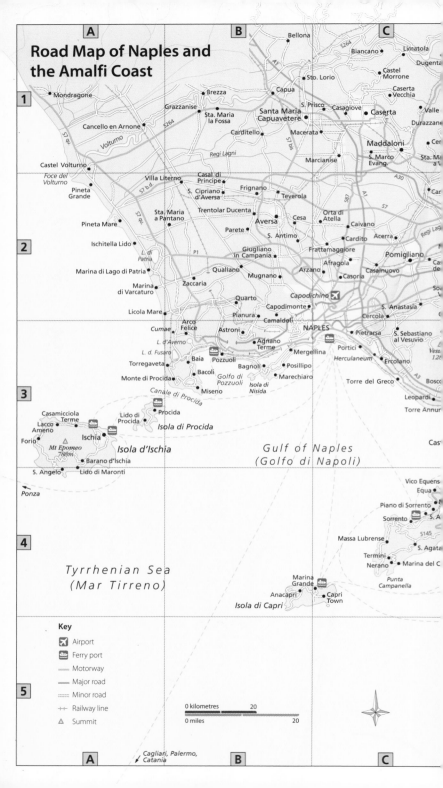